AN ANATOMY OF WITCHCRAFT

Much has been written on witchcraft by historians, theologians, philosophers, and anthropologists, but nothing by scientists. This book aims to reappraise witchcraft by applying to it the advances in cognitive sciences.

The book is divided into four parts. Part I ("Deep History") deals with human emotions and the drive to represent witches as evil female agents. Part II ("Historical Times") focuses on those rare state and church repressions of malefice, which, surprisingly, did not feature in Islamic lands. Modern urbanization dealt a blow to the rural civilizations where accusations of witchcraft were rife. Part III ("In the Laboratory") applies neuroscience to specific case studies to investigate the personification of misfortune, the millenary stereotype witch = woman, the reality of evil, and the phenomenon of treasure hunting. Part IV ("Millenials") wonders whether intentional malefic hatred is a closed chapter in the history of humanity.

An Anatomy of Witchcraft is ideal reading for students and scholars. Given its interdisciplinary nature, the book will be of interest to scholars from many fields including evolutionary psychology, anthropology, women's history, and cognitive sciences.

Oscar Di Simplicio is a former lecturer in early modern history at the University of Florence. His previous publications include several books and articles that explore the history of witchcraft, the witch-hunts, and the neuropsychological origins of witchcraft cognition. He lives in Siena.

Martina Di Simplicio is a clinical senior lecturer in psychiatry at Imperial College London with expertise spanning cognitive neuroscience, clinical psychiatry, and digital technologies. Her research seeks to understand the cognitive mechanisms that underlie emotional distress, support resilience, and drive successful treatment of mental disorders.

ROUTLEDGE STUDIES IN THE HISTORY OF WITCHCRAFT, DEMONOLOGY AND MAGIC

For more information about this series, please visit: https://www.routledge.com/ Routledge-Studies-in-the-History-of-Witchcraft-Demonology-and-Magic/book-series/RSHWDM

AN ANATOMY OF WITCHCRAFT

Between Cognitive Sciences and History

Oscar Di Simplicio and Martina Di Simplicio

Routledge
Taylor & Francis Group

LONDON AND NEW YORK

Designed cover image: Burning of witches in medieval times, historical engraving of 1883. Sunny Celeste / Alamy Stock Photo.

First published 2024
by Routledge
4 Park Square, Milton Park, Abingdon, Oxon OX14 4RN

and by Routledge
605 Third Avenue, New York, NY 10158

Routledge is an imprint of the Taylor & Francis Group, an informa business

British Library Cataloguing-in-Publication Data
A catalogue record for this book is available from the British Library

ISBN: 978-1-032-53933-1 (hbk)
ISBN: 978-1-032-53934-8 (pbk)
ISBN: 978-1-003-41437-7 (ebk)

DOI: 10.4324/9781003414377

Typeset in Bembo
by Taylor & Francis Books

To Gabriele Rebecca Beatrice
For Daša

CONTENTS

PREFACE

Father and daughter … In the arts, from theater to cinema to music, it is not uncommon to come across parental pairs. They are less frequent in humanities and scientific fields, but in these disciplines also the association finds fertile ground in a shared technical language that prepares the atmosphere for possible joint work.

This is not our case. Father and daughter could not have had a more distant if not opposite intellectual formation. On one hand, a historian's archival papers. On the other, specialized laboratories: humanistic culture and scientific culture separated by convention. How did father and daughter manage to overcome disciplinary closure and generational distance? Looking back for a chance opportunity, an episode emerges almost a couple of decades earlier.

Something unexpected happened in Florence during a lecture in the history department. A course on early modern witch hunting had reached the critical junction of therapeutic magic and the young physician, Martina, was asked for a contribution on the concept of diagnosis and the features of differential medical analysis, a lethal blow to would-be witch diseases.

Our plan was wrong. Stimulated perhaps by the age of the host, almost a peer, the students turned the debate into an unexpected direction. The history of medicine soon dropped, the topicality of heated contemporary diatribes on the "unorthodox," "magical" remedies against cancer still agitating the web, took over. And the class kept asking why magical beliefs persist eventually venturing into absolute questions, and wandering around them mercilessly: were there really witches? Were they doing harm on purpose? Were they always women? Why are such convictions still with us? And so on.

We returned home perplexed. The episode settled in the brain convolutions. Ten years later it emerged: didn't those Millennials signal something, a need for information, for a deeper, new cognitive approach?

***

"The further back you can look, the farther forward you can see."[1] This vivid observation by Winston Churchill is the answer and summarizes the method and purpose of our book: to investigate the origin and persistence of humans' intentional malefic witchcraft from a neurobiological and historical perspective. We position the book in the wake of the recent flowering of cognitive science to improve our understanding of lasting issues in human life. To do this, we will deal with a basic scientific theme: the tendency of the mind to orient *Homo sapiens* towards ideas contrary to facts, such as magic and religion, monozygotic twins. This propensity can be observed since the beginning of documented history, however today the knowledge acquired on the phases and processes of brain formation allows an anatomy of the phenomenon to be studied in a chronological dimension that delves into the mists of prehistory.

In the Thirties of the past century, an anthropologist, reflecting on the modes of reasoning of a tribe in central Africa, observed that one cannot see into the head of a man as in a broadly woven basket.[2] This is no longer the case. The accumulation of experiments on brain matter allows us to move in the opposite direction and to scrutinize the inside of men's heads. Neuroscientists, biologists, and cognitive psychologists have deepened the knowledge of the relationship between mind and body and expanded our comprehension of how human beings think and act, endowed with a nature that intertwines genetic inheritance with the cultural process. A favorable situation is looming to reappraise what philosophers, theologians and historians have written on magic and religious appearances, overcoming a "real split between the way in which a person considers the world from the point of view of science and how he sees it reflected in humanities."[3] In traditional explanations of the past, magic and religious creation stories have been blended with the humanities to attribute meaning to our species. "Now that science has given us a clear outline of the human epic, we can anticipate a more fruitful interaction between the sciences and the humanities"; "it has become increasingly evident – although far from conclusively proven – that the biological sciences are not separated from humanistic explanations of aesthetics and moral reasoning, at least not by the divide of seismic proportions formerly accepted."[4] Over the last seventy years historians of witchcraft searching for an explanation of the phenomenon multiplied their social scientific approach appealing to several disciplines. Biology and brain sciences were left out. We are trying to fill this void.

***

What do we offer to the reader? To begin with, a premise. Brain's imaginative operations are due to a neuro-electrical event, a product of its nervous mechanisms: it is a "commonplace among scientists that mental life consists of patterns of activity in the tissues of the brain"; any given phenomenon is the result of how the cerebral matter works.[5] Perception, memory, and emotions lead back to the activity of an incorporated organ, inserted in a context subject to changes in an environment, in all its physical and biological characteristics. We consider, then, witchcraft to be a cerebral representation, the result of the functioning of the organ of thought: it consists of a cluster of ideas which direct human agency. Evil, understood as malefice, is the focus of our study: in its historical development it is quite often synonymous with witchcraft, which not surprisingly the common sense defined as a material, physical or moral damage intentionally inflicted on someone by mysterious means. Searching for its biological drive, for its origin and persistence in a brain process, has involved going beyond the sacred boundaries of written documentation, dividing our work into four sections.

Part I, "Deep History," deals with human emotions and drives through an outline of the evolutionary anatomical completion of the grey matter: fear, anger, empathy, shame, envy, sex, seeking. Applying recent advances in cognitive science to their internal dynamics allows us to glimpse the origin of evil, to nearly grasp the embryogenesis of witchcraft's mainly female sex feature, and the slow engendering of the "natural control" of malefic individuals that clarifies a so far persistent question: why are the extensive bloody persecutions of witchcraft rare over the millennia?

In Part II, "Historical Times," the real malefic agency is met, for a long time sporadically persecuted by the judicial systems. The advent of monotheistic religions did not introduce too great changes; but quite surprisingly witchcraft underwent sudden ruthless repressions by an early modern State and Church, only in certain areas of the Old Continent and for a limited number of years. Surprisingly, Islamic lands remained immune from the phenomenon. These random extensive witch burnings seem to appear as a short circuit between nature and culture that challenges easy interpretations. Still, two realities emerge with some precision from the trials: the persistence of the natural control of witchcraft and the sex of the victims, mainly women.

Part III, "In the Laboratory," applies the results of cognitive science advancements to specific situations: the personalization of misfortune, the evil-eye, the contagious idea of treasure hunts, the millennial cliché witch = woman, are cases charged with feelings and emotions and where to look for a confirmation of otherwise unverifiable hypotheses.

Part IV, "Millennials," marked by the centuries-old end of State and Church formal prosecution of witchcraft, wonders whether in the third millennium AD cosmogony masked forms of malefic agency are anything but a closed chapter in the history of man, as the universality of the expression "witch hunt" suggests. Whatever the case, if today we start to understand how our brain takes us there, we can be better equipped to cope with real or imagined difficulties.

The book began as an adversarial collaboration. Pairing cryptic written testimonies of emotions with evidence from scientific laboratories is fraught with serious risks. Once a problem has been identified, in seeking its solution the method of the neuroscientist and the historian do not differ but the means to weigh the validity of an explanation do. Our examination will present controversial aspects, for failings of the authors and their inevitable idiosyncrasies, overcome by a common hypothetical approach to the matter.

However, there is more: in human affairs a substantial contradiction is intrinsic to the *Homo* species, tossed about in a dynamic between nature and culture. It is in general precisely from this discordant movement that a lesson is to be learned: too many important realities remain hidden, things are never what they seem: a possible consequence of man's epistemic limitations?

Notes

1 "Prime Minister Among the Physicians," in *The Lancet*, 243, 1944, 342; doi.org/10.1016/S0140-6736(00)45452-8.
2 E. Evans-Pritchard, *Witchcraft, Oracles and Magic Among the Azande*, Oxford, 1937.
3 G. M. Edelman, *Second Nature: Brain Science and Human Knowledge*, New Haven, 2006, xv.
4 E. O. Wilson, "The Meaning of Human Existence," in *Darwin's Bridge: Uniting the Humanities and Sciences*, J. Carrol, D. P. McAdams, and E. O. Wilson, eds, Oxford, 2016; and id., in *On Human Nature: Evolution, Diversity, Psychology, Ethics, Politics and Religion*, M. Tibayrenc and F. J. Ayala, eds, Cambridge, MA, 2017, xxi.
5 S. Pinker, *Enlightenment Now: The Case for Reason, Science, Humanim and Progress*, London, 2018, 3.

ACKNOWLEDGMENTS

Our intellectual debt is primarily indicated by the prominence scholars receive in the footnotes. But we owe much more to others. Gregory Hanlon was tireless in supporting us in the project and read an initial draft. Robin Briggs undertook the trouble of reading the *ur* text in Italian and recommended the translation. Edward Bever read an early English draft and advocated its publication. Psychiatrist and neuroscientist friends and colleagues supported the endeavor with their curiosity and surprise. We hope we have not disappointed anyone.

ACKNOWLEDGMENTS

PART I
Deep History

Six to seven million years away, in the north-eastern area of Mother Africa, the separation of an evolutionary trajectory transformed the great primates into a human species. Two images, from the alluring opening scenes of Stanley Kubrick's *2001: A Space Odyssey*, illustrate the event. A tall black monolith stands out on the screen; below are grouped chimpanzees, possibly bonobos. A stronger alpha male stands on two feet, grabs a large bone, and wields it in the air: actions full of meaning. The erect stature heralds a new species and the plot of a future interwoven with domination, hierarchy, and a lasting cooperation. The biology of *Homo*'s brain transformations attempts to show how the primate man was led to counterfactual meditations.

DOI: 10.4324/9781003414377-1

1

TOWARDS *HOMO SAPIENS*

> Men see in all things a spirit, a sense that allows the recognition of dangerous actions and enemies; [for them] all things are full of spirit; the whole world is animated; space is full of semi-divine beings, demons or spirits, ambiguous terms valid for good or bad.[1]

Giordano Bruno, a sixteenth-century philosopher aware of witchcraft realities, alludes to a mind configuration whose persistence has neuropsychological roots that go back to prehistory. How and why are such ideas formed in man? To explain this, the anatomical specification of human brain, a result of hundreds of thousands of years of living in a hostile environment, is the underlying theme of our investigation on the intentionality of evil in one of its many disguises and cognitive complexity, the malefice (*maleficium*).

Time Begins

In the beginning there was only fear and wonder, Descartes' primal "passion."[2] Sky and earth appeared to the small group of hominins as a theater of opposing forces in struggle: light and darkness, heat and cold, well-being and malaise. These beings experienced a symbiotic relationship with the surrounding reality, a sense of belonging to the whole, and the world, animate and inanimate, beneficial or harmful, participated in their life. They ignored the dichotomy between good and evil; their common sense did not need to explain the external universe, but this presented continuous critical issues related to natural phenomena and in the activities carried out to survive and in interpersonal relationships it happened they ran into material and mental difficulties. What were their reactions in response to a variety of complicated or negative situations? We do not know. Primitives left no evidence of the meaning of existence. During prehistory, the growth of vague

DOI: 10.4324/9781003414377-2

speculative thought can be deduced from traces of bivouacs, from rudimentary tools and weapons, from remains of burials, from the coloring of clothing and ornamental objects, from graffiti and wall paintings. Still, the meditations of men and women are obscure. A knowledge gap hard to fill.

In our study, to investigate the genesis and persistence of witchcraft means to ask ourselves about the meaning of harsh facts, damage and suffering, which sometimes mysteriously appear in life. However, the ramifications of this cerebral representation are multiple and move in directions also far removed from the concepts of harm and pain. A neuroanatomy of witchcraft implies that other aspects that motivate it, such as knowledge and desire, are weighed, whether "it consists [...] only in the appetite or desire to obtain what is lacking or what we already enjoy," Spinoza noted.[3]

Many magical practices responded, then, to various mundane concerns, such as searching for lost or stolen objects, missing persons, seeking for love, predicting the sex of an unborn child. All these practices are called the common tradition of magic, because "they were widely used and not limited to any specific group of people."[4] Historians discuss how to define the multiple meanings assumed by this counterfactual propensity of the human brain. Different names are assigned to the phenomenon, in its concrete historical manifestations: magic, witchcraft, sorcery.

This is a subtle point: because the relationship between magic and witchcraft is complex and the two terms end up taking on a synonymous value. Ultimately, "both magic and witchcraft overlapped in the ways in which they were discussed, conceptualized, and practiced, but aspects of both could exist without the other."[5] Magic, witchcraft, and sorcery had, then, similar blurred characteristics, evolved over time and could be interchangeable, regarding their reference to damage and suffering, to *maleficium*.

In historical times, human efforts to dominate the anguish produced by fear of disease and death, the will and desire to live and satisfy cognitive anxieties, left extensive traces. Using David Hume's well-known passage on religion, we argue that witchcraft was born from an interest in life events and from the incessant wavering of hopes and fears that besiege the human mind.[6] After the end of the Pleistocene, for millennia, little would happen in human activities without the search for explanations starting from counterfactual convictions.

Ecological Niche and Biological Perspective

History of the earth, and the space revolutions which the first men and women experienced, is touched upon in the book with limited hints. The climatic variations that occurred on the planet like the one that, more than a handful of millions of years away, narrowed the African forest surfaces, forcing Stanley Kubrick's great ape to leave brothers and sisters – devoid of prefrontal lobes – in the native habitat and walk straight into the Serengeti plains, are not dealt with.[7] Also, *Homo habilis*'s technological improvements are neglected; they are discontinuous due to ecological factors, not easy to reconstruct in detail even if essential to understand how manual skill, with the creation of stone tools and weapons, advanced the species. Instead, our attention is reserved to a biological perspective. Brain transformations, which in the shorter time span of a couple of million years led primate man to abstract thought, will act as proxy for lack of documentation.[8]

***

As it is, ontogenetic life begins from the moment in which differentiating cells give rise to the formation of the organ of thought, and research on its biological nature have advanced our knowledge. All mental functions – from the simplest reflex to the most creative acts connected to language, music, and art – are performed by specialized neural circuits located in different regions of the brain.[9]

Our gray matter evolved to meet the needs of species continuation. With the discovery of the hand, the upright gait, the control of the fire and the invention of cooking, *Homo* was subjected to great cognitive efforts.[10] Increase in cranial capacity and brain mass are believed to be in connection with improvements in the diet. Cooking their food, *Homo* species "overcame the energetic constraints that otherwise apply to larger apes."[11] The brain is a great devourer of energy and advances in food preparation may have promoted its constant growth.[12] Progress was simultaneous, Charles Darwin thought. He was wrong, it seems, on this point, because later studies would ascertain a primacy of bipedalism. Nobody knows if the erect walking gave rise to selective pressures that stimulated brain growth, even if the hypothesis is probable.[13]

We will not insist on the priority of one gait over another; too many things about upright walking still remain uncertain.[14] Instead, let us mention the probability that for a "long period *Homo* had as a model not tigers but hyenas," feeding on the leftovers of predators.[15] Additionally, one point is worth underlining: a change in diet, such as the increase in meat consumption, greatly favored cells that produce dopamine, a neuro-modulator stimulating action, search for information, curiosity, repetition of actions we like.[16] When John Maynard Keynes in his *General Theory*'s famous passage writes of man's animal spirits, he spots a peculiarity of cerebral functioning: "There is [an] instability due to the characteristic of human nature that a large portion of our positive activities depend on a spontaneous optimism [...] the result of animal spirits – a spontaneous impulse to action rather than inaction."[17] Animal spirits, solicited by a dopaminergic effect, were a stimulus to future alchemical adventures of many wizards. Later in this book we encounter a bizarre human economic behavior, the compulsive urge to seek treasures hidden underground (see Chapter 27).

It is necessary to keep focusing on the human ecological niche, at the individual and species level, without fear of naturalistic determinism. Because prehistoric men and women lived in sensate ecologies, clung to soil, close to plants, sun, rain; they observed and imitated animals and tried to tame them.[18] *Homo* appropriates as many things as possible that were around him and the only way available to him so far was his deep involvement in the reality surrounding him. He interprets the world with semiotic abilities that future myth would credit to Prometheus' teaching, the titan friend of humanity, on the day he "showed [...] the rising of the stars and the clues and their sunsets, so difficult to understand."[19] In this symbiotic relationship man has a limited sense of his own individual being. He does not distinguish himself from what surrounds him, everything belongs to him, and he is a part of everything, a cell of a complex organism. The matter around him, living or not, appears animated and alive, part of a network of sentience; the presence and action of invisible powers pervade his mind, and he feels the antithetical laws of life and death. *Homo* considers animal and plant nature as part of the society to which he belongs, in a social connection. Woods from which people drew sustenance are meant as essences with an autonomous will of agency.[20] The attitude of a twentieth-century Mbuti pygmy is significant and can be projected into the Pleistocene past: before planning on hunting, they wondered if it could "please the forest."[21] A sensitivity to trees' emotions that did not require sensors, holograms, and scanners of our present millennium.[22]

The Pleistocene universe, not unlike that of contemporary aboriginals, is full of incorporeal entities; there is a continuity between the living, those who preceded them and those who will come; between humans, plants and animals; between natural creatures and spirits. The space around is not empty but inhabited; movements of the air and shadows hide presences. People are immersed in a flow that connects times and places; they are a node of a network, not isolated individuals, enclosed in a separate space-time.[23] The assumption "that man and nature were closed in a world that interacted" dates back to the dawn of our species and remains until the late Renaissance, the age of witch hunts.[24] There was an intimate relationship between knowledge of plant world and its practical use with repercussions in therapeutic spells, constant examples of which are found in Shakespeare, happily remembered as "the boy from the Greenwood."[25] Ultimately, primitive man fears equally all that is visible and invisible. His psyche is structured by developing mechanisms of plastic regulation, functional to the species continuation, subject to adaptations due to environmental changes and climatic oscillations.

The Essential Factor: The Ape Dilemma

"Nature red of fangs and claws" marked prehistoric times.[26] Tough gentiles (*duri gentili*), as Gianbattista Vico called primitives, long before they thought to "see the gods";[27] well before asking themselves about surrounding realities pervaded by fearsome supernatural agents; in short, far away in the pit of Pleistocene time, hominins harbored an inner torment inherited from when they communicated with each other through gestures, postures, looks, guttural emissions. Primatology suggests such a situation in which fear, anxiety, anger, and curiosity are mixed, with the expression "ape problem." Crouching in prairies or under vaults not yet painted, hominins must have wondered: what are those dense thickets hiding down there? Do they conceal ferocious beasts? Are there any females? Are there males like us or of greater vigor? Do they know things we ignore? And what are their intentions? Are they aggressive or peaceful?

We must reconstruct a primal thinking, namely our ancestors' mental assumptions, to understand why they acted as they did.[28] The constant state of alarm generated by the ape syndrome is a *hub* of our investigation. Primitive mechanisms for processing information, retained from evolutionary experience, prejudice *Homo sapiens*'s judgements about people who differ from him. Cognitive psychology has reconstructed the stages of brain functioning that lead to the formation of judgment under conditions of uncertainty.[29] Hypotheses have been formulated about two types of cognition that regulate human conduct: (a) *fast thinking*, which, pressed by emotion (fear), equips the mind to automatically react in risky situations; (b) *slow thinking*, conscious and reasoning, which reorganizes and processes information by harnessing the free impulses of fast reaction. Slow and fast thought in a metaphor have become the bearer who holds the reins of the elephant. When humans developed language and reasoning the brain reorganized to develop the carrier/bearer (language-based reasoning).[30] *Homo sapiens* inherited the neural mechanisms that evolved to provide threat level assessments, and that never went away.[31] The fast system has obvious evolutionary advantages for survival but it has side effects, because solicitations of fast and slow thinking neural mechanisms, as later explored in Chapter 21, imprinted an attitude on man to reason in causal terms eventually personalizing the blame for negative occurrences, such as malefices.

History of the brain acting as a heuristic substitute has limitations which invite caution. Although joint efforts of paleontologists, archaeologists, geneticists, and neuroscientists have inaugurated a new field of study called cognitive archeology, phases underlying the new discipline are too remote and their indeterminacy is inevitable. Temporal sequences of brain organization continue to remain vague; details of environmental pressures generating neural ramifications, synapses, impulses, associations, and responses equipping *Homo* species for adverse ecological niches, are sadly missing.[32] One metaphor describes man's skull as a toolbox assembled over time by the blind process of evolution by natural selection.[33] Yet an additional, perhaps better, definition of the brain remains that of its intrinsic plasticity, prompted by the ability to act typical of humans.[34] Activities related to hunting and fishing, defense and aggression, collection of edible and curative plants, construction of tools, discovery of fire, family kinship and organization enrich the neuronal and cultural evolution of various types of *Homo*, which will end up much later being strengthened and multiplied by language:

> Human consciences proceeded as a consequence of their activity; acting to carry out their life plans, people reproduced the social and symbolic conditions for the activity, from the most abstract cultural structures to the most particular details of how a particular task was to be completed.[35]

More must have happened. Driven by stimuli from savannas and further insidious habitats, the mind developed various inclinations that allowed it to notice those things that had greatest relevance for ancestors' reproductive success. The tendency to see intentional agents everywhere in nature provides the basic cognitive scheme for believing in supernatural agents that transcend the usual limitations of the laws of nature.[36] In an unpredictable ecological niche and under pressure of physically present realities, hominins' questioning the existence of virtual essences exerted a cognitive effort that leads to cerebral neo-cortexes of higher dimensions, enhancing intellectual abilities. They were on their way to constructing future counterfactual ideas.

Caution is required. This seems like a probable scenario to us but details relating to brain anatomical evolution are unknown. Establishing an exact prehistoric account of its development, due to the fragmentary nature of the available evidence, remains problematic.

Notes

1 Giordano Bruno, *De magia*, 1590 (?).
2 L. Daston, K. Park, *Wonders and the Order of Nature, 1150–1750*, New York, 1998, 13.
3 Baruch Spinoza, *Breve trattato su Dio, l'uomo e il suo bene* [*Short Treatise on God, Man and His Wellbeing*], in Id., *Opere*, F. Mignini, ed., Milano, 2007, 138.
4 R. Kieckhefer, *Magic in the Middle Ages*, Cambridge, 1989, 56; C. Rider, "Common Magic," in *The Cambridge History of Magic and Witchcraft in the West: From Antiquity to the Present*, D. J. Collins, S. J., eds., Cambridge, 2015, 303.
5 See K. Edwards, "The Interrelationship of Magic and Witchcraft," in *The Routledge History of Witchcraft*, J. Dillinger, ed., London, 2021, 257. Historians debate: see C. Tuczay, "Sorcery," and W. Stephens, "Witch and Witchcraft Definitions of," in *The Encyclopedia of Witchcraft: The Western Tradition* (hereafter *EW*), R. Golden, ed., IV, Santa Barbara, CA, 2006, 1061–1064; 1200–1205.
6 David Hume, *The Natural History of Religion*, 1757.
7 Africa played a pivotal role in the evolution of man; D. Reich, *Who We Are and How We Got Here. Ancient DNA and the New Science of the Human Past*, Oxford, 2018, ch. 3. The physical environment was exceptionally variable during our emergence as species; see D. Sloan Wilson, *Darwin's Cathedral. Evolution, Religion, and the Nature of Society*, Chicago, IL, 2002, 31. Paleoclimatology shows that during the Pleistocene the variations and inclinations of our planet around its axis contribute to constantly changing the quantity and distribution of the energy we receive from the sun. These mechanisms, known as orbital forcing, created glacial interludes lasting millennia; K. Harper, *The Fate of Rome: Climate, Diseases and the End of an Empire*, Princeton, NJ, 2017.
8 "An enquiry into the deep history of humans is driven by two themes: one the one hand, brain growth, *encephalization*, and on the other, an increase in *global settlement*"; C. Gamble, *Settling the Earth: The Archeology of Deep Human History*, Cambridge, 2016, 3.
9 Investigations of cognitive neuroscience in the decades at the turn of the twentieth century owe a lot to the studies on the nervous system of a sea snail, *Aplysia californica*, helping to elaborate the links between the brain and the external environment; see. E. R. Kandel, *In Search of Memory: The Emergence of a New Science of Mind*, New York, 2006.
10 Various lithic tools discovered in Kenya, dating back to 3.3 million years, testify to a prevalent instrumental intelligence; S. Harmand et al., in *Nature*, 521, 2015, 310–313.
11 S. Herculano-Houzel, "Remarkable but Not Extraordinary: The Evolution of Human Brain," in *A Most Interesting Problem: What Darwin's Descent of Man Got it Right and Wrong about Human Evolution*, J. M. De Silva, ed., with an introduction by J. Browne, Princeton, NJ, 2021, 57.
12 R. Wrangham, *Catching Fire: How Cooking Made Us Human*, London, 2009.
13 R. Dawkins, *A Devil's Chaplan*, Boston, MA, 2003. The fossil evidence suggests that bipedal walking preceded tool use by millions of years, therefore adapting reason for bipedalism remains a mystery; see Y. Haile-Selassie, "Charles Darwin and the Fossil Evidence for Human Evolution," and "A Reflection on Darwin's Chapter 4: On the

Manner of Development of Man from Some Lower Form," in *A Most Interesting Problem*, 82–102.

14 H. Gee, *The Accidental Species: Misunderstandings of Human Evolution*, Chicago, 2013.

15 R. Calasso, *Il cacciatore celeste*, Milano, 2016, 158.

16 G. Rotilio, *Il migratore onnivoro: Storia e geografia della nutrizione umana*, Roma, 2012.

17 J. M. Keynes, *The General Theory of Employment, Interest and Money*. London, 1936, 161.

18 R. Pierotti, B. R. Fogg, *The First Domestication: How Wolves and Humans Coevolved*, New Haven, CT, 2017.

19 Aeschylus, *Prometheus Bound*, 457–458; C. Calame, *Prometeo genetista: Profitti delle tecniche e metafore della scienza*, Palermo, 2016, 32.

20 No surprise that tree cult testimonies are spread across the planet. See J. Frazer, *The Golden Bough: A Study in Magic and Religion*, London, 1922, chapters 9 and 10.

21 This is the tribe studied by C. M. Turnbull, *The Mbuti Pygmies: An Ethnographic Survey*, New York, 1965. D. Sloan Wilson, *Darwin's Cathedral*, 43.

22 *The Language of Plants: Science, Philosophy, Literature*, M. Gagliano, J. Ryan, P. Vieira, eds., Minneapolis, MN, 2017.

23 P. Coppo, *Guaritori di follia. Storie dell'altopiano Dogon*, Torino, 1994.

24 K. Thomas, *Man and the Natural World: Changing Attitudes in England 1500–1800*, London, 1983, 75.

25 J. Bate, *Soul of the Age: The Life, Mind and World of William Shakespeare*, London, 2009, 36–59.

26 Alfred, Lord Tennyson, *In Memoriam A. H. H.*

27 Gianbattista Vico invites to solicit analysis with inventiveness, to enter the fantasies of the first men through which they thought to see the Gods; Id., *Principi di Scienza Nuova*, in Id., *Opere*, F. Nicolini, ed., VII, [399], Milano, 1953, 515.

28 A. T. Beck, *Prisoners of Hate: The Cognitive Basis of Anger, Hostility, and Violence*, New York, 2000, 30–34. We owe Emily A. Holmes the indication of Beck's work.

29 A. Tversky, D. Kahneman, "The Framing of Decision and the Psychology of Choice," in *Science*, 185, 1974; now in D. Kahneman, *Thinking, Fast and Slow*, London, 2011.

30 J. Haidt, *The Righteous Mind. Why Good People Are Divided by Politics and Religion*, London, 2012, ch. 2.

31 D. Kahneman, *Thinking, Fast and Slow*.

32 E. O. Wilson, *The Social Conquest of Earth*, New York, 2012, ch. 21.

33 D. C. Dennett, *Breaking the Spell: Religion as a Natural Phenomenon*, London, 2007.

34 C. Calame, *Prometeo genetista*, 60–65; A. Favole, S. Allovio, "Plasticità e incompletezza tra etnografie e neuroscienze," in *Forme di umanità*, F. Remotti, ed., Milano, 2002, 167–205.

35 J. Robb, *The Early Mediterranean Village: Agency, Material Culture, and Social Change in Neolitic Italy*, Cambridge, 2007, 245.

36 R. Trivers, *The Folly of Fools: The Logic of Deceit and Self-Deception*, New York, 2011, ch. 12.

2

RECIPROCAL ALTRUISM

The dawn of the human species illustrated by Stanley Kubrick's imagination was followed, in the depth of some million years, by stasis, retreats and progressions of hominin types – about twenty – among which couple bonds and stable reproductive relationships emerged, seed of the primitive forms of human kinship. This was a critical step, because in the primordial state of nature there was never a moment in which human beings existed as isolated individuals. The great apes, who preceded us, developed extensive social skills. Let us still remember that point of arrival and separation from anthropomorphic apes, left behind to reproduce in forest areas. Upon discovering bipedal walking, hominins revolutionized their relationship with space, beginning to expand into new areas and then, following other changes, left Africa for new continents.[1] Their walking upright in the savannahs involved a modification of social behavior, prefiguring greater forms of cooperation to defend themselves from predators and enabling big game hunting. The bipedal posture could also promote gestural communication by disclosing a whole set of precursors that involved the interpretation of gestures by the self and others.[2]

A Leap Forward: The Development of Mental Modules

How did those social units of a few dozen individuals behave in the face of obstacles and dangers coming from their peers and from the harsh ecological context?[3] One answer can be sought by reasoning on the assumption that mental modules had developed in the brain: mechanisms that have evolved in order to react in a specific way to specific stimuli present in the environment, giving rise to a specialized recognition system of every animated thing.[4] These modules are to be thought of as innate cogs regulating human way of thinking. Something is innate, even if it were nothing more than the mechanisms that accomplish learning,[5] an innateness not specified in every detail, but which changes thanks to the neural plasticity that led to the definition of "plastic brain."[6]

DOI: 10.4324/9781003414377-3

As representative of mind modularity, the following features have been proposed: the detection of impostors; reasoning; language; ToM (the theory of mind that allows you to adopt an intentional attitude towards other agents); orientation in space; emotional systems such as fear, disgust, jealousy, etc.; face recognition; choice of partner; the use of tools; recognition of emotions from facial expression, etc. Such a concept of massive modularity presupposes the existence of dozens or hundreds of distinct neural circuits, which globally mediate all the main cognitive activities, each of which has evolved during human existence to govern certain activities. Using some other known metaphors, this modularity is like a Swiss army knife, because it has tools suitable for special purposes; or to small switches located in the skulls of all animals. Each switch is activated by a pattern, which is important for survival in an ecological niche. When it detects a situation, it emits a signal that can change the animal's behavior in an adaptive sense. A cognitive module born of evolution represents an adaptation to a series of phenomena that have created problems or opportunities; it has the function of processing a certain type of stimulus or input, like a snake or a human face.[7] These metaphors are apt to describe forms of adaptation to ancient threats and opportunities present in social life. Their usefulness was to attract the attention of individuals to certain types of events (for example acts of cruelty or disrespect or selfishness), immediately triggering intuitive reactions and even specific emotions (for example, sympathy or anger).[8]

Focusing on the insecurity of life increases our understanding of primitives. The critical circumstances that occurred activated reflections, or systems of specific inferences by area. It is possible that some mechanisms that structure our experiences, such as the sudden bouncing in front of something animated, perceived as a danger, did not require previous knowledge to activate and only subsequently they were categorized in a particular way.[9] It was not a question of forms of knowledge but perhaps innate abilities. Let us be clear about innatism: nature gives us a considerably complex brain, but one that can be considered predisposed (biologically pre-arranged, prewired) - flexible and subject to change - rather than programmed (biologically programmed, hardwired), fixed and immutable. That is, nature provides a first draft which experience then revises.[10] In the course of life, human groups cared about certain situations: the deductive reasoning that emerged through an evolutionary selection equipping them to act, progressed. These were re-actions that led to fight, to escape, to explore which dark active forces lay concealed in their habitat; much later they would lead to cooperation, increasing chances of survival and genetic continuation. Brain neo-cortexes and neural circuits, that is modules such as reciprocity or dominance hierarchy to carry out these specific tasks that will be subject to the ecological modifications of subsequent phases, developed over time.[11] The temporal dimension that took place for the construction of the organ of thought was enormous. In a few million years there was a gradual approach and the final reaching of a limit point, the exceeding of a threshold of cognitive ability.[12]

***

It is unsafe to move in such an extensive chronology.[13] Moreover, two opposite reflections cannot be avoided: we are faced with the frustrating awareness of the occasional and fragmentary evidence available, with the inevitable prospect of formulating fragile reconstructions easily refuted by equally fragile objections. How many accelerations were favored by the vicissitudes of the type of *Homo* (*ergaster*, it is believed), which crossed the Serengeti, is vaguely known. The first systematic hunter of large prey, with a brain born to run, increased its weight (from 800–1000 to about 1300 grams), developing prefrontal lobes and augmenting its transformation into an organ for thinking. After the turn of a million years ago, the light points improve. Evolution set about making a couple of crucial advances.

The beginning of modern human cognition started with a first leap forward, datable to six or seven hundred thousand years ago, with a development of the brain towards what primatologists call a shared intentionality. Perhaps our ancestor's familiarity with the animal world could have induced a "lupification of human behavior [...] There are indications that the human social and even ethical system [...] considered by many at least in theory as one of the highest achievements of humanity, was invented by the canids."[14] A fine hypothesis.

Whatever the case, a genetic foundation is believed to be at the root of cooperative drive.[15] This can be asserted after the first studies of human genome regulatory sequences, in which instructions for the development of our organism are written. There is no doubt that human primates have always been emotional creatures who felt and expressed joy, sadness, anger, and fear transmitted by facial expressions and postures.[16] Hominins seem to have progressed by developing a congenital endowment of affections towards forms of voluntary cooperation culminating in the more mature aspects of reciprocal altruism of *Homo sapiens* 200,000 years ago. This altruism has its roots in the care and attention of parents to their children and continues to embrace all those who are related by kinship (kin selection). Brain areas involved in this mutual support would be part of a legacy as old as the evolutionary line of mammals.[17] It is difficult to have reliable proof of this, though.

Better founded, there is an evolutionary line that includes empathy, one of the most powerful social emotions, destined to affect the future of our species and its cultural and material achievements. It is around the last phase of Pleistocene that *Homo sapiens*'s ritual practices probably took shape, aimed at favoring good weather, hunting, courtship, childbirth, and war, to propitiating the "intentional agents": those benevolent or malevolent mysterious higher energies, believed to be able to fulfil the needs of the group.[18] These strong feelings in the forthcoming agrarian societies lead to long lasting neighborhood bonds through common working pattern.[19]

Sapiens reached this stage through empathy, wrote David Hume almost two and a half centuries ago: through a certain kindness, however small, infused into our chest; a spark of friendship for mankind; a "particle of the dove," mixed in our structure, next to the elements of the wolf and the snake.[20] Empathy, understood as a biological endowment, proves capable of pushing us in search of a universal intimacy, a sense of belonging to the whole. The search for a universal intimacy is the very essence of what we call transcendence.[21]

***

"Despite much theorizing, the evolutionary reasons why humans cooperate extensively with unrelated individuals are still largely unknown. While reciprocity explains many instances of non-kin cooperation, much remains to be understood."[22] The reason why our species moved towards cooperative altruism is probably connected with the "free rider" problem:

> Briefly stated, although if everyone cooperates, we are all better off, it is generally thought that the individual has a better chance of success if she or he does not cooperate but enlists the help of altruists without returning the favor. Since selective pressures on genes act on individuals rather than for groups, this scenario argues against genes predisposing to altruistic behaviors becoming common.[23]

And even less known are the prehistoric contextual conditions under which gender differences in empathy may have developed.[24] Moreover, Hume's lucky perception is abused. Those neurons that produce the emotional empathy are nevertheless susceptible to develop something else, revealing a dark side, with perverse psychological repercussions. Witchcraft situations abound with the opposite face of this emotion.

A Prehistoric Moral Economy

As the millennia passed, less questionable information becomes available. Gradually, *Homo* became good at team play and began to value others as potential collaborative partners and to be socially selective since choosing a poor partner meant less food. Cheaters and slackers were kept away, and bullies rendered powerless.[25] It was an increased perceptive capacity, an incipient aptitude to share mental representations of common tasks such as hunting or gathering food or looking after offspring or defending oneself from aggressive neighbors. For reasons that still elude at some point in human evolution, individuals capable of collaborating with each other found themselves possessing an adaptive advantage.[26]

Despite this, Paleolithic forms of cooperation lend themselves to conflicting interpretations that cannot be omitted from the analysis. It is not clear to what extent biological and social evolution may have favored an egalitarian balance in prehistory. Specifically, what happened when Stanley Kubrick's alpha male heirs "became embedded in groups whose members were armed with stone weapons and able to balance their influence by forming coalitions"?[27] Primatologists point out that these confrontational attitudes were very important, because they foreshadowed new developments in the practice of social group control against dominant individuals, directing humans towards the formation of a conscience and a sense of what is right and wrong through rules. In the end "the social preferences of the groups could powerfully influence the gene pool, and as soon as [*Homo*] began to blush with shame this certainly meant that the evolution of a conscious self-control was well under way."[28]

Once the animal forms of domination and hierarchy were eroded it is believed that they were not automatically replaced by new inequalities based, for example, on ownership. In this way, a subsistence based on foraging and an egalitarian moral economy would develop, favored by a mental attitude that ignored economic growth and limited the concentration of wealth. On the other hand, it is likely that "prehistoric populations should not always be represented as egalitarian as the experience of contemporary hunter–gatherers seems to suggest."[29] It is even admissible that wandering and semi-sedentary groups were able to regulate the possession of the land putting into practice a primordial act of occupation of the territory, from which to derive a series of very precise, rigorous and respected rules of behavior. Primordial forms of possession maybe connected to the supply of food and water or shelter.

Albeit lack of certainty, in reconstructing hominins' way of reasoning we intend to draw attention to a specific behavior pattern that can be described as a form of egalitarian moral economy, conceivable as the response humans give to the perception that the natural environment from which they derive a livelihood is a common good and must be protected with norms and customs against non-cooperative subjects (free riders), upon whom punishments hung. Karl Polanyi's studies, over half a century ago, highlighted the immutability of man as a social being. The preservation of social ties is of crucial importance, first because by not respecting the accepted code of honor or generosity the individual cuts himself off from the community and is expelled.[30] In a certain sense, a prehistoric moral economy is configured as a theory of human conduct at the origin of morality. Everything that is a source of solidarity is moral, everything that forces man to regulate his movements on something other than his selfishness is moral, too, as Émile Durkheim had already stated.[31] Morality: that is, moral feelings not only as a product of social facts but which exist within the mind, the outcome of reciprocal altruism; a succession of small acts revolving around a practical concept of common use of natural resources behind which an evolutionary mechanism is recognizable. A persistent moral economy, an emotional thread that silently runs through history and reaches the feared contemporary dissipation of the common good of nature that presupposes it.

The awareness that each member of the group was a participant in the same idea was a decisive path towards sociability; the beginning of an ethical sense often inauspicious for those who did not adhere to it. Aloofness was frowned upon. When the human brain began to function following a mutual help logic, the rules of life were revolutionized. About two hundred thousand years ago the phase in which *Homo sapiens* would develop the ability to represent what others think and how they could (re)act, began. Neural circuits consolidated making an altruistic, moral way of doing innate and intuitive, because it guarantees better reproductive success. The evolutionary energy produced by shared intentionality and reciprocal altruism materialized in an interactive social monitoring.

But again, our ancestors' tendency to supportive alliances for the common management of resources should not be stretched to excessive conclusions.[32] The instinctual attitude of hunter–gatherers to egalitarianism is to be harmonized with another predisposition: men, like the primates from which they descend, live within a hierarchy of dominance.[33] Also, before getting to the largest of the improvements made by *Homo sapiens*, language, let's remember that the general consensus of studies on the reconstruction above does not intend to cover the existence of discordant realities. This force of evolution which led to mutual altruism hides an opposite side: because being opportunists and parasites (namely, free riders) could lend itself to the achievement of selfish, individualistic ends, and these cannot be ruled out as having been just as adaptive as a guarantee of success.

The Sense of Time

The succession in time of socializing experiences accelerated another acquisition of no small moment in *Homo sapiens*. The innate inclination to familiarize and the biological completion of the brain had to root the mechanisms of time orientation in the organ, started who knows how long before. Augustine of Hippo, wondering about the nature of time, wondered doubtfully: "Who will give us a short and easy definition?"[34] Over the centuries, many ideas and beliefs have followed one another, up to contemporary Physics for which time does not exist. Neurobiology disagrees and believes that it is a product of brain functioning.[35] Created by a nervous, electrochemical event, the perception of time (connected to the pre-frontal cortical areas, and then, gradually, to other areas until it reached the memory centers and the limbic system of affect, etc., etc.) was made up of durations, intervals, waits, breaks that flow in a spatial reality not so much physical as in a psychosocial mode full of emotional, affective, social, practical meanings. Thanks to the sense of time sharpened by the vision of the dead, subsequently conveyed by language (much later reinforced by seasons spent tilling fields), these modern human beings invented cosmogonies and enriched them in continuous narratives.

***

Defending oneself from predators no less than from conspecifics was a priority, too. However reproductive success of this humanity was also forged in protecting itself from adverse weather conditions and the erratic sequence of bad and good weather influenced their thinking, well before Neolithic times with the development of agriculture. Did *Homo* fantasize about entities that were masters of the atmosphere? It is not to be considered accidental that one of the most common projections of historical magical-religious ideas is to have imagined the existence of deities believed to be creators of storms and bad weather – like Baal or the Hadad Semitic deities – according to a psychological mechanism that transforms a series of random phenomena into a causal process.[36] And a collective fantasy, dating back to the eighth and ninth centuries, dark ages of the Christian era, seems to come from the Paleolithic. It is registered by the archbishop Agobard of Lyons, a Visigoth clergyman, in a sermon (*De grandine et tonitruis*/On hail and thunders):

In our country almost all people, both the nobles and the common people, in the city as in the countryside, old and young, believe that hail and thunder can be created by men [...]. We have all seen and heard that many people are victims of this madness and slaves of these foolish beliefs, so they believe and say that there is a country called *Magonia* (land of magicians?). From this country ships would be sent in the clouds, with which they would then transport those fruits that the hail snatches away from the trees and which would be lost in the storm in that country; those seafarers of the ether would then compensate the magicians of the storms to receive cereals and fruit in exchange.[37]

These thought predispositions regarding the existence of someone or something superior, having the ability to alter physical forces, arise from the relationships of our ancestors with such a primeval habitat. A Latin poet, Lucretius Caro, poetized how man came to religion and invented overlying beings:

Now what cause has spread among the multitudes the gods [...] is certainly not difficult to explain with words [...] Because [... men] thought them much superior [...] because in their sleep they saw them perform many wonderful actions without being fatigued. In addition, they saw the events of the sky and the various seasons of the year taking place in a fixed order, nor could they understand from what causes this proceeded. So, they had the only escape for themselves to entrust everything to the gods and to think that everything would yield to their sign.[38]

Cognitive psychology today reaches identical conclusions by insisting on our specific brain inclinations. The mind imagines a pantheon of invisible agents that cause the weather conditions and various other fortunate or unfortunate circumstances. Voilà: here is the birth of supernatural agents as a by-product of a highly adaptive cognitive module.[39]

Speaking: The Holy Grail of Evolution

Pressed by the force of nature, the action of the *Homo* found impetus in new "emotional, material and symbolic resources [which] create the all-round social being" at the end of the Paleolithic.[40] Fifty thousand years ago *Homo sapiens* made significant achievements for the formation of a modern mind with the discovery of language. This time reference will recur. Not less arbitrary than other dates (60,000 or 70,000 years ago), it has a symbolic value, alluding to the time when a more extensive use of vocal communication was made by populations with larger and anatomically completed brain.

There are doubts that a larger brain mass led to language, though. This is the case of *Homo neanderthalensis*, who began to infiltrate Europe from the Fertile Crescent.[41] However, the Neanderthals' capacity for producing an articulated language is still uncertain, despite having a voluminous brain, supposedly bigger than that of *Sapiens* (estimated at 1.2–1.4 kg).[42] Not surprisingly, William Golding's literary imagination made the cousins of ours communicate in a rudimentary way and through forms of telepathy.[43]

The Neanderthals aside, we cannot help but wonder what kind of sounds and gestures hunter/gatherer bands used before being able to speak. There was a time when our ancestors lacked language despite having a complex range of emotions and the need to influence the behavior of others.[44] How *Homo* first types communicated with each other is an occasion for heated academic debate.[45] It is probable that the language of the first humans was preceded by formulating metaphors, by their nature rich from the associative point of view, but relatively imprecise.[46]

The technical aspect of language origins remains a controversial perhaps insoluble puzzle. It is more important to underline that a generalized use of speaking represents the first stage of the changes in communication qualifying some turns of *Sapiens* existence, like the social control played by chatting about things that are not always futile such as gossip about who behaved well or badly.[47] Once the social potential of speaking was discovered, an unstoppable series of explosions of creativity and diversity followed.[48] Language was the Grail of human social evolution and, once established, attributed almost magical powers to the human species, expanding its conceptual power.[49] From the discovery of the sacred cup came an increased impulse towards magic and religion, whose evolutionary dimension was that of keeping primitive nuclei united by favoring collective interest over inextricable individualistic tendencies. Cognitive enhancements consolidated, allowing groups to expand by favoring further mutual aid and planning elaborate actions – hunting, gathering, mating, alliances, war – which facilitated reproductive success. Unfortunately, all this is not directly investigable. An unbridgeable hiatus of some tens of thousands of years, starting from the conventional chronology (50,000 years ago), prevents a reconstruction of *Homo sapiens*'s relations with supernatural agents invoked with songs and dances by magicians or proto priests.

To partially fill this gap, it must be said that in those two, three, four tens of thousands of years, testimonies of different quality but similar in meaning have come down to us. We refer to experiences of amazing manual activities, to wall paintings found in prehistoric caves, a visual translation of needs and desires that are difficult to ascertain.

The Cave of a Sorcerer: A Basis of Civil Society?

One day, a day that lasted no less than forty thousand years, men of Paleolithic began to draw.[50] Some 400 caves have traces of Paleolithic art. Though in recent decades the earliest evidence has become much older than previously thought, any inquiry into the origins of paleoart should rather focus on *why* rather than on *when*.[51] Who were these *Sapiens* endowed with pictorial talent? Nothing about their individuality will ever be known, and it is good to think in terms of living ensembles, small formations formed by families, kinships, social lives characterized by distinctions of age and role, cultural beings who inhabited landscapes invested with symbolic meanings.

Studies to arrive at an understanding of the polychrome decorations of these caverns have multiplied after the 1994 discovery of the Chauvet cave in the Ardèche department of France. In fact, heavy burdens weighed on the minds of men when in September 1940, in the Dordogne department, some French boys discovered the caves of Lascaux.

Interpretations on the meaning of the late Paleolithic figurative language are a controversial issue, but few scholars doubt those artists had the same sort of brains as we have, with appreciation noting the expression of a modern, mature, cognitively clear mind.[52] Why did the ancient gentiles fresco their homes? Let us distinguish. Cave graffiti are related to various themes: they primarily depict large animals but in smaller numbers there are stylized human figures, handprints, and anthropomorphic subjects, such as lion men or men with deer heads, perhaps shamans. It may be that these artistic expressions were aimed at a utilitarian representation of an important moment in daily life, such as hunting.

Uncertainties remain about which stimuli motivated the inspiration of those ancestors. From anthropomorphic signs and figures, not without some twisting, one may get the impression of a prehistoric art penchant for eros.[53] Not a few sketches reproduce parts of the body relating to sex: pubic triangles, phalluses. The sexual allusions of the Rubenesque statuette called Venus of Hohle Fels, sculpted with a possible propitiatory intent, are no different.[54] It can be reasonably assumed that anxieties and emotions, result of experiences lived or handed down by obscure bards, ended up being transformed into emblematic images.

Some unrealistic figures, almost chimeras, imply the presence, in caverns that may also function as ceremonial centers, of some sorcerer or shaman or proto-priest, negotiator with the immanent forces of the universe.[55] Certain areas of the caves were probably reserved for special male people, early anticipation of the future historical gender discrimination which gave men the privilege of contact with divinity. Maybe embryonic cosmogonies would already have been under construction, proceeding by accumulation, in temporal sequences veiled from us. Still, "Beware of art, culture, religion" and sex remain the most important warning.[56]

***

Whatever happened, an invitation to interpretive caution came from an eminent psychiatrist and philosopher of the past century, Karl Jaspers. Because in a very narrow sense it could be argued that from burial places, from ornaments, from painted utensils, from relatively fine musical wind instruments, from buildings and even from wall graffiti, from all this, in short, we only get a very vague idea, to say nothing, of the soul, of the inner attitude, of the beliefs, of the spiritual movement of prehistoric men.[57] And yet, if the builders and early worshippers of the Göbekly Tepe's monumental magic, a religious structure, dating about 11,500 years ago, were hunters–gatherers, then we face the possibility that an organized magic, religious activity predated the agricultural civilizations.[58] The dawn of historical times is not so far away and the first Mesopotamian agrarian societies in their Pantheon attest to the coexistence of magical and religious reasoning. Therefore, an excessive interpretative reticence is of no help.

We take for granted that, though the symbolic associations of wall art escape us, the caves were frescoed by men who had already developed sophisticated linguistic and technical skills. Precisely this fact leads us to underline something else, that their admirable imagination was situated into a broader cultural context and was expression of social relations and kinship.[59] Oscar Wilde's ingenuity captured the idea: there must have been more than hunting, painting, and rituals. As it happens, each personal experience became a story of deeds accomplished or boasted about. The writer wondered:

> Who was he who first, without going out on the hard hunt, told the astonished cavemen, at sunset, how he had dragged the megatherium out of the purple darkness of his jasper cave, or killed the mammoth in single combat to bring back its golden tusks, we cannot say it, nor did any of our modern anthropologists have the courage to tell us, despite their much-vaunted doctrine? [Whatever] his name and his race he certainly was the founder of social relations. He is the very basis of civil society.[60]

In fact, depictions and stories of hunting performances allude to a life in common in those caves, to occasions for play, dialogue, and communication on other urgent matters around which collective existence revolved: reproduction, and the intelligence of things.

In this direction of reasoning, we return to the Holy Grail of evolution. From language visions of the world and much more sprouted up. A programmed necessity of the human instinct to stay close was consolidated. A need to communicate, expressed in practices thousands of years old and in this sense genetically adaptive, took hold: it was an evolutionary sequence that from gestures, postures, looks, and sounds went as far as the language. No doubt, prevailing occasions of the first requests for information concerned *Homo* basic "appetites": hunger, thirst, sex, play. However, what cannot be excluded is the curiosity to collect small news from which the pleasure of simple conversation was formed. As already mentioned, exchanging small talk on aspects considered marginal in life constitutes a non-secondary connotation of the cognitive and emotional abilities and propensities of humans; an adaptive tendency as a nourishment essential to survive for social interaction. Also, it is in such contexts that the mental conformism marginalizing individualists and free riders of every human group was produced and sustained. In vigils and spaces of collective service, people would meet to exchange information and evaluations: acts and concrete situations would be described, compared to similar cases of the past and evaluated. In this process, norms are created, giving rise to forms of egalitarian justice. On the other hand, the same aptitude for chatter and spontaneous relish for gossip, subtly used by all human societies to unmask any moral violation of norms established by custom, may act as a disruptive factor degenerating into malice or slander or envy, a constant hotbed of suspicions of witchcraft agency. A thousand years later, the evangelizing missions of the Jesuit fathers will fight against this pernicious taste of man.

Notes

1 G. Manzi, *L'evoluzione umana*, Bologna, 2007, 65. Recent research on great apes considers the hypothesis that our ancestors used bipedalism both on the ground and to move between trees; see A. Roberts, S. Thorpe, "Challenges to human uniqueness: bipedalism, birth and brains," in *Journal of Zoology*, 292, 2014. See S. L. Lewis, M. A. Maslin, *The Human Planet. How We Created the Anthropocene*, New Haven, 2018.

2 B. Chapais, *Primaval Kinship: How Pair-Bonding Gave Birth to Human Society*, Cambridge, MA, 2008; G. Edelman, *Wider than the Sky: The Phenomenal Gift of Consciousness*, London, 2004.

3 R. Dunbar, "Coevolution of Neocortex Size, Group Size, and language in Humans," in *Behavioral and Brain Sciences*, 16, 1993, 681–735. Dunbar suggests an evolution of three groups of different sizes: overnight camp; band or village; tribe; respectively of 38, 148 and 155 individuals.

4 M. Gazzaniga, *Human: The Science Behind What Makes Your Brain Unique*, New York, 2009; G. Origgi, "Evoluzione e modularità concettuale," in *Scienze della mente*, A. M. Borghi, T. Iachini, eds., Bologna, 2000, 31–45.

5 S. Pinker, *The Blank Slate: The Modern Denial of Human Nature*, London, 2002; M. Gazzaniga, *Human*.

6 The topic of neuroplasticity, in all its aspects, is important but "radiates an optimism" against which one must be cautious; see R. Sapolsky, *Behave: The Biology of Humans at Our Best and Worst*, London, 2017, 137–153.

7 D. Sperber, in *Mapping the Mind: Domain Specificity in Cognition and Culture*, L. Hirschfeld, S. A. Gelman, eds., Cambridge, 1994, 39–67; D. Sperber, L. Hirschfeld, "The Cognitive Foundations of Cultural Stability and Diversity," in *Trends in Cognitive Science*, 8, 1, 2004, 40–46.

8 J. Haidt, *Righteous Mind*, ch. 6.

9 P. Boyer & C. Barrett, "Evolved Intuitive Ontology: Integrating Neural, Behavioral and Developmental Aspects of Domain-Specificity," in, *Handbook of Evolutionary Psychology*, D. Buss, ed., Hoboken, NJ, 2005, 96–118.

10 G. Marcus, *The Birth of Mind: How a Tiny Number of Genes Creates the Complexities of Human Though*, New York, 2006.

11 M. M. Gazzaniga, *Human*.

12 E. O. Wilson, *The Social Conquest*.

13 M. Tomasello, *Origins of Human Communication*, Cambridge, MA, 2009, *passim*; J. Diamond, *Guns, Germs and Steel: The Fates of Human Societies*, London, 1997.

14 R. Pierotti, B. R. Fogg, *The First Domestication*. See T. Flannery, "Raised by Wolves," *The New York Review of Books* (*NYR*), April 5, 2018. "Wolves that were able to approach and feed on human waste around settlements would have a huge advantage […] They chose us," see B. Hare, "The Darwinian Road to Morality," in *A Most Interesting Problem*, 76.

15 R. Sapolsky, *Behave*.

16 S. Mithen, *The Singing Neanderthals: The Origins of Music, Language, Mind and Body*, Harvard, 2007.

17 F. de Waal, *The Age of Empathy: Nature's Lessons for a Kinder Society*, New York, 2009.

18 About religion, some unfortunate hypotheses have been formulated about a location in the brain of an area of the divine. No brain area responsible for such behavior has been identified. Religious ideas, like the magical one, must be understood as underlying a system of neural networks responsible for the connections between emotions, abstract thought, generation of causal links, anticipations of the future and so on. See G. Northoff, "Localization versus Holism and Intrinsic versus Extrinsic Views of the Brain," in *Minerva Psichiatrica*, 55, 2014, 1–15.

19 For "the social history of an idea: that of neighborhood," see A. Wood, *Faith, Hope, and Charity. English Neighborhoods, 1500–1640*, Cambridge, 2021, viii.

20 David Hume, *An Enquiry Concerning the Principles of Morals*, 1751.

21 J. Rifkin, *The Empathic Civilization: The Race to Global Consciousness in a World in Crisis*, New York, 2009, ch. 15.

22 See D. Smith, M. Dyble, K. Major et al., "A Friend in Need is a Friend Indeed: Need-Based Sharing, Rather than Cooperative Assortment, Predicts Experimental Resource Transfers among Agta Hunter–Gatherers," in *Evolution and Human Behavior*, 49, 1, 2019, 82–89.

23 See T. M. Reimers, B. Oakley, "Empathy, Theory of Mind, Cognition, Morality, and Altruism," in *On Human Nature*, 360.

24 A research based on present time situations shows that women rated higher in empathy than men in all experimental conditions: see C. S. Löffler, T. Greitemeyer, "Are Women the More Empathetic Gender? The Effects of Gender Role Expectations," *Current Psychology*, 2021, https://doi.org/10.1007/s12144-020-01260-8

25 C. Boehm, "Bullies: Redefining the Human Free Rider Problem," in *Darwin's Bridge*; N. Raihani, *The Social Instinct: How Cooperation Shaped the World*, London, 2021, 141–156.

26 M. Tomasello, *Origins*.

27 W. Scheidel, *The Great Leveller: Violence and the History of Inequality from the Stone Age to the Twenty-first Century*, Princeton, NJ, 2017, 28.

28 C. Boehm, *Moral Origins: The Evolution of Virtue, Altruism and Shame*, New York, 2013, 113, 177.

29 Ibid., 30. "To use modern hunter–gatherer societies a-simplistic analogs for our early hominin ancestors represents an anachronistic dead end': K. Widerquist, "The Evolution of Equality: Rethinking Variability and Egalitarianism Among Modern Forager Societies' *Ethnoarcheology*, 2015, https://works.bepress.com/widerquist/53/.

30 K. Polanyi, *Primitive, Archaic, and Modern Economies: Essays of Karl Polanyi*, G. Dalton, ed., New York, 1980.

31 É. Durkheim, *The Division of Labor in Society* (1893), New York, 1997; J. Haidt, *Righteous Mind*, ch. 11.

32 C. van Schaik, M. Kai: "Our ancestors evolved a preference for egalitarianism, equity and justice, an obsession with reputation, and a preference to collaborate with trusted – along with the ability to forgo these preferences if profitable opportunities arise," in *NYR*, "Letters," Dec. 22, 2016.

33 J. Haidt, *Righteous Mind*. For a counter-history of the origin of democracy and the destruction of the egalitarianism characteristic among hunter gatherers see the review article: B. Reiter, "The African Origin of Democracy," *Academic Letters*, Article 414, 2021. https://doi.org/10.20935/AL414.

34 St. Augustin, *Confessions*, XI, 14. 37.

35 D. Buonomano, *Your Brain Is a Time Machine: The Neuroscience and Physics of Time*, New York- London, 2017.

36 W. Behringer, *Storia culturale del clima: Dall'era glaciale al riscaldamento globale*, Torino, 2013, 85.

37 A. Borst, *Forme di vita nel Medioevo*, Napoli, 1990, 397.

38 Lucretius, *De rerum natura*, V. 1179–1185. Our translation.

39 J. Haidt, *Righteous Mind*, ch. 11.

40 C. Gamble, *Paleolithic Societies of Europe*, Cambridge, 1999, 351.

41 About Neanderthalensis, hybridized with the African type that supplanted him, knowledge has increased after the reconstruction of his genome: S. Pääbo, *Neanderthal Man: In Search of Lost Genomes*, New York, 2014.

42 D. Reich, *Who We Are*, 26.

43 W. Golding, *The Inheritors*, London, 1955. Golding had studied natural history.

44 S. Mithen, *The Singing Neanderthals*.

45 "The steady growth of hominin cranial capacity during the Lower and Middle Paleolithic supported the emergence of controlled vocalization, orchestrated mimetic techniques, deductive tracking skills and memory traces (exogrammatic) stored outside the brain as consciously-sequenced information packages meant to stabilize abstract calibration of

realities': G. F. Steiner, "Holocene Crossroads – Managing the Risk of Cultural Evolution," in *IFIRAR Quarterly*, Sep 2018, 10, https://doi.org10.5281/zenodo.2348143.

46 G. Edelman, *Second Nature*, ch. 6. Darwin saw in music a possible root of verbal language: see Charles Darwin, *The Descent of Man*, 1871, and *The Expression of Emotions in Man and Animals*, 1872. Dissent in studies remains vehement. See S. Pinker, *How the Mind Works*, New York, 1996; S. Mithen, *The Singing Neanderthals.*

47 C. Boehm, *Moral Origins*, 240–246.

48 M. Tomasello, *Origins.*

49 E. O. Wilson, *The Social Conquest*, ch. 22.

50 R. Calasso, *Il cacciatore celeste*, 27.

51 G. F. Steiner, "Holocene Crossroads," 12.

52 J. D. Lewis-Williams, "Art for the Living," in *The Oxford Handbook of The Archeology and Anthropology of Hunters-Gatherers*, V. Cummings, P. Jordan, M. Zvelebil, eds., Oxford, 2014, 625–642; E. R. Kandel, *The Age of the Insight: The Quest to Understand the Unconscious in Art, Mind, and Brain, from Vienna 1900 to the Present*, New York, 2012. According to a recent thesis, the psyche of wall painting artists was still evolving; their mental development resembled that of autistic minds, a savant autism: N. Humphrey, "Cave art, autism and the evolution of the human mind," in *Cambridge Archeological Journal*, 8, 1998, 165–191.

53 R. Dale Guthrie, *The Nature of Paleolithic Art*, Chicago, 2005.

54 Discovered in southern Germany, also dating back to the same period, made from the ivory of a mammoth; P. Mellars, "Archeology: Origins of the Female Image," in *Nature*, 459, 2009, 176–177; M. Blume, *Evolutionary Studies of Religiosity and Religions, started by Charles Darwin*, Lecture at the 13th Congress of the European Society for Evolutionary Biology (ESEB), Tübingen University, August 22, 2011.

55 A. Leroi-Gourhan, "The Religion of the Caves: Magic or Metaphysics?," in *The MIT Press*, 37, 1986, 6–17; E. Gombrich, "The Miracle at Chauvet," in *NYR*, 43, 1996.

56 See G. Rigal, *Le temps sacré des caverns: De Chauvet à Lascaux: Les hipothèses de la science*, Paris, 2016, ch. 1.

57 K. Jaspers, *The Origin and Goal of History*, Westport, CT, 1977.

58 A. Norenzayan, *Big Gods: How Religion Transformed Cooperation and Conflict*, Princeton, NJ, 2013, 120.

59 L. M. Brady, J. J. Bradley, A. Kearney, "Rock Art as Cultural Expressions of Social Relationships and Kinship," in *The Archeology and Anthropology of Rock Art*, B. David, I. J. McNiven, eds., Oxford, 2018, 671–694.

60 Oscar Wilde, *The Decay of Lying*, 1889, in *Essays*, H. Pearson, ed., London, 1950.

3

PREHISTORIC WOMEN

This chapter faces a thorny problem: where are women in the Pleistocene narrative? Traditionally, by a scholar convention, hominins are referred to by male
gender. But having mentioned "the care and attention of parents to their children"
(p. 12), a spontaneous question arises: isn't the scientific discourse on Prehistory too
sparing of references to women?

A patent androcentrism has characterized anthropological archeology. Yet, given
that evolution has not chosen the simple and efficient way of having offspring from
females without any genetic contribution from males, it is women who do most of
the work.[1] Females disproportionately bear the burden of reproduction. They give
birth, breastfeed, contribute to the food support of the group and, hardly doubtful,
were among the objects of exchange of major value.[2] And there is more, especially
important for our book, if future studies manage to overcome a limited knowledge:
some substantial deductions could derive from a link between the development of
female brain and women's inflated role in witchcraft cases. Shouldn't we weigh up
the hypothesis that the neurobiology of female brain predisposes women to a larger
possession of emotional attributes?

***

On the distribution of activities by sex in groups of hunter–gatherers, scholars
belonging to different disciplines are beginning to question the real dimensions of
women's work. Despite reticent if not silent prehistoric material objects, to
hypothesize that female occupations may have been broader and more significant
than has been established to date is likely correct. However, to test the conjecture
is hard. Because the archaeological data, which in most cases are not specific as to
gender, are difficult to interpret and will slow down the process of giving credit
to women for the contributions they made in prehistoric times. It is to be hoped
that a "new breed of paleoanthropologists, trained to decipher fossils and stone

DOI: 10.4324/9781003414377-4

tools but also to study the subsistence strategies of living hunter–gatherers" will better explore this critical aspect of prehistory.[3]

Recent studies conducted on approximately a hundred contemporary hunter/gatherer communities can be used to observe archeological finds with more attentive eyes:

> while hunting was practiced almost exclusively by males, it was inefficient as a means of providing food. Meat from kills is available at irregular intervals. The !Kung Bushmen of Botswana hunt vigorously for a week and rest for three weeks thereafter. It is the gathering of food by women and not the hunting by men that feeds present-day aboriginals. The hunting of men contributes twenty percent to food, but women regularly produce eighty percent of the tribe's total food consumption.[4]

Among the !Kung of the Kalahari, plant food provides 60–80% by weight of the total nourishment and has a high yield in respect to calories procured per unit of time spent in the harvesting activity (240 calories per hour) compared to hunting (100 calories per hour), marked by long waits and failures. In essence, the contribution of women to the group survival seems to be decisive.[5]

Can these research perspectives be transferred backwards among prehistoric human beings?[6] A strong obstacle consists in contextualizing them: in specific times, spaces, and typologies of *Homo*. Take, for example, *Homo ergaster*, present about 1.9–0.9 million years ago. In that extended period, while crossing the African territories abundant in fauna, the Ergaster probably developed an appropriate stone technology and specialized in the role of hunter. But the post-kill phase has been relatively ignored by archeologists. Maybe much of the food processing aspect was managed by women. They may have been prominent in converting animal carcasses into vital subsistence products and in developing technologies for storage and preservation.[7] Whatever the case, this is certainly a critical point in the evolution of early hominids. We wonder if sophisticated technologies could make us glimpse whether new divisions of work and arrangements of social relations took place within growing couple ties. Constraints, one might suppose, favored by a tendency of females/gatherers to remain faithful to a single man. The competition between males was thus greatly diminished, because of a strong reduction in sexual dimorphism, which was now replaced by permanent material (and affective?) couple ties and new and deeper paternal feelings. Pair-bonding and increased sex egalitarianism may have had a transformative effect on human social organization.[8] Whether biological functionalism from the very beginning would have directed *Homo* towards the monogamous, nuclear family remains a much more questionable hypothesis.[9]

***

Did the hypothetical rebalancing in the role of food supply and storage played by men and women lay the foundations for greater sexual equality between hunter–gatherers? The conjecture is supported by current studies. Our prehistoric ancestors are often portrayed as savages wielding spears, but scientists think that early human societies are likely to have been founded on enlightened egalitarian principles.[10] In contemporary hunter–gatherer tribes, men and women tended to have equal influence on where and with whom their group should live. These findings challenge the idea that sexual equality is a recent invention, suggesting that it has been the norm for humans for most of our evolutionary history. "A gender equality may have been a boon to survival and played an important role in shaping human society and evolution."[11]

Be that as it may – and a happy connotation of paleontology, biological anthropology, archaeology, medical anthropology, and cultural anthropology is that of reserving continuous surprises that make previous acquisitions obsolete within a few years – new evaluations are welcome but cannot ignore a primal fact: *Homo* remained heirs of primates.[12] The morphological differences between male and female are the result of million years of evolution.

Women's "Lengthy Past"

Taken for granted that the stronger anatomical structure of men qualified them to protect the group as well as to defend their inborn machismo, and eventually leading to asymmetries of power status and prestige, caution is to be advocated "in any analysis that characterize women in terms of proscription, marginalization, or exclusion."[13] Perhaps, women and men negotiated their existence in hunter–gatherer societies, making decisions that facilitated their lives and livelihoods; probably, food storage activities were women's spaces within hunter–gatherer communities. It should be noted that such specialized arenas appear to be a distant anticipation of the woman's confinement within home as depicted in Xenophon's *Oeconomicus* (Chapter 24). Is it the result of a negotiation? In any case, it is another proscription on women, after the one, previously hypothesized (p. 18), which forbade them to access the sacred.

***

Future research on gender might certainly benefit from a more critical evaluation of familiar tropes such as women exclusion and marginalization.[14] The beginning of a *gynecopoiesis* – how a woman is made – has prehistoric roots. Whatever the dimensions of the specialization of *Homo ergaster* and his successors in hunter/defender were, once he became *Sapiens*, he paved the way for the future female condition, inaugurating a spatial separation, channeling women into a specification of functions and sociality, relegating them no less to a complex of subordinations that ended up making them a male sexual property. Homer's Achilles alludes to this robbery aim of tribal wars when commenting: "days of blood I spend fighting, fighting against strong men, for their females."[15] A conclusion seems inevitable: the origins of a patriarchal society lie far back in time, long before the advent of agrarian civilizations.[16]

The blind poet's words symbolize women's future destiny. We label it as a double standard bias, expanding its meaning beyond the sphere of sexual conduct, to describe treatment whereby women are given less latitude than men. The logic of the double standard of behavior between the two sexes is clear: the value of male property was diminished using anyone who was not the legitimate owner. The concept, deep-seated in the worldview of agricultural societies, enhances the husband's control over his wife. It is a known history that the double standard rationale, moving from the sphere of sexuality, has marked the marginalization of women in every sphere of activity for millennia up to present days. These topics are later explored by addressing them from the angle relating to the formation of the cliché witch = woman, in Chapter 24.

Therefore, the question that should be addressed concerns how males came to control resources. Here is the historical problem and answering it makes the case for a deep history.[17] Now, a consideration related to a biological hypothesis is to be anticipated. In the evolutionary perspective that interests us here, performing separate functions for hundreds of millennia could have further influenced brain neurobiology, ultimately shaping the attributes of female social emotions.

***

In a fine illustration of a twentieth-century !Kung aboriginal, a woman is shown while breastfeeding an infant and holding by hand a toddler. The powerful image of women's natural superiority in nurturance would be also valid in a Pleistocene environment.[18] A careful reflection on it raises a problem on which exploration is not conclusive: namely have the laws of nature led to an inaccurate coincidence of the male and female brain functioning and to a greater inclination towards emotional traits in women?

When asked about personality and psychological characteristics (such as empathy) women and men differ reliably. However, when this is assessed using more objective behavioral measures, male/female similarities in cognition outperform differences. Women appear to do on average slightly better than men at recognizing emotions from non-verbal cues (and slightly worse at visual spatial tasks and navigation).[19] These findings have noteworthy limitations, of which we will mention two. First, many studies fail to account for confounders and context, for example: training and self-confidence in one's task-specific ability influences performance and may have skewed the data we have so far.[20] Second the literature on sex/gender differences suffers greatly (possibly even more than the general neurosciences field) from a bias towards only reporting differences and not similarities.[21] Even accepting the relative evidence of higher female emotion-processing abilities, neurosciences struggle to determine the extent of its biological basis. The presence of sex/gender-based differences in the brain (after correcting for non-biological factors) is unresolved. Rather, there is consensus around refuting accounts of brain sexual "dimorphism." Instead, the debate is open when it comes to the impact on behavior of quite small male/female differences: in the structure of specific regions (e.g., the amygdala); in how brain areas are connected and in how they may respond differently to, for example, emotional stimuli (i.e., large syntheses of studies to date mostly show inconsistent patterns in such male/female differences).

The brain has properties determined by the influence of steroid hormones during the early development and puberty, and in females during the period of birth and breastfeeding with the consequence that some areas may show a greater degree of feminization than others.[22] Whether this is trivial compared to social and cultural imprints remains debated. The more research delves into the detail, the more environment and experiences appear to strongly shape how these sex-based brain differences are expressed. As cognitive sciences strive to overcome a profound "replication crisis" technology advances should facilitate the large-scale data integrating all biopsychosocial factors that are needed to unravel these questions. Even more difficult as the "wiring" emerges itself from complex environment–gene interplay.

Hence, while caution is paramount in theory in cannot be excluded that a certain degree of "essential difference" in the human endowment of social emotions could be confirmed, with potentially incendiary implications for our book.[23] It certainly remains difficult to test the existence of factors underpinning aspects of a social sub-ordination of women wired in the brain rather than culturally inherited. Even more difficult as the "wiring" emerges itself from complex environment-gene interplay. Scientific research struggles to achieve certainties: "There is no universal model for how the genetic and hormonal components of sex play a role in influencing the brain and behavior."[24] Nonetheless, in the chapters that follow, the hypothesis that there is an association of a greater female endowment of social emotions with the millennial stereotype of the equation witch = woman, cannot be excluded a priori.

Notes

1 R. Trivers, *The Folly*, ch. 5.
2 M. T. Seielstad, E. Minch, L. Cavalli-Sforza, "Genetic Evidence for a Higher Female Migration Rate in Humans," in *Nature Genetics*, 20, 1998, 278–280.
3 S. Hrdy, *Mothers and Others: The Evolutionary Origins of Mutual Understanding*, Cambridge, MA, 2009, 148; *Women in Paleolithic & Neolithic Times*, web.clark.edu/afisher/HIST251/prehistory%202.pdf.
4 Ibid.
5 M. Ehrenberg, *Women in Prehistory*, Norman, 1989.
6 B. Hayden, "Observing Prehistoric Women," in C. Claassen, ed., *Exploring Gender through Archaeology*, Madison, 1992, 33–48.
7 R. Jarvenpa, H. J. Brumbach, "Hunter–Gatherer Gender and Identity," in *The Oxford Handbook of the Archeology and Anthropology of Hunter–Gatherers*, 1266–1288; K. Sterling, "Man the Hunter, Woman the Gatherer? The Impact of Gender Studies on Hunter–Gatherer Research," ibid., 151–176.
8 M. Dyble et al., "Sex Equality Can Explain the Unique Social Structure of Hunter–Gatherer Bands," *Science*, April 2015, unpublished.
9 K. Hawkes, "Mating, Parenting and the Evolution of Human Pair Bonds," in *Kinship and Behavior in Primates*, B. Chapais- C. Berman, eds., Oxford, 2004, 443–473; S. Hrdy, *Mothers and Others*, 143–171.
10 M. Dyble, R. Mace, N. Chaudhary, "Human Behavior: Sex Equality Can Explain the Unique Social Structure of Hunter–Gatherer Bands," in *Science*, 348, 2015, 796–798.
11 Male assistance became important during the period when women were breastfeeding: F. W. Marlowe, "A Critical Period for Provisioning by Hadza Men: Implication for Pair Bonding," in *Evolution and Human Behavior*, 24, 2003, 217–229.

12 A. K. Hill, D.H. Bailey, D.A. Puts, "Gorillas in Our Midst? Human Sexual Dimorphism and Contest Competition in Men," in *On Human Nature*, 235–244; E. E. Spinapolice, "From Primitivism to a Contemporary View of Pre-history: A New Tale," in O. Raggio, "Forum: On the Condition of Dialogue between Sister Disciplines. Forty-four Years after Marshall Sahlins' Stone Age Economics," in *Quaderni storici*, 151, 1, 2016, 290–300, doi: 10.1408/84148.

13 R. Jarvenpa, H. J. Brumbach, "Hunter–Gatherer Gender and Identity."

14 Ibid.

15 Homer, *Iliad*, IX, 326–327. Our translation. See J. Gottschall, *The Rape of Troy: Evolution, Violence and the World of Homer*, Cambridge, 2008.

16 B. Smuts, "The Evolutionary Origins of Patriarchy," in *Human Nature*, 6, 1, 1995, 1–32.

17 C. Gamble, *Settling the Earth*; Id., "The Death of Prehistory," in *Quaderni Storici*, 151, 1, April 2016.

18 See the illustration in S. B. Hrdy, *Mother Nature. Natural Selection and the Female of the Species*, London, 1999, 99.

19 G. Rippon, R. Jordan-Young, A. Kaiser, C. Fine, "Recommendations for Sex/Gender Neuroimaging Research: Key Principles and Implications for Research Design, Analysis, and Interpretation," in *Front Hum Neurosci* (Frontiers in Human Neuroscience), 8, 650, 2014, doi:10.3389/fnhum.2014.00650.

20 L. Arrighi, M. Hausmann, "Spatial Anxiety and Self-Confidence Mediate Sex/Gender Differences in Mental Rotation," in *Learning & Memory*, 29, 9, 2022, 312–320. doi:10.1101/lm.053596.122.

21 L. Eliot, A. Ahmed, H. Khan, J. Patel, "Dump the 'Dimorphism': Comprehensive Synthesis of Human Brain Studies Reveals Few Male–Female Differences Beyond Size," in *Neuroscience & Behavioral Reviews*, 125, 2021, 667–697, doi:10.1016/j.neubiorev.2021.02.026. A reply: M. Hirnstein, M. Hausmann, "Sex/Gender Differences in the Brain Are Not Trivial: A Commentary on Eliot et al.," in *Neurosci Biobehav Rev*, 130, 2021, 408–409. doi:10.1016/j.neubiorev.2021.09.012.

22 J. R. Rainville, T. Lipuma, GE. Hodes, "Translating the Transcriptome: Sex Differences in the Mechanisms of Depression and Stress, Revisited," in *Biol Psychiatry* (Biological Psychiatry), 91, 1, 2022, 25–35. doi:10.1016/j.biopsych.2021.02.003.

23 S. Baron-Cohen, *The Essential Difference: Men, Women and the Extreme Male Brain*, London, 2004.

24 C. Fine, *Testosterone Rex: Unmaking the Myths of Our Gendered Minds*, London, 2017, 61.

4

PRIMARY EMOTIONS

Fear and Anger

At the end of prehistory, when societies based on work in the fields emerged 10,000 or 12,000 years ago, some space of human mental constructions was occupied by an aggregate of beliefs devoted to a lasting future, religion and witchcraft. In previous pages we asked ourselves how and why *Homo sapiens*'s brain had reached a stage of speculative thinking that led minds to invent cosmogonies populated by mysterious entities, in which good and wicked ideas are intertwined. Of this cognitive human drive, we recover the original nucleus, the "ape problem," the syndrome that brings fear and anger to center stage and explains why people reacted the way they did when faced with the fear of evil.

Fear Created Gods and Magicians

But before dealing with a dissection of a primary emotion let us move forward to the centrality of fear in historical times, when nothing or little was known about brain anatomy. The embryogenesis of magic and religious convictions is captured by an assumption expressed concisely by the Roman poet Publius Statius: *primus in orbe deos fecit timor* (fear first made gods in the world). The maxim synthetizes man's mind mechanism that places hominins' most ancient experienced primary emotion, fear, at the root of religion: a modern and functional insight that highlights divinity's neuropsychological derivations.[1] The long common path of magic and religion authorizes one to interpolate the poet: *primus in orbe deos [et magos] invenit timor*. A human cowardice in the face of gods, a *deisidaimonia*, as treated in classicism, which leads to the conclusion that "it is really fear that drives superstitious behavior: and in this sense Theophrastus and Plutarch were right."[2]

Gods and magicians, therefore. We start from here, always keeping in mind a warning: "magic remains a special case, and its relationship with religion has not been resolved at all."[3] A lasting future is reserved for Statius's intuition. The

DOI: 10.4324/9781003414377-5

concept crosses pagan and Christian ages. In early modern times, almost at the end of the witch hunts, it finds substance in Baruch Spinoza's comments and then in David Hume's:

> If men could direct their affairs with firm purpose or if luck were always kind to them, they would not be prey to any superstition. But often they end up in situations so difficult that they cannot formulate any action plan and, usually, for the sake of the uncertain goods of fortune [...] they oscillate miserably between hope and fear: so, their soul is almost always totally inclined to believe anything. When in doubt, a small impulse is enough to push them in one or another direction; and this happens even more easily when, agitated by hope or fear, they stop, ensnared [...] The cause for which superstition is born, takes root and grows, is therefore fear.[4]
>
> But it must be always admitted that [...] terror is the first principle of religion.[5]

Our digression closes with the testimony of an aboriginal given to a French ethnologist at the beginning of the twentieth century. In the words of an Eskimo shaman, healer, and magician, Aaona, we recapture *Homo*'s emotional scenario.

> We do not believe, but we are afraid. All our habits come from life and are directed towards life [...] We do not believe anything. We fear the spirit of the earth which generates bad weather and which we must fight to snatch our nourishment from the sea and the earth. We fear Sila, the god of the moon and Takanakapsaluk the great woman who lives at the bottom of the sea and reigns over marine animals [...] We fear the disease that we encounter every day around us [...] We fear the evil spirits of life, those of the air, of the sea, of the earth, which can help some evil shamans to harm their fellow men. We fear the souls of the dead and those of the animals we have killed [...] And we are so ignorant, despite all our shamans, that anything unusual scares us. We fear all that we see around us, and likewise fear all the invisible things that are likewise around us, we fear all that we have heard in the tales and myths of our ancestors. Therefore, we have our customs.[6]

Aaona's dramatic cosmogony describes the eternal canvas of witchcraft agency; and prefigures themes around which witch trials unfold: anguish, bad weather, sustenance, disease, wicked magicians, evil spirits, souls of the dead, stories handed down.

We decode the short passage in neural terms. The opening, we do not believe, but we are afraid, summarizes human mental evolution, because emotional factors precede and dominate in the life of prehistoric man. Fear had a more remote evolutionary history than other primary emotions, bringing into play reaction mechanisms in all repetitive daily situations (search for nourishment, mating, hiding places and shelter) during which individual and group safety was in jeopardy. In the shaman's story, a further alarm must be added to the list of fearsome virtual entities. In the ancestral past, to an even prevalent extent, fear came from fellow men whose presence kept aroused a congenital anxiety about the purpose of human actions: group selection raised hominins to peaks of solidarity and fear. Every tribe knew very well that if it was not armed and not on guard its very existence was in danger.[7] Gang assaults, followed by murders and territorial expansions aimed at greater access to resources and females, were a million-year-long strategy.[8] Fear therefore produced a lasting effect, transforming *Homo* into modern social beings who enhanced their chances of survival through the solidarity of kinship.

***

The conceptual harmony of Statius, Spinoza, and Aaona, a poet, a philosopher, and a shaman, anticipates the research of neuroscience on the function performed by primary emotions in the evolution of human gray matter.[9] The role of magic appears homologous to that of religion and qualifies as a mental milestone of our species in the face of pressing anguish and insistent questions of primitives dominated by the harshness of survival. Defensive, operational aspects of such ideas are configured as the brain's prerogative; an ability to deduce causes, agents, and intentions, to predict dangers and formulate causal explanations of predictive value, that is, useful for survival.

The combination of "deos [et magos]" was for a long time a foregone conclusion, a dichotomy that ambiguously expresses connected tensions. However, it is no good to exceed in homologation, because first Mesopotamian testimonies of documented history already outline a timid parting of ways of witchcraft and religion, started who knows when. Several millennia still pass and in biblical and Greco-Roman societies religion claims distinct objectives and affirms a persistent primacy, not exempt from refusals. Because as far as practical aspects of all institutionalized cults are concerned – to protect, comfort, fulfill, heal – it will always be a contested or at least circumvented primacy.[10] If religion cannot heal, one can turn elsewhere to magic. The Roman playwright Plautus alludes to it in a comedy. In *Curculio* ("Weevil"), Cappadoce no longer believes in the therapeutic virtues of divinity and exclaims: "I am determined to leave the temple immediately because I have understood Asclepius' decision: he does not care about me, nor does he care to save me."[11]

A Primacy: The Amygdala

At this point neurobiology occupies a central stage. Deepening the genesis and persistence of witchcraft conviction requires a careful consideration of the brain map. Behind the previously evoked cultural references to fear there is a specific anatomical reality, namely the amygdala, giving it a temporal precedence that almost assigns it a supremacy in the control and management of human emotions.

Not surprisingly, "most of what we know about the neurobiology of emotion comes from studying primary emotions," and fear paved the way for a knowledge of the "emotional brain," a biological phenomenon that dates to the history of life's earliest days.[12] The communication between nervous tissue cells, the synaptic transmission, which is the basis of fear, has been preserved over the course of evolution. The part of the brain called the amygdala is responsible for the "fear system," and small almond-shaped synapses are predisposed to respond to salient signals by receiving an impulse and transforming it into effect, by virtue of which the individual, when perceiving a danger at a neural level, produces reactions that increase their chances of survival. This primary emotion can be interpreted as the result of a biological evolution, which lasted for a few million years, to protect the life during which the organ was ordered with schemes aimed at learning fears that had a meaning in the Stone Age. And the only way in which evolution can transmit this information from the past into the present mind is through genes.

How have things turned out? During the Pleistocene, the probable modifications of the brain were determined by environmental conditions that increased the chances of our ancestors to reproduce by developing the mental modules, already mentioned, to adapt to circumstances.[13] Slow cognitive processes were activated, conferring an instinctual ability to recognize impending dangers from sounds, noises, physiognomies, postures, staring gazes. In comparison to anthropomorphic apes, natural selection had favored hominins, endowing them with the whites of their eyes. Thanks to the sclera, gaze direction can be identified by capturing the intentions of others. Seeing, for a primitive, is like a sense of touch extension; his eyes are fingers that grasp and can do more, as we show later, when dealing with the evil eye (Chapter 22): the pathogenic ray that wounds and kills, a true form of "optical witchcraft."[14]

The role of the amygdala is now quite well known: it is not limited to generating fear or even emotions in general but is a "detector of salience and biological relevance."[15] The small structure is connected to the visual system through afferent pathways that transmit signals in a fast but unsophisticated way; in this way the information that arrives from the eyes to the amygdala loses in detail but gains in speed. Thus, the amygdala measures the coarse characteristics of the stimuli sufficient to identify whether they stand out from the environmental context, or how potentially important they are. If a stimulus appears new, different, or relevant, the amygdala transmits the signal to the cortices that direct attention or begins to prepare motor responses even before the granular and precise information on that same stimulus becomes conscious to the superior visual cortices.

Let us focus on stimuli that can signal a danger. What stands out is the ability of the amygdala and the salience network of which it is the center, to develop in people the skill to sense and forewarn danger. Permanence of this biological endowment should be emphasized; it gives meaning to the repetitive cases occurring in witchcraft trials when the offended and the offender (or the mediator between the two) confront each other, studying each other reciprocally, scrutinizing the slightest movements of the face's hidden intentions. The physiological basis of fear conditions human beings by providing them with an intelligent awareness, an internal guide in the relationship between the subject and their circumstances, a signal that lights up (the amygdala's discharge) every time something changes in the environment, when the gaze of others shifts. This brain apparatus combines two ways in which critical situations are fixed by responding to "species-specific dangers and to those learned by individuals in the course of their lives," and profoundly influences human behavior.[16]

When fear is too strong it produces perverse side effects: instead of saving our lives it then becomes a stress factor, which, in the long run, destroys life both mentally and physically.[17] Deleterious experiences in which numerous protagonists of witchcraft trials incur. The outcome of the physiological preconditions appears to be a conditioning from fear stimuli that tend to be refractory to change but not immutable. If a previously neutral stimulus (the rustle of the leaves) is followed by bad luck (the attack of a predator), that stimulus remains conditioned by fear, and its recurrence automatically activates the neural trace. Once again, the amygdala is at the center of the cerebral circuit that mediates this mechanism together with the hippocampus which encodes the context (the forest, but not the bushes inside the village) in which the association between stimulus and damage determines fear.[18] These associations can be forgotten, yet fear memories just as easily remain in the brain and are reactivated during existence, as we know today.

Historians encounter the negative consequences of such mind upheavals in dealing with *maleficium* and the panic caused by witch-hunting. In moments of life involving rash scares, individual or collective, the decision-making process in the face of risks created by the influence of a dangerous person is dictated by a final mental input that depends on emotion, on the dismay that triggers violent response. The neurobiological foundation sets in motion mechanisms of (re)action which do have their own rationality and which in the analysis of the phenomenon allow us to approach the root of the intricate psychological connection between the witch and her victims.

Anger: Reactive, Proactive

If anxiety and dismay have a biological purpose in protecting life, the current of impulses that through the amygdala generates fear cannot be separated from anger. This emotion also has "an ancient biological basis, linked to the survival instinct, in particular to the aggressive response to possible threats."[19] Aristotle, reflecting on the fear that arises from thinking of impending doom, with words adaptable to the psychological dynamics of the mutual ill will that is established between victim and offender in witchcraft situations, defined the combination fear/anger as a pain or a disturbance due to a mental image of a possible future painful or destructive misfortune that is so close that it can be considered imminent.[20] A mechanism is thus revealed: the fear that bad deeds of selfish subjects would have destructive effects on the group to which one belongs, provoking an immediate neural reaction whose outlet in primitive communities, as in cases of malefic agency, seems to have been rage with a probable consequent physical elimination of such individuals, thus overcoming the paralyzing inertia of terror. During evolution, from a neurobiological point of view, the process appears clear: parts of the brain involved in the regulation of emotions (the prefrontal cortex and in particular the orbito-frontal cortex that modulate the function of the amygdala) intervened by playing "an important role in controlling anger and controlling the reactions that arise from it," thus allowing people to respond in a non-mechanical way to actions that trigger ire.[21]

The cognitive component is crucial to our argument. Aggression could lead to killing profiteers who exploit the cooperation of others but do not reciprocate. It is useful to distinguish between a reactive aggression and a pro-active one; the first is "prominent among males struggling for hegemony"; the second "characterized by premeditation" and triggered by various reasons including the achievement of a gain.[22] These forms of violence took place in a neural space which was unknown in ancient times. All this seems obvious: today we can clarify that the space in which a witchcraft crisis explodes is a consequence of emotional processes, of previous evaluations that take place outside awareness, that is, unconsciously.[23] *Fast thinking* reacts immediately to threatening situations. Anger was functional to survival.

It is pivotal to focus on how anger triggering reactions were overcome. The formation of human consciousness, understood from the perspective of an interaction between nature and culture, highlights the slow development of "changed cerebral mechanisms of emotion [...] In effect, one of the key purposes of our educational development is to interpose a non-automatic evaluative step between causative objects and emotional responses."[24] In this way, although with procedures that are not without constant contradictions, man tries to go beyond spontaneous reactions by making *slow thinking* intervene. The significance of this psychological development unfolds in future human settlements. Scattered hunter–gatherer groups, abandoning African prehistory, moved towards a residential stability in villages populated by other groups of non-relatives. They were *Sapiens*, who had reached the stage of cultural and material advancement of pre-Axial civilizations (biblical and pagan).[25] We believe that automatic reactions – or proactive aggression – of Pleistocene ancestors, based on the automatic circuits of fear and wrath, to eliminate opportunists and evil people, might prove dysfunctional in a context characterized by the coexistence of family stocks of different origin and culture.[26]

The Role of Culture: From *Thinking Fast* to *Thinking Slow*

In the matter of consilience between disciplines, we are at a new junction in our investigation. Neurobiology provides the tools for understanding the cognitive node, hardly explored by historical research and difficult to solve with only the craft of the Greek goddess Clio. We allude to the "natural control" of witchcraft.[27] In primitive communities, the control of negative individualities that occurred before through an altruistic and pro-active punishment of free riders, performing the adaptive function of holding small groups together, later underwent further adaptations during the transition to proto-historic societies. The neural legacy of Prehistory reactive/pro-active automatism is forced to interact with more complex human contexts and altruistic punishments are accompanied or replaced by a no less adaptive mediation. A disguised governance of ill-disposed subjects will be present in the entire historical trajectory of witchcraft. Among the sedentary populations in the agricultural age, alternative "informal," not drastic, solutions root coexistence with those who were morally ambiguous and potentially dangerous. It should be noted that these are choices inclined not only to stem rash retaliations but to contain their transfer to the surrogate intervention (ultimately also vindictive) of the "formal" state or church justice that developed as normative encodings of fear and anger, as well.

If our analysis is correct, further reasoning on the role of free riders can be ventured. How could this social typology be concretely imagined? Free riders could impersonate different realities. Non-cooperative behavior aroused malevolence, resentment, and even violent hostility, which could lead to ruptures of neighborhood familiarity which in turn could trigger vengeful reactions. However free riders were the same as non-conformists, that is people who, while cooperating, mind their own business and reject sociable attitudes, have a propensity to live in seclusion, with isolation that is not free from risks (Chapter 25). Whatever the types, a common denominator stands: they tend to withdraw. And here lies a historical problem: aloofness. Because it does not go unnoticed: "Whoever withdraws, in fact, if it was not deliberately to do evil, was doomed in spite of himself to do it inevitably, by his very isolation which made him more vulnerable to attacks."[28] Separateness could be the consequence of a desire to play a role of social utility (curator, soothsayer, connoisseur of mineral/plant nature) whose outcome eventually marginalized losers. It is not misleading to assume that inherent to this Prehistoric social figuration positive/negative critical potentialities bequeathed to historical times, existed.

***

[T]he orbital cortex, then (together with its ventromedial neighbor), is involved in various pacifying faculties of the human mind, including self-control, sympathy towards others, and sensitivity towards norms and conventions. For all these reasons, the orbital cortex is a fairly primitive part of the brain.[29]

In the individual formation (ontogenesis), brain plasticity properties subject to interaction with the environment and societal life allow and favor adaptation. It is probable that this biological development implies an evolutionary convenience.[30] Nevertheless, the rooting of the non-automatic learned evaluative steps, typical of *slow thinking* was characterized by the continuous stop-and-go that persisted during the civilization process from Prehistory through ancient, medieval, modern and contemporary world. We don't think it accidental that for an exceptionally long time a sudden anger, served as self-preservation in the face of danger, continued to be considered an emotion not characterized in a negative way.[31] In Cervantes's novel Don Quixote apologized to his faithful servant, Sancho Panza: "[forgive] the blows I gave you in ire; because men cannot repress first impulses."[32] Not otherwise, the impulsive "fist," in response to a provocation, to which Pope Francis (Jorge Mario Bergoglio) alluded in a public conversation, comes from afar and possesses a neural logic.[33] Anger was little diminished by its reputation for irrationality and took the form of moral aggression applicable in dynamics that arise after sudden misfortunes and damage and the subsequent triggering of malefice accusations.

Let us use an oxymoron that would not please Descartes: anger can be defined as an intelligent emotion, entangled in witchcraft phenomena, induced by physical stimuli established in the course of evolution or learned by association, but always triggered from the outside, by a person, an animal, an object, a situation, even when evoked by the memory, by the recollection or by the anticipation of an event experienced or told on the many occasions of a sociality that was once much more widespread. When external threatening stimuli present themselves to the visual or auditory regions of the brain, they open locks that trigger the emotional state. The result is a peculiar way of reasoning in which, to put it again in Descartes's words, thought will appear conditioned by an intelligent and disparaging "malin génie," which seeks compensation for the damage received in vindictive rage. Malignant genius that the brain imagines and from which it draws even without a direct visual stimulus. The widely held opinion of anger as a hot-blooded emotion, on the contrary, in retaliation for the damage suffered, often takes the form of a meal served cold.

The timing of recurring psychological mechanisms described in witchcraft trials highlights the dynamic between *fast thinking* and *slow thinking*, when threats uttered by some, and the inevitable reactions of fear or rage of others are recorded. This is a situation often defined as "refused charity syndrome." If in a community help is denied to a neighbor and they walk away muttering threatening words such as you will regret it, if a misfortune strikes someone who refused alms, after some time they blame whoever articulated those hostile words and seeks, finds satisfaction in the vengeful anger of a witchcraft accusation. What happened in the accuser's mind? A re-elaboration of facts that caused the damage is automatically activated, leading to the "personalization of damage." A mental process to be deepened in Chapter 21.

Seeing and Hearing Past Emotions

Guided by the amygdala, through a chemical interaction between body and mind, fear and anger had been specified in man as armed sentries; neural systems interacting with what is seen, heard, perceived.[34] Fear and anger come as biologically determined processes and adaptations, dependent on innately predisposed brain devices established through a long evolutionary history.[35] Despite this, their manifestation – in breathing rhythm, in facial muscles alteration, in voice timbre variations, in body and hands postures and in eyes movements – will be modified thanks to learning and culture which interact with the plasticity of the brain organ.

No surprise that the primacy of seeing and hearing is once again established (see Chapter 22, on the evil eye). Unfortunately, they are marginal senses among Clio's conventional tools! Trial reports allow us to inadequately perceive actors' emotions in the drama triggered by a witch aggression. Yet, they rarely may have been disguised and were visible on the face and in the eyes as a guarantee against retaliatory threats from those who are afraid.[36] Trial minutes reveal that protagonists react with a state of mental confusion not in the face of concrete data but rather of what is thought the antagonist has done or can do. An observer of great and minor human events like Niccolò Machiavelli pointed to these cerebral tricks by writing: "The generality of men feed on what appears as much as on what is: indeed, many times they are moved more by things that appear than by things that are."[37] The attempt to look beyond or behind appearances can be today labelled as a form of mind reading to which we shall return. Our aim is to solicit judicial sources through the hermeneutics offered by what is already known of brain neural functioning, thus trying to overcome the explanatory gaps imposed by the archival papers. Judicial transcripts constitute a *sui generis* film clip, devoid of actors' voices and faces. Omissions subtracting emotions that cannot be hidden in live hearings.

A consilience among disciplines may have "wide implications for historians, because it overturns humanists' unscientific claims that culture alone determines human actions and that culture is unstable everywhere, constantly subject to change and transformation."[38] It is clear, for example, that fear has a physiology like all emotions. This aspect, biology, has always been a difficulty for historians,[39] even if Marc Bloch had already suggested that they eat everything, like the ogre from a fable, because the state of the texts and even more our research methods insufficient acuteness, limit our ambitions.[40]

Perplexity over the protracted separation between scientific culture and humanistic culture has recently led to observations that if historians had access to the psychological states of the protagonists of the past, they would in turn be able to construct more coherent narratives.[41] Anthropologists wonder how much is lost "when one works predominantly with written sources as in the case of many historians."[42] A knowledge of brain functioning helps to venture a speculation that these "paper criminals" harbor malefic intentionality, on their actual will to commit *maleficia* that we are investigating.[43]

A few decades ago, a regret of two historians was truly anticipatory and significant. It was an externalization in the concluding pages of their research on the collective psychodrama of the Salem Village witchcraft trials in 1692. Our sympathy for the authors' laments is obvious and for this very reason remembered:

> If we had had the opportunity to know [the protagonists] better – to hear the timbre of their voices, to grasp the alternation of emotions on their faces, of following them in some moments of their life of which no trace remains – we would have been able to perceive with even greater intensity the living flavor of their individual being.[44]

Notes

1 Publius Papinius Statius, *Thebaid*, III, 661.
2 H. Bowden, "Before Superstition and After: Theophrastus and Plutarch on Deisidaimonia," in *The Religion of Fools? Superstition Past and Present*, S. A. Smith, A. Knight, eds., Past & Present Supplement, 3, Oxford, 2008, 71.
3 W. Burkert, "The Problem of Ritual Killing," in *Violent Origins: Walter Burkert, René Girard, and Jonathan Z. Smith on Ritual Killing and Cultural Formation*, R. G. Hamerton-Kelly, ed., Redwood (Cal.), 1987, 161.
4 Baruch Spinoza, *Trattato teologico-politico, Prefazione* (Tractatus Theologico-Politicus), 1, 4, in Id., *Opere*, 427, 428. Our translation.
5 David Hume, *The Natural History of Religion*.

6   L. Levy-Bruhl, *Le surnaturel et la nature dans la mentalité primitive*, Paris, 1931, xx–xxi. Our translation. The cosmological traits drawn by the aboriginal "naturally recur in individuals through humanity although they are given a different cultural expression in particular times and places." See R. Hutton, *Shamans: Siberian Spirituality and Western Imagination*, London, 2001, 149.

7   E. O. Wilson, *The Social Conquest*, ch. 8.

8   H. Trivers. *The Folly*, ch. 11.

9   Bronislaw Malinowski, a founding father of anthropology, sees magical and malefic actions as the result of anxious reactions, of oppressive emotions or obsessive desire based on a universal psychophysiological mechanism; see Id., *Magic, Science and Religion*, Whitefish, 2010.

10 Today we learn, almost with certainty, "from dozens and dozens of accurate studies conducted with healthy and sick subjects […] that religious practice is positively correlated with health." See R. Trivers, *The Folly*, ch. 11; and B. Y. Lee, A. B. Newberg, "Religion and Health: A Review and Critical Analysis," in *Zygon*, IX, 2005, 443–468.

11 The implications of Plautus' tirade are evident and can be projected back and forth in time; E. R. Dodds, *The Greeks and the Irrational* (1951), Oakland, 2004.

12 A. Damasio, *Looking for Spinoza: Joy, Sorrow, and the Feeling Brain*, San Diego, CA, 2003, 45; J. LeDoux, *The Emotional Brain: The Mysterious Underpinning of Emotional Life*, New York, 1998. On interrelations between *fear* and *anxiety*, Id., *Anxious: The Modern Mind in the Age of Anxiety*, London, 2015.

13 D. Sperber, *Explaining Culture: A Naturalistic Approach*, Cambridge, MA, 1999. It is known that we must consider not only the differentiation of brain activity but above all the integration of the various functionally separated brain regions: G. Edelman, *Wider than the Sky*.

14 D. G. Gilmore, *Aggression and Community: Paradoxes of Andalusian Culture*, New Haven, CT, 1987, 168.

15 R. Adolphs, "Fear, Faces and the Human Amygdala," in *Current Opinion in Neurobiology*, 18, 2008, 166–72.

16 J. LeDoux, *The Synaptic Self: How Our Brain Becomes Who We Are*, New York, 2002, 10.

17 A. Damasio, *Self Comes to Mind: Constructing the Conscious Mind*, New York, 2010. Emotion is an integral part of the processes of reasoning and decision, for better or for worse. What is certain is that it does not seem at all that reason can work better without the influence of emotion. On the contrary, emotion is likely to support reasoning, especially when it comes to personal and social issues that involve risks and conflicts; Id., *The Feeling of What Happens. Body and Emotions in the Making of Consciousness*, San Diego, 1999.

18 S. Maren, K. Luan Phan, I. Liberzon, "The Contextual Brain: Implications for Fear Conditioning, Extinction and Psychopathology," in *Nature Review Neuroscience*, 14, 2013, 417–28.

19 R. Bodei, *Ira. La passione furente*, Bologna, 2011, 9.

20 Aristotle, *Rethoric*, II, part II.

21 M. Sitskoorn, *I sette peccati capitali del cervello*, Roma, 2012, 101; R. Douglas Fields, *Why We Snap*, New York, 2015.

22 R. Wrangham, *The Goodness Paradox: How Evolution Made Us Both More and Less Violent*, London, 2019, 24–29.

23 J. LeDoux, *The Emotional Brain*.

24 A. Damasio, *Looking for Spinoza*, 54–55.

25 The term axial proposed by the German psychiatrist and philosopher Karl Jaspers refers to an interpretation of the history of humanity, in the period between 800 and 200 BC.

26 Studies conducted on the Gibuti tribe (Papua, New Guinea) show that they establish whether an individual's violent behavior is intolerable and, if it is, for the good of the tribe, the individual is killed. S. L. Lewis, M. A. Maslin, *The Human Planet*.

27 The concept of witchcraft natural control was anticipated by the Scottish historian C. Larner, "Natural and Unnatural Method of Witchcraft Control," in Id, *Witchcraft and Religion: The Politics of Popular Beliefs*, Oxford, 1984, 127–139.

28   G. Duby, "L'émergence de l'individu. Situation de la solitude XIe–XIIIe," in *Histoire de la vie privée*, 2, *De l'Europe féodale à la Renaissance*, P. Ariès and G. Duby, eds., Paris, 1985, 504.

29   S. Pinker, *The Better Angels of Our Nature: Why Violence Has Declined*, London, 2011, 506.

30   A. Damasio, *Descartes' Error: Emotion, Reason, and the Human Brain*, New York, 1994, ch. 5.

31   M. McGuire, "Moralistic Aggression, Processing Mechanism, and the Brain. The Biological Foundations of the Sense of Justice," in *The Sense of Justice: Biological Foundations of Law*, R. D. Masters, M. Gruter, eds., London, 1992, 31–46.

32   Miguel de Cervantes, *Don Quixote of La Mancha*, I, ch. 30.

33   In a speech by pope Francis in Manila, on January 16, 2015.

34   S. Baron-Cohen, *Zero Degrees of Empathy: A New Theory of Human Cruelty*, New York, 2011, 26–27.

35   A. Damasio, *Self Comes to Mind*.

36   Charles Darwin, *The Expression of Emotions*.

37   Niccolò Machiavelli, *Discourses on Livy*, I, ch. 25 (trans.: H. C. Mansfield, N. Tarcov).

38   G. Hanlon, "The Decline of Violence in the West: From Cultural to Post-Cultural History," in *The English Historical Review*, 128, 2013, 368.

39   J. Bourke, *Fear: A Cultural History*, London, 2005.

40   M. Bloch, *Feudal Society*, London, 2014, II, ch. 2. Important breaches are finally opening: See *The American Historical Review*, 119, 2014, pp. 1492–1629: "AHR Roundtable: History Meets Biology: Introduction"; J. L. Brooke, C. Spencer Larsen, "The Nurture of Nature: Genetics, Epigenetics, and Environment in Human Biohistory"; E. Russell, "Coevolutionary History"; R. Roth, "Emotions, Facultative Adaptation, and the History of Homicide"; K. Harper, "The Sentimental Family: A Biohistorical Perspective"; W. Scheidel, "Evolutionary Psychology and the Historian"; L. Hunt, "The Self and Its History"; J. Adeney Thomas, "History and Biology in the Anthropocene: Problems of Scale, Problems of Value"; N. Macleod, "Historical Inquiry as a Distributed, Nomothetic, Evolutionary Discipline"; M. D. Gordin, "Evidence and the Instability of Biology." Some walls are still erected: J. Plamper has "a mission [*sic*]." He tries to warn Clio of the dangers of following the path of other human sciences and of taking recklessly from experimental psychology, especially in the neuroscientific incarnation, in Id, *The History of Emotions: An Introduction*, Oxford, 2015, 163.

41   J. Kagan, *The Three Cultures: Natural Sciences, Social Sciences, and the Humanities in the 21st Century*, 2009.

42   P. Geschiere, "Witchcraft and the Danger of Intimacy," in *Emotions in the History of Witchcraft*, L. Kounine, M. Ostling, eds., Manchester, 2016, 213.

43   The definition of "paper criminals" in S. Luzzatto, *Max Fox o le relazioni pericolose*, Torino, 2019, 3.

44   P. Boyer, S. Nissenbaum, *Salem Possessed: The Social Origins of Witchcraft*, Cambridge, MA, 1974. Historians will need a fertile imagination to apply C. Gilligan's listening guide to their mute paper sources; Ead., "The Listening Guide Method of Psychological Inquiry," in *Qualitative Psychology*, 2, 1, 69–77.

5

SOCIAL EMOTIONS

Empathy–Shame–Envy

Ten thousand or twelve thousand years ago, with the advent of agricultural civilization, the preconditions for the development of evil witchcraft found favorable ground in villages where interrelated groupings of people created the conditions for the activation of the entire range of all social emotions. Much further on, the witchcraft trials of the early modern age will abound with information on the protagonists of malefices, mostly women, that still await in-depth studies (Chapter 24). But emotions have a long past in the construction of the individual self that transcends the sacred boundaries of recorded history. *Homo sapiens* progressed following a much more elaborate script in the diversified human environments of the late Pleistocene. It was a change of scenery with more complex roles for humans.

Empathy

A "Particle of the Dove"

Maleficium analysis enters a real labyrinth, because the impulse to do evil is entangled in the microcircuits of the brain tissue and the negative drive of acting maliciously is held back by a compassionate emotion already encountered, empathy.[1] Evolution has endowed our brain with checks and balances and the automatism of a bad act produced by fear and anger is countered by empathic altruism, a prerequisite of ultra-sociality.[2]

The metaphor suggested by a primatologist can help us understand. Empathy is composed of various layers like a Matryoshka, the commonly known Russian doll, at the core of which there is the ancient tendency to match the emotional state of others (an emotional contagion). Around this core, evolution has built increasingly sophisticated capabilities, such as concern for the condition of others and the assumption of their point of view.[3] Matryoshka's external layer leads to reciprocal altruism.

DOI: 10.4324/9781003414377-6

Psychopaths, for example, do not seem to have the deepest layer of Matryoshka. They understand the wishes and needs of others, but do not care. Their learning curve of emotions and behaviors is altered by this deficiency. Diagnosing psychopathy in past criminals is obviously impossible. A clue to determine the syndrome perhaps comes from the repetition of immoral, bad actions, which have neutralized amygdala reactions contrary to evil doing.[4] Or, other people are predisposed to this lack of emotional contagion.

Recent studies suggest that another small brain area, the insula anterior section, is dysfunctional in subjects with characteristics at risk of psychopathy. The insula performs the function of associating body sensations with the emotional experience, a key aspect of our emotional vocabulary. In children and adolescents who have "non-emotional-indifferent" (callous-unemotional) personality segments, potential antecedents of psychopathic traits in adults can be seen.[5] This brain area proves less active in response to the smile of those who are nearby, and the less the insula is activated, the less individuals feel the instinct (usually contagious) to laugh together.[6] Insula activity deficit is also manifested when these same "callous-unemotional" adolescents are asked to imagine how guilty they would feel for carrying out hypothetical acts that violate simple moral norms. It may be that the neural deficit implies the lack of emotional involvement in doing evil, in the face of an intact ability for rational judgment regarding the morality of actions.[7] These deficits in adolescents at risk or before an actual psychopathy occurs (which may never manifest itself) suggest that feeling neither remorse nor empathy is more the origin than the consequence of repeated malicious actions. Such a sociopathic predisposition seems to have a relatively important genetic component, which is more easily transformed into antisociality only in the presence of adverse environmental (socio-economic) conditions.[8] This is a doubt to be later addressed in a specific situation (Chapter 27).

If research suggests that empathy development (or its failure to develop) is partly innate, the result of a biological program, we are only at the first Matryoshka layer that goes from the comprehension of the emotions of the others to voluntary cooperation and reaches the point of reciprocal altruism. Opinions remain conflicting because it cannot be excluded that empathic help conceals a hidden selfish interest.[9]

Seeing and Perceiving: How Empathy Is Produced

More must be said about Hume's "particle of the dove." Visual experiences mark the beginning of everything. Repeated observation of others' conduct led to the growth in the psyche of this emotion, which was destined to have a great influence. Unsurprisingly, the cognitive neuroscience drive includes sight, the foremost of our senses. Investigation on the brain's optical perception consolidates the idea that humans are a visual species, which hears with the eyes. Seeing is often equivalent to understanding and understanding is equivalent to seeing. In the analysis of the magic world it has been considered necessary "to move on from demonology to look at contemporary epistemology, more generally, concentrating on what seemed to be at stakes in so many cases of, and argument about, witchcraft – what people saw."[10] In village and urban neighborhoods, where inhabitants externalize fears of incumbent malefices, much is missed if we neglect a full-bodied truism: sight was their primary organ of knowledge.

Sight, to dig deep into this concept, is used to perceive, to favor appropriate actions and understand those of our fellow men. In the dynamics of human relations, few moments provide an intensity of signals like a face-to-face meeting. In our mediocratic civilization, the perception of facial signals is multiplied by the close-up of cameras, relentless in revealing internal anxiety. The close-up of his sweating face cost Richard Nixon the White House in the televised debate against John F. Kennedy on September 26, 1960, a broadcast watched by more than 50 million people. In documents without images, such as witchcraft trials, anxieties hidden in fleeting glances or different corporal gestures do not appear. The human ability to read other people's thoughts in their face (mind reading) is an important step in the study of interpersonal contacts and represents a salient moment in the development of witchcraft cases in small communities characterized by constant interactions between people.

This mind-reading ability is the activity of representing the specific mental states of others, for example, their perceptions, goals, beliefs, expectations and the like. "It is agreed that all normal humans develop [this] ability [...], a system of representation often called folk psychology."[11] The perception of faces is one of our most developed visual skills. Studies in evolutionary psychology have reconstructed micro expressions resulting from the attempt to mask emotions from the gaze of strangers, a necessity that is not infrequently crucial in relationships between individuals.

Mind Reading: Some Historical Examples

A key weapon for those who held all forms of economic, political, religious and witchcraft power, from a monarch to a minister to a parish priest to a witch to a cunning man, was the ability to grasp the secret thoughts and unspeakable intentions of people to tame or punish or correct or condition their volition. The extraordinary villainous agency of a parish priest who for decades tyrannized over the inhabitants of Montorgiali, a seventeenth-century Sienese-state village, with feigned seductions and crimes, would be less understandable if not interpreted in the light of this cerebral faculty.[12] Montaigne's words fit the case of that obscure priest and the episodes of daily life in which malefic subjects interact with people: "man exercises himself, he trains himself in this [lying] as to an exercise of honor; since dissimulation is among the most remarkable qualities of this century."[13] At a very high level, always with the same purpose of managing power relations, deception was vital for the exercise of command to be able to foresee, to penetrate "the mask, with which most men usually cover their faces [and] the artifices, which they usually use to disguise themselves and hide their flaws."[14] Literary creations deliver these psychological excavations to us. Readers of Alexandre Dumas's masterpiece, *The Three Musketeers*, have certainly been impressed by Cardinal Richelieu's penetrating gaze on the aspiring musketeer:

The cardinal rested his elbow on his manuscript, his cheek on his hand, and looked at the young man for a moment. No one had a more profoundly scrutinizing eye than Cardinal Richelieu, and d'Artagnan felt that gaze run through his veins like a fever ...[15]

... bringing out signs that are difficult to hide in the face and tone of voice. Although no less difficult to interpret, as the Othello error repeatedly warns, because the Moor badly read Desdemona's mimicry and then her tears, intended as a reaction to the news of the alleged lover Cassio's death.[16]

But to go back to the Cardinal. What happened in the hypertrophic brain of Louis XIII's minister, "wonder of nature"? This is a question that he, a self-styled nineteenth-century French craniologist, who dealt with it in specific studies, must have asked himself.[17] Today neuroscience could suggest an interpretation of the Cardinal's faculties of domination: Armand-Jean du Plessis was favored by a prodigious dexterity in mind reading, by his innate and exercised intuitive ability to insinuate himself into the heads of others. Anyone who wants to successfully direct human actions will show an aptitude to anticipate the development of an action before it is thought of because he himself designs it, simulating the mental state of others, activating his emotional systems in the brain.[18] A sorcerer boasted of this in the Tuscan village of Radicondoli in 1572, penetrating the thoughts of women gathered around with his eyes. We will meet him later (Chapter 26).

Mirror Neurons and Vitality Forms

When someone else's action is observed, it intrudes into our emotional system, and we know what the other is doing without any cognitive effort because a motor pattern like that of the person carrying out the action is set in motion within us. According to recent research, people's sensations stimulate a specific type of neurons in our brain, called "mirror neurons," which are activated and cause neurons to be stimulated in other cortical motor areas.[19] Such a theory promises to be reductionist in the best sense of the term: an important and mysterious phenomenon – our care for others – explained by a more basic psychological mechanism, empathy, in turn rendered possible by a precise brain mechanism.[20] This is a principle considered by some to be entirely valid for all emotional systems, by which we understand what others do and feel because our brain automatically mimics the actions of others and the intricate network of sensations associated with them.[21] Imagine a baby who sees his mother frown and cry: it is plausible that this activates the mirror neuron system and the baby's brain will produce an automatic simulation of all the unpleasant physiological sensations related to crying. A fracture of these mechanisms – infants who often do not look at their mother's face – could contribute to the onset of empathic deficits.[22]

Once again, individual developmental psychology is used as a source of hypotheses to understand evolution. This mirror faculty would have developed with the evolutionary acceleration leading to the goal of shared intentionality, during the Pleistocene grand finale. We speculate that our psyche has evolved to imagine what the other feels and is able to feel empathy. Seeing someone get hurt activates almost the same areas in the brain that are triggered when we feel suffering. These areas are part of pain circuits and the circuits that connect body emotions and sensations, for example the anterior section of the insula, and the anterior and medial part of the cingulate cortex.[23] It is believed that when we observe someone suffering, our synapses produce a simulation of pain, and this allows us to understand the feelings of the other. It has been shown that the pain circuit of both men and women is less active in the face of the suffering of an unpleasant person and more active in the face of a person we care for.

Empathy manifests itself because of observing people's bodily and psychological experiences. Through an "embodied simulation" we enter into resonance with someone by establishing a dialectical relationship between body and mind, subject and object.[24] For example, when meeting someone we look at his face and his eyes and have an immediate impression of his state of mind and intentions, and without realizing it we are ready to meet him, in turn expressing our orientation in the face and the body. By entering into relationships with others, we intuitively evaluate their emotions and states of mind, their state of health and illness based on the vitality that is expressed through movements; this evaluation takes place in a short period of time.

It also seems that the empathic system is solicited by the vision of someone experiencing happiness. If this is the case, developing this neural network would have had the advantage of stimulating behaviors that support cohesion and balance disruptive ways of doing such as those triggered by an apparently only harmful emotion like envy. Another person's happiness instead of making us envious could make us happy and genuinely happy for them. Increasing the empathic system could counter that bittersweet tendency to enjoy travails of others, because if the other is hit by a misfortune, through the action of the neural network linked to empathy we would feel sincere pain. And let us add: empathy most likely contributes significantly to the manifestation of sympathy and compassion, two feelings involved in socially pleasing integrations. A comparison of the golden rule, typical of all organized religions, opens a way for a better understanding of how morality works in the brain: the principle of treating others as you want to be treated sounds like the universal foundation of all ethics. In neural terms it is a "forced empathy."[25]

***

Particular interest is given to the "forms of vitality" of which an action is composed revealing its neural basis.[26] These vitality forms are the way we interact. We can offer something to a person in a kind or rude way. We can ask a motorist to stop, making the stop gesture in a gentle or abrupt manner. How we perform these actions depends on our internal state. In our relationships with someone we communicate this disposition continuously. As always in acting, alongside an active aspect there is the opposite one, that of recognizing the actions of others. By observing the vitality forms we understand if the agent's mood is kind or aggressive if he or she performs a certain action willingly or not. From the neural point of view, the representation of this form seems to have a specific neural basis. This time the central section of the insula, connected to the motor and memory circuits, suggests that the *how* is intrinsic to the understanding of the action as much as the *what*, this a fundamental aspect to remember. Such an aspect, the how, is in fact a fundamental element of social inclusion (as shown in Chapter 26). The how is the most important aspect of a gesture, from the point of view of the quality of human relationships. This is evident in those historical cases already defined as a refused charity syndrome: the how of request and refusal, sometime denied to archival papers by the scribe's recordings.

The cerebral element "which is closest to empathy, in the sense of compassion, is neither a cortex piece nor a subcortical organ but a hormonal bonding system. Oxytocin (technically that neuropeptide that can act as a hormone) produced by the hypothalamus acts on the emotional systems of the brain [ending up with] affecting the rest of the body. The original evolutionary function was to ignite the components of motherhood [...] but the hormone's ability to reduce the fear of the proximity of other creatures" favored other forms of affiliation that include sympathy and trust between unrelated people.[27]

We see today that the empathic neural mechanism can be manipulated in various ways. By strengthening the appropriate brain circuits, we could curb ill-will and the propensity to rejoice in the misfortunes of others and thus discourage aggressive competitive techniques such as those of harming others by gossiping or acting behind their backs.[28] The necessary knowledge to develop empathy towards others lacking it, both in the case of happiness and pain, is unknown.

Yet, such goals are by no means new in history. "There were deep cultural sanctions against envy, anger and hatred."[29] An insistent preaching effort of seventeenth- and eighteenth-century Jesuit evangelizing missions, repeated annually in Italy and in German Catholic regions, consisted in aiming with patience to restore peace and the Christian spirit to communities divided by factions. Tensions and grudges that arose between those who suspected malignancy in their close neighbors and those who were suspected unfold a perverse mixture of envy, fear, anger, hatred and revenge, emotions that catalyze witchcraft ideas. For rural dwellers, the repeated appearances of missionaries constituted an acculturating experience whose psychological impact cannot be underestimated from the point of view concerning us here. No description of a visit omits remarks that "peace" was made between hostile parties. Missionaries sometimes attracted thousands of participants. We would like to listen to their sermons. People came out so stunned by the sermons, doctrines, and good deaths, with such horror of their sins, with such confusion and shame of their choices that they themselves told us that they could neither sleep nor eat nor rejoice. On the contrary, not even asleep they quieted down, seeming now to see the devil who in terrible forms ran to their waist to strangle them and drag them to hell.[30]

Witchcraft cases abound with epidemics of dreams and collective denunciations which are a mine for scholars of the neurobiology of emotions, hard to excavate, and concerning predominantly female contexts. Well, the tenacious Jesuit fathers, unaware of synapses, mirror neurons, forms of vitality and oxytocin, enhanced the empathy of thousands of faithful by arousing great moments of widespread apprehension with theatrical mastery, aiming to develop a community feeling that would get rid of gossip and slander. That is not all. In this account we should include that some side effects of those terrifying sermons were to exacerbate ailments linked to a specific fear: the fear of divinity is just what the good fathers set for themselves.

The intent of the Jesuit missions to re-establish a fraternal atmosphere between the local factions, discloses a psychological reality on which neuroscience is debating today: the existence of a dark side of empathy. The problem with empathy is that it "is too parochial [...] It can be switched on and off, or thrown into reverse, by our construal of the relationship we have with a person."[31] The critical point of emotion consists in its "nature as a spotlight [...] and spotlights have a narrow focus" and end up making us feel really close only to those who resemble us, ending up opposing "us" to "them."[32] Certainly the opaque side of emotion does not affect its propulsive role in the domestication of humans, whose line of development must be seen in the path that from the high levels of cooperation leads to the establishment of a village governance made up of customs, norms and rights and duties.

This dark side represents another critical moment in our discourse on the *maleficium*. In fact, it highlights that, in witchcraft situations with blasts of collective dismay and accusations of damage, a discrimination that extinguishes the compassionate impulse is activated in the minds of those we perceive as different. The aftermath of the empathic system collapse are brought out in Chapter 25. We grasp the change by reflecting on shame.

Shame

Redness – recalls Charles Darwin – is the most characteristic expression of man and the most human of all expressions. Monkeys turn red with anger, but it would take a significant amount of indisputable evidence to convince us that any animal can blush with shame.[33] It would be important to be able to determine at what point these bodily signals began to appear in humans. Also, its biological basis is ignored, a gap in the understanding of the emotion. We ask ourselves: "Why should an expression of embarrassment, shame or shyness be highly visible when these emotions are associated with hiding, keeping aloof, covering up?"[34]

Blushing and Guilt

A correlation of redness with the moral dimensions of shame would seem evident, being the phenomenon associated with guilt. Sociality had led to new neural modifications. Tribal environments qualified by high cooperation favored the evolution of a set of new social instincts adapted to the life of such groups, of new emotions, such as shame and guilt, which increase the likelihood of norms being respected.[35] Failure to comply with generic rules of conduct or more stringent social norms agreed and sanctioned by custom, due to the unanimous blame that could follow, is likely to be held back by a sense of shame, aligning the potential individualism of some people to the majority of the group. Different attitudes created an embarrassment signaled by facial redness, a body language that biology hesitates to explain. Shame comes from being observed, and one reacts to emotion not only by tending to withdraw or hide, but also by imitating someone through a chameleon-like psychological behavior eager for social approval. A human desire for consent is illustrated with sarcasm by the vicissitudes of Leonard Zelig (Woody Allen) who conforms to disparate people with whom he enters into a relationship.[36]

Following or violating your own group rules could become a life-and-death affair in small communities. Shame, pushing to align one's reasoning with others, slows down the indulgent and charitable inclination leading to connect with others and tolerating those differences that do not result in too blatant violation of norms. The role of shame in historical times therefore lends itself to conflicting considerations. Studies on the domestication of our *inner demons* (such as violent reactions generated by rage) highlight shame's heavy socio-psychological obstacle, which limits the compassionate impact of individuals and groups, preventing the rebalancing of emotions aroused by panic attacks and anger. In situations activated by anxiety and suspicion of impending malefic deeds, it is never easy to measure the psychological component of this emotion that produces alignments among people. We fail to discern how the shame rate goes from protective against violation to dysfunctional. When minds are homologated, a seedbed is slowly generated for jealousy and the envy of the different, activating angry aggressions towards profiteers and non-conformist people, mavericks, individualists never completely absent in human groupings. In the eyes of the social analyst, an evaluation of this slippery emotion appears complicated because, as mentioned, it positively influences the community ethic by discouraging transgression of agreed upon customs. Single cases are cryptic due to the opacity of the sources but thinking in aggregate terms a negative impact does not escape. The degeneration of shame into defensive resentment manifests itself as an attitude that acts on a collective basis. Examples come from contagious complaints punctuating early modern Europe by witchcraft accusations and trials. Could violence therefore be associated with shame, a psychological process produced by diversity? It is useful to further reflect on the connection.

From an intrapersonal perspective, shame can become a feeling from which psychopathological developments of profound suffering germinate. In contexts of psychiatric pathology, shame acts like a boulder that stands in the way of overcoming traumas and adverse experiences and is the opposite of self-compassion. Therapeutically, the emotion is in fact unhinged through a slow work of (re)construction of acceptance and compassion towards oneself, a self-compassion that implies welcoming misfortunes, mistakes, and the dark sides of one's psyche.[37] Recent studies have begun to quantitatively measure the relationship between shame and aggression in non-pathological contexts, confirming the clinical experience where deep feelings of shame and low self-esteem related to disorders with frequent manifestations of both hetero and self-directed aggression.[38] The use of virtual reality holds promise for generating experimental settings that will let neurosciences better explore these emotions and action tendencies in interpersonal scenarios.[39]

As already mentioned, we know little about the neurobiological basis of shame.[40] Our knowledge about the role of shame as an engine of the absence of intrapsychic compassion and of more or less psychopathological aggression reinforces the idea that an understanding of the dynamics of emotion at group level can lead to the argument that human contexts have oscillated between a compassionate relationship with those who are different or deviants and the hard option by marginalizing and punishing them. At the moment, it is certainly risky for a historical reconstruction to measure whether the cultures of shame, throughout history, have been the most aggressive and violent, because they block the empathic impulse and, with this, the ability to experience other people's suffering and react with acts of compassion.[41] In the early modern age onsets of rancorous witchcraft accusations are recorded, an alternation of micro and macro mental conflicts precisely in centuries which, compared to previous ages, should attest to a general growth of Hume's "particle of the dove." For cognitive psychology, neuroscience and historians, the attempt to understand the supposed malaise of society becomes a challenge.

We must bring up now the most ambiguous and fearful "affection" of humans: envy.

Envy

Invidia infelix ranks extremely high on a scale of factors that measure the intensity of the emotions activated by witchcraft.[42] Neuroscience will have to get out of the difficult predicament by defining it scientifically unless they resign and consider it merely as "an unfortunate facet of human nature."[43] Francis Bacon grasped the disruptive impact:

> We have not seen any feeling as fascinating or bewitching as love and envy. Both create overwhelming desires, are immediately composed into fantasies and suggestions and easily take possession of the eye, especially in the presence of the objects that lead to irresistible attraction, assuming that it exists […] The act of envy has something magic about it, so there is no other cure than magic, that is to resolve the evil eye (as it is defined) and throw it on another.[44]

The English polymath, proposing to transfer the spell by which one is struck to another person, alludes to an anti-magical strategy that recurs frequently in trials. The emphasis placed on the eyes, on the gaze cast on people or things has been previously anticipated. However, we postpone the association of envy with the oblique gaze and the staring gaze, that ancient link in close connection with the concept of the evil eye, further below.

A Purposeless Affection?

It is puzzling to proceed with the analysis of this emotion which influences the sight and reasoning of the observer. It has already been noticed that by moving away from primary emotions of fear and anger, cognitive and neurobiological sciences encounter greater problems in dealing with more complex feelings such as empathy, shame, and envy. And the latter is practically an intractable matter. Without too much originality evolutionary psychology presents its advantages: it plays a key role in survival, motivates realization, is useful for self-awareness and for others, and warns us of inequalities that, if nurtured, can cause a notable increase in violence.[45] These are propositions to be reconciled with opposite ones describing envy as useless:

> It seems to serve none of the purposes of other emotions. Unlike emergency emotions like fear and anger, it is not for survival; unlike pride and joy, it does not serve the aspiration, fulfillment, quality of life; unlike guilt and shame, it serves no conscience or community.[46]

Ultimately, in the frequent pauses of his madness, Don Quixote makes the point by reminding Sancho Panza: "All vices contain some enticement, but that of envy contains nothing but disgust, rancor, rage."[47]

A source of ruinous animosity, envy fuels incessant social tensions in relatives and neighborhoods, fostering resentment and accusations of bewitchment. It has an elusive nature and does not reveal itself through external signals. If it is generally true that our face and our acts warn those who look at us of what is happening in our head, by revealing our intentions, this is badly done with the "green-eyed monster."[48] Charles Darwin in *The Expression of the Emotions* could not include an image reproducing this unhappy emotion. He had to emphasize that when envy manifests itself in visible actions this happens because anger will have taken its place. It is almost impossible for painters to portray suspicion, jealousy, envy unless they use additional elements to help understand the situation; and poets use vague and imaginative expressions.[49]

Envy is invisible. It should not be considered a stretch to identify in it a common thread of human dynamics that end up feeding the witchcraft agency. As Spinoza observed, "Envy is the same as hatred or sadness, an affection from which man's power to act, that is, his drive, is repressed."[50] Envy is unfathomable. Never confessed, this bitter passion resists inspection by the most attentive eyes. Because, as we read in *Billy Budd*, "its lodgment is in the heart, no degree of intellect supplies a guarantee against it."[51]

Nice try, Melville! Your comment may have generated great confusion in many. If true, it would be a great disaster for neuroscience and its expensive technological equipment. With all due respect to the novelist's intense pages, although the biological basis of emotion is far from deciphered to date, recent studies conducted with functional magnetic resonances have been able to precisely identify the areas of the brain involved in envy that are the site of conflicting feelings inherent in the pain circuit. "Envy stimulates the pain system of the brain so it is linked to a painful sensation. This pain can be alleviated by the tendency to enjoy the misfortunes of others, a feeling linked to the pleasure system."[52] And in the rich articulations of the brain, in fact, a mere enjoyment of our neighbor's misfortunes is glimpsed:

> When misfortune strikes an advantaged person and helps to narrow the gap of a relative performance in an important area, discouragement or pain is reduced and induces a pleasant sensation. This pleasure for the misfortune of another corresponds to the activation of the ventral striatum and the medial orbitofrontal cortex.[53]

Dissecting the Feeling

And again, it should be noted that nothing new exists under the sun. Ovid had already arrived there in a hexameter of his unsurpassed journey into the fantastic world of gods and men: "Without a shadow of a smile, if not moved by the misfortune of others."[54] Quotes could be multiplied and seem to indicate that envy has a long history. How deep? References to the cerebral organic basis of emotion (the ventral striatum) can lead to doubts about the nature of the good savage. Were the primitives envious in the end? What happened in the caves of Lascaux or Chauvet two thousand generations ago? What sort of glances did Vico's big beasts (*bestioni*) exchange? Was there room for envy in prehistoric altruism, when these two words (mine and yours) – to put it again in Cervantes's words – "were ignored by the living"?[55]

Let us be wary, here. Comparative ethnology studies demonstrate the pervasiveness of envy among contemporary aboriginal societies and this fact can be logically projected backwards. The same research on developmental psychology leads to support the universality of jealousy between siblings within hunter-gatherer families. Disposition to envy would be acquired for the most part during the active and passive experience of fraternal jealousy.[56] That the passion of envy was rooted in the individual from childbirth could not be escaped St. Augustine, who in the *Confessions* recalls: "I have seen and met a jealous child: he did not speak yet but was already looking livid with grim eyes at his brother milk."[57] The reflection sheds light on the destructive force of disharmony within the intimacy of family and relatives. Witchcraft trials are rife with it.[58]

Evolutionary psychology opens predictable scenarios by defining envy as a genetically heritable trait: it plays a role in survival, motivating the achievement of results, serves the awareness of the self and the other and warns us of iniquity which, if fed, can lead to an intensification of violence.[59] Other studies deepen the point. In fact, arguing that it was "such an emotional adaptation that was shaped by selection to signal a strategic interference in the search for the acquisition of resources," they approach a crucial point.[60] Because in this meaning we run into the eternal drama afflicting humans, that relating to food supply. *Primum vivere, deinde philosofari* ("first live, then talk about philosophy") is worth remembering. It is no coincidence that according to Augustine's authoritative testimony, the first reason for envy was that of food.[61]

We therefore insist on a foregone conclusion: it is easy to realize the decisive importance that food has had in the history of evolution for the formation of envy and the mechanisms used to prevent it.[62] Envy, already inherent in kinship nuclei, extends to the proximity between human groups of some increased numerical consistency leading a substantially stable life. In the psychological conflicts generated by contagious accusations of witchcraft it is generally noted that envy does not arise from a great disproportion between us and another person but on the contrary from our being close to her.[63] If we keep in mind that in past peasant civilizations society was thought to be a closed economic system where the gain of one individual occurred at the expense of another, it followed that "social health was seen and based on a shared poverty criterion, a delicate balance in which relative positions change as little as possible."[64]

In conclusion, envy, whatever its gender peculiarities, is confirmed as a corrupting force, an essential source of conflicts that took place before humans developed embryos of normative systems that were opposed to individualistic initiatives; an emotion that by forcing members of a neighborhood or village to submit to community norms immobilizes consciences in a homogenization conceived and practiced precisely as an antidote to the destructive power of the unhappy passion.

The Problem

There is also something else configured in the organ of thought that we must not exclude. Surely the "green-eyed monster" applies everywhere (from amorous competition to the economic one) and with anyone, without any distinction between men and women. But the data of witchcraft studies make the analysis more complicated. As we have seen, the social contexts of early modern witch hunting denote an extraordinarily strong pre-eminence of women among the accused and the convicted in percentages ranging between 70% and 80%. How do we want to interpret this pattern that stubbornly presents witchcraft situations as a matter of women's milieu and affairs? Shouldn't we weigh up the previously advanced hypothesis that the neurobiology of female brain denotes pronounced emotional attributes predisposing women to envy, the most intense of the emotions aroused by witchcraft, to repeat Francis Bacon's thought? After all, if irony be allowed, neuroscience would discover hot water:

> From Greek myths to medieval iconography, to modern philosophy, there seems to be a sort of tacit and transversal consensus [...] The identification of envy = woman [turns out] to be one of those constants that endure in space and time by crossing cultures and civilizations.[65]

Does this not support that "essential difference" of the female brain at the root of the persistent witch = woman cliché (Chapter 24)?

Notes

1 Sometimes the terms empathy and compassion are used synonymously. In fact, the link between empathy (understood as a reflection in the feelings of the other) and compassion (feeling close to others and behaving in a kind way) is more indefinite than one might think: see P. Bloom, *Just Babies: The Origins of Good and Evil*, New York, 2013.

2 D. W. Pfaff, *The Neurosciences of Fair Play: Why We (Usually) Follow the Golden Rule*, New York, 2007. On operational theory of empathy see E. O. Wilson, *The Social Conquest*, ch. 24.

3 F. de Waal, *The Age of Empathy*, ch. 7.

4 A. Shenhav, J. D. Greene, "Integrative Moral Judgment: Dissociating the Roles of the Amygdala and Ventromedial Prefrontal Cortex," in *Journal Neuroscience*, 34, 2014, 4741–4749.

5 These are personality traits that manifest themselves from childhood, defined by limited empathy, the absence of a sense of guilt, superficial affectivity; See www.psychologica lscience.org/observer/callous-unemotional-traits-in-children.

6 E. O'Nions, C. F. Lima, S. K. Scott, R. Roberts, E. J. McCrory, E. Viding, "Reduced Laughter Contagion in Boys at Risk for Psychopathy," in *Current Biology*, 27, 2017, 3049–3055.

7 A. Seara-Cardoso, C. L. Sebastian, E. McCrory, L. Foulkes, M. Buon, JP. Roiser, E. Viding, "Anticipation of Guilt for Everyday Moral Transgressions: The Role of the Anterior Insula and the Influence of Interpersonal Psychopathic Traits," in *Scientific Reports*, 36273, 2016.

8 E. Viding, E. McCrory, A. Seara-Cardoso, "Psychopathy," in *Curr Biol*, 24, 2014, 871–874. doi: 10.1016/j.cub.2014.06.055.

9 M. Hoffman, C. Hilbe, M. A. Nowak, "The Signal-Burying Game Can Explain Why We Obscure Positive Traits and Good Deeds," in *Nat Hum Behav* (Nature Human Behavior), 2, 2018, 397–404. doi: 10.1038/s41562–018–0354-z.

10 See S. Clark, in M. Tauziet, "Rationalizing the Irrational. Interview with Stuart Clark," in *Magic Ritual and Witchcraft*, 5, 2010, 225.

11 V. Gallese, A. Goldman, "Mirror Neurons and the Simulation Theory of Mind-Reading," in *Trends in Cognitive Sciences*, 2, 1998, 495.

12 ODS, *Luxuria. Eros e violenza nel Seicento*, Roma, 2011.

13 Michel de Montaigne, *Essais*, II, ch. XVIII.

14 Richelieu, *Testament politique ou Les Maximes d'État de Monsieur le Cardinal de Richelieu*, VII, D. Dessert, ed., Paris, 1990, 63.

15 Alexandre Dumas, *Les Trois Mousquetaires*, Paris, 1968, ch. XL.

16 P. Ekman, *Telling Lies: Clues to Deceit in the Marketplace, Politics, and Marriage*, New York & London, 1988; W. Shakespeare, *Othello*, V, II.

17 C. Jouhaud, *La main de Richelieu ou le pouvoir cardinal*, Paris, 1991, 46–47.

18 M. Gazzaniga, *The Ethical Brain: The Science of Our Moral Dilemmas*, New York, 2005.

19 G. Rizzolati, L. Craighero, "The Mirror-Neuron System," in *Annual Review of Neuroscience*, 27, 2004, 169–192. See V. Gallese, L. Fadiga, L. Fogassi, G. Rizzolati, "Action Recognition in the Premotor Cortex," in *Brain*, 119, 1996, 593–609.

20 P. Bloom, *Just Babies*.

21 Each new scientific discovery raises enthusiasm, discussion, criticism. And mirror neurons have been called into question in relation to a multitude of human capacities, diseases and phenomena, in some cases in a reasonable way, in others not; see G. Hickock, *The Myth of Mirror Neurons: The Real Neuroscience of Communication and Cognition*, New York, 2014.

22 E. Viding, E. McCrory, A. Seara-Cardoso, "Psychopathy."

23 B. Bernhardt, T. Singer, "The Neural Basis of Empathy," in *Annual Review of Neuroscience*, 35, 2012, 1–23.

24 V. Gallese, C. Sinigaglia, "What is So Special about Embodied Simulation?," in *Trends in Cognitive Sciences*, 15, 2011, 512–519.

25 E. O. Wilson, *The Social Conquest*, ch. 24.

26 *Vitality form* is a concept introduced by D. Stern. See G. Di Cesare, C. Di Dio, M.J. Rochat, C. Sinigaglia, N. Bruschweiler-Stern, D. N. Stern, G. Rizzolati, "The Neural Correlates of 'Vitality Form' Recognition: An fMRI Study," in *Soc Cogn Affect Neurosci* (Social Cognitive and Affective Neuroscience), 9, 2014, 951–60.

27 Ibid., 957.

28 T. Singer, "Neuronal Basis of Empathy and Fairness," in *Novartis Foundation Symposium*, 278, 2007, DOI: 10.1002/9780470030585, ch. 3; T. Singer, B. Seymour, J. P. O'Doherty, K. E. Stephan, R. J. Dolan, C. D. Frith, "Empathic Neural Responses Are Modulated by the Perceived Fairness of Others," in *Nature*, 439, 2006, 466–469; M. Sitskoorn, *I sette peccati capitali*, 57.

29 L. Roper, *Witch Craze: Terror and Fantasy in Baroque Germany*, New Haven, 2006, 62.

30 Oscar Di Simplicio (hereafter, ODS), *Autunno della stregoneria. Maleficio e magia nell'Italia moderna*, Bologna, 2005, 366.

31 S. Pinker, *The Better Angels*, 591.

32 P. Bloom, *Against Empathy: The Case for Rational Compassion*, New York, 2016, 31. "Human empathy is bounded and fickle," N. Raihani, *The Social Instinct*, 131.

33 C. Darwin, *The Expression of Emotions*.

34 W. Ray Crozier, Peter J. de Jong, eds., *The Psychological Significance of the Blush*, Cambridge, 2012, 1–2.

35 P. J. Richerson, R. Boyd, *Not by Genes Alone: How Culture Transformed Human Evolution*, Chicago, IL, 2005, ch. 6.

36 We refer to *Zelig* (1983) interpreted and directed by Woody Allen.

37 P. Gilbert, *The Compassionate Mind. A New Approach to Life's Challenges*, London, 2009.

38 For example, in several samples of adolescents the predisposition to feel shame seems to predict a future and dangerous antisociality at age 18–20; J. Stuewig, J. P. Tangney, S. Kendall, J. B. Folk, C. R. Meyer, R. L Dearing, "Children's Proneness to Shame and Guilt Predict Risky and Illegal Behaviors in Young Adulthood," in *Child Psychiatry Hum Dev*, 46, 2015, 217–27. doi: 10.1007/s10578-014-0467-1.; S. Roos, E. V. Hodges, C. Salmivalli, "Do Guilt- and Shame-Proneness Differentially Predict Prosocial, Aggressive, and Withdrawn Behaviors during Early Adolescence?," in *Development Psychology*, 50, 2014, 941–6. doi: 10.1037/a0033904. 2013 Jul 29.

39 S. Duan, L. Valmaggia, D. Fennema, J. Moll, R. Zahn, "Remote Virtual Reality Assessment Elucidates Self-Blame-Related Action Tendencies in Depression," *J Psychiatr Res* (Journal of Psychiatric Research), 2023 Mar 6;161:77–83. doi: 10.1016/j.jpsy-chires.2023.02.031. Epub ahead of print. PMID: 36905843.

40 A few more theories have been formulated on the neural systems that could drive the opposite pole – always intrapersonal – of self-compassion/esteem. In particular, the opium-idergic system (endorphins) regulating the perception of pain and pleasure is brought into play. These protein hormones are our internal pain reliever system that produces a general sense of psychophysical well-being, so typical after physical activity such as jogging. Our sophisticated capacity for emotional self-soothing is linked to the opium-idergic complex, when in face of adversity we can console ourselves with a walk, a song or welcoming a hug. For the moment this is little more than a fascinating working hypothesis: that is, that a dysregulation of endorphins, perhaps matured in correspondence with trauma or lack of stable attachment figures in childhood, makes some people more vulnerable to shame and makes it more difficult for them forgive oneself for one's misfortunes, oversights, gaps, misdeeds… and continue to live. Perhaps the same mechanism of relationships between trauma, shame and self-soothing difficulties generates aggression on an interpersonal level.

41 J. Rifkin, *The Empathic Civilization*, ch. 4.

42 Virgil, *Georgics*, III, 37.

43 Bertrand Russell, *The Conquest of Happiness*, New York, 1930.

44 Francis Bacon, *Of Envy*.

45 M. D. Hauser, *Moral Minds. The Nature of Right and Wrong*, New York, 2009.

46 W. Gaylin, *Hatred: The Psychological Descent into Violence*, New York, 2003, 65.

47 Miguel de Cervantes, *Don Quixote*, II, 8.

48 "O, beware, my lord, of jealousy; / It is the green-ey'd monster, which doth mock/ The meat it feeds on"; Shakespeare, *Othello*, 3, sc. 3, 165–67. Shakespeare rather alludes to the neighboring feeling of jealousy.

49 See Ch. Darwin, *The Expression of the Emotions*.

50 Baruch Spinoza, *Etica*, III, LV, D, in Id, *Opere*, p. 948.

51 Herman Melville, *Billy Budd, Sailor*, London, 1924, ch. 12.

52 M. Sitskoorn, *I sette peccati capitali*, 54–55.

53 See H. Takahashi, M. Kato, M. Matsuura, D. Mobbs, T. Suhara, Y. Okubo, "When Your Pain Is My Gain: Neural Correlates of Envy and Schadenfreude," in *Science*, 323, 2009, 937–939; see also S. G. Shamay-Tsoory, Y. Tibi-Elhanany and J. Aharon-Peretz, "The Green-Eyed Monster and Malicious Joy: The Neuroanatomical Bases of Envy and Gloating (Schadenfreude)," in *Brain*, 130, 2007, 1663–1678.

54 Ovid, *Metamorphoses*, II, v. 778. On *Schadenfreude*, Lucretius's stoic utopianism differs from Ovid; Id. *De Rerum*, II, v. 3.

55 Miguel de Cervantes, *Don Quixote*, I, 11.

56 H. Schoeck, *Envy: A Theory of Social Behavior*, New York, 1969, ch. 2.

57 Augustine, *Confessions*, I.7.11.

58 See J. Demos, *The Enemy Within: 2000 Years of Witch-Hunting in the Western World*, New York, 2008, 3; P. Geschiere's *Witchcraft, Intimacy & Trust: Africa in Comparison*, Chicago-London, 2013.

59 M. Hauser, *Moral Minds*.

60 S. E. Hill, D. M. Buss, "The Evolutionary Psychology of Envy," in *Envy: Theory and Research*, R. Smith, ed., New York, 2008, 60–70.

61 It would be useful to investigate a second brain, the enteric one, connected to the cranial one by the vagus nerve, and to some of its specific additional endowments which, by secreting psychoactive substances, influence moods. Food and sex are engineered to produce dopamine bursts that please our mind.

62 H. Schoeck, *Envy*, ch. 3.

63 David Hume, *An Enquiry Concerning the Principles of Morals*.

64 G. M. Foster, "The Anatomy of Envy: A Study in Symbolic Behavior," in *Current Anthropology*, 13, 1972, 168.

65 E. Pulcini, *Invidia: La passione triste*, Bologna, 2011, 118.

6

DRIVES

Eros

While over hundreds of thousands of years complex "affects," such as empathy shame and envy, completed the brain evolutionary trajectory, *Homo* was being confronted with two powerful *impulses*: eros and seeking.[1] Sex takes precedence. But how do we approach the subject?

How to Write about Sex?

We are in fact reluctant to start a discussion of eros by looking for a definition. Scholars have often grappled with the subject, showing how over the centuries various aspects of the impulse (erotic, romantic, heterosexual, homosexual, maternal/paternal, etc.) have been organized by customs, religion, socialization, economic calculations, laws of states. A conclusion was drawn, to be summarized in a well-known adage: "The past is a foreign country. They do things differently there."[2] A categorical and in a certain sense incontrovertible assertion transforms the sentence into faith-like statement: for historians it is absolutely imperative to avoid any anachronism.[3]

There is, however, too much reliance on dogmas! Evolutionary psychology has dealt major blows to such certainty and in no territory like eros is this axiom proving shakier, upsetting some of the excesses of cultural reductionism, which mask the biological foundations of eros. And the stubborn vitality of that drive finds repeated confirmations in millennia-old love magic testimonies.

In his later years Sigmund Freud, summing up the condition of man in civilization, formulated a clear aim: "The question of the purpose of human life has been raised countless times; it has never yet received a satisfactory answer and perhaps does not admit of one. Some of those who have asked it have added that if it should turn out that life has no purpose, it would lose all value for them." And then he asked himself: what do men "demand of life and wish to achieve in it? The answer to this can hardly be in doubt. They strive after happiness; they want to become happy and to remain so."[4]

DOI: 10.4324/9781003414377-7

But what satisfies humans? And, over time, have humanity's main yearnings changed? An attempt to reconstruct early modern English retrospective ethnography has identified six fundamental values that more or less consciously concerned them: "military prowess, work, wealth, reputation, personal relationships and the afterlife."[5] The choice can be extended to the whole of humanity. This chapter is interested in personal relationships that in those centuries would possibly have received a more explicit formulation with the word love (*eros*).

Evolutionary Strategies: From Cave Painting to Courbet

Throughout the entire Paleolithic era, the ends of life should be understood as dictated by struggle for survival, reproduction and continuation of the species. In our case, *eros* is defined as an aggregate of bio-social dynamics aimed at selecting a suitable partner for one's propagation. Maybe, in truth, our hominins were the first voyeurs, because moving away from the forest habitat they would develop bipedal walking in order to be sexually visible.[6] A characteristic that made up for the disappearance of feminine estrum.

The genitals' visual seduction aside, it is a foregone conclusion that man's conduct and creative mind must have been conditioned by the sexual sphere since primordial times. No surprise then that erotic representations in art have a very long tradition, among which an exaltation of sexuality stands out. Biased by an evolutionary history that tends to trace the beginning of everything, let us here note that few celebrations of eroticism possess the evocative power that Gustave Courbet gave in 1862 to one of his female nudes: *The Origin of the World*. Sometimes all things in the world seem to hold together: the painting followed Charles Darwin's *Origin of Species* (1859) – and *The Descent of Man* (1871) was in gestation for decades.[7] No cabal of dates! There is no evidence of an evolutionary influence to inspire the provocative icon. Nonetheless, the primeval suggestion of Courbet's famous painting, reproducing thighs, vagina, abdomen and breasts of his favorite model, serves to connect to the wall graffiti at Chauvet, to that supposed sorcerer's cave where a hybrid, anthropomorphic being, like a bison, is represented in the act of mounting a large human vulva.

Also, add repeated stylizations of male and female sexual organs and, at Lascaux, the shaman with the head of a bird and an erect penis; the Venus of Hohle Fels, and others similar, with an exaggerated "nature" and thighs. As previously noted, the series of anatomical details seem to attest to more than a marginal interest in genitals of those ancestors. Neuroscience is now willing to suggest updated interpretations of eroticism and artistic creativity in relation to brain development. The socio-cultural roots remain obscure, but it can be argued that they are connected to specialized brain circuits that make them powerful, suggestive, and lasting.[8]

And yet, in our context, the *eros* we must focus on remains difficult to understand. From evolutionary psychology, rapid conjectures are advanced on the symbolic value of these late Pleistocene artistic expressions. Artifacts and the depictions of male and female attributes could constitute early evidence of love spell, connected to courtship and mating relationships of tribal groups. In stylized phalluses and pubis, some possible exhibitionisms are glimpsed, fitness indicators for a choice. Nor should alpha-male narcissism be excluded, connected to an innate ancestral polygamy, dominating a small primitive community life, that selects attractive women predisposed by anatomy to mating (and sexual enjoyment) to survive and reproduce successfully.[9]

Analyze as you wish, sex, "heaven" and "hell," is sought, and the essence of witchcraft volition consists in obtaining what one does not possess. Specialized literature on love magic clearly explains male/female endeavors to manipulate eros's pathogenic force for their own ends. In the vast sea of erotic spells multiple rituals converge, from poems to curses to bifid filters, to exert power over the coveted subject emotions and sexual desires, or to destroy them in a rival, making him impotent. From the ancient world to early modern age trials, Mediterranean Europe has maintained evidence of these stubborn attempts to coerce mind and body of others. We come across an eros that seems to have no history; not to be confused with the multiple, changing expressions of a feeling, subject to selective, culturally determined forms of social approval. First, its neural aspects must be brought into focus.

A Timeless *Eros*

> All men are born unaware of the causes of things, and all have an appetite to seek their own profit, of which they are aware. From this it follows in the first place that men believe they are free because they are aware of their volitions and their appetites, while they do not even dream about the causes from which they are willing to desire and want, because they are unaware of them.[10]

Who anticipated all this? Still him, Spinoza: perceptive, enigmatic. On the one hand, he shows that the desire to live – sometimes he calls it *cupiditas* – appears to be the essence/substance of man whose efforts are directed towards that end; on the other hand, he reveals that, out of ignorance, man does not see his appetite serves something else, the conservation of the species, but not exclusively.[11]

Take romantic love. Studies on the sentiment remain few compared to other areas of human psychology. A brain network underlying both maternal-infantile and adult attachment is clearly identified, two systems that from an evolutionary point of view both perform the function of keeping two people together for a certain (relatively long) period of their life. Among others, brain areas come into play such as the anterior cingulate gyrus, the insula, the striatum, the nucleus accumbens, rich in neurons that release dopamine and are responsible for the human and animal "reward system."[12] Studies of animal breeds considered serial monogamous from a biological point of view show that the release of dopamine and the stimulation of dopaminergic type D2 receptors in the nucleus accumbens promote the formation of the monogamous pair, while if these receptors are pharmacologically blocked the animal ceases to express preference for a single partner.[13] Stimulation of this same receptor with the so-called dopaminergic agonists promotes substance abuse in cocaine-dependent rats. Of course, it appears evolutionarily crucial that forming couple bonds might be also underpinned by reinforcement mechanisms shared with simpler stimuli (such as pleasure-inducing substances) to maintain the commitment necessary for rearing offspring. In short, falling in love would derive from some deep-buried emotional mechanism that we inherited from distant ancestors who developed it before acquiring language;[14] or it obeys the assumption that *Homo* are structured to survive and reproduce their genes.

During evolution, brain areas responsible for regulating responses to sexual stimuli soon appeared. The unconscious strategies that men and women put in place to win and keep a partner were the result of adaptive solutions to the problems of stable mating for the continuation of the species and ended up winning in history.[15] We try to list them. Considering a possible scarcity of partners, the selective pressure exerted by rituals of eros's procedures would have played a role in brain growth and in the evolution of language;[16] the concept of beauty and the sense of attraction would be inscribed in the genes, directed by programs imprinted in brain circuits over thousands of generations. The highest value attributed by men to some female physical attributes, such as sinuous roundness, possesses an evolutionary coherence and the selection would have favored the males who chose women with greater reproductive probabilities. Men would become particularly receptive to the signs of youth, to women who possessed infantile features: big eyes, small nose, small chin, abundant hair, etc. But is that all accurate? Perhaps, evolutionary psychology is jumping to conclusions forcing interpretations that give off a smell of determinism.

***

Let us focus on falling in love and weigh the evident parallelism of two distant investigations. First, in the Christian era's third millennium, contemporary neuroscientists who experiment and work in the laboratory, extricating themselves from neurons, neurotransmitters, hormones, sophisticated equipment. As already mentioned, it is the dyadic bond between animals (we are not the only serial monogamists) that has offered researchers a way to examine something akin to the affection of love among humans. If neurosciences were looking for a mascot, it would certainly find it in a rural rodent, the pretty prairie vole (*Microtus ochrogaster*).[17]

The mechanism leading to couple bonds (to make people fall in love), when the oxytocin and vasopressin receptors are stimulated in appropriate brain sites, has been reproduced by studying this prairie vole. It seems conceivable that – to some extent – in an automatic and natural way a similar chemistry is triggered among human beings and these receptors stimulated in the medial region of the amygdala are involved in forming links to those closest to them.[18] Furthermore, by intervening with genetic techniques on the level of vasopressin, it is possible to transform polygamous species into monogamous ones.[19] The action of these hormones occurs at least in part through the stimulation of reward circuits already described in the laboratory, the choice of a partner induced by oxytocin is lost if D2 receptors for dopamine are blocked, and vice versa. The hormone oxytocin, whose levels increase in the critical stages of motherhood, during childbirth and breastfeeding, when active in the body generates an atmosphere of relaxation with implications for sexual relationships and its prosocial effects. This is what happens in twentieth and twenty-first centuries neuroscientists' laboratories.[20]

Second, we discover that generations of our ancestors, who knows how soon before the artists of wall paintings, were convinced of the energy possessed by a large repertoire of (magic) acts whose rituals were able to release the power contained in vegetable, mineral, and animal substances. Let the Bard once again tell us about this ancestral heritage. What else does that force hidden in a "western flower" hit by a Cupid's arrow and which induces a suggestive effect represent? The king of the fairies, Oberon, reveals the secret to Puck, in *A Midsummer Night's Dream*:

> And maidens call it love-in-idleness.
> Fetch me that flower; the herb I shew'd thee once:
> The juice of it on sleeping eye-lids laid
> Will make or man or woman madly dote
> Upon the next live creature that it sees.[21]

In the past, resorting to the love filter of the Shakespearean elf, people unaware of synapses and neurons denoted a consciousness of the vigor that a substance endowed with supposed magical power has to deeply influence the choice of individuals, to penetrate their nervous system and upset their normal physiological functioning. Today, neurobiology's hybris penetrates the laws of nature using the techniques of functional magnetic resonance imaging (fMRI).[22]

In the 1990s, from a famous study showing that after a single dose of intranasal oxytocin, cooperation and generosity in the game increased, neuroscientists sought to determine whether oxytocin is the neuropeptide magic filter of trust in neighbors and human cooperation.[23] Some works have shown, for example, how oxytocin decreases the amygdala's response (yes, the amygdala itself!) to fear stimuli and how an infusion of oxytocin is able to improve the ability to decode emotions from the gaze of others. In short, in the neurobiology of falling in love we find pleasure, dependence, trust (blind, alas, to our natural fear of the unknown), interpretation of glances. However, as it often happens with the progress of research not all the magic attributed to oxytocin has been replicated and the prosocial effects of this neuropeptide appear more complex and more elusive, subject to individual variables and the environmental context.[24] Ultimately, triggered by a floral filter or by the secretion of oxytocin, the physiological reactions and the cognitive processes that follow appear to escape the control of volition. Neuroscience and the conclusions of literary invention do not seem far apart.[25] Clearly, individuals would act driven by unconscious motivations imprinted over time because maximizing chances of generating and raising viable offspring. All this turns out to be admissible.

***

Spinoza's emphasis on human unawareness should be examined in the light of evolutionary biology. Our ancestors knew nothing of the neurobiological roots of appetites but were aware of the morbid force of *eros*. Before the great Marrano philosopher there was no lack of illustrious ancestors from which an unconscious genetic determinism appears. Horatio Flacco, in the *Epistulae*, recalls the impossibility of breaking free of one's habits: "You can drive out Nature with a pitchfork, but it always returns."[26] A similar allusion can be found in Shakespeare's *Anthony and Cleopatra*, when Lepidus, in dialogue with Caesar Octavian, makes a comment on Antony's lust: "His vices [...] are inherited rather than taken; it was not he who chose them. He can't change them."[27]

Antony's lasciviousness offers an opportunity to question ourselves about another aspect of life, the satisfaction of sexuality. Multiform cases of love magic and its binding spells confirm that volition cannot be configured as the outcome of a cluster of modules that leave free will powerless. Cognitive and neurobiological sciences, by reasoning on aggregate data, can prove the universal regularities of human conduct. On the other hand, flexibility and fickleness, that is, the ability to change and choose, are part of a regularity of biological behavior. The same disciplines do not miss an unpredictable variable of ours: human beings are structured to violate their own predispositions. A seventeenth-century Sienese nobleman and memoirist, unaware of neuroscience, saw aptly when writing in his family papers that "love and madness have no law."[28]

Accurately, desires are blind to forces that explain their existence. Sexual desire exists because it leads to the conception of a child, but the psychology of the sexual urge is not connected to any interest in conception.[29] So here comes the question that has always conflicted with reasoning: why do humans have sex? It is trivial to observe, with all due respect to Spinoza *et al.*, that everyone does it for a lot of reasons. A substantial motivational autonomy leads to sexual intercourse.[30] For its part, historical research documents that love magic filters are not prepared by obeying an unconscious genetic calculation but are often aimed simply "at a good fuck."[31] In technical terms: non-reproductive sexuality performs an exaptative function by fulfilling a social function; not unlike the feathers of birds born to regulate body temperature and then adapted to serve on the fly.[32]

A good lay. After all, wasn't that the goal of Ammonius, an obscure figure, whose jealous carnal passion has been conveyed to us by a second-century AD cursing tablet, coming from Egypt?

> I oblige you, Theodoti, daughter of Eus, by the tail of the snake, the mouth of the crocodile, the horns of the goat, the venom of the asp, the whiskers of the cat, the penis (appendage) of god, so that you cannot ever be able to have sex with another man, that you can't be fucked or sodomized or that you can't have oral sex, and that you can't do anything that gives you pleasure with another man other than just me, Ammonius, son of Hermitari, [...] and that she can bring her thigh to my thigh, her genitals to my genitals, to have sex with me for the duration of her life.[33]

Such vehemence! Thanks, Ammonius, with the magic of a cursing tablet you have explained the practical reasons for your jealous carnal craving, without any further evolutionary motivation. However, things are never simple. It cannot be excluded that lust developed to push for sexuality, even violent, that has a reproductive purpose.

We do not want to lay sexuality on a Procrustean bed by bending it to different interpretations.[34] Yet this aspect of "machismo sexual behavior" which opens onto a hateful theme, bringing into question sexual violence against women in prehistoric times cannot be overlooked. Obviously, its dimensions are ignored but there is no doubt that rape is a masculine demeanor "understandable from the advantageous point of view of the genetic interests that shaped human desires and feelings in the course of evolution."[35] To label Paleolithic hunters/foragers as gangs of rapists is certainly out of the question, but the suspicion is not unfounded. And unfortunately, before the sensitivity of mankind began to be shaped by the humanism of the Enlightenment, Ovid's unfortunate *vis grata puellae* had muddied the relationship between the sexes. A potential cognitive distortion spans centuries and reaches as far as the words of Da Ponte and the music of Mozart: "Beat, beat, oh handsome Masetto your poor Zerlina / I will stay here as a little sheep to wait for your blows."[36] In the hypothalamus, proximity and overlapping of areas involved in sexuality and aggression help explain why these two instinctive drives can be so easily merged.[37] Such violence in sexual approaches has received an arguable evolutionary interpretation in the theory called the Savanna principle: "Beaten women and their violent partners have more children than the rest of the general population."[38]

The frequency of prehistoric sexual violence remains a chapter still to be written. We resign ourselves to ignorance, keeping two points firm. First: however inconvenient it is, evolution does not obey any interpretative pseudo-correctness other than that of research. The drive of human males to maximize their reproductive success is shown by a key factor, namely the competition between males for direct access to females. From this follows the "dizzying common male violence against women for forced sex or in response to rejection."[39] Second: human brain plasticity facilitates social learning capable of containing a prevaricating violence in the relationship between the sexes, but the slowness of such an educational development is known, as the magical tricks that women used to protect themselves from the beating and coercion of husbands and lovers amply demonstrate. From voodoo dolls to curse tablets, the millennial history of these flourishing spells in the Mediterranean area is configured as "a universal human response to danger or impending disaster," and the remarkable similarities refer to memetic replicas (cultural borrowings) from societies that invented such rituals first.[40]

Immutable Constants

Have emotions and impulses undergone significant changes with the passing of historical ages? In the continuous interplay between nature and culture the possible stresses triggered by brain areas related to *eros* do not affect every behavior. The cerebral predisposition of those who are eager to love is reconciled with a multi-plicity of factors. Appetites and feelings are part of a discourse that "depends on nonautomated governance in a social and cultural space."[41] It must be repeated: research shows that the adaptations influencing human psychology for continuing the species largely come to terms with institutions and moral codes.[42] However, it remains difficult to establish what role brain plasticity played in such a dialectic. We know that on an individual level the organ structure changes with experience. Opportunities in life and any form of learning influence thinking, emotions, and ways of doing. Much more can medications that by integrating or substituting desire are expanding the time frame of sexuality.[43] Nor can synaptic connections and genetic structural modifications be excluded.[44] According to recent findings now replicated, an individual's genes can be made active or silent by environmental factors such as repeated trauma or food deprivation.[45] In an unpredictable and continuously moving dynamic field, neurobiological propensity and cultural ties continue to face each other, to fight, leaving us uncertain about the outcome of the confrontation.

Some constants over time, sinking into direct experiences of our brain, are truly bewildering. Consider a parallel between two episodes more than three centuries apart. They insist on the atavistic belief that seminal or menstrual fluids or pubic hair have vigor to influence the psyche. In 1617, Giulia Chiappina, a young Tuscan peasant, was accused of witchcraft. The inquisitor friar, made suspicious by the contents in a small box found in her house during the search, asked her about it. The woman replied:

> Inside are Antognaccio's member hairs that I was holding; [because] he had shorn my nature [pubis], and he carried the hairs in his bag, and I sheared his hairs and kept them in that little box for memory. Those hairs that are in the box I keep them for love that I brought to the said Antognaccio, and for memory.[46]

Observed, touched, relived through mind maps, those organic remains through body and brain chemical sequences whose neural aspects would not escape today thanks to neuroimaging studies, really strengthened faithful Giulia's love, and, by reproducing past electrical discharges, replaced it.

Now is the turn of the cultivated twentieth century. What do we have? The hard reality of centuries-old convictions rises to the surface, and the vitality released by menstrual bloodstains in a handkerchief entangles the sight of a famous man, Arturo Toscanini. What visual representations did they evoke, what hormonal earthquake, what enchantment did they produce while he was pocketing his lover's menstrual-soaked handkerchief, to enhance his stamina while conducting an orchestra from the podium?

> I received our Holy Shroud just as I was climbing the stairs of the theater. I directed the concert keeping it jealously hidden in my pocket [...] It is you who lead me to such excesses [...] If only you had seen me when my eyes were staring at that diaphanous veil with the splashes of your blood ...[47]

Notes

1 Drives, motivations, emotions, and feelings were an ensemble Spinoza called *affects*.
2 This is the beginning of L. P. Hartley's novel, *The Go-Between*, 1953, also known for the script reduction by Harold Pinter and the film adaptation by Joseph Losey (1971).
3 R. Darnton, "How to Become a Celebrity," in *NYR*, May 21, 2015.
4 S. Freud, *Civilization and Its Discontents* (1930), Aylesbury, 2000, 7–8. Freud was 73 when he wrote the essay.
5 K. Thomas, *The Ends of Life. Roads to Fulfilment in Early Modern England*, Oxford, 2009, 2.
6 H. Gee, *The Accidental Species: Misunderstanding of Human Evolution*, Chicago, 2013.
7 Courbet's client was an Ottoman diplomat, collector of erotic art.
8 E. R. Kandel, *The Age of the Insight*.
9 G. Miller, *The Mating Mind: How Sexual Choice Shaped the Evolution of Human Nature*, New York, 2000.
10 Spinoza, *Etica* (Ethics), I, *Appendice* (Appendix), in Id., *Opere*, 827.
11 Spinoza, *Etica*, III, Proposizione IX, Scolio, 907.
12 A. de Boer et al., "Love Is More Than Just a Kiss: A Neurobiological Perspective on Love and Affection," in *Neuroscience*, 201, 2012, 114–24.
13 H. E. Fisher, *Anatomy of Love: The Natural History of Monogamy, Adultery and Divorce*, New York, 1992, 432.
14 R. Dunbar, *The Science of Love and Betrayal*.
15 D. M. Buss, *The Evolution of Desire: Strategies of Human Mating*, New York, 1994.
16 G. Miller, *Sexual Selection and Human Evolution*.
17 See K. M. Pessin, "Seduction, Super-Responders, and Hyper-Trusters. The Biology of Affiliative Behaviour," in *Pathological Altruism*, B. Oakley, A. Knafo, G. Madhavan, D. Sloan Wilson, eds., foreword by F. J. Ayala, Oxford, 2012, 349.
18 J. LeDoux, *The Synaptic Self*. "The Emotional Ties and Romantic Love Can Be Traced Back to Similar Biological Descriptions," in A. Damasio, *Looking for Spinoza*, 88–96.
19 See M. Lim, Z. Wang, D. Olazobal, X. Ren, et. alii, "Enhanced partner preference in a promiscuous species by manipulating the expression of a single gene," *Nature*, 429, 2004, 754–757; H. Wang, F. Duclot, Yan Liu, Z. Wang & M. Kabbaj, "Histone Deacetylase Inhibitors Facilitate Partner Preference Formation in Female Prairie Voles," in *Nature Neuroscience*, 16, 2013, 919–924. The debate on how oxytocin can act on different species is open: J.L. Goodson, "Deconstructing Sociality, Social Evolution and Relevant Nonapeptide Functions," in *Psychoneuroendocrinology*, 2013, 38, 465–78.
20 L. Young, B. Alexander, *The Chemistry between Us: Love, Sex, and the Science of Attraction*, London, 2012.
21 Shakespeare, *A Midsummer Night's Dream*, II, sc. I, 170–173.
22 A. Damasio, *Self Comes to Mind*.
23 M. Kosfeld et al., "Oxytocin Increases Trust in Humans," in *Nature*, 435, 2005, 673–77.
24 M. Di Simplicio and C. J. Harmer, "Oxytocin and Emotion Processing," in *Journal of Psychopharmacology*, 30, 2016, 1156–9.
25 And the complexity of biology itself ends up dampening accusations of determinism. M. R. Cunningham, "Measuring the Physical in Physical Attractiveness: Quasi Experiments on the Sociobiology of Female Social Beauty," in *The Journal of Personality and Social Psychology*, 50, 1986, 925–935. On the sociological theory relating to sexual selection see the sarcasm of V. S. Ramachadran, "Why Do Gentlemen Prefer Blondes," in *Medical Hypotheses*, 48, 1997, 19–20.
26 "Naturam expelles furca, tamen usque recurret," Horace, *Epistulae*, I, 10, 24. Lucretian traces seem obvious: *De rerum*, III, vv. 307–309.
27 Shakespeare, *Antony and Cleopatra*, I, iv, 12–15.
28 ODS, *Autunno*, 62.
29 P. Bloom, *Just Babies*.
30 F. de Waal, *The Age of Empathy*.

31   S. Blackburn, *Lust: The Seven Deadly Sins*, Oxford, 2005; N. Eldredge, *Why We Do It: Rethinking Sex and The Selfish Gene*, 2004.

32   Exaptation describes the change in the function of a trait during evolution.

33   *Papiri Greci Magici*: tablet quoted in D. Ogden, *Magic, Witchcraft, and Ghosts in the Greek and Roman World. A Sourcebook*, Oxford, 2002, 231.

34   *Sul letto di Procuste. Introduzione alla sociologia della sessualità*, C. Cipolla, ed., Torino, 1996.

35   S. Pinker, *The Better Angels*, 395.

36   Ovid, *Ars amatoria*, L. I, 1. 673–674; "Batti, batti, o bel Masetto, la tua povera Zerlina; starò qui come agnellina le tue botte ad aspettar," Wolfgang Amadeus Mozart, *Don Giovanni*, I, iv.

37   E. R. Kandel, *The Disordered Mind (What Unusual Brains Tell Us About Ourselves)*, New York, 2018.

38   S. Kawanaza, "Battered Women, Happy Genes. There Is No Such Thing as Altruism, Pathological or Otherwise," in *Pathological Altruism*, 313. Dissent abounds.

39   R. Sapolsky, *Behave*, 376.

40   C. A. Faraone, "Binding and Burying the Forces of Evil: The Defensive Use of 'Voodoo Dolls' in Ancient Greece," in *Classical Antiquity*, 10, 1991, 198. The earliest examples of figurines come from the Giza necropolis and date from the Sixth Dynasty (about 2300 BC); J. Meerloo, *Intuition and the Evil Eye*, Wassedore, 1971.

41   A. Damasio, *Looking for Spinoza*, 167.

42   L. Stone, "Sexuality," in Id., *The Past and the Present Revisited*, London, 1987, 344–382.

43   Chemistry, with sildenafil citrate (Viagra), approved by the American Food and Drug Administration on March 27, 1998, entered the history of *eros*, following the commercialization of the contraceptive pill, operational since the 1960s.

44   T. D. Albright, T. M. Jessel, E. R. Kandel, M. I. Posner, "Neuroscience. A Century of Progress and the Mysteries that Remain," in E. R. Kandel, *Psychiatry, Psychoanalysis and the New Biology of Mind*, Washington and London, 2005, ch. 6.

45   N. Wade, *A Troublesome Inheritance: Genes, Race and Human History*, New York, 2014, ch. 3.

46   ODS, *Autunno*, 153.

47   On the evening of November 14, 1936, for a concert in Vienna. See *The Letters of Arturo Toscanini*, H. Sachs, ed., New York, 2002, *ad diem*.

7

DRIVES

Seeking

Fifty thousand years ago, *Homo sapiens*'s brain, having acquired verbal communication potential, is presumed to have reached its completion. Emotions and stimuli were now better integrated into the most admirable of cerebral endowments, the impulse to seek, know and choose. Of the many thousands of years that envelop prehistory in darkness, those relating to the end of the Paleolithic are the densest of cognitive enhancements. What had happened in the head of cave painters, those Oscar Wilde's founders "of social relations," over the millennia preceding, for example, a Sumerian literary text such as the *Epic of Gilgamesh*, conceived around 2100 BC, in which sex, love, anger, violence and spells are encountered?[1] The Babylonian myth of Creation illustrates the magic conception of kinship and the alliance of man with strange and monstrous animals; it summarizes the story of his fears and contains the conflict between religious ideas and the magic conception of evil entities. Plots intertwined in his head, handed down only orally.

Seeking, but What?

The hiatus in our knowledge related to human brain modifications makes its negative impact feel stronger, because it falls on the heuristic of a more complex "impulse." Seeking, the need to know, came as an urgency no less vigorous than other human "appetites" but lacking a specific, clear unifying direction, comparable to that promoted by primary emotions. What were they looking for those *Sapiens*?

The development of speculative thinking must have accelerated. At some point in the late Paleolithic, tribal rituals, incomplete antecedents of magical-religious ideas, began to give birth to something else, through successive eruptions of imagination. Something that for a long time had proceeded alongside fear, being inseparable from it. The direction of a brain development from which the mental

DOI: 10.4324/9781003414377-8

predisposition to question itself on non-visible, not physically attackable, unknown phenomena is identified and fixed.

A vicious circle of human reasoning reappears: a return to the starting point, to those mysterious agencies present in the earth that stimulated the human search for strategic information. The primordial "ape problem," that is, the syndrome revolving around the fear of insidious living beings, hidden by the trees, assumed a compelling heuristic force. The trend of mental evolution would seem to be the following: seeking and knowing in order to survive and continue one's species, making choices. This basic drive directed pre-humans and *Homo sapiens*. The idea that there were hidden realities in the cosmos was wired into the brain of the species by natural selection: "Only those who suspected that a predator might be hiding behind the rustle of branches survived long enough to transmit their genetic information."[2] A constant investigation, because nature was an encrypted writing full of illusory realities. It "had its own language organized and created by itself," which blurred understanding.[3] Men would thus be forced, by brain structure programming, to investigate the meaning of what is happening around them, what awaits them in life. It is precisely from observing the things of creation that those indications come, those multiple signs of the universe whose origin *Homo* tries to interpret, clouding causal relationships, uncertain about the intervention of mere chance.[4]

The thrust exerted by the ape dilemma led to a push towards distinct knowledge, to the formulation of cosmogonies.[5] Magic-religious principles, as pertaining to knowledge, were the product of this brain functioning, the compulsory outlet of a mental system oriented towards the vital need to know, common to all humans.[6] It would pass from philosophy to technology to science, variants of an identical drive: the need to learn, the drive to obtain what one does not have, which constitutes the "very essence of man."[7] A "hunger," which in the form of a conscious perception is commonly called desire; a set of impulses and motivations also nourishing insidious suspicions that malefic agencies of our fellow men or supernatural entities may hide behind sudden and inexplicable misfortunes. This is the twisted cognitive complexity of evil witchcraft or malefice.

Supernatural Entities

If multiple unknown forces were acting on the earth, it was vital to try to establish contact with them.[8] The scenario envisaged by the continuous advancements of cognitive sciences and neuroscience insists on the innate tendency to develop concepts according to certain schemes: "Supernaturalistic beliefs have their roots in some mechanisms [...] which are an integral part of our normal cognitive processes."[9] Even in the early days of humanity, disease, physical decay and death (the sight of the dead) produced questions and emotions difficult to master. The experience of other people passing away stimulates imaginary relationships with the unknown.[10] The first evidence of cemeteries with traces of rituals dates to about ninety-five thousand years ago. At that time, or even earlier, the living must have wondered: where do all these dead go? The answer must have been obvious right away. The perception of changing seasons and their repetition in a circular pattern of birth–death–rebirth may have led them to consider death as entry into another world. With visions stimulated by the drugs of some shaman the dead continued to live and in dreams they regularly reunited with the living in the world created by the brain.[11] Additionally, these dead could be angry with the living, because their passing had occurred in some violent way; and "once invented, the category of the restless gave rise to numerous tales, actually ghost stories."[12] How many deities (positive / negative) appeared in this way in man's imaginary palimpsest, induced by hallucinating trances, or by dreams? We ignore it.

***

Two hundred thousand years ago, in that stage of evolution that saw the probable appearance of *Homo sapiens*, magic-religious ideas would have germinated. In which way? Cognitive anthropology and evolutionary psychology ask the theory of mind functions for help. This function allows individuals to infer the mental states of the others by attributing thoughts and conjectures to them, and attributing an agency to physical phenomena, to the alternating of seasons, to storms, to earthquakes.[13] Mind reading, which passes our mental state to abstract essences, is activated.[14] From an evolutionary perspective:

> [I]t is better to be sure rather than sorry with reference to the identification of agency in conditions of uncertainty. This cognitive propensity favored the emergence of malevolent deities in every culture, just as the Darwinian compensatory propensity to cling to those who take care of us favored the appearance of benevolent deities.[15]

The admissible hypothesis is that in the absence of knowledge and the ability to explain cosmic events in another way, the brain possessed a strong predisposition to interpret external stimuli as human-like agents. This led us to attribute our mental faculties to natural forces. When groups of hominins became more numerous and created larger communities practicing evolutionary strategies of high-level cooperation, perhaps the seeds of a further critical passage emerged. This transfers a similar (cooperative) mental state to supernatural entities: that of great gods who monitor human conduct. In this hypothesis, the steps leading to the psychological transfer from social monitoring to supernatural monitoring exercised by superior and undisciplinable powers, remain difficult to discern.[16] Less uncertain is the proposal that genetic transmission made these forms of proto-morality adaptive. To demonstrate this remains a question that stands as a challenge for scholars.[17]

Gods, Magicians, Scepsis: Secondary Brain Products

If the above reconstruction works, Statius's verses are corroborated. Fear would have favored a continuous enrichment of mental activity. Emotion and simulation often seem inextricably linked, as demonstrated by experimental studies comparing the power of mental images at eliciting feelings to other forms of thought.[18] Magical beliefs, not different from religious ones, are a spin-off of the brain that seeks, guesses and simulates, and include emotionally charged components formed in regions of the brain to which the conscious mind has no access. Natural selection has marked them with a compelling quality free of mere facts.[19] Multiplied by the infinite possibilities of verbal communication, they ended up opening the way to the invention of cosmogonies, to gods, demons, fantastic narratives of *Magonia* in high skies already encountered. In this perspective that outlines how human instinct forges beneficial and malefic entities, witchcraft is specified as intelligence and action: that is, on one hand, a way of perceiving the world, of giving it meaning, understanding it; on the other, a selfish will to bend it to its own ends.

But have all human beings since prehistoric times sought a relationship with supernatural realities? We do not know how to answer. This question alluding to skepticism is possibly top of the list for coefficient of difficulty encountered in elaborating the themes of the book. However, let us not be surprised by the side effects of this human drive to seek. In fact, why should an alternative epistemological position not derive from human curiosity and perplexity? Can neurobiology and cognitive sciences give up and conclude that "the question is very likely to remain unresolved"?[20] Or argue that unbelief "is generally the result of deliberate vigorous work against our natural cognitive disposition [toward religion],"[21] and that "as many evolutionary scientists have proposed, [...] religion had an advantage starting point on atheism and science in the human brain"?[22]

A head start? We are just not convinced, and favor an interpretation that emphasizes something else. The same urgency to observe the environment in order to know it, dominate and predict it, and the meta-cognitive abilities to scrutinize one's own thoughts, led and continue to lead some individuals to dissect and distrust what is real, questioning it in the present and not projecting it into future.

What is this seeking in the end? Where do magicians, gods, doubts, or indifference about counterfactual entities come from? We do not want to suggest that generating gods, demons and witches is the distorted solution of an organ built for guessing; on the contrary, it is the almost inevitable outcome, a secondary product of the tireless work of this approximately 1300 grams of gelatinous mass. Let us discuss more the *predictive, simulator* and *creative* brain.

The Predictive Brain

We will speculate even more closely on magic and the neurobiological foundations of religion. Can the generation of unreal explanatory hypotheses be a predictable secondary product (spin off) of our nervous system? It is difficult to resist such a suggestion that comes from the most recent brain computational and cognitive models. In summary, these models propose that the brain is a tool for "guessing" in a recursive and increasingly refined way.[23] What does this mean? From a Kantian point of view, our nervous system does not record reality as it is, but the information we take for valid from the environment is the solution of a probabilistic calculation of the brain that integrates two systems. On the one hand, the imprecise signals from our peripheral sensory systems arrive, which through the primary sensory areas of the brain communicate to the higher cortical areas – for example, the prefrontal cortex – (*bottom-up communication*). On the other hand, the higher cortices (such as the prefrontal cortex) contain the traces of previous information on which basis they formed knowledge of the regularities of the surrounding conditions, and these traces generated by the previous knowledge build the meaning of each new sensory stimulus, filtering and correcting the specifics of what is perceived by the senses from time to time (*top-down communication*). Our brain creates a model of the present reality that is continuously updated by new environmental information from the periphery (*bottom-up*). The new incoming stimuli meet the expectations created by the previous knowledge with which they are compared (*top-down*): and the result of this comparison between bottom-up and top-down is a signal that corrects the brain's expectations about the meaning of a stimulus based on previous knowledge: the so-called "prediction error."

Each new environmental stimulus or inner event generates a prediction-error that potentially corrects the anticipation, and if necessary, updates the knowledge. In the brain this signal is given by the firing of dopaminergic neurons.[24] One way experimental psychologists study these manifestations is by creating laboratory games like gambling. To win you need to learn what the winner of a pair of cards is. During the game, suddenly the trump card can change, violating the learned rule of association between stimulus and reward, and it is now that in functional magnetic resonance imaging (fMRI) brain activity can be observed indicating the prediction-error signal, as from Evans-Pritchard's inside a broadly woven basket.[25] When a prediction is violated, the brain shifts attention to the new stimulus, learns and acquires more details by amplifying cognitive effort. When there is no violation, the brain assumes that it has encoded the first basic information well and moves on, without having to waste cognitive resources decoding the details of something it already knows. In a continuous balance of tested, confirmed and corrected novelties and advances, our "predictive brain" creates probable, plastic and mobile knowledge, decodes the environment, and learns its regularities.[26]

That is what is to be expected. There is nothing other than the truth of our senses continuously anticipated, harmonized, corrected and reshaped by our brain's integrative functions. In the most advanced predictive brain thesis, all brain functions (not just sensory systems) follow this computational model, which continually tests hypotheses and corrects them. It is an energy saving system, because a precise calculation of everything that happens continuously outside and inside us would not be possible, with a continuous margin of error, when the balance that integrates surprise and regularity is not well settled. For example, it gives too much weight to internal rules already learned or vice versa to the alleged novelties of environmental signals; when it becomes too rigid or too malleable and unable to learn simplifying rules and filter the relevant ones among thousands of environmental signals, then computational flaws in the brain appear. It is hypothesized, for example, that auditory hallucinations (to be encountered later, an internal thought mistaken for an external voice)[27] are the consequence of one of these flaws in our probabilistic balance, as well as the cognitive distortions of the absolute pessimism of depression into which a "stiffened" nervous system is no longer able to give benign interpretations of the environment.[28]

The Simulator Brain

Returning to belief and skepticism, a macro aspect of this apparatus of multiple continuous micro prediction-errors pushes our predictive brain to the extreme and demonstrates its adaptive power. This aspect seems relevant to us for understanding the mechanisms supporting the magic-religious ideas. In fact, not only do we learn to guess which card is most often associated with a prize, and win the game, but using the same system calculating the probability between bottom-up and top-down we can predict what will happen next time we enter the bar to have a coffee, when all neighbors stop for a chat with the newspaper. We can simulate what emotions we will feel if we stop smiling, offer them a coffee and then integrate into the conversation, and what happens if we just throw two coins on the counter with our head down. We can thus decide what to do based on our mood if we need company to recover from a tiring day or if we want to avoid a person to whom we owe money.

If at an unconscious level the brain performs continuous micro-simulations, at a conscious level we continuously simulate plausible future situations, producing mental images that draw on memories, but also that make up counterfactual and fantasy plots (see the treasure hunting phenomenon later in Chapter 27). We create, more or less voluntarily, multisensory simulations that have the ability to evoke the same emotions and the same physiological responses of actually perceived experiences and stimuli.[29] The brain does not distinguish much difference between figurations of the mind and perceived stimuli, an adaptive cunning fundamental to simulate every theoretical occurrence hidden around the corner in such a realistic way as to be really ready to face the future.[30] This extreme simulation ability to "train mentally" will not surprise a dancer or a high jumper: it is proven that the simulated repetition of specific motor sequences improves their execution. However, the power of the cognitive function of simulation goes far beyond, so much so that it has been hypothesized that acquiring the ability to simulate possible future events (starting from the knowledge contained in memory) was a key step in increasing evolutionary fitness and humans' chances of survival.[31] The more refined our abilities to simulate and imagine "it seems almost real," the more we will be able to navigate the future, especially that which, starting from the Paleolithic, is made up of increasingly complex social relations.

Not only this. Using imagination to anticipate the future helps to regulate the emotions of the present, to dominate impulses, to achieve long-distance goals. It will come as no surprise that it is a cognitive tool that sometimes becomes blocked and distorted. In the grip of anxiety, the depictions of catastrophic future scenarios amplify worries to the point of paralyzing action; in depression, suicidal thoughts become more intense when they are accompanied by mental images that simulate the final act or its consequences. In those who abuse substances, vivid mental representations, such as the pleasure of a cigarette, increase the craving and the likelihood of smoking.[32]

Brain Creativity

Faced with the pervasive and penetrating attitude of the human mind to simulate, we ask ourselves: do witches, soothsayers and shamans not perform the function of externalizing this simulating and predictive faculty, regulating it, harnessing it? In addition, can't our simulator brain naturally lead us to believe that a strongly imagined will or emotion generates real results? Once again, the indications of experimental psychology are suggestive. Imagining a behavior can increase the probability of implementing it (including voting in elections!).[33] We borrow, in a simulation, the words of a patient:

> It is like a scene from a movie that pops up in my head and goes in a loop without me being able to stop it anymore. [...] I imagine my professor who enters the doctoral students' room screaming, red in the face with raised eyebrows and telling me "How did you go wrong with that experiment? [...] you blew all the data!" [...] I feel terrified, humiliated, a failure, yet my professor is truly kind and has never yelled at anyone, but since I have that image in my head, I have not gone to a reception anymore and I cannot go through the corridor of his office [...] What if it really happens? I know it is not real, but I feel it as such.[34]

Similar mental ruminations produced by suggestions of witchcraft environments are common currency in trial testimonies, albeit cryptically expressed (see below, Case study 6 and 7). Therefore, it is enticing to speculate that the magic-religious ideas are not only the product of a brain made to know but also of a brain that knows by guessing, by adjusting prediction and error. It is an intricate neural system that often overcomes environmental challenges by imagining, simulating, playing in advance where it does not know and cannot know. Maybe to the point of constructing ideas that violate common expectations.

In summary, paths to extricate ourselves from the problem of gods, magicians, and the beginning of skepticism are to be looked for in the convolutions of the pre-frontal cortex, in the labyrinth of the complexity of cerebral propensities. Precisely that drive, that is, the impulse to verify the realities of the "ape problem" allowed separate mental spaces to open up for abstract considerations (the result of the same game of prediction and error but calibrated differently? At the moment this remains only speculation). Considerations that, leading to carelessness or extraneousness or to an obstinate refusal to bow to the conformity of the majority, led to an incessant rational search.

After all, be it permitted, it comes naturally to imitate, by adapting it, a celebrated tirade of Humphrey Bogart: "This is the brain, baby. The brain!" All the amazing brain creativity, and we can't help it.[35] Nothing but the outcome of an incessant search and choice, as if the status of *Homo* consisted of a concept of incessant *anthropopoiesis*, the self-building process of social being.[36]

Notes

1   The first traces of the Epic were brought to light in the ruins of the library of Ashurbanipal in Nineveh in the mid-nineteenth century.
2   L. M. Krauss, "The Universe: The Important Stuff Is Invisible," in *NYR*, March 10, 2016.
3   Thomas Mann, *Doctor Faustus*, London, 1999, ch. 3.
4   W. Burkert, *Creation of the Sacred. Tracks of Biology in Early Religions*, Cambridge, MA, 1998, ch. 7.
5   G. Luck, "Witches and Sorcerers in Classical Literature," in *Witchcraft and Magic in Europe*, B. Ankarloo, S. Clark, eds., 2; V. Flint, R. Gordon, G. Luck, D. Ogden, *Ancient Greece and Rome*, London, 1999, 96.
6   P. Boyer, *Religion Explained. The Human Instincts that Fashion Gods, Spirits and Ancestors*, London, 2002; S. Atran, *In Gods We Trust: The Evolutionary Landscape of Religion (Evolution and Cognition)*, Oxford, 2002. S. Harris insists on the functional neurobiology of belief, Id., *The Moral Landscape: How Science Can Determine Human Values*, New York, 2010, and S. Harris, S. A. Sheth, M. S. Cohen, "Functional Neuroimaging of Belief, Disbelief, and Uncertainty," in *Annals of Neurology*, 63, 2008, 141–147.
7   Spinoza, *Etica*, III, 9, scolium, in Id, *Opere*, 907.
8   S. Atran, A. Norenzayan, "Religion's Evolutionary Landscape: Counterintuition, Commitment, Compassion, Communion," in *Behavioral and Brain Sciences*, 27, 2004, 1–18; Commentary, 19–41; authors' response, 42–57; P. Boyer, B. Bergstrom, "Evolutionary Perspectives on Religion," in *The Annual Review of Anthropology*, 2008, 37, 111–130.
9   V. Girotto, T. Pievani, G. Vallortigara, *Nati per credere: Perché il nostro cervello sembra predisposto a fraintendere la teoria di Darwin*, Torino, 2008, 97.
10   W. Burkert, *Creation of the Sacred*, ch. 1.
11   E. O. Wilson, *The Social Conquest*, ch. 25.
12   R. Gordon, "Imagining Greek and Roman Magic," in *Ancient Greece and Rome*, 176.
13   The evolutionary hypothesis for the theory of mind is social intelligence also known as Machiavellian intelligence. This excess intelligence may have been beneficial for social manipulation, deception, and cooperation. This suggests a slightly independent evolutionary history of mindreading ability; see R. I. M. Dunbar, "The Social Brain Hypothesis and its Implication for Social Evolution," in *Annals of Human Biology*, 36, 2009, 562–572.
14   A. Norenzayan, *Big Gods*, 13–32.
15   S. Atran, A. Norenzayan, "Religion's Evolutionary Landscape," 7; S. Atran, *In Gods We Trust*, 267.
16   A. Norenzayan, *Big Gods*.
17   D. Sloan Wilson, E. O. Wilson, "Rethinking the Theoretical Foundations of Sociobiology," in *The Quarterly Review of Biology*, 82, 2007, 327–348; N. Wade, *The Faith Instinct: How Religion Evolved and Why It Endures*, London, 2009, 62–74.
18   A. Mathews, V. Ridgeway, E. A. Holmes, "Feels Like the Real Thing: Imagery Is Both More Realistic and Emotional than Verbal Thought," in *Cognition and Emotion*, 27, 2013, 217–29.
19   J. Haidt, *Righteous Mind*, ch. 6; N. Wade, *The Faith Instinct*, 13–37.
20   P. Boyer, *Religion Explained*, 366.
21   Id., "Religion: Bound to Believe?," in *Nature*, 455, 2008, 1038–1039.
22   A. Norenzayan, *Big Gods*, 191.
23   K. Friston, "The Free-Energy Principle: A Unified Brain Theory," in *Nat Rev Neuroscience* (Nature Reviews Neuroscience), 11, 2010, 127–138.
24   Through a precise signal emitted by the neurons that release dopamine. See W. Schultz, "Dopamine Reward Prediction-Error Signaling: A Two-Component Response," in *Nat Rev Neuroscience*, 17, 2016, 183–195, doi: 10.1038/nrn.2015.26.
25   In animals this can be recorded directly through electrodes implanted in the brain's dopaminergic areas.
26   K. Friston, "The Free-Energy Principle."

27 P. C. Fletcher, C. D. Frith, "Perceiving is Believing: A Bayesian Approach to Explaining the Positive Symptoms of Schizophrenia," in *Nat Rev Neuroscience*, 10, 2009, 48–58, doi: 10. 1038/nrn2536.

28 Q. J. Huys, N. D. Daw, P. Dayan, "Depression: A Decision-Theoretic Analysis," in *Ann Rev Neuroscience* (Annual Review of Neuroscience), 38, 2015, 1–23, doi: 10. 1146.

29 J. L. Ji, S. B. Heyes, C. MacLeod, E. A. Holmes, "Emotional Mental Imagery as Simulation of Reality: Fear and Beyond-A Tribute to Peter Lang," in *Behavior Therapy*, 47, 2016, 702–719.

30 J. Pearson, T. Naselaris, E. A. Holmes and S. M. Kosslyn, "Mental Imagery: Functional Mechanisms and Clinical Applications," in *Trends in Cognitive Neurosciences*, 19, 2015, 590–602.

31 T. Suddendorf, D. R. Addis, M. C. Corballis, "Mental Time Travel and the Shaping of the Human Mind," in *Philosophical Transactions of the Royal Society*, in *Biological Sciences*, 364, 2009, 1317–24. doi: 10.1098/rstb.2008.0301.

32 J. L. Ji, E. A. Holmes, D. Kavanagh, C. MacLeod, M. Di Simplicio, "Mental Imagery in Psychiatry: Conceptual and Clinical Implications," in *CNS Spectrum*, 2019, 24, 114–126.

33 Libby et al., "Picture Yourself at the Polls: Visual Perspective in Mental Imagery Affects Self-Perception and Behaviour," in *Psychological Science*, 18, 2007, 193–198.

34 E. A. Holmes, S. A. Hales, K. Young, M. Di Simplicio, *Imagery-Based Cognitive Therapy for Bipolar Disorder and Mood Instability*, New York, 2019.

35 That is Ed Hutchenson's (Humphrey Bogart) phone line in Richard Brooks's *Deadline*: "That's the press, baby. The press! And there's nothing you can do about it."

36 C. Calame, *Prometeo genetista*, 65.

8

EVOLVED AND ABANDONED

A Standstill Psychology?

In April 2003, the official announcement of the completion of the Genome project (99.7%) spread around the world and in May 2006 the last human chromosome sequence was published in the journal *Nature*. It looked like a new dawn for human science. Genomics has profoundly changed the field of human evolutionary genetics. Cognitive horizons opened by new discoveries keep uncertainties alive. Is our innate social psychology really the one that was bequeathed to us by our Pleistocene ancestors? Did the brain of those men who frescoed so many caves remain intact for millennia? If the human mind was modeled in the reality of predation, perhaps Paleolithic hardships did not definitively forge our ancestral adaptations, as cognitive archeology studies tend to show.

The Genome Project and Human Nature

Without overwhelming convictions, evolutionary biology and paleoanthropology lean towards the conjecture that from the Neolithic onwards there would have been an opportunity for significant changes in the brain. The interaction between biology and culture produces adaptations following changes in the climate, diet, exposure to pathogens. With the transition from Paleolithic to Neolithic, the gradual spread of agriculture and the expansion of available calories, societies incorporated important aspects of human biology and the changes created a new neurophysiological ecosystem, a field of evolutionary adaptation in which customs and habits that generate new neural configurations or that alter the states of the body-brain system have been able to evolve in unpredictable ways.[1] A well-known example of genes and culture coevolution is that of lactose digestion in adults. Mutations to the lactase enzyme have made milk digestible in some populations.[2] However, many other characteristics (from skin to body, from hemoglobin to alcohol tolerance) that bring advantages in specific environments must be added. Why on earth should the human mind, and only the

DOI: 10.4324/9781003414377-9

human mind, have remained frozen for thousands of generations instead? "Evolved and abandoned? "[3] In short, there does not seem to be a good reason why our brain – 2 percent of body mass that absorbs 20 percent of energy – should "be exempt from this adaptive process."[4]

Certainly, the basic connotation of the organ previously referred to, the synapses plasticity, makes it susceptible to future adjustments, so much so that we can affirm that the discovery of its plasticity has struck a blow to the nature-culture balance.[5] Maybe we should even discuss a *Homo plasticus*.[6] How far plasticity can lead is unclear. To date, epigenetic studies are not able to demonstrate that new individual experiences, by changing the physical structure of the brain and its functional organization (physiology) are genetically transmissible or selectable.[7] However, it seems plausible to question whether the variation in historical age of terrestrial ecosystems, produced by agrarian civilizations and the subsequent impact on neurophysiology, along with the changes added in information and communication technologies, played a role in readjusting humans thought processes. But how to test such sequences?

***

The stakes are high. To proceed in order: the environment changes genes, or rather the expression of the genes in an individual. If and how this process may be relevant at a species level, has a more uncertain answer, though. On one hand, according to the conventional knowledge of evolutionary psychology, the human brain, "in the sense of a cognitive and emotional repertoire," would have remained constant over the few thousand years of recorded history.[8] Exactly, evolved and abandoned: a complex organ like our brain took millions of years to develop.

On the other hand, further and more radical studies tend to demonstrate that the human mind was "biologically formed by recent environments added to the ancient ones."[9] The number of generations the human genome needs to respond to new selective pressures is not well known. The difficulty lies in finding an appropriate time scale. Genes turn on and off continuously in response to conditions such as stress, famine, or disease; they are dynamic genes that build people determined to expose themselves to new climates, predators, parasites, food sources, social structures and forms of war.[10] In this sense it is now known that the brain hardware can change during a person's life. But it is quite another story to hypothesize changes at the species level.

A time scale is urgently needed. In the depth of prehistory, chronology does not work very well, and demography, which cannot be ignored, is in worse waters due to its inaccuracy. What numbers do we have? Around 100,000 years ago *Homo sapiens* could have amounted to 10,000 individuals, who reached 500,000 seventy thousand years later, to rise to the level of 5/6 million at the beginning of the Neolithic, 10,000 years ago. In addition, in the following millennia, the population growth rate until the birth of Christ went from 1.25 to 7.62, bringing the planet's inhabitants to 250 million.[11] Such a surge in population density triggered a considerable number of genetic mutations whose traits have been identified.[12] Let us therefore ask ourselves: in that whirling waltz of genes and culture co-evolution, did the genetic partner not even move a step? At the same time the cultural partner began to dance to the new rhythm created by the energy-communication revolutions that follow one another after the advent of agriculture, the invention of writing and then of printing. How is it possible that the genetic mutation has not also given a "touch up" to our brains and behaviors when our social environment has undergone the most radical transformation in the history of primates?[13] Yet recent anthropological studies suggest that changes in allelic frequencies (variants of a gene) were determined precisely by the impact on the environment of human cultural practices: such as those already encountered in dealing with reciprocal altruism and the psychological needs of *Homo sapiens* groups, 200,000 years ago. Geneticists are beginning to consider culture as one source of pressure on genes, with no reason to exclude from this mechanism the multiple genes responsible for brain architecture and function.

A Touch-Up to the Brain?

We reread the quote: a "touch-up" to the brain. The assumption is strong and implications for our topic may not be ruled out. In the end, the synapses of modern-age witch-hunting protagonists may not have been identical to those of ancestors of few thousand years before. An adventurous hypothesis. Let us call time-out, as in a basketball game, to better face the critical moment of a match.

Nature/culture dialectical interaction is to be carefully examined. In fact, we are about to take a new direction in reasoning. Magical-religious mental representations have been interpreted as the response of an evolution that equipped the brain to prefer cognitive options consistent with humanity's universal proclivity of finding information for the needs of life, carrying out probabilistic calculations and simulations aimed at continuing the species, defeating the pain, overcoming death. These options were the way out of primordial inclinations who knows how far away. A succession of phases can be postulated here. Starting about a million years ago, our innate hyperactive recognition system interacted with the new behavioral innovations of ethical value (reciprocal altruism) triggering an adaptive genetic response that selected a cognitive propensity to seek and simulate. From the synergistic field produced by shared intentionality and from tribal ultra-sociality, magical/religious ideas would have evolved in the imminent *Homo sapiens*.

A sequence of phases that may have been "the stratified result of primary adaptations, collateral effects, non-adaptations and readjustments that occurred both in our biological evolution and in our cultural evolution."[14] The distribution across space and the tenacious persistence of such powerful ideas would have been favored by a natural selection of a genetic type which privileged a psychological tendency that was somehow reached. Starting from a more advanced moment, around 50,000 years ago, the orientation of our mind to seek, inform, choose, imagine, socialize, and narrate took on the task of passing on stories, cult practices and beliefs heard in the narratives and myths of ancestors, as said by Aaona, the shaman. The genetic basis of our shaman's brain predisposition is obvious: the entire human behavior has a genetic component, and everything was fixed in the final stretch of the Pleistocene.

Nevertheless, it is necessary to insist: reconstruction does not seem to stop there. Thinking in terms of the co-evolution of genes and culture makes our discourse much more intricate. In the end an uncomfortable but basic question arises: how different in instinct and emotions did men become over time? When a new factor of change is introduced by the mutation of the ecological niche, a restructuring due to the mutual adaptation between mental modules and social practices seems conceivable.[15] It is desirable that studies of the human genome continue to describe the selective pressures it has been subjected to in historical ages, setting the brave goal of editing humanity.[16] It is already known that genes can respond much more quickly to environmental changes even in the span of a few tens of centuries.[17] We must therefore investigate whether human evolution was recent, intense and local.[18] Influences of recent genetic selection "involve the functioning of the nervous system so that they could, in theory, have an effect on cognition and emotions."[19] In the short duration of recorded history, new social interrelations materialized in some principles that redefine the conduct of the individual in expanded communities. Human choices interface with the evolutionary course by finding opportunities that can favor a synaptic adaptation.

***

Time-out has elapsed. We do not believe perplexities posed by the allusion of a "touch-up" to the brain have been eliminated. Nor can the opposite be excluded: early modern synapses may have been subject to change, or not, and yet this does not imply an immediate link with either the predominant pacific natural control of witchcraft or with the witch hunting. But then, despite its evolutionary advantages, causality be cursed! Our spite seeks comfort in the reflection of an evolutionary biologist: much of the variation in social complexity around the social actors of those centuries is beyond our comprehension, at least in causal terms.[20]

For long, the change variations of human synapses in the moments of the construction of consciousness will be ignored.[21] The biological perspective shows that the brain shapes culture, which shapes the brain. It is called coevolution.[22] And in this regard, "probably the most important fact about genetics and culture is the delayed maturation of the frontal cortex in childhood […], the genetic programming of the young frontal cortex to be freer from genes from other brain regions, and thus be sculpted instead by environment, to sop up cultural norms."[23]

Notes

1 D. L. Smail, *On Deep History and The Brain*, Oakland, 2007.
2 P. J. Richerson, R. Boyd, *Not by Genes Alone*.
3 T. Pievani, *Evoluti e abbandonati. Sesso, politica, morale: Darwin spiega proprio tutto?*, Torino, 2014, 72–73.
4 W. Scheidel, *Evolutionary Psychology*, 1565.

5 S. Pinker, *Blank Slate.*

6 V. S. Ramachandran, *The Tell-Tale Brain: A Neuroscientist's Quest for What Makes Us Human,* New York, 2012.

7 C. Nagy, G. Turecki, "Transgenerational Epigenetic Inheritance: An Open Discussion," in *Epigenomics,* 7, 2015, 781–790, doi:10.2217/epi.15.46.

8 S. Pinker, *The Better Angels of Our Nature,* 612.

9 Ibid, 615–617.

10 J. Haidt, *Righteous Mind,* ch. 9.

11 D. Christian, *Maps of Time: An Introduction to Big History,* Berkeley, CA, 2002, 143.

12 J. F. Pickrell, "Signals of Recent Positive Selection in a Worldwide Sample of Human Population," in *Genoma Research,* 2009, 19, 826–837.

13 J. Haidt, *Righteous Mind,* ch. 9. The metaphor on dance is taken from Richerson and Boyd, *Not by Genes Alone.*

14 V. Girotto, T. Pievani, G. Vallortigara, *Nati per credere,* 176.

15 J. Haidt, *Righteous Mind,* ch. 9.

16 D. Reich, *Who We Are*; K. Davies, *Editing Humanity: The Crispr Revolution and the New Era of Genome Editing,* New York, 2020.

17 K. N. Laland, J. Odling-Smee, S. Myles, "Howe Culture Shaped the Human Genome: Bringing Genetics and Human Sciences Together," in *Nature Reviews Genetics,* 11, 2010, 137–148.

18 N. Wade, *A Troublesome Inheritance,* ch. 1.

19 S. Pinker, *The Better Angels of Our Nature,* 614.

20 R. Trivers, *The Folly,* ch. 14; C. Rovelli, *Helgoland,* Milano, 2020, 185, and *passim.*

21 The strength of synapses can vary throughout the course of existence: see A. Damasio, *Descartes' Error,* ch. 5. J. P. Changeux summarizes his point of view on the strength of synaptic proliferations with the expression "deep epigenetic tangle," in the sense that the predisposition of genes to behave in a certain way yields to the cultural pressures of the environment; see Id, *Geni e cultura,* G. D'Agostino, ed., Palermo, 2007.

22 There is a new approach to gene-culture coevolution. "The conclusions of this paper should not be seen as contradicting but, rather, as complementing the tenets of dual inheritance theory which only seem to cover half of the spectrum of cultural evolution. On one hand, DIT (gene-culture coevolution theory) strives to project the mechanisms of biological evolution on culture but, on the other hand, it ignores the decisive role that neoteny seems to have played in our biological evolution. Therefore, any theory of cultural evolution that does not include neoteny as a component is incomplete. I have attempted to correct this shortcoming by showing that neoteny has a cultural extension that should be acknowledged and added to the variables upon which the equations of gene-culture coevolution theory are constructed"; see G. F. Steiner, "Holocene Crossroads," 80.

23 R. Sapolsky, *Behave,* 326.

9

LOOKING FOR WITCHCRAFT

What did the initial witchcraft act set out to do? "I would like to know the cause of the first ill will," St. Augustine wondered.[1] And who was the first witch?

These are absurd questions because origins are never known. Absurd yet inevitable because the human mind has always been attracted by their charm. It is "the superstition of the single cause," an ambiguous "embryogenetic obsession" in which the question of beginnings and that of causes end up merging.[2] Imagining a genesis of witchcraft agency in communities without literacy is then a challenge.

The Formative Antecedents

Concretely, to this end, we must focus on the essential, regular, and repetitive circumstances typical of the bands of hunters/gatherers expanded into chiefdoms and tended to sedentary lifestyles; situations involving nurturing, courtship, reproduction, protection, alliances, play, competition, strife, and wars. "The continuous impact of these recurring trans-cultural relationships sculpted the mechanism of the human mind that aimed at solving problems," including suffering and damage, often inexplicable.[3] What could an adaptation between mental modules and social practices have meant for our distant ancestors? Without written texts, a Paleolithic chiefdom's description of events must necessarily proceed by approximation, arguing in terms of degrees of probability.

One question arises before others: how was power, which is a pivotal feature of witchcraft and religion, formed and organized there? How did a magician or a chief impose himself? It is not new, noted Hobbes, that men have always resorted to "violence in order to seize people, women, children and livestock of other men."[4] However among the reasons why a subject becomes a guiding figure, in addition to certain visible bodily qualities that qualify him as a patriarchal alpha-male dominating the territory, we must identify other ones:

DOI: 10.4324/9781003414377-10

One of the many reasons why some people become leaders and other followers [...] has little to do with knowledge or skill and a lot to do with how certain physical traits and the manner of a given individual promote certain emotional responses in others.[5]

Against the background of a generic human predisposition to follow and obey, we can advance the hypothesis that one day, within numerically consistent groupings, males of different psychological caliber emerged. The command strategies of late Paleolithic chiefdom implied the strengthening of mental properties that were decisive for those who acted within a political or magic and religious sphere. In community social relations, the desire to influence the conduct of others through one's guidance depended on rarely documentable character enhancement. A nineteenth-century autobiographical testimony suggests the probable lines of such a psychological strategy in tribal circles: "Okonkwo never openly showed any emotion other than an emotion of anger. Showing affection and attachment was a sign of weakness; the only thing worth showing was strength."[6] The message is clear: strength, power, leadership.

This is not only about physical vigor, but also about shrewd minds that made people excel in interpersonal dynamics. Euripides' Tiresias tells us that such mental superiority and the knowledge of the natural world were the "result of a sophisticated investigation."[7] In these guiding characters we can identify the very distant prototypes of our Aaona, with deer heads, interpreters of a phenomenal reality dominated by virtual entities in high sky. They could be the first to believe that these dreamt up (why not?) supernatural beings in human features, but more powerful because they were supposed to tame the climate, "had to be venerated and kept happy with sacred ceremonies."[8] These must have been recurring rituals, with a frequency of actions, gestures and dances aimed at specific purposes.

As a result, music came into play, the latest in evolution, it is believed. "Singing and dancing are significant elements of all hunter/gatherer societies."[9] We are in the presence of a set of sounds, songs, gestures motivated by anxiety and aimed at achieving a certain purpose, overcoming material and psychological impediments. We must imagine the effect determined by a concomitance of stimuli producing a large release of endorphins, with beneficial effects on the immune system and considered adaptive from an evolutionary point of view as creators of a sense of belonging that increased the group potential to survive. Reflecting on the foundations of religious life Durkheim wrote about the psychological effervescence that is unleashed by these practical ceremonials. The mere fact of agglomeration acts as a stimulant of exceptional power. As soon as individuals are gathered, a kind of electricity arises from their juxtaposition which quickly transports them to an extraordinary level of exaltation.[10] They are rituals generating phases of euphoria that enhance community bonds and produce states of happiness due to the action of endogenous neurotransmitters in the brain; an almost universal "biotechnology" to create a sense of unity.[11] In historical times sources are available that speculate on an impalpable ecstatic pleasure transmitted by magical religious rituals, music, rhythmic movements.[12] Euripides still helps:

[Enter Cadmus, dressed in clothing for the Dionysian ritual]
Cadmus. We must sing his praise, as much as we can,
for this Dionysus is my daughter's child.
Now he's revealed himself a god to men.
Where must I go and dance? Where do I get
to move my feet and shake my old gray head?
You must guide me, Tiresias, one old man
leading another, for you're the expert here.
O I'll never tire of waving this thyrsus,
day and night, striking the ground. What rapture!
Now we can forget that we're old men.[13]

These insights are confirmed in recent psychology studies which show that euphoria and a sense of collective identity generate changes in social bonds capable of producing beneficial effects on the mental and physical health of participants.[14] These solicitations were followed or accompanied by an increasingly better organized and systematized number of habits, codified acts and formulas deliberately executed and perceptively understood as "formative antecedents" of magic agency.[15] An amount of customs reveals the essentially psychological value of this act, the result of pressure on the emotional and fantasy faculties. Pre-magical-religious anticipations that aim to interpret or resolve or facilitate all sorts of negative situations by soliciting the mediation of otherworldly essences.

We want to suppose that in the genesis of these rituals the cognitive form already mentioned, that is the manifestation of the most intense emotions as mental images, played a role. It seems plausible that moments of high emotional intensity trigger *flashforwards*, that is, mental images of future events, *best guesses* of the brain in response to an uncertain and unknown emotional scenario. These ante-litteram magicians were those who conveyed collective visions, harnessing the power of future simulation perhaps as an adaptive way to channel the group's fear, desire and need to know[16], then retained this prerogative or power when the collective ritual was over. We will argue later, in Chapter 27, that such visions can constitute a palpable cognitive agency in a handful of men involved in an adventurous search for buried treasures. What they imagined (because they wanted it, because they feared it, because they tried to guess what could happen) felt real. And whether it is real or not, it does not matter because so strong is the emotional energy of the image that you have to behave as if it were. It seems plausible that such an individual psychological mechanism, wired into the human cognitive apparatus, has become a collective conviction, with particularly gifted people suitable for directing it.

Voilà! This is the development of magical-religious convictions; this is how first shamans, would-be priests and magicians, who are somehow distant ancestors of the world protagonists of witchcraft crossing trial sources in future millennia, must have acted. As already noted, in this direction their agency played multiple roles that made up for or supplemented the (prehistoric, ancient, medieval, and modern ages) insufficient base of scientific and technological knowledge. It is a pity not to know more, because witchcraft embryogenesis is located there, in situations that in historical times are defined by scholars as divination or protective or healing or erotic or malefic magic cases.

Was Witchcraft a Maladaptation?

The men exchanging stories about their life experiences in painted caves were still far from concretizing magical-religious practices in distinct social institutions. Let us try to reconstruct the moments when different profiles of a magician and a proto priest are formed. If there was no original demarcation of situations characterizing magic and religion, we believe that a probable border line is identifiable. In the common mental state defining the two phenomena there is an inherent differential peculiarity that will lead to their separation. We schematize for clarity.

There are four common situations: relating:

1. relating to mental representations of non-physical agencies (spirits, ancestors, gods, etc.);
2. relating to artifacts associated with such ideas (statuettes, amulets, symbolic markings);
3. relating to ritual practices, with songs and dances, referring to non-physical agencies; and
4. relating to attempts to come together with non-cooperative people.

Common circumstances stop here. "Moral intuitions as well as explicit moral agreements connecting people in particular groups to non-physical agency" are excluded.[17]

And here is the difficulty. Despite these primordial moral intuitions, we have few doubts that in the explicit ethics of this point a great San Andreas Fault must be situated, doomed to shake the magic-religious connection for an exceedingly long time up to the definitive abyss dug between the two ideas. Pivotal to the difference between witchcraft and religious belief would be the "moral intuitions," namely, how to solve the damage, suffering, evil plaguing mankind.

That an explanation of the difference between the two convictions is to be sought within this interpretative line may be indicated by later historical testimonies. From what we know of the Sumer-Babylonian Pantheon, "the gods were expected to punish the wicked and protect the righteous against everything evil: demons, illness, witchcraft and bad luck in general."[18]

Had something then happened in the neural circuits of *Sapiens* in that handful of tens of thousands of years – marked by the wall paintings – in which we presume the separation between the twin beliefs – witchcraft and religion – began to take shape? DNA studies promise to shed genetic light on the great change in human behavior indicated by archaeological finds from the Upper Paleolithic.[19] Answering the question has a crucial relevance, because it follows from it that religion was adaptive and genetically supported, while what opposes it, such as magic devoid of moral intuitions, would be a testimony of a counterproductive conduct produced by the difficulties of life. And in this line of reasoning, witchcraft would be nothing more than "a simple example of a maladaptive cultural variant."[20] So, witchcraft as a maladaptation? We are not convinced of this, and the disagreement is clarified later in the next chapter.

***

In an exceptionally long meantime, chiefdoms were further expanding. About twenty thousand years ago, approaching the last glacial melt of Pleistocene, adventurous *Sapiens* on their way from the Serengeti savannas towards the Fertile Crescent, were about to reach a critical outcome with the gradual abandonment of hunting, fishing and gathering slowly replaced by agriculture. Hunters/gatherers moved on to work in the fields, a change conventionally understood by scholars as a great advancement of civilization. But why did agriculture take so long to arrive? If the gods of that hyper Urania *Magonia*, which by now is familiar to us, from the high skies had better looked around, it would not have escaped them that Arctic ice was melting, since a favorable conjuncture in the orbital cycles had led to a sharp and decisive increase in temperatures.[21] Twelve thousand years ago, such "orbital forcing" helped Sapiens bring the planet into a fortunate climatic oscillation, due to natural causes, which inaugurated the Holocene and its benevolence towards agrarian civilizations.

Was this current geological epoch really benevolent? Let's listen to the contrary voice of a Greek poet. Eight centuries before the birth of Christ, Hesiod, nostalgic for an egalitarian moral economy, asked himself: was this transition to agriculture a progress? Was it a reconquered paradise, a new ecological and social golden age favored by the increase in the average annual temperature of 7°C in the space of a few decades?[22] Or did agriculture, as his verses complain, come as a curse for future generations of men, the worst mistake in the history of humans?[23]

> ... I could not have lived with the fifth lineage
> of men, but had died before or were born later,
> because now the race is of iron; never during the day
> they will cease from fatigue and trouble, never at night,
> heartbroken; and harsh pains the gods will send to them.[24]

Notes

1 Augustin, *The City of God*, L. 12.6.
2 M. Bloch, *The Historian's Craft: Reflections on the Nature and Uses of History and the Techniques and Methods of Those Who Write It*, London, 1964, ch. 1, and ch. 5.
3 *The Adapted Mind: Evolutionary Psychology and the Generation of Culture*, J. H. Barkow, L. Cosmides, J. Tooby, eds., New York, 1992, 88–89; R. Briggs, *Witches & Neighbors: The Social and Cultural Context of European Witchcraft*, Oxford, 2002, 340–342.
4 T. Hobbes, *Leviathan*, XIII. See R. Wrangham and D. Peterson, *Demonic Males: Apes and the Origins of Human Violence*, Boston, MA, 1996.

5 A. Damasio, *Looking for Spinoza*, 48.
6 Chinua Achebe, *Things Fall Apart*, in *The African Trilogy*, introduction by Chimamanda Ngozi Adichie, London, 2010, 22. Author's life shows a resolute Igbo man rising in command position, when Nigeria suffered the impact of Christianity and colonialism in the 1890s.
7 Tiresia, in Euripides' *Bacchae*, [first episode].
8 E. O. Wilson, *The Social Conquest*, ch. 25.
9 Ibid. For historical times, see B. Ehrenreich, *Dancing in the Streets. A History of Collective Joy*, New York, 2007; W. H. McNeil, "Shall We Dance," in *NYR*, September 27, 2007.
10 É. Durkheim, *The Elementary Forms of the Religious Life*, London, 1915.
11 J. Haidt, *Righteous Mind*, ch. 10.
12 "Historians in general will begin to realize the value of considering music much more relevant in their quest to deepen our understanding of past cultures [...] Music needs to be more fully integrated into the grand design of history – cultural, social and intellectual." See P. Gouk: review of S. F. Williams, *Damnable Practices: Witches, Dangerous Women, and Music in Seventeenth-Century English Broadside Ballads*, London, 2015, in *H-Music*, June, 2017, www.h-et.org/reviews/showrev.php?id=49648.
13 Euripides, *Bacchae*, translated by J. Johnston, Nanaimo, 2003, vv. 228–239.
14 N. Hopkins, S. Reicher, "The Psychology of Health and Well-being in Mass Gatherings: A Review and a Research Agenda," in *Journal Epidemiology Global Health*, 6, 2016, 49–57. This is the Mag Mehla Festival which gathers thousands of pilgrims in northern India every year.
15 W. Burkert, *Creation of the Sacred*.
16 V. Wardell, M.D. Grilli, D. Palombo, "Simulating the Best and Worst of Times: The Powers and Perils of Emotional Simulation," in *Memory*, 30(9), 2022, 1212–1225. doi: 10.1080/09658211.2022.2088796.
17 P. Boyer, B. Bergstrom, "Evolutionary Perspective on Religion," in *The Annual Review of Anthropology*, 37, 2008, 112.
18 M.-L. Thomsen, "Witchcraft and Magic in Ancient Mesopotamia," in *Witchcraft and Magic in Europe*, 1, F. H. Cryer, M.-L. Thomsen, *Biblical and Pagan Societies*, London, 2001, 10–11.
19 D. Reich, *Who We Are*.
20 P. J. Richerson, R. Boyd, *Not by Genes Alone*, ch. 5.
21 K. Harper, *The Fate of Rome*.
22 C. Broodbank, *The Making of the Middle Sea: A History of the Mediterranean from the Beginning to the Emergence of the Classical World*, London, 2015, ch. 5; W. Behringer, *Storia culturale del clima*, 66.
23 The advent of agriculture has been called "one of the greatest blunders of all time"; see J. Diamond, in *Discover*, May 1987, 64–66; but he is less drastic on the successes of the advent of agriculture in, Id., *Arms, steel and diseases*. Provocative R. Sapolsky, too: "agriculture was one of the all-time human blunders," in Id., *Behave*, 326. It is a never-ending debate. The controversial side-effect of granaries on civilization is highlighted by D. Graeber- D. Wengrow, *The Dawn of Everything. A New History of Humanity*, New York, 2021, and reviewed by K. A. Appiah, "Digging for Utopia," *NYR*, December 16, 2021; D. Wengrow and K. A. Appiah, "The Roots of Inequality: An Exchange," *NYR*, January 13, 2022.
24 Hesiod, *Theogony*, vv. 175–180, our translation.

10

DEFINING EVIL WITCHCRAFT

How do we define evil witchcraft? Was it the opposite of the previously remembered moral intuitions connecting people to non-physical agencies? To answer is like stepping into a tortuous maze. It is fair to admit, we will not be able to get out with the clarity desired. As a partial comfort of the resulting sense of frustration, we propose keeping in mind the coincident warning of a neuroscientist and a classical philologist: "it is time to say goodbye to simplicity"; that is, we must resist "the temptation to simplify what is not simple."[1]

***

The anatomy of evil witchcraft brings out an incertitude about our supposed dichotomy: are we good or bad? Doubts persist as showed by some lasting legends built around the meaning of reciprocal altruism, on the idea of an egalitarian primitive society where small groups of our ancestors shared scarce resources. What happened to the Golden Age myth whose protagonists would not have reasoned in terms of "mine and yours"? What about the "naïveté originelle"? An Erasmian praise foreshadowed in Michel de Montaigne as well as in Cervantes, whose ingenious hidalgo in one of his philosophizing moments asserted that "in that pious age […], to obtain his daily food, one had only to raise his hand and pick it" from trees, or from mother earth's bowels not yet profaned by plows.[2] In fact, the primeval goodness of Adam's lineage conception, made famous by young Jean-Jacques Rousseau's *Discours sur l'origine et les fondements de inégalité parmi les hommes* (1755), has always been a vision of the past good for poets, novelists and social utopians.

We want to go beyond the Genevan philosopher's perception of a prehistoric moral economy, because modern biology, paleontology and cognitive sciences as a whole greatly enrich our understanding of *sapiens*'s essence, of which reciprocal altruism is but a minority partner. The profound history of the primitive hordes hides cruel events, discordant from those that tell of the corruption of a self-styled original harmony.

DOI: 10.4324/9781003414377-11

Preverbal Meaning of Evil

With Hesiod's fifth lineage of men, the peasants, our investigation enters the territory of documented history and tries to account for the critical core of witchcraft, for damage and unexpected, mysterious suffering, that is, for evil.

According to a Flemish proverb, wickedness is the daughter of familiarity. When we read that Grotius was convinced that in the natural state there were no bad people, one cannot help saying that he was thinking of the remote creatures of the golden age. But the opposite is true: wickedness arises from the low fences that separate gardens, in the narrow alleys where people are pressed shoulder to shoulder, where the trees of one shade the vineyard of another.[3]

Hugo Grotius's words contain a kernel of truth with an evolutionary flavor. If malefic witchcraft was born from familiarity, something happened in the mind of the hunter–gatherers when leaving their native land of northwestern Africa, they began their long march towards the Fertile Crescent. We must stop and ask: what was evil for *Homo*? What was malefic volition?

The topic cannot be tackled head-on, with an unlikely definition. Evil comes in too many forms. We will carry out the "story very backwards, taking it back to its first source,"[4] asking a question presupposing a different cognitive scheme. And that is: in prehistoric time, how could the concept have been conceived by *Homo*, whose interpersonal relationships oscillated between a violent opportunistic egoism and a tendency towards cooperation?

In the simplest sense that occurs, we are referring to a definition of evil understood as a negative event, as a misfortune without any specific moral implication. In fact, evil is defined by its opposite, good, perceived as something that benefits the individual and the group. Perhaps the future ethical dualism between good and evil arose from the dualism between the pleasant and the unpleasant, between the useful and the harmful. Then evil could perhaps "be understood [by adopting] a naturalistic, unintentional vocabulary, not [to] avoid responsibility, but [to] find new lexicons to assume it."[5] In the conscience of primitives there is still no distinction between the two spheres of morality and the usefulness. Good is what is useful, bad is what is harmful.[6] Therefore, having removed the word from its inextricable ethical connotations, to understand it we will have to try to describe the social contexts that germinated it.

It seems easy to infer that the distinction between good and evil is rooted in biology. Far, far back in the Pleistocene depths, hominins had encountered the elementary problems of existence inherent in life and death, pleasure and pain, related to defense from dangers and to the integrity and health of the organism and to the satisfaction of impulses and motivations (hunger, thirst, eros, curiosity, play): primordial feelings that reflect the current state of the body.[7] We will never know what happened, but certainly "we have to go back to that point at which evil is preverbal [...] not semantically identified and yet implicitly recognized as a human destructiveness."[8]

For million years, the search for food, for the protection from hostile conspecifics and for predators and for shelter from natural elements left our ancestors little time for moral speculation, too expensive in terms of mental energy. Let these states associated with pain and pleasure hold our attention. Later, in less distant millennia, when *Homo heidelbergensis* began to practice shared intentionality, pleasure and pain (good and bad) channeled the species towards an ultra-sociality from which behavioral rules (pre-moral) will be elaborated. In the previous chapter, references to evil found an organic contextualization of its impulses within a neurobiology of those social emotions – empathy, shame, envy – which completes the trajectory of the evolution of the *Homo sapiens* brain. Now it is important to focus on a point: since this was a social world, the specific situations that groups often had to deal with involved other individuals and some of these situations involved what we consider moral or ethical aspects.[9]

Towards "Morality": Relational Models, Evolution, and Causality

Among the many types of hominins, approaching the prevalence of *Homo sapiens*, the neural circuits of the brain which tended to make him a subject inclined to sociality specified relational models based on the creation of various associations. Patterns were formed which can be referred (a) to relations within kinship and the closest conspecifics, (b) to spatial contexts, such as residences or hunting places, and (c) to resources, such as food or land or work or sex. The acquisition of ideas of pleasure/pain and useful/harmful occurred together with the learning of these relational models, but there is no pleasure/pain and no useful/harmful without cause/effect. That is, to arrive at the ethical concepts of good and evil these *Sapiens* had to pass from the interpretation of natural phenomena and human occurrences through categories of cause and effect. Let us pause briefly to see what insights can come from neuroscience to understand the formation of the concepts of cause–effect and of good–evil in larger communities.

***

Neuroscience is at the root of the study of how the brain constructs the concept of cause, first questioning the simplest levels of causal relationships. The current hypothesis is that cause and effect emerge primarily from the perception of specific temporal and spatial characteristics between two stimuli. Brain specific areas map spatial contiguities, and it is believed that the rhythm of neuronal discharges encodes the passage of time and the perception of duration and temporal consequentiality.[10] Neuroimaging studies suggest the attractive idea that the concepts of temporal contiguity and causal link are superimposed and not always distinct in their neural coding. As if to say that for us and even more so for our ancestors, even at the dawn of abstract thought, it was "difficult not to have the experience of causality when they thought about the temporal component of events ."[11] To give an example:

> If I sneeze and a nearby lamp lights up in my office, I can perceive a causal relationship between these two events based on their spatial and temporal

contiguity, but I know well that sneezing does not turn on the light. That is, I have experience of the "perceptual illusion" of causality.[12]

Evolution would have selected the nervous mechanism of time to endow us with a sense of causality, an incredible evolutionary advantage. It is unknown how an order of reality is created in individual consciences that goes from space to time to morality. Again, we speculate that once those larger social ensembles were constituted, the same associative mechanisms regulating physical causal illusions could distort temporal contiguities, transforming them into causal links in the sphere of interpersonal and social relationships, and that this mechanism played a role in the construction of a first collective conduct of the group and in the slow development of ideas about what or who was valid or harmful.

In substance, we suggest that in the phase we are talking about, a path towards morality is envisaged, linked to determining what and who causes negative events (evil), a path intrinsically vulnerable to cognitive distortion operated by human brain mechanisms. At the mercy of such sophisticated yet fallacious cognitive tools, Pleistocene man learned to be a cooperative member in groups that had grown in number due to the incorporation of new relatives that made the assimilation of these norms more difficult but necessary, then bequeathed genetically to future generations. From neuro-philosophy comes a specialized definition of ethics, which consists in adapting to the aforementioned relational models: "Morality appears [...] to be a natural phenomenon – constrained by the forces of natural selection, rooted in neurobiology, shaped by local ecology and modified by cultural developments."[13] Much later in time it is significant to note, for example, that studies of Greco-Roman antiquity confirm there was a "vital, ethological importance of morality: everyone was required to respect the imperatives and prohibitions of the community."[14] Those who violated the terms of those relations were seen as antisocial elements and became the likely targets of proto-moralistic reactions and anger: free riders who intentionally broke rules and customs. Neuroscience has posed the problem of the mental origins of this deliberate non-cooperation of the opportunists by proposing to identify the functioning of a biological mechanism that can lead to such "dishonesty." Understood as an intrinsic component of the social world, dishonesty seems to take the form of a series of small breaches in a moral code that gradually widens, increases with repetition: "a biological mechanism that sustains a slippery slope: this which begins as a series of small acts of dishonesty can escalate into larger transgressions ."[15] In many biographies of criminals such drifts would perhaps stand out.[16]

To conclude. Those who strayed from shared social rules ran the risk of having the causes of damage/injury attributed to them and hence the possibility of being labelled as subjects predisposed to do evil, putting their own existence at risk. During the last phase of deep history, a cooperative (moral) attitude will become adaptive, benefiting the species. Evolutionary psychology argues that evolution shaped culture by influencing cultural variants that are learned, remembered, and taught, and thus helping to determine which ones persist and spread.[17] The explanation looks good. We wish we could be satisfied and close the paragraph with a smiley face ...

Free-Ridership: The Option between Being a Victim or Acting as Witch?

But yet, *something* does not quite fit. Perhaps there is no reader who would not send "but yet" to hell, as the proud Cleopatra, when learning of Antony's marriage to Octavia: because "it mortifies the good that precedes. Fie upon but yet."[18] Unfortunately, they are to be accepted as intrinsic ingredients of a scientific explanation. What is meant by this *something* is soon said: by placing altruism in an adaptive evolutionary perspective, things do not entirely add up when selfish ways of acting are met. The free riders' selfishness persisted throughout evolution and its intentional negative and malefic volition represents one aspect of human nature.

We approach the difficult argument by proposing the following consideration. The species' genes, imprinted by emotions organic to the goal of survival, have collected the adaptive suggestions of the habitat. The human disposition to enter into relationships with others, leading to an agreed sociality, produced the recurrent mixtures of alert fear curiosity desire, previously exemplified by alluding to the "ape problem," in which we have also identified the neural preconditions for the activation of magical and religious ideas. The rationale of magic and religion is the culmination of brain functioning aimed at equipping man with the tools to survive and reproduce through a growing questioning about how things of the world work. And through that questioning encountering and generating malefic agency. The accumulation of magical–religious formative antecedents ends up by structuring itself into increasingly complex cosmogonies, in a virtual mental world bringing about a probable adaptive advantage. Admitting this and granted that the reconstruction of the mechanism pushing *Homo* to create theoretical and counterfactual scenarios is acceptable, the next obstacle challenging cognitive and neurobiological sciences remains the malefic agency, or rather the antisocial behavior layered with magical attributes.

From the point of view of evolutionary fitness, the human brain equipped itself for the construction of social networks based on reciprocity. Precisely for the purposes of such fitness, the reason for the antisocial egoism of parasite free riders remains unclear. It therefore seems inevitable to ask: within our interpretative framework, given that an altruistic behavior (a moral sense) would have promoted a better adaptation to the environment for the survival and continuation of small clan groups, how does it happen that man alienates others and drives away with individualistic and in some cases evil actions? An uncomfortable, permanent conundrum. And, much later, a dilemma made more difficult by the silence of our trial sources. They hide the concrete possibility, for a free rider, that the use of an evil agency was the result of a rational decision: the choice of witchcraft over victimhood to exploit the power attributed to him or her. This is a hot spot in the analysis of witch agency. The questions of whether the individual actually carried bewitching acts or whether they had any self-awareness of being a witch are not "irrelevant."[19] We never meet "a person who either is born with or achieves an inherent character of evil. In this case, it is not an unconscious mystical quality, it is gained by a conscious act."[20] Alas, the option is buried in the depth of individual mind.

Before risking an interpretation, we review the primitive communities again. Small human ensembles function as living organisms and one prerequisite to survival was to maintain coordination and cooperative balance between the internal components. Members of each sedentary group are aware of the presence of some asocial individuals, profiteers qualified by an adverse (selfish) desire that threatens group coexistence. How would groups have behaved towards these profiteers? Did they get rid of them by evicting or killing them? By once again reviewing the wall paintings and the repeated stylizations of human beings, often armed, we look for a graphic allusion to fratricidal killings. Not in vain, as shown by Rock Spain drawings, dating back to 8500 years ago, representing figurines holding bows and arrows directed towards a figurine lying on the ground hit by darts. Does the scene want to allude to an execution?[21] Given what we know about today's foragers, it is likely that the victim was a member of the same group – a deviant who went against the moral code and may well have broken the egalitarian rules. The probable ostracism and ferocious lynching of ill-disposed opportunists can be inferred from other investigations, too.

Prehistoric Executions of Witches

Scholars' evaluations of fratricidal conflict among primitives are discordant. In this field no certainties are reached and to judge from occasional finds of prehistoric human skulls bearing signs of suspicious fractures appears risky. Less doubtful is that a systematic application, for hundreds of thousands of years, of such lethal social control would have removed genes from the genetic pool:

> Aggressive (and originally non-moral) social sanctions shaped an early human genome to give us evolutionary consciousness, and that extended control of chea-ters (free riders) had another important effect. In turn, the suppression of cheaters paved the way for the evolution of altruism [...] These three great developments, taken all together, can be seen as *the scientific history of the origins of morality.* [22]

The explanation might work. Confirmation comes from applying a regressive method, projecting the drastic social discipline practiced by some Aboriginals backwards into prehistoric times. As shown from a careful analysis of fifty native societies, the capital punishment for malicious sorcery was on average three times that of the punishment for other specific deviances, like cunning deviance or sexual transgression. For sure "we get a partial idea of how often capital punishment has taken place over the past century or so. But keep in mind that we will be seeing only the tip of the iceberg."[23] Data leads to some retrospective considerations: they witness a ruthless community practice to get rid of loafers and cheaters.[24] It is important to emphasize the significant statistical impact of witchcraft intimidation, equal to just under 50 percent of the overall figure. Conspicuous remnants of harsh tribal justice towards malefic subjects must also have been the experience of ancient, medieval and early modern societies.[25]

***

Let us go back to free riders. Despite the fleeting documentary consistency, interpersonal dynamics activated by their role have led us to a previous conjecture: to understand them as possible embryo of malefic agency. "The typical witch [free rider] is to some extent an outsider and is marked as other because he or she deviates in various ways from social and biological norms."[26] Another point in common between the free riders and the witch could be identified in their harmful, selfish intentionality. On the one hand, the opportunism of cheaters damages the common good; on the other hand, purposeful envious witchcraft also affects individuals and the community. We will never be able to know whether among human skeletons with smashed heads there are individuals executed because they were expert in evil spells. Conversely, we do not exclude that, around these elusive human types, future generations could have built narratives of archetypes, according to the mythopoetic fecundity of a *bottom-up* projection.

Notwithstanding deep history's uncertainties, in settlements where new aggregates of relatives converged profiteers probably increased in number, ending by multiplying the suppression of parasites to maintain a high level of cooperation and the impact on the gene pool. This reconstruction is satisfying if one thinks in terms of "groups." On the other hand, it appears evident that it does not solve the enigma of the origin and purpose of the individual evil agency, which from the point of view of evolution would seem to remain an incoherent human cognitive ramification. The only plausible explanation would be that free riders' potential deviance is somehow configured as an alternative reproductive strategy for a better interaction between their genetic heritage and the environmental circumstances that advise against mutual support. Ultimately, some fitness advantages could be hidden in selfish individualism, bordering even on psychopathy.[27]

Impulse to Antisociality or Witchcraft as Maladaptation?

How to comment? The scene is quite shaky. In short, how can things be? It is difficult to find a single evolutionary line. Would hostile volitions reveal selfish ends that have a genetic basis?

> The significant point is not that a particular aggregate of genes (or genetic heritage) causes a certain behavior, but the genetic differences between individuals [...] are linked to behavioral differences which, from time to time, translate into the fact that certain individuals have greater reproductive success than others.[28]

The hypothesis of selfish genes presents us with the question we will return to several times: what makes a person antisocial (or malefic)? A reference to a well-known study could prove instructive and keep us balanced on the uncertain dividing line between a-sociality and evil. In a recent survey conducted in New Zealand, a consistent interaction between genetic inheritance and family environment emerged from a selection of 442 sociopathic young people (out of a sample of 1047) from difficult families where they had been mistreated. A significant number of them were found to possess low activity genetic variants (genes producing a protein in a minor form) of the MAO-A enzyme which contributes to regulating the level of some neurotransmitters in the brain and this lower activity would have made antisocial genes. In short: the combination (and presumed interaction) between genetic predisposition and the abuse suffered would be associated with antisocial behaviors.[29] Decades after this initial finding, what we know about the MAO-A depicts the intricate and still partly elusive nature of what makes a complex behavioral phenotype such as aggression (with the contribution of gene-gene interactions, hormones, environmental factors, sex, race etc.).[30]

Alas! To resolve the dilemma on the impulse to evil in a prehistoric or historical past, the explanatory hypothesis which identifies the virtual ill doing in a quantity of MAO-A enzyme produced by a specific genetic variant cannot be used. It would then remain to explain how this was adaptive. How then to jump the obstacle?

Given the enormous weight of the problem for associated life, there is no lack of interdisciplinary attempts to reconstruct mental states predisposing particular individuals to antisocial actions. In discussing the relationship between ethics and biology, a mediation was sought between: (a) a conception of human nature considered essentially selfish/evil and goodness (morality) as a simple cultural covering, a patina; (b) a vision focused on altruism, the founding basis of ethics; (c) an interpretation viewing human moral infrastructure rooted in man's genes (functional, that is, to the continuation of the species) but subject to systematic corruption (which generates some deficit), that is, to a deviation from morality.[31]

This latter point possesses an undisputed cogency to attempt a broader interpretation of contexts in which deviant agency and accusations of witchcraft are formed, because it brings the discourse back to the role played by fear and anger in addressing human conduct. Our moral judgments can be subtly undermined by emotional factors. A latent and only partially conscious sense of hostility towards a rival can prejudice our judgment as to whether he is guilty of a crime. We can sincerely be convinced that our opinion (as an imputation) is the result of a cognitive process (namely, rational) but in fact the emotional influence can be decisive and has been programmed by natural selection to be so. *Fast thinking*, in short, acts automatically; emotions influence our behaviors. We overemphasize our righteousness.

Favoring this line, we are brought back to the beginnings, to the Roman poet Statius and the dynamic field generating fear between victims and perps of damage. However, let us not stray too far from the problem concerning the adaptive advantages of selfish individualism. If a series of adaptive moral behaviors arose from cooperative acting of primitives, because they guaranteed better reproductive success (as well as a precondition for the idea of religion), the behavior that allowed parasitic free riders is also adaptive. It is not clear why selfishness and propensity for evil should be interpreted as a maladaptation and not as a genetically transmitted adaptive trait. We believe that it is a fruitful direction of investigation to understand intentional evil as an action taken to resolve psychological impulses produced by envy; or to gratify deeper genetic inclinations for antisocial actions that remain a mystery to neuroscience. There is the possibility (Chapters 25 and 26) that the evil agency of witchcraft "is the weapon of fierce competition between individuals and small parental groups that involve winners and losers."[32] And we add that on a more general level, defining witchcraft as a simple example of maladaptive cultural variant, contradicts the shared assumption that the evolutionary roots of adaptation and supposed maladaptation are identical. Seeing witchcraft as the outlet of false and often deleterious beliefs means not taking into account that the function of beliefs is sometimes not easy to understand, and a lot of work is required before being allowed to generalize.[33]

The Seed of Evil: Human Nature from Thucydides to Darwin

Understanding the roots of human iniquity remains a distant goal, trapped as we are in that tortuous maze and afraid of not finding a way out. The ability to do evil is perhaps nothing more than an option of the organic constitution of the brain; it would be a side of our essence. Drawing a clear, aseptic profile of human nature, Thucydides left us with a bitter taste in the mouth, describing fratricidal massacres that occurred in Corcyra (present-day Corfu) in 427 BC:

> Many serious disasters struck the cities torn by civil war, which always happen and always will happen as long as human nature remains the same [...] The life of the city at that juncture was upset, and human nature, which usually commits evil, violating the laws, prevailed against the laws, and was pleased to show that, unable to control its own anger, is stronger than justice and enemy of any higher value.[34]

For the great Athenian, man's evil inclination arises as an objective fact. Before the Jewish-Christian conception of God, Greek thought noted the cognitive obstacles concerning the existence of imperfection, catastrophes, evil and undeserved suffering.[35] Monotheistic religions, in the desperate mission of penetrating the contradictions of theodicy, will speak of absolute evil. Augustine of Hippo's statement is well known. He writes in the *Confessions*, "I wanted to do a gratuitous evil, without having any other reason to be evil than evil."[36] The saint's reflection shifted to the slippery ground of transcendence. Today some would doubt whether it makes sense to assert that we behave cruelly because we are carrying a mysterious entity called malice, wickedness or the like.[37] Yet the logic of the Saint is puzzling.

The fact that evil is intrinsic to human action is a persistent perception. When nothing was known about genetics, synapses, neurons and modules and they were absent from the common linguistic heritage, the many faces of human nature could be referred to with different lemmas or phrases, qualifying it as anger, instinct, "thirsty evil," "poésie énigmatique." Many centuries after St. Augustine,

Montaigne appears uncertain as to how to define it: "Did I not find in Plato that divine phrase that nature is nothing but an enigmatic poem?"[38] But refractory to metaphysical considerations, he glimpses something basic, constitutive, immutable in evil: "Nature itself, I fear, has instilled in man some instinct towards inhumanity."[39] Two other souls of the age, Cervantes and Shakespeare, appear in harmony. In a short story the Spaniard notes: "I am not surprised, Braganza, since, in the same way that hurting comes from an instinct, it is quite easy to learn how to do it."[40] Across the Channel, the Bard notes in *Measure for Measure*: "Our instincts, rats that gobble their poison, are thirsty for blood."[41]

We must turn to the Enlightenment to find insights of modern neurobiology. The great thinkers of the Age of Reason and the Enlightenment were scientists, avid theorists in the sciences of human nature. They were cognitive neuroscientists of their times who tried to explain thought and emotion in terms of the physical mechanisms of the nervous system. And they were social psychologists who wrote about moral feelings that keep us united, selfish passions that inflame us, and the obstacles of narrowness of views that make our best prepared plans useless. These thinkers are even more remarkable in that they gave life to their ideas in the absence of formal theories and empirical data. The words neuron, hormone, and gene had no meaning to them.[42] In David Hume and Adam Smith, asociality and altruism had robust roots connected to primary emotions. Hate, resentment and revenge "are regarded as necessary parts of the character of human nature," Smith observed in *Theory of Moral Sentiments*.[43] Emanuel Kant's reflections go in the same direction. For the Prussian philosopher, radical evil was seen as an innate tendency of man but activated by basic elements of human life such as material deprivation, disease, and death.[44] After Darwin, evolutionary biology tried to get out of the mists, replacing the word nature with expressions such as the amoral force of natural selection. Even today, despite great advance in neuroscience research the territories of what would be called antisocial personality and its "extreme variant" of psychopathy are a minefield. In the wide spaces embraced by such a thorny notion, neurobiology and cognitive science studies proceed slowly. Consider scientists' attempts to interpret mental disorders caused by a mixture of egocentrism and lack of empathy: their inescapable conclusion is that the relatively few subjects suffering from psychopathy, aware of the difference between good and evil, persist in deviating without caring for it.[45] The finding seems well suited to an actor's line that has become a cult object: "Some men just want to watch the world burn."[46] Perhaps it's a standstill. However, some insight comes from developmental studies that suggest there might be different trajectories leading to psychopathic features: some more routed in neurocognitive dysfunction of basic emotions such as fear and linked to genetic variants involving abnormal functioning of the oxytocin system, while others with the same phenotype do not exhibit such abnormalities but have a childhood maltreatment history and a physiological profile typical of chronic stress exposure.[47] And since our reflections aim at discovering evil volition links (natural, cultural), these insights lend the opportunity to probe whether an emotional deficit has not occurred in the mental functioning of individual offenders, indifferent to good and evil, in our witchcraft context.

Are We Good or Bad?

Several schools of thought remain discordant: does goodness or evil prevail in *Homo sapiens*? Darwin in his *Autobiography* asks himself whether the world is good or bad.[48] Doubts about the real existence of an innate moral grammar lead to abuse of the nature/culture cliché.[49] Do people owe more to one or the other? For naturalists, we are substantially determined by the interaction between body and brain and their innate functioning starting from the neuronal mechanisms repeating themselves precisely from the origins of the species. Experimental evidence of specific hypotheses that can unpack and demonstrate this approach continues to be sought. Theories propose that the dilemma of the human cooperation principle

> is permitted not by specialized cognitive modules that have evolved for this purpose, but rather through a parsimonious evolutionary re-proposition of basic cognitive mechanisms, such as learning what is useful, discovering threats, self-projection and response selections that already existed.[50]

This must be reconciled with the widespread diffusion of reciprocal altruism that exists "even in the presence of significant incentives to behave selfishly … [And this is] a lasting evolutionary mystery."[51] A mystery, indeed. It remains controversial why selection has prevented learning only what is beneficial to genetic fitness.[52] According to a strict rule in the social evolution of genes, selfish individuals prevail over altruistic individuals while groups of altruists defeat groups of selfish individuals.[53] This is a picture from which we can derive the conclusion that "our genetic nature is primarily selfish, secondarily nepotistic and only moderately inclined to support acts of altruism."[54]

All in all, we are faced with an inevitable contradictory situation given the persisting conceptual uncertainties that make it difficult to explain how the brain produces the mind. The goal of understanding volition will require an integrated analysis. A favorable territory for investigation seems to be malefic witchcraft, that is, the intentional damage inflicted on someone's health or property. The logical obstacle consists in comprehending the alleged volition. The relationship between evil and the will occupies a leading position in the history of ethics. Can man voluntarily do evil? The Bard's answer was dubious: "We knew not / The doctrine of ill-doing."[55]

The classical age of witch-hunting, testimonies coming from the Italian or German or English or Scottish countryside, lead us to reiterate that "it would be wrong to suggest that all persons accused of witchcraft had had malevolent thoughts about their neighbors. But a substantial proportion of them certainly had."[56] Early modern witchcraft trials are not without evidence of the real practices of malefices: spells were actually cast and some really tried to harm or kill people or animals, or to destroy crops or property, using hidden means.[57] Everything we know about European villages shows that they were pervaded by feuds and factions organized around kinship groups. Such interpersonal animosity that paradoxically coexists with a strong communal solidarity found an outlet in acts of hatred (individual, collective). A social atmosphere that generated haters, to keep up with the lexicon of a disconcerting contemporary phenomenon.

Intentional *maleficium* had not escaped scholars. Today, the brain decade revolution (the 90s) despite all its limitations allows us to try to interpret witchcraft in neurobiological terms, because "there is probably something in the minds of men that often generates this … let's call it a cultural institution."[58] In fact, suspicion about the existence of a *mens rea* represents a likely thread in witchcraft trials, albeit very hidden. Understanding what cerebral realities lie behind those malevolent thoughts is a challenge. Causes of a social fact are not to be sought exclusively among its antecedent social facts but also among conscious mental states predisposing an individual to action. Of course, not every criminal act represents a *maleficium*, although a thin line separates it from damage performed in anonymity out of envy, resentment, retaliation, greed or other.[59] It only remains to explore this point later in Chapter 25, being alerted by St. Augustine: "seek not […] the efficient cause of an evil will [because] there is no efficient cause but deficiency […] Try to discover this defect's causes […] is equivalent to wanting to see the darkness or hear silence."[60]

Deficiency? Aren't we used to thinking of evil as absence and deprivation of good? Conversely, we should be convinced that it has a face that is not mere lack but affirmation of a *mens rea*. But despite this, in obvious contradiction, the very word deficiency provides an additional clue to brain sciences to reconstruct how the corrosion of an individual empathic gradient can end up leading to evil.

***

It will not be easy to summarize malevolent agency. Having rejected a transcendent category such as evil, it must then be admitted there should be no mystery about its sources. It resides in brain mechanisms, and has allowed humans to prevail in the struggle for survival. Reasoning in terms of a biologically based epistemology, the concept of evil is formed in connection with the experience of suffering and harm and subsequently, once language is discovered, it is translated into expressions of social relations. Primary emotions provided man with the impulses to create his magnificent conceptual castle.[61] Evil agency seems to come from an internal gap in the individual genetic constitution keeping the predisposition to selfishness, familism and altruism in a fluctuating imbalance. It may be that for hundreds of thousands of years in human groupings there has been the automatic killing of those who did not cooperate. From an evolutionary point of view, it seems likely that "deviant behavior punishment is older than the appreciation of virtue."[62] The cerebral transformations of our Pleistocene ancestors, placing the neurobiology of ethical sentiments (of good and evil) in such an expanded temporal dimension, bring out those adaptive forms of high degrees of cooperation that in the shorter term of history will organize themselves into values of positive coexistence, customs, and laws.

And anyway, for this very reason the fate of free riders, parasitic cheaters as well as potential proto witches, was not sealed forever. *Homo sapiens*'s propensity for ultra-sociality took a further step forward by activating the *thinking slow* in specific social and cultural spaces. This was a "non-automatic" (learned) regulation of immediate reactions (of the *thinking fast*) occurring when people are pressed by primary emotions: fear and anger, with the corollary of repressive agency. Same problem (harm/suffering), same goal (getting rid of it), different solution. Cognitive modules predisposed by neural bases were triggered, eventually materializing in social practices aimed at avoiding traumatizing solutions for communal living, such as the systematic killing of profiteers. The action of culture in turn interacts with synaptic connections with new outcomes. One of the greatest social adaptations of the human species was the ability to organize cooperation to resolve the inevitable conflicts inherent in our social psychology.[63] Admittedly, the self-regulation of cases of witchcraft without the interference of the authorities had a long-lasting tradition in Europe. But this informal method "has been largely overlooked in the secondary literature, though it must be pointed out that the phenomenon has been known for some time in German folkloristic literature, and there are quite astonishing and extensive parallels in the English ethnological literature."[64] The intelligence of a historical problem such as the natural control of evil witchcraft (*maleficium*), anticipated by dealing with anger, is poorly grasped in documented history for lack of information. We must look for its roots in the territory of neurobiology and in the contrasting relationship between *thinking fast* and *thinking slow*.

Notes

1 G. Edelman, *Wider than the Sky*; E. R. Dodds, *The Greeks and the Irrational*.
2 Michel de Montaigne, *Essays*, L. I, ch. XXXI, *On Cannibals*; Erasmus, *In Praise of Folly*, XXXII; M. de Cervantes, *Don Quixote*, I, 11.
3 G. Steiner, *Malice*, Oxford, 1952, 16.
4 "Altius omnem expediam prima repetens ab origine famam," Virgil, *Georgics*, IV, 285–286.
5 E. Morin, *In cielo come in terra: Storia filosofica del male*, Roma, 2011, 287.
6 H. Kelsen, *Society and Nature: A Sociological Enquiry*, New York, 2009, *passim*.
7 A. Damasio, *Self Comes to Mind*.
8 D. Parkin, "Entitling Evil: Muslim and non-Muslim in Coastal Kenya," in *The Anthropology of Evil*, D. Parkin, ed., Oxford, 1985, 237–238.
9 M. S. Gazzaniga, *Human*.
10 It remains uncertain whether this is a property of only some neuronal populations; moreover, a single network of brain areas seems to be involved in determining both physical and social causal links; see J. Bios, A. Chatterjee, T. Kircher, B. Straube, "Neural Correlates of Causality Judgment in Physical and Social Context – The Reversed Effects of Space and Time," in *Neuro Image*, 63, 2012, 882–893.
11 A. Kranjecl, E. R. Cardillo, M. Lehet, and A. Chatterjee, "Deconstructing Events: The Neural Bases for Space, Time, and Causality," in *Journal Cogn Neurosci* (Journal of Cognitive Neuroscience), 24, 2012, 1–16.
12 Ibid. See J. Baedke's report of *Expanding Views of Evolution and Causality Workshop*: "Cause and Process in Evolution," Konrad Lorenz Institute for Evolution and Cognition Research (KLI), Vienna, May 11–14, 2017, in *J Gen Philos Sci* (Journal for General Philosophy of Science). DOI 10.1007/s10838–017–937.
13 P. S. Churchland, *Braintrust: What Neuroscience Tells Us about Morality*, Princeton , NJ, 2011, 191.
14 P. Veyne, *L'impero greco-romano*, Milano, 2007, 395.

15 N. Garret, S. C. Lazzarro, D. Ariely, T. Sharot, "The Brain Adapts to Dishonesty," in *Nature Neuroscience*, 19, 2016, 1727–1732. doi:10.1038/nn.4426.

16 In the career of a serial contemporary impostor, we find exemplified such a mental construction: how from minor deceptions it is possible to slip into major misdeeds up to "overtake the Rubicon" towards a mature crime; S. Luzzatto, *Max Fox*, 51, 62, 65 and *passim*.

17 P. J. Richerson-R. Boyd, *Not by Genes Alone*, ch. 7.

18 "I do not like 'But yet', it does allay / The good precedence, fie upon 'But yet'." Cleopatra in *Antony and Cleopatra*, II, v, vv. 50–51,

19 É. Pócs, *Between the Living and the Dead: A Perspective on Witches and Seers in the Early Modern, Age*, Budapest, 1999, 9.

20 P. Brown, "Sorcery, Demons, and the Rise of Christianity from Late Antiquity into the Middle Ages," in *Witchcraft: Confessions and Accusations*, M. Douglas, ed., London, 1970, 35.

21 See G. Nash, "Assessing Rank and Warfare Strategy in Prehistoric Hunter-Gatherer Society: A Study of Representational Warrior Figures in Rock-Art from the Spanish Levant," in M. Parker Pearson, I. J. Thorpe, eds., *Warfare, Violence and Slavery in Prehistory*, Oxford, 2005, 75–86.

22 C. Boehm, *Moral Origins*, 83 (our italics).

23 Ibid., 84.

24 In the past, in the highlands of New Guinea, out of ten deaths at least one was due to the execution of a person accused of witchcraft (usually male): R. Wrangham, D. Pilbeam, B. Hare, "Convergent Paedomorphism in Bonobos, Domesticated Animal and Humans: The Role of Selection for Reduced Aggression" (unpublished).

25 There are, for example, well-founded suspicions of merciless lynching in the most marginalized mountain areas of Europe such as Catalonia, the Balkan Mountains, the Scottish Highlands, whose inhabitants have left hardly any written documents.

26 M. Ramsay, *Professional and Popular Medicine in France, 1730–1830. The Social World of Medical Practice*, Cambridge, 1988, 270.

27 C. Boehm, *Moral Origins*, 28.

28 S. Shultz, R. Dunbar, "The Evolution of Social Brain: Anthropoid Primates Contrast with Other Primates," in *Proceedings of the Royal Society*, Biological Sciences, 274, 2007, 2429–36.

29 A. Caspi, J. McClay, T. E. Moffit, et alii, "Role of Genotype in the Cycle of Violence in Maltreated Children," in *Science*, 297, 2002, 851–854. Debate is open: C. Aslund, N. Nordquist, E. Comasco, J. Leppert, "Maltreatment, MAO-A, and Delinquency: Sex Differences in Gene-Environment Interaction in a Large Population-Based Cohort of Adolescent," in *Behaviour Genetics*, 41, 2011, 262–272. See also: I. Ouellet-Morin, S. M. Côté, F. Vitaro, M. Hébert, R. Carbonneau, É. Lacourse, G. Turecki, R. E. Tremblay, "Effects of the MAOA Gene and Levels of Exposure to Violence on Antisocial Outcomes," in *The British Journal of Psychiatry*, Oct 2015, bjp.bp.114.162081; doi: 10.1192/bjp.bp.114.162081; A. Raine, *The Anatomy of Violence: The Biological Roots of Crime*, New York, 2013.

30 N.J. Kolla, M. Bortolato. "The Role of Monoamine Oxidase A in the Neurobiology of Aggressive, Antisocial, and Violent Behavior: A Tale of Mice and Men," in *Prog Neurobiol.* 194, 101875, 2020, doi: 10.1016/j.pneurobio.2020.101875.

31 F. de Waal, *Primates and Philosophers: How Morality Evolved*, Princeton, 2006. The four philosophers were R. Wright, Ch. Korsgaard, P. Kitcher, and P. Singer.

32 W. Irons, "The Intertwined Roles of Genes and Culture in Human Evolution," in *Zygon*, 44, 2009, 311–319.

33 P. J. Richerson, R. Boyd, *Not by Genes Alone*, ch. 5.

34 Thucydides, *The War of the Peloponnesians and the Athenians*, L. III, 82, 84; L. I, 22. 4. Our translation.

35 S. Nadler, *The Best of All Possible Worlds: A Story of Philosophers, God, and Evil*, New York, 2008.

36 St. Augustine, *Confessions*, II, 4. 9.

37 G. Jervis, *Pensare diritto, pensare storto: Introduzione alle illusioni sociali*, Torino, 2006, 17.

38 Michel de Montaigne, *Essais*, L. II, ch. XII. Montaigne misinterprets Plato for whom every poem is, by its nature, enigmatic.

39 Ivi, L. II, ch. XI.

40 Miguel de Cervantes, *The Novel of the Colloquy of the Dogs*, in Id., *Exemplary Stories*, Yale, 2016.

41 "Our nature [...] do pursue a thirsty evil"; Shakespeare, *Measure for Measure*, I, iii, vv. 13–15.

42 S. Pinker, "Science Is Not Your Enemy," in *New Republic*, August 7, 2013; and the debate: S. Pinker and L. Wieseltier, "Science vs. the Humanities," *Ivi*, September 27, 2013.

43 Adam Smith, *The Theory of Moral Sentiments*, Cambridge, 2004, I, s. II, ch. 3, 3.

44 Emmanuel Kant, *Religion within the Limits of Reason Alone*, Cambridge, 1961.

45 M. Cima, F. Tonnaer, M.D. Hauser, "Psychopaths Know Right from Wrong but Don't Care," in *Social Cognitive and Affective Neuroscience*, 5, 2010, 59–67.

46 "Some men aren't looking for anything logical, like money. They can't be bought, bullied, reasoned, or negotiated with. Some men just want to watch the world burn." Thus, Michael Caine, in C. Nolan's *The Dark Knight* (2008).

47 S.A. De Brito, A.E. Forth, A.R. Baskin-Sommers, et al. "Psychopathy," in *Nat Rev Dis Primers*, 2021, **7**, 49, doi: 10.1038/s41572-021-00282-1.

48 C. Darwin, *The Autobiography of Charles Darwin 1809–1882*, New York, 1993.

49 R. Dawkins, *A Devil's Chaplain*.

50 J. W. Buckholtz, R. Marois, "The Roots of Modern Justice: Cognitive and Neural Foundations of Social Norms and their Enforcement," in *Nature Neuroscience*, 15, 2012, 660.

51 Ibid., 665.

52 P. J. Richerson, R. Boyd, *Not by Genes Alone*.

53 E. O. Wilson, *The Social Conquest*.

54 C. Boehm, *Moral Origins*, 205. The "first rule" of reciprocal altruism, sort of: see E. Wilson, *Half-Earth. Our Planet's Fight for Life*, New York, 2016.

55 M. Mori, *Volontà*, in *I concetti del male*, P. P. Portinaro, ed., Torino, 2002. Shakespeare, *The Winter's Tale*, I, ii, vv. 69–70.

56 K. Thomas, *Religion and the Decline of Magic: Studies in Popular Beliefs in Sixteenth-and Seventeenth Century England*, Harmondsworth, 1973, 624; and extensively in E. Bever, *The Realities of Witchcraft and Popular Magic in Early Modern Europe: Culture, Cognition, and Everyday Life*, Basingstoke, 2008.

57 N. Cohn, *Europe's Inner Demons: The Demonization of Christians in Medieval Christendom*, London, 1993.

58 J. Haidt, *Righteous Mind*, ch. 1.

59 Arsons, for instance, keep alive such a fear; see K. Thomas, *Religion*, 635–637; G. K. Waite, "Sixteenth-Century Religious Reform and the Witch-hunts," in *The Oxford Handbook of Witchcraft in Early Modern Europe and Colonial America*, B. P. Levack, ed., Oxford, 2013, 501.

60 St. Augustine, *The City of God*, L. 12. 7.

61 G. M. Edelman, G. Tononi, *A Universe of Consciousness: How Matter becomes Imagination*, New York, 2000.

62 C. Boehm, *Moral Origins*, 19.

63 P. J. Richerson, R. Boyd, *Not by Genes Alone*.

64 W. Behringer, *Witchcraft Persecutions in Bavaria: Popular Magic, Religious Zealotry and Reason of State in Early Modern Europe*, Cambridge, 1997, 89; Id., *Witches and Witch-Hunts*, 37.

11

REDEFINING EVIL WITCHCRAFT

The dilemma remains: primary and secondary emotions turn the essence of malefic witchcraft into a puzzle. It is impossible to get over the mental tangle in which empathy, shame and envy confront each other. The comprehension of historical context is sometimes unavoidably confused because the neurosciences themselves prove that brain reality is structured in such a way as to produce "the best and worst of human behavior."[1] So, a question arises spontaneously: what happens to empathy, the brighter side of human nature, mixed in our structure?

> It [...] cannot be disputed, that there is some benevolence, however small, infused into our bosom; some spark of friendship for humankind; some particle of the dove, kneaded into our frame, along with the elements of the wolf and serpent.[2]

Nature has predisposed its best angels to curb our darkest impulses, but it is still essential to ask: why do brain systems responsible for detecting, functioning, and producing emotions and empathy fail?[3] Neuroscience has not yet provided an answer and does not shy away from investigating. But since the essence and ends of evil remain obscure, a frontal attack is avoided and the conundrum approached obliquely, with the knight's move in chess.

***

By setting the goal of looking for evil's neurobiological roots, a methodological proposal to redefine it, deprived of metaphysical implications, is welcome. Evil has been replaced with lack of empathy.[4] As it is, the emotion can be turned on, producing positive sensations when someone is sick. Or it turns off and even reverses. Revenge is triggered as an effect of negative empathy. Due to these peculiarities, for the purpose of understanding the reality of evil it may prove useful

DOI: 10.4324/9781003414377-12

to accept an extended definition of empathy, to be understood as "our ability to identify what someone else thinks or feels, and respond to his or her thoughts and feelings with an appropriate emotion."[5] It does not go unnoticed that in this interpretation there are at least two stages: that of recognizing the emotions of others and that of responding to them. Imagine, then, that for circumstances of life, that over the years for some reason a person's empathy – Hume's "particle of the dove" – has undergone degradation and cannot respond with appropriate emotion to critical situations that may arise. How does the human psyche react in such situations? Let us see how neuroscience and historical investigation face the problem.

For scientists, this possible erosion that occurs slowly has been faced head on and presents a spectrum of plausible solutions. Studies on the anatomical abnormality of a smaller amygdala or related to other brain lesions have in fact been placed at the center of studies on the emotional brain.[6] Research conducted with the aforementioned fMRI techniques suggest that in psychopaths many emotional areas, including the amygdala and the ventromedial pre-frontal cortex, react weakly to emotional stimuli.[7] A more recent sophistication of brain imaging opens up new perspectives on the neurobiological basis of deviance and criminality.[8] And as we have seen, a reduced functioning of another area, the insula, could underlie forms of weakened emotional contagion in line with the many shades of evil.[9]

For historians, on the other hand, paths of interpretation are restricted by the intrinsic limits of the sources. How do we discover cases of people possibly suffering from psychopathy for whom evil is an end in itself? Later, in Chapter 26, the empathy erosion hypothesis is dealt with in depth. But we start thinking about it here. Reconstructing individual social emotions is a challenge rarely supported by the judicial material received.[10] The empathy of witchcraft psychodrama protagonists is unstable, it depends on an internal struggle within their personality, on troubles that are not easy to grasp in the remaining trial files. Nonetheless, neuroscience invites historians to dare, adding to intuitions coming from literary creations, which contain superb archives of annotations on social relations that are anything but ornamental. Anton Chekhov's remarks on the "frowning and sad glances of sly eyes" of envy, malevolence or hatred stimulate our interpretations no less than fMRI.[11] The conflicting intimacy of the peasant family, seed bed of slander, greed, and envy, does not escape literature as much as the acumen of the seventeenth-century Jesuits' evangelical missions. In what sense, then, can shifting attention from evil to the lack of empathy provide a better intelligence of this disturbing human connotation? Some trials evoke the social situations leading to the "making of the witch" concept and the role played by emotions in such a mental construction. Once triggered, the idea of the witch activates oscillating reactions in all protagonists. The sense of time and causality, those *Homo sapiens*'s great acquisitions, dominate the judicial sources. The memory of a suffered curse is subject to an oscillation of reliving, waits, intervals, permanence and breaks affecting emotional reactions. On the one hand, there is a variation in the empathy rate in those who have first suspicions of a neighbor, which can result in direct accusations. On the other hand, in the suspected, the surrounding atmosphere of distrust generates a growing aversion (an empathic deficit) eventually leading to a malefic agency, acted or threatened, to be understood as an intentional defensive and offensive drive to harm or manipulate others using the very occult malevolent powers attributed to him or her. An outcome that can be considered as the decision – buried in the labyrinth of individual consciousness – to be a witch rather than a victim.

Notes

1 S. Pinker, *The Better Angels of Our Nature*, 497.
2 D. Hume, *An Enquiry Concerning the Principle of Morals*, London, 1751/1777.
3 E. R. Kandel, *The Age of the Insight*.
4 S. Baron-Cohen, *Zero Degrees of Empathy*, ix.
5 Ibid., 11.
6 Neuroscience has its hero, Phineas Gage, an American railroad worker. In 1848, during some excavation works in Vermont, due to an explosion, a long iron bar pierced his cheekbone, penetrated the brain, pierced the cranial vault. The shaft, while damaging the prefrontal cortex, did not prevent Gage from getting up. He lost his left eye but was later able to resume work and survived for years. But he had become a different person. The foreman, amiable and cordial with his workmates, had turned into an unpredictable drunkard addicted to gambling and blasphemy; he behaved like an antisocial individual, devoid of empathic inspiration. Today's diagnosis believes that the part of the brain (amygdala and hypothalamus) that regulates the emotional and cognitive aspects of behavior was damaged. See. J. S. Beer, D. Scabini, R. T. Knight, "Orbitofrontal Cortex and Social Behavior: Integrating Self-Monitoring and Emotion-Cognition Interactions," in *Journal Cogn Neurosci*, 18, 2006, 871–879.
7 R. J. R. Blair, "The Amygdala and Ventromedial Prefrontal Cortex in Morality and Psychopathy," in *Trends in Cognitive Sciences*, 11, 2008, 387–392.
8 Extensively in A. Raine, *The Anatomy of Crime*, ch. 11, and *passim*.
9 E. Viding, *Psychopathy*. See A. Denise, *Critica della ragione empatica: Fenomenologia dell'altruismo e della crudeltà*, Bologna, 2020, 209–231.
10 M. Gaskill, *The Ruin of All Witches: Life and Death in the New World*, London, 2022; the author in his narrative "filled gaps imaginatively and made plausible inferences," 233.
11 See Chekhov's short-story masterpiece, "Peasants."

PART II

Historical Times

Homo sapiens multiplies and travels. He faces new challenges, illustrated by an imaginary figurative cycle. Frescoes cross the millennia showing tilled fields, temples, aqueducts, sacred emblems (Jews, Christians, Muslims), cathedrals, towers, presses, chimneys. Humans familiarize further with space, and the changes in the environment produced by work and information technology correspond to an adaptation of their psychology, bent by new types of coexistence. Religion ends up uniting people around one God. Magic persists and plays a substitute role when causes of suffering and evil escape common understanding. How did people behave when faced with the reality of evil? A ghost lurks in the records of witchcraft trials, the natural control of *maleficium*. This legacy of reciprocal altruism remained operative for a long time, containing the use of massive witch killings.

DOI: 10.4324/9781003414377-13

12

VISIONS OF THE WORLD

We will, then, follow the footsteps left by witchcraft in the mental architecture of man by crossing the fictional panel of frescoes, an allegory of advances promoted by agrarian societies. It is useful to consider the handful of millennia preceding the classic period of the witch hunts – the sixteenth and seventeenth centuries – as a succession of cosmogonies characterizing ancient, medieval, and early modern age. A slow change in communication contexts distinguishes these visions, with overlaps and passages from mainly oral cultures to written ones, up to the invention of printing. In each of these phases the function of witchcraft, a sort of panacea for various conjunctures, is ingrained in the system of thought of the current civilization, with varying intensities that are difficult to measure. From one phase to another, people's mental repositioning occurs, mostly due to residential mobility, potentially corrosive of magical beliefs when men move from countryside to cities, as we will later see.

A few more words on the concept of cosmogony. Summarized for our purpose, the notion has a broad spectrum of meanings and alludes to embedded psychological structures. That is, it wants to embrace a plurality of assumptions, of rules concerning the life of people and which lead to a social grammar made up of absorbed and internalized values relating to universal categories. Let us see some of the main ones: the concept of space, time, knowledge, relationship between man and nature, between man and man, man and woman, are recognizable: universals presiding over daily life and orienting it. Each historical age had something different to say about the idea of a social space and time, about what is meant by legitimate knowledge, about how relationships are structured in a community.[1] These universal concepts are certainly not new topics. "Those who deal with history involuntarily apply [them]. They can remain uncritical, even unconscious, and therefore undisputed. In the methods of historical thinking they tend to be assumed as obvious."[2] During the millennia of recorded history – from the first Sumerian cuneiform tablets dating back

DOI: 10.4324/9781003414377-14

about 3500 years, to the early modern great witch-hunts – in the passage from one era to another, the universals are subject to overlapping, to some acceleration, to setbacks; in short, to a sort of inertial motion, remembering that "properly there are no periods in history but only in historians."[3] The result is the coexistence of dominant ideologies with others that are only manifest and others simply latent. We will examine them quickly.

Witchcraft: An Ingrained Idea

As previously argued, the embedding of magic and religion in the cosmogony of recorded history has biological roots: Publius Statius's verses, "fecit deos [et magos] timor," introduce the subject. A perception that stood out because human suffering and desires are marked with the constant oscillations of humans between the search for solutions offered by refuge in faith and use of witchcraft or science. Within these fluctuations great shifts are recognizable, during which dominant systems of ideas, to be labelled as the official religions, were developed, and ended up taking root.

Prehistoric phases of the ambiguous proximity between religious and magical practices were punctuated by an essential transition whose stakes are clear: achieving a privileged relationship with the supernatural. The turning point towards a parting of ways took place on this very point. It is a conceptual axis in which the problem of power is implicit; a turn presupposing the action of individual charism to make the influence of magical and religious concepts authoritative, which, in a self-nurturing spiral, will enhance that charism. Through rituals, in a trance atmosphere made up of sounds, dances, songs, this exclusive relationship is structured, becomes a prerogative of specialists (shamans, priests) and materializes in some situational models. In retrospect the factual pillars of religion's dominance are clear, implying a prominent role played by men, rarely by women; a primacy of spaces putting a center (the city) before a periphery (the countryside); a hierarchy of times that, legitimizing daytime hours, privileges values carried out in areas managed by the urban elites. On these founding premises between Antiquity, the Middle Ages and the early modern era, the religious palimpsests underwent a radical change. The monopoly of the relations with otherworldly essences resulted in material realizations still visible today. When the meager economies of hunter–gatherers yielded to the growing returns of agriculture, the privileged contact with religion was celebrated with works embodying transcendent and civic values.

Human magical propensities adapted, overtly inserted in these human events, nourishing a mental embeddedness that repositioned and shaped with changing spatial, socio-economic, political, and cultural contexts. Adaptations: we are not able to assess whether in the transition from the ancient to the medieval and early modern world there were increases or decreases in the embedding of witchcraft, a phenomenon impossible to measure. Adaptation, after the decline of the Roman Empire, could mean the beginning of a subordinate and parasitic positioning with respect to the religious event profoundly revolutionized by its monotheistic transformation. Adaptation, during Humanism and Renaissance, could mean the beginning of a slow retreat towards vast countryside–mountain territories, leaving city centers to the hegemony of social elites.

Latent Ideas: Skepticism

But wouldn't we ask if all humans felt the need to question the existence of transcendent entities in the Paleolithic mists? This uncomfortable doubt leaves a cognitive problem that challenges neuroscience and evolutionary psychology uncovered: namely that of unbelief. On one hand, humans appear to be belief-forming machines;[4] on the other, there is a parallel brain inclination that incessantly moves towards knowledge. The ape dilemma not only leads to the invention of supernatural essences but produces a further effort to seek. Regarding transcendent concepts, it is plausible that doubt coexists with indifference. Ambivalence towards magic and religion appears as a general trend in human societies, and skepticism and even agnosticism would be recurrent traits in pre-literate societies, whose presence has been poorly studied.[5]

In the past, it is problematic to document an indifference towards transcendence that is not of educated origin. Studies on popular religion show that among the illiterate there are subjects with a background of life whose disregard for the supernatural came from mere empiricism, from observations of the animal, plant, mineral universe, the result of daily practices that endowed them with concreteness devoid of other implications.[6] In deep history the magic-religious tendencies of *Homo sapiens* did perhaps not have an incessant and total predominance over the psychology of individuals. Interdisciplinary studies of the mind argue that unbelief does not always seem to require a solid or explicit cognitive effort. Many non-believers simply do not bother spending time thinking about religious ideas. Later on, a latent and hidden formation of a culturally motivated skepticism involved "hard intellectual work that had to fight against the same counterfactual intuitions and replace them with newer concepts."[7] In the Axial age, between 800 and 200 BC, when synapses of peoples bordering the Mediterranean Sea performed spectacular achievements of intelligence, a current of thought emerged that left its first written traces and for a couple of millennia skeptical concepts entered the cosmogonic backdrop in a position of latency, much in the background with respect to the manifest domain of magic and religion.

Ultimately, the embedding of witchcraft in human minds was not total and in the "small and isolated communities, where life and culture are so closely connected as to be the same thing," there were those who managed to escape the shackles of prevailing cognition.[8] It took about fifteen centuries of stop and go to arrive at a new positioning of intellectually qualified skepticism. The readjustment of the imbalance gradually brings out a new attitude of knowledge and understanding. Within a couple of centuries, in intriguing coincidence with sixteenth-seventeenth-century witch hunts, in the world of European urban elites an epistemological drama, defined by a skeptical crisis, selective according to a hierarchy of spaces and social classes, is produced. The radiation, favored by the anti-magic potentialities inherent in the rational city, produced somewhat divergent results.[9] On one side, Montaigne's perplexed observations emerged from the growing waves of doubts, theisms and atheism, on the other, amid twisted decades dripping with blood certainties, a thinker like Jean Bodin wrote the *Démonomanie des sorciers* (1580) asserting the extermination of witches as a bulwark in defense of absolute monarchy.

Notes

1 J. Galtung, E. Rudeng, T. Heiestad, "On the Last 2,500 years in Western History, and Some Remarks on the Coming 500," in P. Burke, ed., *The New Companion Cambridge Modern History*, Cambridge, 1976, 318–361; A. J. Gurevič, *Medieval Popular Culture*, Cambridge, 1990.
2 K. Jaspers, *Origin*.
3 E. R. Dodds, *Pagan and Christian in an Age of Anxiety: Some Aspects of Religious Experience from Marcus Aurelius to Constantine*, Cambridge, 1965, 3.
4 M. Gazzaniga, *The Ethical Brain: The Science of Our Moral Dilemmas*, New York, 2005.
5 "In literate societies skepticism may achieve written expression as a doctrine but it is also present in oral cultures as one element of their world view [...] In so-called traditional societies, not everyone believes everything; indeed many myths incorporate a measure of disbelief." See J. Goody, *The Theft of History*, New York, 2006, 245.
6 Traces of them can be found in the criminal causes that the Church of the Counter-Reformation instructed on people resisting the Easter precepts, intercepting conflicting voices that in response to personal experiences attested to a personal vision of things. See ODS, *Peccato penitenza perdono. Siena 1575–1800: La formazione della coscienza nell'Italia moderna*, Milano, 1995, 226–241.
7 A. Norenzayan, *Big Gods*, 176–177.
8 *Witchcraft and Magic in Europe*, B. Ankarloo, S. Clark, eds., 2, xvi.
9 "The controversies over witchcraft occurred in an era of skeptical crises, [but] philosophical skepticism cannot be shown to have exerted an appreciable influence on the decline of witch hunts," W. Stephens, "The Sceptical Tradition," in *The Oxford Handbook of Witchcraft*, 120.

13

WITCHCRAFT AND POWER

The long sixteenth century was yet to come. It is now necessary to verify which realities concealed the embedding of witchcraft in past cosmogonies, and to delve into previously scattered references to the concept of power.

> The beliefs that refer to the magical world, religion and witchcraft are beliefs inherent in power. The source of power and the degree of dependence that an individual is prey to or can manipulate is the focus of any belief system.[1]

There is a clear Weberian nuance in this perception. It refers to the passages from *Economy and Society* where magic, religious and political charisma is alluded to, underlining a specific gift of body and spirit by virtue of which the magical-religious power is maintained until those who use it achieve success. A strength, this gift, based on emotional conviction of the importance and value of religious, ethical, artistic, scientific events and actions; of the heroic character of asceticism or war, of judicial wisdom, of magical virtue or of any other kind of manifestation.[2] This transformation of the individual authority towards an elevation to charisma has been glimpsed in prehistoric times when particular individuals (shamans, priests, leaders, sorcerers, witches) found agency ("power") in animated or inanimate substances, in living or dead people in which one sought advice and from which one received the energy and the power to benefit or harm others.

None of this is new to anyone studying the beginnings of magic-religious convictions. Our intention is to highlight the little explored side of this magic power and how it is organized in historical societies.

The general lines were indicated by Max Weber himself and are those of its retreating with the progressive development of permanent institutional formations, that is, of official religions and state structures.[3] Yet, despite witchcraft's retreat, its contiguity with religion in everyday life generated equivocal promiscuity and

DOI: 10.4324/9781003414377-15

frequent tensions. A closeness constantly concerned with harm, illness, desire. Who could interpret and resolve the worries occasioned by sudden, mysterious, undecipherable, unnatural, or intentionally caused misfortunes? Some individuals had the knowledge/magical power to undo and remedy the devastation caused by *maleficia*. We believe the leverage of these specialists over time was articulated into a system, not structured but concrete, to help people cope with witchcraft agency.

The Power of Cursing and Staring

Before outlining the characteristics of a witchcraft system, we need to clarify what the power of witches consisted of. Admittedly cursing was their main weapon: uttering or mumbling often inaudible threats a witch reinforced her status. The association of witches and curses has been a staple of historical investigation for years, since the appearance of two seminal monographs in the early seventies of past century.[4] All of this is obvious, but that is not our point.

Because those were situations that led to a clash between two parties in the open. Conversely, to further understand the agency of curse it is necessary to focus on the hidden force of unexpressed threats.

We must figure the constant village sociability in which subjects suspected and feared of having the power to threaten evil were inserted, often for generations, and never or rarely the outcome of a break of relationship occurred. We will see later, as we tackle the classical age of witch hunts, that large parts of the Continent bear no evidence of the refused charity syndrome pervading early modern witch trials. Why? Surely, even among those populations there were feared subjects believed to have the power to do evil. And people resorted to solutions that remain difficult to study due to lack of documentation, but that did not imply falling out with potential fearsome individuals.

Such dissimulated use of the power of cursing was accompanied by another natural endowment of these dangerous co-villagers: the force of the staring gaze. But how to trace this power of the eyes in the past? We try to get to grips with the point in Chapter 22.

The Natural Control of Witchcraft: A System

As it is, historians have not come to terms with an anomaly they know well: why doubts towards people considered to be evil agents "could lie latent for months, even years, and it was only when a number of different factors coincided that an official accusation might be levelled"?[5] The way in which a set of arrangements for a control of malefic agency may have developed, dates back to the closing millennia of prehistory. Continuing to use the 50,000 years ago as a chronological watershed, we have figured above a transition from a preverbal phase of evil to a phase in which it was semantically identified, and perhaps some negative deeds/ situations were labeled as witchcraft and people suspected of having perpetrated them. In essence, evil and witchcraft existed "long before any word that made

those concepts familiar [...] In Homer and other archaic literatures and documentation, there is abundant evidence of 'a magical world before magic'."[6]

Evolutionary biology teaches that there has never been a period in *Homo* species
in which he existed as an isolated individual. *Sapiens*'s success was due to their
ability to organize cooperation by establishing deep relationships with fellow men.
One of the greatest social adaptations of humans will be the elaboration of moral
norms and laws, together with the development of judicial systems, a response to
the detection of imbalances caused by social behaviors that endangered individuals
and the group.[7] But this is the future, the development of our civilization. In the
millennia leading up to Protohistory, faced with the cognitive complexity of *maleficium*, a pragmatic solution had to be realized within village governance to solve
the problem it created: the recourse to mediation through the experts who could
and knew how to make up for what inexplicably happened. These social figurations (in historical times: *indovini, cunning men/women, charmers, curanderos, devins-
guérisseurs, toverdokters, Hexenmeisters*) whose sex is difficult to ascertain, gave life to a
system: an informal/natural mechanism of control, arbitration and resolution of
problems, operating in opposition or in parallel with other local powers, such as,
for example, the kind of official ministers of the ongoing cult, and without
resorting to regulatory solutions or norms/laws in the process of being constituted.
When the first hydraulic-agrarian communities of the Middle East pre-state societies formed, human domestication was accelerated, Fertile Crescent people consolidated the progress with the advent of the first forms of writing. Norms were
produced to rebalance antecedent solutions no longer adequate to resolve conflicts
generated by human social psychology in which egoism, familism and altruism
competed. The complexity of new human aggregations led to the elaboration
within a few thousand years of that Hammurabi code in which significant passages
against *maleficium* are registered:

> If a man or woman has made magical preparations and found evidence in
> their hand (and) against them, the maker of the magical preparations shall be
> put to death.
>
> The man who saw the magic preparations being made (and) heard from the
> mouth of an eyewitness the magic preparations, who said to him (saying) "I
> myself saw this," comes forward as a witness-having-heard and tell the king; if
> what he said to the king is denied by eyewitnesses he will make a statement in
> the presence of Taurus, the son of the sun God saying, "On my oath, he said
> it," and then go free [...][8]
>
> If a man has accused another man of witchcraft but has not proved the
> charge [through witnesses], the one against whom the accusation of witchcraft
> was brought will go to the river of ordeal and be subjected to the ordeal, and
> if the river sinks him his accuser will seize his house. If the river ordeal acquits
> that man and he comes out safe, the one who presented the accusation of
> witchcraft will be put to death; he who jumped into the river will take pos-
> session of the accuser's house ...[9]

And here a problem arises: almost no trace of the application of the Hammurabi laws has been found. For what reason? If our reconstruction is correct, undistorted by documentary silence, people inherited the practice of containing witchcraft by avoiding head-on collisions between opposing parties. It is likely that resorting to laws against alleged perpetrators of spells would have caused splits in heterogeneous communities, presenting serious risks of retaliation in cases of the accused's innocence by relatives who would have asked for it. The habits of informal control of witchcraft agency particularly active in small-scale societies would have taken hold due to the nature of interpersonal relationships (often of kinship) in each tribe. It had become the prevailing code of stratified societies which, faced with the complexities of *maleficium*, pragmatically operated using protagonists and methods of the system.[10] Even the use of strong anti-magical solutions to counteract the malefic spells is a concrete testimony of the natural control of witchcraft. Mercury's words to Ulysses to help him avoid Circe's fatal deceptions allude to it:

> Come on, I want to free you from the dangers and save you
> Here, with this beneficial herb in Circe's house
> enter; his power will prevent you from the bad day [...]

> So saying, the Argyphon gave me the grass,
> tearing it from the ground and its nature showed me;
> the root was black, the flower was like milk,
> "molu" gods call it.[11]

Homer's hexameters record a settled custom. The winged god, by delivering the magical plant to his protégé, provided us with what is to be considered "the first attestation of the concept of opposing witchcraft with witchcraft."[12]

There is no denying that historical ages should abound with official, formal judicial actions against *maleficia*. On the contrary, these were rare. Agrarian civilizations were accustomed to village governance of their prehistoric ancestors. Unluckily, pagan and biblical sources have left almost nothing on protagonists of the system, and very few Greek and Latin ones. We need to get to the sixteenth- and seventeenth-century persecutions to find continuous traces of the anti-witchcraft's actors.[13] Their social function, which also responded to solving many practical needs of people in addition to tracking down witches and forcing them to withdraw the spells they cast, has been examined by historians.[14] They formed a group of practitioners, ambiguously welcome, who endure the course of recorded history almost invisibly. In the space of those two centuries something went wrong, triggering a dynamic in which the control of the evil spell took, at times, a different turn passing into the hands of Church and State justice according to a glowing evolutionary line in which "the witch hunt replaced the witch finder, the state replaced magic."[15]

Historical research has neglected the underground influence of the informal natural control of witchcraft. To us, it seems to come from the prehistoric past; it had roots in the mechanisms of brain activity, in that shared intentionality that prepared the ground for a better integration between *fast thinking* violent solutions and the *slow thinking* mediations, made inevitable by the cognitive enigma of *maleficia*.

Notes

1   C. Larner, "Natural and Unnatural Method," in *Witchcraft and Religion*, 138.
2   M. Weber, *Economy and Society*, Berkeley, CA, 1978, I, P. 1, ch. 3.
3   Ibid.
4   A. Macfarlane, *Witchcraft in Tudor and Stuart England: A Regional and Comparative Study*, London, 1999; and K. Thomas, *Religion and the Decline of Magic*. In a study of contemporary Irish people penchant for cursing, a proclivity that goes back millennia, the phenomenon – mostly spoken maledictions for smiting evildoers – is assumed "to help to explain why, during the early modern period, Ireland experienced no 'witch craze' with just a handful of trials"; see T. Waters, "Irish Cursing and the Art of magic, 1750–2018," in *Past and Present*, 247, 1, 113–149.
5   L. Kounine, *Imagining the Witch: Emotions, Gender, and Selfhood in Early Modern Germany*, Oxford, 2018, 38.
6   R. Gordon, *Imagining Greek and Roman Magic*, 165.
7   A. Damasio, *Self Comes to Mind*, ch. 11; F. Fukuyama, *The Origins of Political Order: From Prehuman Times to the French Revolution*, London, 2012, 34–38.
8   "The Middle Assyrian Laws §47"; see M.-L. Thomsen, "Witchcraft and Magic in Ancient Mesopotamia," in B. Ankarloo, S. Clark, eds, *Witchcraft and Magic in Europe*, 1, F. H. Cryer, M.-L. Thomsen, *Biblical and Pagan Societies*, London, 2001, 18–30.
9   Codex Hammurapi §2; The Middle Assyrian Laws § 47; See M.-L. Thomsen, *Witchcraft and Magic*, 25, 26. At a closer exam Hammurabic norms and the Assyrian laws tells more. The above laws were not "directly occupied with the penalty for witchcraft but rather with the problems of proving a charge concerning witchcraft." An indirect confirmation of the existence of an informal system to address the problems posed by the existence of occult crime: M.-L. Thomsen, *Biblical and Pagan Societies*.
10   J. Diamond, *The World until Yesterday: What Can We Learn from Traditional Societies?*, London, 2013, ch. 9.
11   Homer, *Odyssey*, X, vv. 285–287. Our translation.
12   D. Ogden, *Circe*, in *EW*, I, 190.
13   Certainly, in peasant communities acts of private revenge were carried out, with the inevitable consequence of retaliations by the relatives of the would-be malefactor. But it is a phenomenon that leaves rare documentary traces.
14   W. Behringer, *Shaman of Oberstdorf: Chonrad Stoeckhlin and the Phantoms of the Night*, Charlottesville, 1998. An anti-witchcraft role could be inferred from C. Ginzburg, *The Night Battles: Witchcraft and Agrarian Cults in the Sixteenth and Seventeenth Centuries*, London, 1983. For a synthesis see O. Davies, *Cunning -Folk. Popular Magic in English History*, London & New York, 2003, 163–186.
15   W. Behringer, *Shaman of Oberstdorf*, 159.

14

A LONG WALK

Towards a Magic–Religion Dichotomy

The First Historical Ancestors

Abandoning the African cradle, our hunters and gatherers, generation after generation in columns marching along the Nile corridor, ended up settling in the river basins of the Middle East and then in the lands washed by the Mediterranean Sea. A set of "fully modern populations under the anatomical profile was present in the region of the Near East";[1] sites provided with ecological advantages promoted the socio-economic and cultural evolution of pagan and biblical societies. In fact, twelve thousand years ago, Planet's adverse forces had loosened their grip, and a climatic *optimum* would open the beginning of agrarian civilizations. Magical–religious beliefs followed the modeling of human behavior in relation to ecological changes in broad sense, in the sphere of the physical and biological.

What do we know about the immigrants who populated the Fertile Crescent? They had already begun to weave networks of connection over significant distances, creating a liberation from proximity and the ability to share a communion of ideas while being distant.[2] Let us venture a risky bird's eye view on demography. The number of men who worked the land eludes us. Perhaps they were smaller; a "reduction in height [...] not necessarily due to malnutrition or disease, but [indicative of] a useful adaptation to an activity with less mobility than foraging ancestors engaged in periodic periods of scarcity."[3] Solid demographic references are lacking, and the existing margin of error can be around 30 percent or more. According to global estimates humans of the entire planet at the time of cave paintings may roughly have been around 5/6 million.[4] According to other estimates we would have a hypothesis of a global population of one or two million individuals during the last glacial maximum, around 20,000 years ago.[5] Unlike what happened during the Pleistocene era, agriculture allowed civilizations to no longer oppose the soil reality but to challenge it by leveraging the physical force derived from various

DOI: 10.4324/9781003414377-16

technological advances. Ancient, medieval, and early modern crops thus became part of an ecosystem subject to the laws of physics. The economic structure could not remove nature by considering it as a given and immutable whole, infinitely capable of supporting human activity. Therefore, the energy revolution caused by major deforestation and clearing had costs. Entropy later presented a bill. Material and cultural improvements sustained by Neolithic progress, when stable work in the fields became the basis of life, populated Europe bringing the number of inhabitants to an unsustainable level of about 35 million around the birth of Christ, altering the balance between resources and population. The entropic debt formed and a multiplicity of factors, including non-human ones (climatic variations, deadly pandemics) ended up weakening the resistance of a too vast Roman empire. Europe's new order produced by the barbarian invasions shows a substantial demographic contraction that lasted for four hundred years, from the sixth to the tenth century AD. At the turning point of the year one thousand, the values of ten centuries earlier returned. Agrarian history rhythmic cycle was ready to restart, supported by new techniques, with effects on urban growth. Crudeness of life dissolved with twelfth and thirteenth centuries urban flowering, and then, after the mid-fourteenth century black plague demographic die-off, the largest early modern urbanization followed, eventually corroding witchcraft embeddedness. However, until the eighteenth century agriculture was the feature of the age.

Middle East Compromises

But let us go back to the immigrants from Serengeti and other African savannas whose marches found a happy end in the great Levant pictured below. In these mother lands Neolithic tools replaced the Paleolithic ones; garden and field cultivation were established and within a few millennia the first farmers expanded to the Atlantic. As already said, a mixture of populations had the good fortune to seize a superlative window of ecological opportunity heralding transformations in society, culture, economy, and human relations with nature.[6] The fortunate circumstance produced a cradle of civilizations previously encountered mentioning the *Epic of Gilgamesh*'s admirable cycle and the Hammurabi code. Something else followed among new people: a collection of far more explosive stories. We will refer to them shortly after hinting at the solutions of a coexistence between the magical and religious beliefs offered by these polytheistic societies.

When the first agrarian civilizations consolidated, the gap between magic and religion widened. It was a move away favored by the adaptive peculiarities of religion. Nevertheless, in the Assyrian-Babylonian mental palimpsest the purpose of those who practiced magic continued to be interchangeable with that of those who followed a religious cult, at least in the utilitarian sense of helping man by overcoming the obstacles of existence. In Mesopotamian lands, the arcana of magical arts were not mocked or understood as superstitious and considered prejudicial in opposition to the official religion. In the few texts available it is glimpsed that an understanding had become inevitable in the form of a pragmatic tolerance towards the attractive power of magical formulas whose definition remains uncertain and can usefully be understood as "more or less a residual category in close proximity to both of 'religion' and of 'medicine'."[7]

Of course, maleficent witchcraft was a whole other story, and theoretically at least it was strictly prohibited. Nevertheless, only one case has been found, "in striking contrast to the comprehensive material concerning incantation, rituals and medical recipes against witchcraft which document a profound fear of being bewitched."[8] Why is that? Our thesis, already set out, is that the resolution of the problems was delegated to mediation provided by the natural control of *maleficium*.

At the current state of knowledge only Sumerian literary texts that tell of wise women who use anti-witchcraft means, like Homer's Ulysses, to cure and purify, can be produced to support the operational function of the system. The only way to circumvent the lack of sources is by proposing an argument *e silentio*. Conventionally considered weak, such reasoning is not without some coherence. So, why were there no cases of trials despite a widespread fear of being bewitched in ancient Mesopotamia? To infer that an informal method of settling witchcraft controversies must have been operational seems to be a reasonable hypothesis.

The situation in Ancient Syria and Palestine is not dissimilar, and sheds more light. Prohibitions recorded in Israelite and Jewish society remained a dead letter: "Episodes of witchcraft usually did not reach the level of a resolution of conflicts through judicial means," perhaps reserved for the elites of society.[9] The absence of formal legal action "in the (relatively abundant) judicial literature of the entire Near East" is disconcerting and in our opinion justified by the practice of private settlements and informal control of malefic deviance: the invisible ghost in historical sources.[10]

The Bible: A Nuclear Explosion

Before leaving the Fertile Crescent we must linger over Syria and Palestine center of varied forms of associated life, which was the breeding ground of a host of religious convictions today forgotten.[11] Indirect evidence of heated conflict comes from the communities of that area: exchanges of accusations between competing groups of the faithful; power conflicts between ethnic nuclei concerning the knot of divination, that is, which priestly elites had the right to enter into a relationship with divinity. A deepening of these disputes, produced by the formation of diversified centers of social power, interpretable as aspects of the building of a state identity, would obviously not be marginal to our purpose. Still, we want to stress something else: that is, the enormous importance acquired by the condemnation and the negative connotation that malefic witchcraft and magic respectively took on in the Old Testament story, in the political conflict in progress. Here the great code was formed, a sacred history built on faith in one God. This is the decisive watershed in the historical development of the control of malefic witchcraft.

The nuclear explosion metaphor of this paragraph alludes in our case to a radioactive fall-out that has been contaminating for centuries. In the history of Western culture, the biblical condemnations marked the fate of witches by defining their damned figure. And magic itself, as anti-witchcraft, is negatively sanctioned. The divine message request for a death sentence in *Exodus* was explicit: "maleficos non patieris vivere" (22.18), according to St. Jerome's Vulgate, a verse debated and tormented by translators into future national languages, turning the noun to the feminine.[12] Leviticus's threats are unequivocal:

> If a person turns to mediums and necromancers, whoring after them, I will set my face against that person and will cut him off from among his people [...] A man or a woman who is a medium or a necromancer shall surely be put to death. They shall be stoned with stones; their blood shall be upon them.[13]

The prohibitions in Deuteronomy are more general:

> anyone who practices divination or tells fortunes or interprets omens, or a sorcerer or a charmer or a medium or a necromancer or one who inquires of the dead, for whoever does these things is an abomination to the Lord.[14]

In essence, by interpolating a famous intuition by Karl Marx, Christianity was able to "produce [persecutions] from its own bowels,"[15] a drift that ended by infringing upon the highest of its teachings, the golden rule, which accentuated the beneficial aspect of retaliation by prescribing: "So whatever you wish that others would do to you, do also to them, for this is the Law and the Prophets."[16]

Notes

1 P. Mellar, "La Confusion Aurignacienne: Disentangling the archeology of modern human dispersal in Europe," in M. Camps and C. Szmidt, eds, *The Mediterranean from 60,000 to 25,000 BP: Turning Points and New Directions*, Oxford, 2009, 348.
2 C. Broodbank, *The Making of the Middle Sea*; C. Gamble, *Paleolitic Societies*.
3 J. Robb, *The Early Mediterranean Village*, 36, 221.
4 C. Clark, *Population Growth and Land Use*, London, 1977, 64.
5 C. Broodbank, *The Making of the Middle Sea*, ch. 4.
6 G. Barbujani, A. Brunelli, *Il giro del mondo*, 120; C. Broodbank, *The Making of the Middle Sea*.
7 B. Ankarloo, S. Clark, eds, *Witchcraft and Magic in Europe,*1, F. H. Cryer, M.-L. Thomsen, *Biblical and Pagan Societies*, XII.
8 M.-L. Thomsen, *Witchcraft and Magic*, 23.
9 F. H. Cryer, "Magic in Ancient Syria-Palestine and in the Old Testament," in *Biblical and Pagan Societies*, 140.
10 Ibid.
11 C. Broodbank, *The Making of the Middle Sea*; G. Russell, *Heirs to Forgotten Kingdoms. Journeys into the Disappearing Religions of the Middle East*, London, 2015.
12 W. Wiporska, *Exodus 22:18 (22:17)*, in *EW*, II. "Do not allow a sorceress to live," *Bible Hub*, English Standard Version (ESV).
13 Leviticus 20.6; 20.27.
14 Deuteronomy 18:10–12 (*Bible Hub*, ESV).
15 The original line has "Judaism," not persecutions; Karl Marx, "Zur Judenfrage," in D. Nirenberg, "Shakespeare's Jewish Questions," in *Renaissance Drama*, 38, 2010, 78.
16 Matthew, 7.12 (*Bible Hub*, ESV).

15

GREECE AND ROME

The Complementarity between Magic and Religion

Christian monotheism is still far away, and meanwhile masterful civilizations have developed around the *Mare nostrum*. Let us leave its southern shores and move towards Greece. In this area, the contiguity between magic and religion materialized according to lasting coexistence, but such relationship over centuries ranging from proto-Homeric Greece to full classicism cannot be reconstructed due to a lack of information.

"The concept of magic began to exist in the Greek-speaking world in the fifth century."[1] The final field of action between the two ideas is clearly known. A preliminary observation will be useful. Religion, whether Greek or Roman, must be envisaged under the sign of multiplicity and there is no room for structured doctrines: it was primarily a matter of political rather than religious discussions. It can be affirmed that during political-social transformations from the period of the city-states to the emergence of Principalities and beyond, a decisive turning point concerning the privileged relationship with the divinity, took place. In the classical age the cult of gods was organized according to some civic agreements sanctioning a pre-eminence whose credentials are given by (a) the beneficial purpose of incorruptible divinities, (b) a daytime period where to carry out rites and sacrifices in specific social urban spaces, and (c) a calendar of feasts officiated mainly by men. Primacy and trend are drawn and mark a distinction: anything deviating from the listed founding values will always represent something different, falling into the category of magic-witchcraft, that is, a practice and a knowledge that are tolerated if they do not challenge the city/state principles. The control or coercive function of what, to simplify, we call central state power will find an uncertain, erratic, uneven enforcement, but the direction of change appears unequivocal: the magical world "ceased to be [...] simply given for granted, and when necessary [it was] convicted [...] examined, challenged, defended."[2]

DOI: 10.4324/9781003414377-17

But once again, the rarity of formal judicial actions for cases of malefice must be emphasized, we believe due to the operational agency of the witchcraft system shrouded in prevailing obscurity.

The System: Blurred Identifications and the Role of Cities

All the actors of witchcraft situations remain enveloped in a substantial opacity: both wrongdoers (witches, women, and men) and those who mediated with them or opposed them. Of the latter, too little is left to venture a sound sociological profile. In a passage from the *Republic* Plato draws the portrait of a self-styled pundit (a góis), that is of a polyvalent expert who combines initiations with private mysteries and black magic.

> Charlatans and fortune-tellers present themselves at the doors of the rich and convince them that with sacrifices and spells they have obtained from the gods the power to remedy the possible injustice of one with games and parties, whether he committed it in person or one of his ancestors; and that if one wants to harm an enemy, he will be able to harm the just as well as the unjust with little expense by means of certain evocations and magical bonds, because, they say, they persuade the gods to serve them.[3]

These few lines summarize the essentials of what is important to know about such experts, pivotal gear of the witchcraft natural control. All of them, scholarly or illiterate, over the millennia of our narration fall within the Athenian philosopher's description.

The góis' declining career can someway be guessed despite the lack of specific judicial documentation. As magic and religion evolved, different occupations opened, with winners and losers contending over who had the right to connect with the gods. On one hand, the winners, the priests of an official cult; on the other, the losers, the top layer of those who worked in the occult, those self-appointed experts with similar functions whose fate, alongside their marginalization, ended up being marked by a probable sapiential degradation. In larger cities they pursued careers whose probable itinerancy depended on the fluctuating reputation they enjoyed. The bottom layers' final positioning completely escapes us.

In villages, the swinging career of mediators and fortune tellers can only be speculated about. We do not know how their magical power was formed. We must imagine individuals who acted using the knowledge acquired by exploring nature plants, animals, and mineral secrets. Perhaps a heterogeneous group of herbalists, curators, smiths, etc., managed to build a significant position by transmitting their know-how through the family. Among these variegated individualities, women, heirs of memories and knowledge of prehistoric gatherers are not to be counted as a notable minority.[4]

Of the many questions to be asked, one seems more urgent: how much did the growth of the city influence the functioning of the witchcraft system? In the Hellenistic period, "urbanization favored intellectual centers [...] and large cities became melting pots [...] Magic, based to a certain extent on imitations and adaptations, greatly benefited from these conditions."[5] Can we presume the witchcraft system underwent some differentiation during those spatial and demographic changes? This assumption is anything but secondary in the interpretation of the phenomenon. Witchcraft social formation is subject to persist or deteriorate depending on the proximity or distance of villages from cities. Basically, if we see things correctly, in the classical era the primacy of a civic religion did not mature beyond a certain threshold the latent elements of urban rationalism (or skepticism), corrosive of counterfactual beliefs. The link between countryside and city, in the history of this social institution, will end up presenting itself with a changed value long after the fall of the Roman empire and medieval dark ages. When the year 1000 is turned, during medieval and early modern urban rebirths, fortune-tellers will continue to have customers in the cities, but in a culturally and socially more articulated communication context their influence slowly evaporated.

The Evil Witch: Fiction, Reality, and Mental Origin of the Image

Cunning men and wise women refer to a magic agency. This is a tricky point: in general, "historians have found it impossible to agree over the question of how many of the accused in witchcraft cases had previously practiced as 'cunning folk' of one kind or another in their communities."[6] But who were the wrongdoers, the witches, actually? "In ancient times, an elderly woman was the witch par excellence"?[7] Perhaps this was imagined by contemporaries. The topos of old superstitious women occurs frequently in literature. A dearth of documentation advises against risking suppositions, though. Statistics are not built on vacuum of data. Unlike early modern Europe, when secular and ecclesiastical judicial records make a quantitative and sociological analysis feasible, distinguishing by sex, age, origin, types of crime, little or none of this is achievable in the ancient world that almost completely ignores formal repressions of the state. How, then, did Greek and Latin immortalize their witches? Where are Circe, Medea, Canidia, Eritto from?[8] The meagre information that can be extracted from these artistic creations points towards the professional qualifications already mentioned (herbalists, curators, fortune tellers) and, implicitly, to their feared metamorphosis into aggressors owing to the ambivalence of magical power in the sphere of health, emblemized by the persuasion that "those who know how to heal also know how to make you sick": *qui scit sanare scit destruere* (Chapters 25 and 26) With all this, do not be deceived by this duplicity, flattening the real life. The therapeutic sphere apart, there were evil people, inclined to cast a deadly spell everywhere. They remain anonymous in the darkness.[9] Nevertheless, let us speculate on how the representation of the witch can be formed.

***

The personification of malefic agency raises a theoretical problem faced by neuroscience: the origin of mental imagery (here, of the witch notion) forks into a top-down or bottom-up genesis.

The idea of a witch: *top-down* thesis. The theory of mind modules and human brain propensity to search for hidden agencies led humans to imagine non-evident, good or bad entities. A belief in the existence of morally ambivalent forces emerged from *Sapiens'* mental events, from his fears of invisible and unreachable essences. A world of demons, forerunners of the witch could be assumed. Mythical demonic creatures offered an ideology employable as the witch's matrix in pagan and Christian Europe's future demonological narratives. It could be added that in some moment, who knows how far away, a humanization of primordial beings might have taken place, and they became the witches of everyday reality.[10] In pantheons that men built for themselves in mythological terms *daimones* may have been nothing more than fallen divinities, as would be the case of Circe, the curly sorceress. Medea belongs to such a typology, herself a minor goddess or priestess of a deity of a more distant age or geographical space.[11]

The *bottom-up* thesis. On the other hand, the "making of the witch" could have followed an opposite path. That is: from the concrete, lived experience of evil ancestral subjects – possibly free riders, too – fantastic stories were created projecting them into the world of myth, into a cosmogony of future demons. There may have been ancestors of Horace's grim Canidia, behind whose actions a witch in flesh and blood can be discerned.[12] Not otherwise Erichtho, Lucan's brutal creation. Erichtho might have been a character based on real people active in a region that already in Neolithic Attica, due to its early concentrations of villages, could boast a primacy in a magical-witchcraft sense.[13] And the greedy witch "never sated with on human flesh" may refer to more distant forms of cannibalism, "a theme present in Greek mythology (Atreus and Thyestes), which dates back to a remote past, when human beings were offered in sacrifice and eaten."[14]

How remote is that past?

> [Biology] takes for granted that there is a range of conditions under which mothers [...] abandon or cannibalize their young, and an even wider range of circumstances in which unrelated males and rival mothers take advantage of the vulnerability of infants.[15]

It seems reasonable, then, to argue that the testimonies inherent in the wide spectrum of Greek and Roman murderous performances – infanticides, cannibalistic blood splatters, night raids – passed in legacy to future centuries with obvious adaptations, increases and subtractions; they are red traces of blood leading back to prehistory and to anthropophagous practices of those ancestors.[16] Man's "inhumanity," which perplexed Montaigne, had primordial roots.

In short, an inverse, *bottom-up* transposition appears sustainable; a chronologically parallel birth, not different from that which saw a myriad of heroes akin to humans, whose exploits survived in oral form. Unfortunately, no theory "manages to embrace the process of *mythopoesis* in all its complexity."[17]

Notes

1 M. Dickie, *Magic and Magicians in the Graeco-Roman World*, London, 2001, 2.

2 R. Gordon, *Imagining Greek and Roman Magic*, 162.

3 Plato, *Republic*, 364b. See F. Graf, *Magic in the Ancient World*, Cambridge, MA, London, 1997.

4 In Greek–Roman age, further evidence of the widespread use of anti-witchcraft comes from the curse-tablets attesting the presence of a dense network of practitioners of beneficial and maleficent magic (men and women) whose levels of experience varied from simple amateurs to ultra-specialists in amorous, therapeutic, divinatory magic, etc. See R. Gordon, *Imagining Greek and Roman Magic*, 178–204; G. Luck, *Witches and Sorcerers*, 61–62.

5 G. Luck, *Witches and Sorcerers*, 157.

6 S. Clark, *Witchcraft and Magic in Early Modern Culture*, in *Witchcraft and Magic in Europe*, 4, B. Ankarloo, S. Clark, W. Monter, *The Period of Witch Trials*, London, 2002, 113.

7 I. Bremmer, "La donna anziana: libertà e indipendenza" ("Old women: Freedom and Independence"), 4. "Le donne anziane e la stregoneria" ("Old Women and Witchcraft"), in *Le donne in Grecia*, G. Arrigoni, ed., Roma-Bari, 2008, 292–293.

8 R. Gordon, *Imagining Greek and Roman Magic*, 178–204.

9 The information on the protagonists of witchcraft remains vague and uneven; "They [...] are seldom the main focus of attention in our literary or historical sources." See M. Dickie, *Magic and Magicians*, 11.

10 E. Pócs, *Between the Living and the Dead*, 16–17.

11 G. Luck, *Witches and Sorcerers*, 111–113.

12 Orazio, *Epodi*, V; *Satire*, VIII. See also L. Cherubini, *Strix. La strega nella cultura romana*, Torino. 2010, 106–114; G. Luck, *Witches and Sorcerers in Classical Literature*, 137–138.

13 Lucan, *Pharsalia*, VI, v. 512. On Tessaly, C. Broodbank, *The Making of the Middle Sea*.

14 Lucan, *Pharsalia*, VI, vv. 707–708; see *Arcana Mundi. Magia e occulto nel mondo greco e romano*, G. Luck, ed., Milano, 1997, 579.

15 S. B. Hrdy, *Mother Nature*, 294.

16 Y. Fernandez-Jalvo, J. Carlos Diez, I. Caceres, "Human Cannibalism in the Early Pleistocene of Europe (Gran Dolina, Sierra de Atapuerca, Burgos, Spain)," in *Journal of Human Evolution*, 37, 1999, 591–622, doi: 10.1006/jhev.1099.0324.

17 *Il mito greco*, II, *Gli eroi*, G. Guidorizzi, ed., Milano, 2012, XII-XIII; and, *Il mito greco*, I, *Gli dèi*, G. Guidorizzi, ed. Milano, 2009, XV.

16

GREECE AND ROME

The Ambiguous State Control of Witchcraft

Athens

The Greek world, passing from city-states to Hellenistic kingdoms, developed socio-political conditions in which the status of witchcraft was defined in relation to the legitimate dominance of an institutionalized cult. The moral supremacy of civic religion was undisputed, but the influential power of magic remained evident and deep-seated in the psychology of collective needs. It did not cause state persecution of any significant dimension, confirming, in our opinion, the natural control of *maleficium* as steadily operational.

Silent sources make even conjectures difficult. In fact, there is lack of evidence of trials brought for damage to people or property.[1] There are traces of legal actions against subjects accused of impiety (*asebeias*). It is significant to note these accusations were directed towards those who tried to influence the will of gods with enchantments. Some judicial proceedings in fourth-century Athens must be interpreted from this perspective. The defendants were women and probably at least one of them, Theoris, was a metec specialist, practicing healing magic. Some generalizations can be drawn.[2] The accusation of impiety was advanced against marginals, and a few experts who moved among private individuals making use of magical-religious knowledge were foreigners settled in Attic cities. Plato clarifies the point, proposing severe punishment for those who "promise to persuade the gods [...] with sacrifice, prayers and conjurations, and undertake to undermine entire families and states from their foundations."[3] But this was the position of a great thinker, an intellectual who despised witchcraft. On concrete ground, what do we have besides a generic aversion to ambiguous activities such as Bacchic mysteries or private ecstatic cults in an urban environment? Magical practices remained in a certain sense under control, due to the existence of specific rules adverse to their evil form. Theoretically, single citizens could have filed a lawsuit

DOI: 10.4324/9781003414377-18

for damage. No traces of it remain. Charges of *maleficia* rarely gave rise to formal trials.[4] Perhaps, the meager contribution of Greece on matter of law did not lead to the creation of a group of magistrates responsible for legal interpretation and hindered the use of such options. This happened in the polis. In villages, the witchcraft system probably persisted absolute.[5]

Rome

As the poet says, "Greece, once conquered, in turn conquered its uncivilized conqueror."[6] But in Hellenistic culture the development of literate urban-hydraulic-agrarian societies had not led to a significant expansion of criminal law. On the contrary, the situation will unfold in a completely different way in Rome. The achievements of its extraordinary juridical civilization raise a problem of discontinuity as regards the relationship between the natural control of the witchcraft deviance and its legal control through the intervention of the State judicial system, aimed at promoting witch hunts to ascertain the crime and identify a culprit.

To immediately understand what is meant by discontinuity we start the story not from Romulus and Remus but from a flash forward over the last century of the Republic. Like a bolt from the sky, Livy's chronicles record that from 184 to 153, at the conclusion of "trials for poisoning," massive executions were ordered by Roman magistrates, in the vicinity of the city and in other parts of Italy, with a number of about 5000 victims. In the face of such a bloody wave of condemnations which arose in sharp breach with Classical and Hellenistic Greece and the Republic's previous centuries,[7] it seems urgent to ask: why did these large killings occur? Before looking for an answer we step back a few hundreds of years and proceed in order.

In matters of Roman anti-witchcraft measures the development had been slow. Two periodizing stages are identifiable, quite distant from each other. The XII Tables law of 450–451 BC clearly intervened against damage caused to other people's property, concerning an action to destroy another's crops through enchantments and to increase one's harvest by stealing that of the neighbor by magical means.[8] Later, the Lex Cornelia of 81 BC dealt with damages inflicted on people's lives. It is likely that previous rules, specific to poisoning cases, extended to deaths caused by spells. It should be noted that in all legal measures the use of magic as such was not questioned, if it did not defy the State. On the contrary, the use of divination in public affairs was challenged and repressed. Law enforcement against *maleficium* seems to have been rare, pointing not only to an obvious tolerance of magic practices but above all to extrajudicial solutions of *maleficium* cases. Admittedly, this situation began to change as the republican period continued.[9] But again, there are few jurisprudential acts and there is no agreement among scholars on the assumption of a creeping trend in legislation towards a prohibition of magical practices.[10] Ultimately, Livy's two reports of bloody events are mysterious flashes out of the blue:

[In 183/184 and then in 180 BC the praetor Quinto Nevio instructed] trials for poisoning, most of which he held outside of Rome in the municipalities and minor localities [...] If we want to believe Valerio Anziate, he condemned about two thousand [people][11]

[About three years later] from the praetor C. Menio, to whom, in addition to the province of Sardinia, the poisoning trials had been assigned beyond a radius of ten thousand steps from Rome, a letter arrived, stating that three thousand people had already been condemned, and that due to the allegations the trials increased.[12]

Allegations of what? We have nothing on the type of crimes reported, nothing on the accusers, nothing about the victims, or would-be witches. Not even torturing the reports with the most fertile of imaginations can anything solid be obtained from the scant Livian lines, little more than two expanded tweets, we would say today, built on the phrase "trials for poisoning." Perhaps, isolated over long centuries of substantial tolerance, it is not rash to affirm that batches of five thousand people are configured as exceptions that confirm the rule of a natural, informal control of evil witchcraft.

Historians have wandered whether the Roman batches show some similarities with the great sixteenth- and seventeenth-century European state- and church-directed witch hunts. A clear-cut answer, whether to confirm or dismiss it, is once again denied by the disconcerting scarcity of sources. To answer, it would be essential to know which types of supposed crimes gave impulse to a likely paranoia of accusations such as to force a plausibly centralized political decision.

In fact, another hypothesis should not be excluded: namely that the carnage was the dramatic tail of more general problems accumulated over the entire decade 190–180 BC.[13] A great repression of the Bacchanalia, which occurred in 186 BC, would seem to complicate the understanding of the following two or three decades. "It is probable that the accusations of veneficium launched during and after the affair secretly reflect the feeling that the Bacchants and their ilk are guilty of the collective misfortunes of the time, more particularly of the pestilentiae."[14] The conjecture that trials for poisoning were the outlet for local witch hunts does not preclude seeing in those extensive repressions a much wider political-religious significance. In other words, the strengthening of the patriarchal order and the male monopoly of public life, which in a series of episodes over different years and culminating in 195 had been disturbed by some manifestations of matrons.[15]

More generally, the fight against the Bacchantes and their misguided magical-religious practice was the occasion for a showdown between two models of relationship with the divinities, that is, between the institutionalized Roman religion and the ecstatic practices of ancestral cults developed in the rituals of the last communities of hunters and gatherers and subsequently handed down. In the deep times of the Pleistocene, the propensity of the species to meet the supernatural through trances procured by dance and songs, stimulated by special neural circuits, was by now structured in the mind. Classical Greece has left ample traces of recurring frenetic orgiastic cults of which Euripides' *Bacchantes* are an emblematic and ambiguous artistic peak as regards the relationship between ecclesiastical and ecstatic. But in Rome the course of civilization had taken a different direction, and no one forgets that the true meaning of the Roman world was by now that of a state unwilling to negotiate its monopoly of the relationship with Gods. Divination had for centuries passed under the control of religion; Homer's Calcante was already receiving its mana from Apollo.

Let us go back to the unruly bacchanalians, who remained confined to private practices. Titus Livy dwells on them with a clear negative opinion:

> [They were] mysteries, to which few were originally initiated [...] The delights of wine and banquets were added to the ritual, so that the minds were more attracted to error. When the fumes of wine, the complicity of the night and the confusion of males and females, children and adults, had erased every limit set by modesty, every kind of depravity began to be committed because everyone found their ready satisfaction for what they were most suited to. [...] If someone was less easy to adapt to dishonor or less determined to such actions, he was sacrificed as a victim.[16]

They were orgies, vividly imagined in Rubens's painting *Baccanale*.[17] The light, the color, the movement of a brilliantly overloaded canvas serve the dramatic moment of those contexts. Rubens's imagination seduces and appears almost the *Historiae*'s pictorial translation. But the allusions to the poisoning trials remain shrouded in darkness. And even on those specific propitiatory cults the information to be used for our topic is not abundant.

Of course, serious massacres took place. Whatever the causes, situations favorable to the onset of witchcraft crises are not unlikely, obeying the sequence mortality → panic → viral spread → accusations → repression. At times such a spiral became perverse in Europe precisely in the centuries when the legal foundations of modern state took shape. Coincidence leading back to the Livian bacchic drunkenness "plague that spreads and insinuates itself every day: now too widespread to be contained within the limits of private interests: it targets the sovereignty of the state."[18] No doubt Jean Bodin, the French political philosopher theorist of the state, would have subscribed to those words.

Notes

1 "No legal speech survives dealing with such a case"; See M. Gordon, *Imagining Greek and Roman Magic*, 248, 250.
2 E. Eidinow, "Pattern of Persecution: 'Witchcraft' Trials in Classical Athens," in *Past and Present*, 208, 2010, 9–35; Ead., *Envy, Poison, & Death: Women on Trial in Classical Athens*, Oxford, 2015.
3 Plato, *Laws*, X, 909b; see F. Graf, *Magic*.
4 F. Graf, "Victimology, or How to Deal with Untimely Death," in K. Stratton, D. S. Kalleres, eds., *Daughters of Hecate: Women and Magic in the Ancient World*, Oxford, 2014, 386–417.

5   "In classical Athens there was no law against magical practice as a whole": G. Andrikopoulos, "Witches in Greece and Rome," in *The Routledge History of Witchcraft*, 3.

6   Horace, *Epistulae*, II.I, v. 156.

7   R. Gordon, *Imagining Greek and Roman Magic*, 254.

8   Ibid., 253.

9   It should be noted a possible transformation inferable from some episodes of sudden deaths, due to suspected poisoning, which occurred in the city in 331 BC (as reported by Livy), and certain magical thefts of messengers (as told by Pliny the Elder in 221 BC), and little else.

10 R. Gordon, *Imagining Greek and Roman Magic*, 259–260; M. Dickie, *Magic and Magicians*, 147–151.

11 Livy, *Historiae*, Libri XXXVI-XL, 39.41, 5–6.

12 Ibid., 40.43., 1–3. Ten thousand steps add up to just under 15 km. Our translation.

13 Ibid., 39.8.1. There are reports of repression of conspiracies organized by Bacchic associations. It was a scourge that spread from Etruria like an epidemic (*velut contagione*); ibid., 8.16.

14 J.-M. Pailler, *Bacchanalia: La répression de 186 av. J.C. à Rome et en Italie*, Rome, 1988, 248–329; N. Cohn, *Europe's Inner Demons*; F. Graf, *Magic*.

15 L. B. Zaidman, "The Religious Role of Roman Women," in *A History of Women in the West*, G. Duby, M. Perrot, P. Schmitt Pantel, eds., Cambridge, MA, 1992.

16 Livy, *Historiae*, 8, 5–7; 13, 11–12.

17 Peter Paul Rubens, *Baccanale* (London, National Gallery).

18 Ibid., Livy, *Historiae*, 16, 3–7.

17

CHRISTIAN TRANSFORMATIONS

The Nuclear Fallout

Why the Evil? From Classical to Christian Theodicy

What happened after the 181 BC trials for poisoning? From this specific point of view reconstructions are uncertain. It is assumed that around the middle of the fourth century AD "a precise *malaise* in the structure of the governing classes of the Roman Empire [...] forced the ubiquitous sorcery beliefs of ancient man to a flash point of accusation."[1] On the other hand "it is far from certain that there was absolute increase in fear of sorcery or in sorcery practices in the Late Roman period."[2] With how many trials and what verdicts? Huge bloody repressions which would have escaped the tweets of any chronicler can be excluded.

The natural control of witchcraft must have persisted. But now, populations gathered in the faith in one God were involved. The conversion of the Roman empire induced a slow adaptation of people's beliefs, favored by the "gradual evolution of the Abrahamic god from a set of bizarre and temperamental warrior tribal gods, into the unitary, supreme, eternally vigilant and moralizing divinity of Judaism and Christianity."[3] Entering monotheism people began to question evil, maleficent people and the injustice of Heaven in a new way.

***

An ethics of religious beliefs could come from the innate, altruistic moral infrastructure that humans are directed to by their cerebral propensity. Man's aspiration towards pro-sociality ended up configuring itself as the mirror of a just world transferred up into the heavens, in which intentional agents monitored and intervened in human conduct. But such fallout of a cognitive projection clashed with life's harshness, often struck by physical suffering and material losses. To what extent could the latest *Sapiens* have been afflicted by this illogicality is obviously a mystery. In search of historical precedents of such a contradiction we are referred to the Hittite or Persian/Sumerian Middle Eastern cosmogonies

DOI: 10.4324/9781003414377-19

which with Zoroastrianism contemplated the coexistence of divinities of good and evil. The horizon did not clarify when the Greek world moralized deities. The best minds began to reflect on the incongruity by asking themselves about the problem of heavenly justice. Between the sixth and fifth centuries BC, the elegiac poet Theognis appropriately explained the problem by invoking Father Zeus:

> How can it be right that he who keeps himself away from injustice and who, avoiding any guilty excess and any perjury, keeps himself just, is not treated justly? Faced with this example, what other mortal would keep the respect of the gods? What feeling would push him when the unjust and guilty man, without fear of the anger of anyone, man or god, insolently displays abundant riches, while the just bear the hard bite of Poverty?[4]

Theognis' pessimism refers to the roots of a complicated theodicy. Reflections on the amorality and justice of classical divinities are enveloped in many perplexities.[5] Admittedly, a way out of the contradiction was offered by the appearance in archaic Greece of a indistinct category of divine beings, called *daimones*, benevolent or malevolent at the discretion of the inconstant *Tyche* (fortune). They were interchangeable with "gods" or more commonly "with lower-level divine figures."[6] The advantage offered by demons was to "separate the good gods of a civic cult from the morally ambivalent divine powers used at the popular level."[7] It was a try to circumvent the paradox of evil. We could accept the top-down thesis that it was them who paved the way for witches, earthly dispensers of material and moral damages. Interpretations vary, though, and one may with some uncertainty argue that, in the Late Roman centuries, "evil demons lifted the burden of guilt and pain from human shoulders." They will be responsible for the evil. A non-negligible legacy for Christianity.[8]

Monoteism and the Devil

In the Christianized late Empire, much was changing from a theoretical point of view, but let us reduce the direction of change into one sentence: the existence of evil will materialize in the personification of an idea reserved for a fateful future, the Devil.

Every religion, except perhaps Buddhism, has developed complicated interpretations about the origins of evil, but those who believe in one God have a greater difficulty to find an answer. In monotheistic religions "the idea of a single prince of evil is dominant."[9] The Judeo-Christian doctrine is a labyrinth and for theologians the reasons for evil end up in a puzzle of an insoluble theodicy. To exonerate the divine responsibility for earthly sufferings scriptural narrative explained its genesis because of man's fallibility, but this always referred to some antecedent temptation that made him fall, like the snake in the garden of Eden, the Devil's ancestor. The negative entity pre-existence, as mentioned, could have come from Persia in the sixth or fifth century BC, deriving from Zoroastrianism.

In essence, evil remains a mystery in Abrahamic religions.[10] There are few and varied ideas of the Devil in the Bible, and the notion of him as "a mighty leader of evil spirits became much more prominent in Jewish apocalyptic literature that exerted a wide influence on the New Testament."[11] And it is in fact in the Gospels that the Devil's power fully emerges in the context of a clash between good and evil. This dualistic opposition is undermined by the story of Satan understood as a rebel angel, condemning the Manichaean vision to defeat. Satan became the incarnation of evil and by delegating malefic powers to his ministers, the witches, he stood as an enemy, a hater of humanity. Will this then be the prevailing theme of the witchcraft convictions of the educated and illiterate classes in a Continent that became Christian with the Edict of Constantine (313 AD)? The story is much more complicated, but we offer a simplification.

**

When Judeo-Christian monotheism accelerated a process of institutionalization, an increasing number of aspects of life fell under the control of the new creeds. The new Faith marked the passage from a mythological consciousness proper to oral cultures to a theological culture proper to written cultures. One God conducted a dialogue with individual consciences emerging from collectivities whose members still had a limited sense of their own being. Actions that could have been seen as deviations from community rules were understood as violations against the chosen creed. The saving vision of Christianity enhanced the human inclination towards compassion.[12] Our neural predisposition to communicate with counter-intuitive, supernatural essences was translated functionally into more codified rites, always aimed at enhancing the protection of people, animals, and plants. Religion and the sacred began to be experienced through practices accompanying men from birth, to adulthood, to death. The constitutive needs of human psyche remained unchanged, but much was added by giving faith an increasingly structured dimension. If the above reconstruction is valid, the largely illiterate populations should have adapted to the changed conceptual, moral, and institutional terrain. It did not go that way.

As a matter of fact, this outlined transformation turns out to be more a trend of future developments of the monotheistic religion. The beginning of it all could not have been more troubled. The new model of the world in the story of the relationship of men with the divinity was built within a devastated, impoverished ecological and human context. The centuries-old climatic *optimum* of the Roman Empire was replaced by an early medieval *pessimum*. Cities were depopulated, work in the fields abandoned. Wilderness regained the upper hand, relegating small groups of inhabitants to farms and a few sites of greater consistency, surrounded by forests, woods, swamps or marshes, where gatherers of wild fruits reappeared as in the early days of humanity. Also, the persistent competition of magic and religion in the practical task of resolving or alleviating physical and psychological suffering must be emphasized: saints invariably present themselves as magicians and healers.[13] Soothsayers mentioned by a chronicler such as Gregory of Tours (538–594 AD) attest to a panacea to remedy material and moral misfortune. In this leap back towards a new Protohistory, individual conduct regarding malefic witchcraft is barely visible.

From Malefic Witches to the Enemies of God

Christianity, in the centuries preceding the age of the witch-hunts, maintained an overall linear attitude towards witchcraft. Augustine of Hippo, according to Scriptures, considered any magic driven by the devil and punishable by death. As already stressed, the importance of the Bible in marking the future destiny of witches remains huge. Half a millennium after the Saint, the *Canon episcopi* (906), an instruction to bishops on the behavior to be assumed towards witchcraft belief confirms that the power to inflict harm and the metamorphosis into animals to perform nocturnal flights in infanticidal missions must be attributed to Satan's deceptions. In the following centuries, diabolism penetrated Christianity as the primary concern of an educated elite, imposing a rigorist tradition. Its driving force has been identified in the tenacious struggle against heretical movements of the Church. In the context of the persecution of Cathars, Waldensians, Jews, and Templars, twisted narratives were elaborated. Various plots were intertwined: witches, Satan's ministers, had made a pact with him, copulated with him, went to worship him by flying on the back of goats in meetings called Sabbaths, practicing infanticides and orgies through rituals of inversion of the Christian ceremonial.

All these ideas, cultivated in literate circles and circulating even among the uneducated classes, formed a "complex process of coalescence, diffusion, fusion and attenuation."[14] Allow us to call it a kind of meme inherited in some of its parts from the classical age and reproduced erratically. As for the distant provenance of what the most terrifying stories contained (such as anthropophagy), it remains buried, using Oscar Wilde's ingenuity, in the minds of "astonished cavemen."[15]

Witches became apostates, adepts of a new sect of enemies of God, humanity, and the State, responsible for infanticide, creators of storms, destroyers of crops and livestock. The crucial decades for the formation of this stereotyped narration have been identified from about 1375 to 1440.[16] The opinion that such a sect conspired against Christian society found a decisive pillar in the Heinrich Kramer's *Malleus maleficarum* (1486) to whom Innocent VIII's papal bull, *Summis Desiderantes affectibus* (1484), premised to the treaty, gave authority, defining witchcraft as a heresy to be fought by any means. Conspiracy of the enemies of Christianity did not have a uniform diffusion in Europe. In the states where it was poorly received (Scandinavian countries, England, Christian-Orthodox lands), the erratic repressive waves were less bloody. It should be emphasized that among common people, in general, the idea of devil worship remained peripheral. It was used by theologians, jurists, and clergy hierarchy. When people were not influenced by ecclesiastical or secular authorities, the demonological conception of the witch was marginal to the ways of reasoning of individuals. The executors of any mysterious misfortune were sought in the daily relationships with some malevolent neighbor and for the resolution of problems people mainly resorted the natural control of witchcraft.

Kramer's *Mein Kampf*

The *Malleus Maleficarum* should be further dealt with. Due to its wide circulation in the sixteenth century and beyond, two points need to be highlighted: the centrality of *maleficium*, and the possibility that the book imprinted a decisive mark in qualifying the crime by sex, understood to be predominantly perpetrated by women.

In Kramer's intentions, *Malleus* was intended to be a compendium of legal proce-dures for witch-hunting, built on his experience as man in office: a Dominican inquisitor moving from one location to another to carry out investigations. Twelve editions of the work appeared between 1486 and 1523. Sixty years followed without any further request from the international legal milieu. When Christian Europe settled into opposing creeds, the demand returned and coincided with the most crucial phase of the so-called European "witch craze." Another 14 editions followed, and it was estimated that around 30,000 copies circulated in Europe. Let us focus on the two points of particular interest here.

First, *maleficium*. The crime represents the core of the treatise and its truly origi-nal contribution, destined for this reason to have a strong influence in the immi-nent unleashing of witch persecutions. A realistic description of the witchcraft system comes straight from Kramer's extensive experience as an inquisitor:

> Sorceresses appear in three kinds, that is, those who cause injuries, but who are unable to cure, those who harm but are unable to heal, those who cure and do not harm [...] and those who harm and heal.[17] [...] How many of them there are! They can always be found every one or two German miles and within this radius these sorcerers seem to heal whatever harm is caused by other sorceresses [...] others can heal only with the consent of the sorceress who inflicted the sorcery.[18]

Second, the witch as a woman. The treatise constituted a breaking point in the fifteenth century demonological tradition that revolved around the Sabbath. Night meetings, sexual promiscuity, obscene adoration of the devil, flying in the air, find marginal mention in the work. The hammering centrality conferred in the treatise, the sequence woman → lust → witchcraft, grasped the common cultural thread of the previous century by developing the latent Dominican misogynism and char-acterized the crime by sex. In fifteenth-century demonological writings the dia-bolical sects lack a marked specificity as to the sex of affiliates. With the *Malleus* Kramer created a conceptual fusion, maybe spurred by the monk's own delusional ravings about dangers potentially inherent in female carnality. It is no coincidence that in 1486 in a bishop's private letter Kramer was defined as a madman suffering from senility.[19]

Was, then, Kramer's battle a paranoid conception of female sexuality? Whatever the case, he won it, according to victim percentages by sex. With unpredictable distant outcome on nineteenth- and twentieth-century psychiatry, based on projections that go from Jean-Martin Charcot to Sigmund Freud. "Influential nineteenth century physicians believed that hysteria – largely, though not exclusively, a female malady – provided the solution to bizarre episodes of witchcraft and convulsionary phenomena in the past."[20] Freud himself admitted that he had read the *Malleus Maleficarum* "diligently" to the point of privately suggesting that if hysterics were homologous to old-fashioned witches, psychiatrists were like witch hunters.[21]

Even today the *Malleus* continues to be printed and read. A check of entry recurrences on the web presents conflicting opinions and reactions that assimilate it to Adolf Hitler's *Mein Kampf* or Mao Zedong's "Little Red Book." However, how much responsibility should be attributed to the infamous libel of a greater diffusion in following centuries of the witch = woman stereotype remains difficult to measure. "The literature on witchcraft conspicuously lacked a sustained interest in the topic of gender [...] High on the agenda of today's social and cultural historians, the witch's female sexuality was low on the agenda of demonologists."[22]

Notes

1 P. Brown, "Sorcery, Demons," 35.
2 Ibid.; see also V. Flint, "The Demonisation of Magic and Sorcery in Late Antiquity: Christian definitions of Pagan Religion," in *The Athlon History*, 2, *Ancient Greece and Rome*, 315–324.
3 A. Norenzayan, *Big Gods*, 133.
4 Theognis (elegiacs), vv. 731–5; see H. Kelsen, *Society and Nature*. Our translation.
5 W. Burkert, *Greek Religion*, Cambridge, MA, 1985, ch. 7.
6 N. Janowitz, "Demons and Witchcraft in the Early Church," in *The Routledge History of Witchcraft*, 36.
7 R. Gordon, *Imagining Greek and Roman Magic*, 176.
8 V. Flint, *The Demonisation of Magic and Sorcery*, 291.
9 J. B. Russel, "Devil," in *EW*, I, 270–274.
10 The single entry "Evil" is missing in the second edition of the *Encyclopedia Judaica*.
11 J. B. Russel, "Devil," in *EW*.
12 J. Rifkin, *Empathic Civilization*; F. de Waal, *The Age of Empathy*.
13 A. Gurevič, *Medieval Popular Culture*.
14 R. Kieckhefer, "The First Wave of Trials for Diabolical Witchcraft," in *The Oxford Handbook of Witchcraft*, 160.
15 An understanding of human evolutionary history contributes to explaining the structure and function of "horror stories"; see M. Clasen, "Terrifying Monsters, Malevolent Ghosts, and Evolved Danger Management Architecture: A Consilient Approach to Horror Fiction," in *Darwin's Bridge*, 184–193.
16 E. Peters, "The Medieval Church and State on Superstition, Magic and Witchcraft: From Augustine to the Sixteenth Century," in *Witchcraft and Magic in Europe*, III, K. Jolly, C. Raudvere, E. Peters, *The Middle Ages*, London, 2002, 233.
17 Henricus Institoris, O. P., Jacobus Sprenger, O. P., *Malleus Maleficarum*, edited and translated by C. S. Mackay, vol. II, *The English Translation*, Cambridge, 2006, II, Ch. Two, 233.
18 Ibid., Part Three, Quaestio II, 358.
19 The bishop of Brescia George Golser wrote: "Ipse realiter mihi delirare videtur"; see H. Kramer (Institoris) *Der Hexenhammer. Malleus Maleficarum*, G. Jerouschek, W. Behringer, W. Tschacher, eds, München, 2004, 63.

20 R. Porter, "Witchcraft and Magic in Enlightenment, Romantic and Liberal Thought," in *Witchcraft and Magic in Europe*, III, M. Gijswijt-Hofstra, B. Levack, R. Porter, *The Eighteenth and Nineteenth Centuries*, London, 1999, 268.

21 Ibid., 271; J. M. Masson, *The Complete Letters of Sigmund Freud to William Fliess (1887–1904)*, Cambridge, Mass., 1985.

22 S. Clark, *Thinking with Demons*, 116–117. But see L. Kounine, *Imagining the Witch*, 188–200. On the feminization of witchcraft, C. Rider, "Magic and Gender," in *The Routledge History of Medieval Magic*, S. Page, C. Rider, eds, New York, 2019, 343–355.

18

EARLY MODERN WITCH-HUNTING

A Cognitive Puzzle?

At the sunset of the fifteenth century, the perverse effects of the biblical fall-out, "Do not allow a sorceress to live" (Exodus 22.18), reached a full maturity sealed by the *Malleus maleficarum*. Despite the conflicting contiguity between magical and religious beliefs, in the thousand years of the Middle Ages magic and witchcraft had not always been a matter of great concern to the lay and ecclesiastical authorities. In the early centuries, the control of witchcraft by the formal judicial structures remained a negligible issue punished with religious penances. From the eleventh to thirteenth centuries, isolated executions of witches were recorded in various European towns and cities. The prevailing silence of medieval chronicles implies that no large-scale repressions occurred.[1]

> Even in the fourteenth and fifteenth century when the problem of magic and witchcraft attracted more attention, the laws and theoretical production concerning them remained a very small part of an immense devotional, legal and theological literature that was mainly reserved for other aspects of the social and spiritual life of European Christianity.[2]

But three huge persecutions (with about 500 victims each or more) took place in the first half of the fifteenth century in Dauphiné, Duchy of Savoy and Valais. Then, after the lull around the age of the Reformation, for about one hundred and fifty years, fires ignited and extinguished irregularly, concentrating in paroxysmal phases in the six decades between the end of the sixteenth century and the 1640s, the period of the witch trials.

***

As an object of research and reflection, this so-called classical age of witch hunts is a topos that has been happily expanding for not much more than a handful of decades. It has been written that books on witchcraft, not unlike witchcraft trials,

DOI: 10.4324/9781003414377-20

come in waves. There is a calm of activity and then they burst forth.[3] In the 2000s, such a multiplication of monographs ended up allowing the publication of syntheses, by individual authors or the result of collective works.[4] In the following paragraphs we intend to reappraise the historical relevance of what appears to have been an erratic series of marginal judicial operations.

To begin with, the repression of witchcraft in the early modern years is not a single event and does not lend itself to a conventional treatment, appropriate to events such as the English revolution or the French revolution, which are usually approached distinguishing by origins, factors precipitants, development, protagonists, results. Historians have tried to identify the factors that triggered these flare-ups, dissatisfied with a single cause. No univocal interpretative criteria (religious, economic, political, climatological) explain the beginning and the end of the golden age of witch-hunts.[5] The propensity of researchers towards multi-causality, however, raises our doubt that upstream of the "many reasons why" there is a complicated cognitive riddle illustrated by a metaphor: the crackling of some burning trees diverts attention from the deafening silence in the whole forest. Historians have shown that the formal prosecution of witches had an uneven spread geographically and chronologically but have devoted scarce attention to the silent areas. We will argue that this silence, namely the very absence of complaints and trials and their marginality in a large part of the Continent, are nothing other than the millennial persistence of the natural control of witchcraft, the possible transmutation of the prehistoric shared intentionality, which made the witchcraft system operational. However, before revisiting the formal repression by State and Church, the human and natural environment in which it took place must be remembered.

A Still Enveloping Nature

In the age of great witch-hunts in Europe some 80 percent of men and women lived in small villages in the countryside. Only towards the end of the nineteenth century did city-dwellers exceed the rural inhabitants. Urbanization should be understood as the key factor eventually undermining the persistence of this cultural institution, witchcraft.

Those extended agrarian spaces were full of "demons and spirits." Giordano Bruno's quote that opened the book invites us to focus on the psychoactive influence of nature. Not too unlike the people of ancient and medieval world, early modern Europeans remained subject to the same emotions, the same hopes, even the same types of distortions in perception and cognitive processes, which generated suggestions typical of a society still overwhelmed by the wonders of natural phenomenon. That primeval awe of our *Sapiens*, characterized no less the people of the early modern age. "René Descartes called wonder the first of the passion, 'a sudden surprise of the soul' which makes it tend to consider attentively those objects which seem to it rare and extraordinary."[6] All this would produce reactions resulting in an accentuated sensitivity, in experiences that took place in wooded areas, in uninhabited places, sometimes in the mountains, as literature and landscape art illustrate and allow to relive. Those "harsh and solitary places" of Sierra Morena swarmed with "throngs of charmers" hostile to Don Quixote's exploits;[7] the enchanted forests where *Orlando furioso*'s characters enter; the woods crossed on horseback by the same Ludovico Ariosto on his diplomatic missions, shuttling between Cardinal Ippolito d'Este and Pope Julius II in the second decade of the sixteenth century. Real-world people acted in such a landscape, in the long duration of a psychotropic nature.

The Nolan philosopher's assumption that humans are part of a sentient world is to be recovered. "Men see," the philosopher reminds us. Seeing occupies a privileged position in our narration because through its function a primacy of knowledge is built.[8] The human brain responds differently to the pervasiveness of landscape. Certain grandeurs such as a chain of mountains can be overwhelming to the point of oppression. Neuroscientific studies increase our understanding of the close connection between people and the places where they live. The brain is at the center of this relationship and the functional magnetic resonance imaging (fMRI) technology open a potential that brings us closer to comprehending the physiological, cognitive, and emotional basis of human actions in ways previously unavailable.

The natural environment has an impact on the anatomy of the brain. People respond to the Sublime of landscapes with amazement and dismay. If we observe certain typical images, such as Alpine peaks, parts of the brain affected by fear (such as the amygdala) and pleasure (such as the *nucleus accumbens*) "respectively respond more strongly or remain inert, while the prefrontal cortex, responsible for abstract reasoning, does most of the work, indicating that we are experiencing more of a cognitive than an emotional reaction."[9] The Swiss painter Henry Füssli, famous for his distressing depictions of nightmares, left us a pertinent note reflecting on Salvator Rosa's Sublime:

> In landscapes he was a genius. His choice is the original scenery of Abruzzo: he delights in ideas of desolation, solitude, and danger, impenetrable forests, rocky or storm-lashed shores; in lonely dells leading to dens and caverns of banditti, alpine ridges, trees blasted by lightnings or sapped by time, or stretching their extravagant arms against a murky sky, louring or shuddering clouds, or suns shorn of their beams.[10]

Perhaps the caves also harbored occasional dropouts, witches. Salvator Rosa was a lover of black witchcraft: there is a parallelism between literary writings, such as the ode *The witch* (1646), and a pictorial work such as *Witches and incantations* (1646), where a ruined tree could be transplanted into any of his disturbing and harsh landscapes. It has been written that mountains thin air arouses hallucinations, and natural phenomena that manifest themselves in abnormal forms easily lead men to believe in demonic intervention.[11] This psychological appearance had not escaped Thomas Mann's imaginary creation. In the *Magic Mountain* Swiss Alps, "[Hans Castorp] strove to see, what he saw was nothing [...] and only occasionally did the ghostly shadows of the phenomenal world surface in that nothingness."[12] And perhaps the same Sierra Morena heights dazzled our La Mancha's hidalgo by transforming windmills into giants, too.

It is certainly true that some witch hunts took place in mountainous and hilly areas. The ghostly shadows hidden in the physicality of pristine territories were nevertheless a form of experience common to many, not peculiar to the inhabitants of specific altitudes.[13] The witchcraft phenomenon maintained the imprinting of spatial contexts where vegetation, woods, rivers, darkness, and light had a heavy impact. The entire historical trajectory of charms appears to be conditioned by an environmental mechanism that acts on individuals, changes their spirits and translates into different receptivity, frame of mind, awareness, practices. In Italy, in the years of the Counter-Reformation and the great anti-magic offensive unleashed by Pope Sixtus V's papal bull *Coeli et Terrae* (1586), more than one fortune-teller would consider himself capable of alleviating the anxiety of people oppressed by the anguish generated by abnormal forms of nature. Maco del Bolgia, a seventy-year-old sorcerer ("stregone") practicing divination and therapeutic magic in the Tuscan area, trapped in the nets of the Inquisition, during the interrogation among his specialties mentioned a "remedy for those who are traveling [...], that he had had some grip or fear or sudden panic for a forest or other."[14] The trials instructed by the State and the Church occurred in this ecological context; they were aimed against people whose main occupation was agriculture and whose way of thinking had remained deeply involved with plant and animal nature.

"Witch Hunt": Definition

The need to reframe how early modern people perceived the world should be taken for granted. Now, before an in-depth analysis of the legal persecutions, let us specify again what is meant by witch hunt, to free the expression from the meaning it has assumed in common discourse, in the language of politics, of mass-media and of ordinary people: a catch phrase for any human imbroglio. The hunt alludes to legal actions taken against individuals suspected of having committed malefices: "Suspicious people are never obvious: they must be found and identified."[15] Hunt is a technical term and finds use in the same lexicon of some protagonist, such as Gata, who, when investigated by the Sienese Inquisition in 1605, remarked: "Like me there can be fifteen or more [...] they can blame both me and others, what do I know, and since they are hunting me so they can hunt others."[16]

The hunts were an amalgamation of thousands of individual criminal cases. They became a complicated event of medium size (from 5 to 10 victims) or large scale (much more than 10 victims) when the condemned sent to the stake confessed, often under torture, the names of conniving partners in the would-be demonic pact.[17] In an ideological code in which witches had become the devil's handmaids and enemies of God, there were rulers who used the argument of repression to consolidate their Christian power through renewed legislation. Historians agree in assigning a critical role to the law.

In Roman law there were solid precedents for repressing the *crimen exceptum*, as opposed to the vagueness of canon law. Early modern European hunts spread when the appropriate legal bases became *more* available in the emerging nation states. On the Continent, these preconditions meant (a) the introduction of the inquisitorial system in place of the accusatory one, both for secular and ecclesiastical justice; (b) the systematic use of torture; (c) the extension of the jurisdiction of the crime to secular courts. The developments are particularly clear in the cases of the French and English monarchies and equally in the lands where the Inquisition controlled local apparatus, such as in the Spanish kingdoms and in the Italian peninsula. "Both the introduction of the inquisitorial procedure in most European jurisdictions and the emergence of secular control over witchcraft were a reflection of state power growth."[18]

Nonetheless, the center-periphery dynamic remained complex because the central apparatus struggled to limit the authority of peripheral powers, sometimes pressed by local requests for punitive interventions. It was pointed out that regions characterized by strong political fragmentation and a weak state building process could have higher percentages of trials and stakes. In any case, the judicial actions ended completely when, in the second half of the seventeenth century, the legal rules were withdrawn or suspended or simply hindered by technicalities that raised the burden of proof against the crime.

Facts

The Data

Early modern age state and church courts supply a substantial number of complaints and trials to historians that allow to reconstruct types of crime and the sociology of criminals. In archive papers, secular or ecclesiastical actions take the form of a flow of reports or accusations that result in the opening of formal inquiries in proportions difficult to ascertain. The calculation of the totals can vary from one third to one seventh. According to recent estimates in Europe, between 1400 and 1775, proceedings were opened on about 100,000 people (flow of complaints amount could fluctuate from 300,000 to 700,000),[19] with several executions ranging between 45,000 and 55,000.

The Crisis Areas

In general, the hunts seem to respond to the criterion of a repetition in places already hit by a previous wave. The succession of stop-and-go, that is, of crisis-pause-crisis invites us to closely weigh how much of the natural control of witchcraft affects these temporal alternations. Each witchcraft crisis implicitly revolves around the endemic/epidemic (or physiological/pathological) dichotomy, which refers to the agency of the witchcraft system whose function was to protect and maintain the homeostatic balance of each community, avoiding dramatic fractures. Like a karst river, the key figures of the system (fortune tellers, diviners, cunning folks, etc.) disappear and reappear in the fragmentation and diversity of historical sources. We have tried to identify their traces back to the origins of documented history when, heirs of the prehistoric reciprocal altruism, the first agrarian civilizations began to leave some written evidence of how they organized village governance. Early modern trials definitively brought the system into the open. Witches did not so often occupy a marginal social or economic status. How could they be members of the community living alongside co-villagers who suspected them? "When people were brought to trial, we often learn that they had a reputation for practicing magic that goes back many years."[20] Why, then, such long impunity?

Most crises followed a model: the impulse to try witches came from the local authorities pressured by village discontentment, with initiatives not exclusive to the popular classes. Here the serious problem regarding State and Church court actions arises. Were formal accusations and trials the result of strong duress or were they the expressions of minor and in any case intermittent social unease? We believe that the natural control evidently replaced the contingent reasons that advised against or prevented recourse to the judicial system. At the beginning of the modern age, procedural changes were introduced that made the crime more easily punishable. Yet the option remained rare. "The formal persecution of witchcraft was often a solution that was resorted to only when other more informal means of agreement had been exhausted."[21] Recourse to the law was expensive and not close by. In villages, personal conflict resolution or other defensive strategies were preferred through mediation, or direct threats against maleficent people, or refuge in prayer, to the point of using a multiplicity of expedients (amulets, superstitious rituals, etc.), signs of a reassuring paranoid obsession to contain the risks of misfortune caused by malicious people or carriers of the evil eye.[22]

Areas without Crisis

"Many places, including places that we know experienced witchcraft prosecutions, remained blank."[23] Given the universality of witchcraft convictions, the absence of judicial proceedings in many parts of the Continent and the British Isles remains unexplained. Let us give a quick example, by hinting at known situations. Spain, Italy, Poland, Netherlands, and Sweden experienced mass witch hunts, but only in limited areas and for short periods of time. In Scotland, France, in the states of Germany, and in the Swiss Confederation they were conducted with great intensity and ferocity. Yet even there the active centers were constantly changing and in other areas witch hunt never took place or was of little importance.[24] In Jura and Cambrésis areas are documented that appear to be exempt. Similar considerations apply to Lorraine and Scotland. In England nearly 60 percent of the allegations are concentrated in Essex, but in the same county some areas were immune. In the middle of Italy, Tuscany and Emilia, in the territories under the jurisdiction of the Sienese and Modenese Inquisition, the number of villages exempt from witchcraft crises equals the number of those where complaints, investigations or trials occurred. In Andalusia, judicial initiatives seem to be absent, leaving a truly improbable impression that southern Spain was free from witches.[25] The listing could go on. "When one considers the overall record [...] Europe as a whole did not surrender in panic to a wave of witch-hunting."[26] Historians are aware of how concentrated hunts occurred "in relatively few specific territories and areas and how in the rest of Europe – across huge expanses of it, in fact – they were sporadic, scarce or had a negligible role."[27] Or the prosecutions were totally non-existent. Yet, legal procedures were also present in the regions not affected by repression and these areas remain terra incognita for research. Yet, in these vast European regions devoid of persecutions, the brains of individuals were not different, people shared the same drives. How then can we account for this deafening silence of so many populations in the face of the reality of malefices?

Judicial Statistics Compared

During periods of intense repression, such as when a chain reaction occurred if diabolism was called into question, witchcraft cases occupied a significant percentage of the time and effort of the prosecution.[28] It ended up generating a misleading historical problem. That the would-be European "witch-craze" was not a preponderant reality finds a sounder confirmation in a comparison of judicial statistics considering the number and type of crimes. In the absence of extensive national comparisons, two sub-regional statistical references relating to England and Italy can be used. From records relating to nine English counties the *maleficium* only in a particularly sensitive area such as Essex between 1620 and 1680 reaches the percentage of 4% compared to crimes against property, homicides and infanticides, while in the remaining eight counties, the percentages range from 1 to 2 percent or are nil.[29] In the Sienese State, between 1580 and 1721 in the sum of the crimes judged by the inquisitorial court and by the local secular justice, the same crime percentage is 1.72 percent.[30]

How do we want to interpret these remarkably similar numerical values from demographically homogeneous areas? Perhaps, it would not be risky to generalize and argue that "the incidence of the accusations of this crime does not in any way correspond to the intrinsic interest in it."[31] Probably, the cases of witchcraft did not clog the courts even in the entire European panorama. And this is precisely because people, except in situations of extreme tension, preferred not to resort to the State or Church for justice but to solve mysterious suffering and damage in another way. For lack of complaints or trials historians have devoted scarce attention to this silence.

The Human Cost

Victims of the hunts are certainly not forgotten. Their meaning will be stripped of an anachronistic concern for a politically correct approach. Given that, in many decades overheated by religious dissent it was easier to be put to death because people were Catholics or Calvinists or Jews or other than witches. According to balanced evaluations in three hundred years there was a bloodbath of witches oscillating between a minimum calculation of 45,000 or of 55,000 victims. We want to focus on these numbers. Historians are asked to be cautious and sensitive when making comparisons about the loss of human life. On the other hand, it is pertinent to note that these figures, diluted in just over three centuries, are modest. The adjective is inappropriate. It acquires meaning when commensurate with orders of magnitude, in terms of violent deaths we encounter in past events such as conflicts of religion, which abounded in the Ancien régime. It would be wrong to belittle the horrendous meaning of the pyres because they have been scaled down from a quantitative point of view. Therefore, we prefer to highlight their striking sociological aspect: on average 70%/ 80% of the people killed (or accused) were women. The heartlands of witch hunts (Scotland, England, Holy Roman Empire, Spain and Italy) were dominated by the stereotype of the female witch.[32] Why this abnormal gender cost? We will discuss this in the specific Chapter 24.

A Cognitive Puzzle

Single cases of witch killing can be traced throughout the documented history of the entire millennial Old Continent, but they are numerically minor episodes. On the other hand, we must agree that for almost one hundred and fifty years, the period of witch trials, there were considerable exceptions of large persecutions. And yet, even in the crisis areas the flames of *fast thinking*, ignited by critical sequences of climate change (the "Little-Ice-Age") → economic conjuncture → mortality crisis → panic, usual in the *ancien régime*, continued to be contrasted by the resistance of *slow thinking*, in the guise of natural control of malefices. And there is more.

On one side, it should be added that the pyres, from the neurobiological point of view, should not have occurred. This if we evaluate human conduct following a likely growth of human species empathic gradient, Hume's already mentioned "particle of the dove." Reflecting on the cognitive horizons opened by the completion of the Genome Project, we have hypothesized that a readjustment of human thought processes could have occurred in the millennia of agricultural civilizations that precede the witch hunt of the early modern age. On the other, the development of possessive individualism penetrating early modern agrarian societies could multiply occasions for envy in close knit communities, corroding the empathic system of a village.

What, then? Is this a cognitive puzzle: a series of brain short circuits in the nature-culture dynamic, in which *fast thinking* momentarily took over the *slow thinking*? No doubt, something is escaping our understanding. We will come back to it, in the closing of the next chapter.

Witchcraft without Stakes

Erratic sixteenth and seventeenth-century witch-hunting left few traces in the eighteenth century and none in the following one, to which the definition "witchcraft without burning" fits well. Actions taken by an Italian secular court between 1815 and 1825 symbolize the change very well. These judges, unlike the Franciscan and Dominican friars of the erstwhile Inquisition, were not interested in knowing people conscience.[33] Reports concerned 13 cases of crimes related to malefices in Tuscany. Situations and social actors of past centuries now familiar to us emerge. We are informed that in smaller towns of The Sienese and Florentine, "chief magicians" were consulted:

> Chief magicians [were consulted] or anti-witches, so defined by the people, for their specialty of being able to ascertain whether there are possible malefic influences at the origin of strange, sudden, and incurable diseases, against which they possess safe remedies. Since they almost always diagnose the existence of a spell, they are the ones who most spread and confirm the reputation of witches of women who have a bad public reputation, or who in any case are considered capable of giving the evil eye. For this reason, once discovered by the authorities or reported by women who see themselves defamed, they are found guilty and punished with jail.[34]

The stage is identical: the diagnosis of spells, identification of witches, recourse to anti-witchcraft based on the resolute certainty that only those who harm can heal. Nothing seems to have changed with respect to the internal dynamics of the witchcraft system as already described. The absence of police raids in the metropolitan centers of Tuscany is worth noting.

The case can be interpreted as the beginning of a slow *de profundis* of witchcraft natural control. As scholars who have experience of the nineteenth-century judicial archives know well, there are other similar cases and forms of primitive justice on the part of exasperated individuals or communities; cases often recorded in the press.[35] Such episodes were listed as local disturbances of public order to be controlled with good governance measures. Few situations were dealt with in the courts.[36]

Ultimately, a detail is worth mentioning, for its emblematic value, related to contemporary medical statistics. It points out that even today infant mortality between the ages of one month and one year in 50 percent of cases is due to the so-called "cot death" syndrome.[37] But already in the nineteenth century no European court could have instructed a trial on such deaths. A decriminalization had already appeared in the second half of the seventeenth century when newborns found dead in their beds began to be evaluated by judges as the killing of an infant by the mother and no longer as the result of the aggression of a witch. The hunts as a legal aberration and judicial affair were over.

However, occasionally "people continued to take the law into their own hands with regard to dealing with witches, and this led to what has been called "witch trials in reverse." These occurred when those physically abused or harassed for being suspected witches prosecuted their tormentors."[38]

Notes

1   W. Behringer, *Witches and Witch-Hunts*, 53–54; N. Cohn, *Europe's Inner Demons*.

2   E. Peters, *The Medieval Church and State on Superstition, Magic and Witchcraft*, 176.

3   A. Macfarlane, "Difficult Women," in *The Times Literary Supplement*, May 13, 1983.

4   *Witchcraft and Magic in Europe*, 6 volumes; *The Encyclopedia of Witchcraft*, 4 volumes; *The Oxford Handbook of Witchcraft; The Routledge History of Witchcraft*.

5   R. Briggs, "'Many reasons why': witchcraft and the problem of multiple explanation," in *Witchcraft in Early Modern Europe: Studies in Culture and Belief*, J. Barry, M. Hexter, G. Roberts, eds., Cambridge, 1996, 64–95; W. Behringer, *Witches and Witch-Hunts*, 83–164; B. Levack, *The Witch-Hunt in Early Modern Europe*, Harlow, 2006[3].

6   L. Daston-K. Park, *Wonders and the Order of Nature*, 13.

7   Miguel de Cervantes, *Don Quixote*, I, 23.

8   F. Faeta, *Le ragioni dello sguardo: Pratiche di osservazione, della rappresentazione e della memoria*, Torino, 2011, 31–33.

9   E. Russel, "How Can Neuroscience Help Us Understand the Past?" in: *Environment, Culture, and the Brain: New Explorations in Neurohistory*, edited by E. Russel, *RCC Perspectives 2012* (Rachel Carson Center for Environment and Society), 6, 2012. 9–13; Id., *Evolutionary History. Uniting History and Biology to Understand Life and Earth*, Cambridge, 2011, 94–98.

10 Salvator Rosa, "Paesaggio con Apollo e la Sibilla Cumana (1650/1660)"; see A. Wilton, "The Sublime in the Old World and the New," in *American Sublime. Landscape Painting in the United States 1820–1880*, A. Wilton, T. Barringer, eds., Tate Britain, London 21 February- 19 May 2002, 12.

11 H. Trevor-Roper, *The European Witch-Craze of the 16th and 17th Centuries*, 1969.

12 Thomas Mann, *The Magic Mountain*, VI.

13 ODS, "Mountains and the Origins of Witchcraft," in *EW*, III, 790–792.

14 ODS, *Autunno*, 204–205.

15 C. Larner, "Crimen Exceptum? The Crime of Witchcraft in Europe," in *Crime and the Law. The Social History of crime in Western Europe since 1500*, V. A. C. Gatrell, B. Lenman, G. Parker, eds., London, 1980, 49–50.

16 ODS, *Autunno*, 179.

17 W. Monter, *Accusations*, in *EW*, I, 3–4.

18 B. Levack, "The Decline and End of Witchcraft Prosecutions," in M. Gijswijt-Hofstra, B. Levack, R. Porter, *The Eighteenth and Nineteenth Centuries*, 88; Id. *The Witch –Hunt*, 74–108.

19 W. Monter, *Accusations*; B. Levack, *Introduction*, in *The Oxford Handbook of Witchcraft*, 5–6.

20 R. Kieckhefer, "Magic and its Hazards in the Late Medieval West," in *The Oxford Handbook of Witchcraft*, 16.

21 J. Sharpe, *Instrument of Darkness: Witchcraft in England, 1550–1750*, Harmondsworth, 1996, 105. On the Continent, most recent studies confirm that few suspicions of witchcraft lead to formal accusations.

22 J. Diamond, *The World until Yesterday*, ch. 9.

23 W. Monter, "Geography of the Witch Hunts," in *EW*, II, 413.

24 N. Cohn, *Europe's Inner Demons*; W. Behringer, *Witches and Witch-Hunts*.

25 "Fully developed European witchcraft was never mentioned in inquisitorial records from such southern Spanish regions as Estremadura, Andalusia, Granada, Murcia, or Valencia, and very rarely in New Castile," W. Monter, "Witchcraft in Iberia," in *The Oxford Book of Witchcraft*, 273.

26 R. Briggs, *Witches & Neighbors*, 345; A. Rowlands, *Witchcraft Narratives in Germany: Rothenburgh, 1561–1652*, Manchester, 2003, 2.

27 B. Ankarloo, S. Clark, *The Period of the Witch Trials*, in *Witchcraft and Magic in Europe*, 4, xiii.

28 B. Levack, "Witchcraft and the Law," in *Witchcraft and Magic in Europe*, 4, 482.

29 Essex Assizes, in "Table1. Indictments for Felony in Nine Counties, Selected Periods, 1550–1749," in J. Sharpe, *Crime in Early Modern England 1550–1750*, London & New

York, 2015, 55. The other counties were: Middlesex Sessions, Sussex Assizes, Hertfordshire Assizes, Cheshire Court, Devon Assizes, Cornwall Assizes, Norfolk and Suffolk Assizes.

30 For Sienese State justice, ODS, *Peccato-Penitenza-Perdono*, 32; for the Inquisition justice; Id., *Sienese New State*, in *EW*, IV, 1035. From a demographic point of view, the two areas were similar, with populations of just over 100,000 inhabitants.

31 J. Sharpe, *Crime*, 56. In Lorraine, one of the areas with the highest persecution rate in Europe in relation to the population, "only a minority of suspects ever came before a court, while many villages never saw a single trial"; R. Briggs, *The Witches of Lorraine*, Oxford, 2007, 382.

32 R. M. Toivo, "Witchcraft and Gender," in *The Routledge History of Witchcraft*, 220.

33 The activity of the Papal Inquisition declined rapidly in the second half of the eighteenth century. The Tuscan branch was closed in 1782.

34 They were incidents in the jurisdiction of the Podesterie of Bagno a Ripoli and Campi, of the Vicariates of Prato, Pescia, San Miniato, San Giovanni, Radda, Montalcino, of the Commissariat of Pistoia and of the Government of Pisa. See L. Maccabruni, "Dall'Inquisizione alla polizia: superstizioni, stregonerie e sortilegi in Toscana negli anni della Restaurazione," in *Stregonerie e streghe nell'Europa moderna*, Pisa, 1996, 482.

35 M. Gijswijt-Hofstra, "Witchcraft after the Witch-trials," in M. Gijswijt-Hofstra, B. Levack, R. Porter, *The Eighteenth and Nineteenth Centuries*, 97–128.

36 See W. Behringer, *Witches and Witch-Hunts*, 222–223; W. de Blécourt, "The Witch, her Victim, the Unwitcher and the Researcher: The Continued Existence of Traditional Witchcraft," in *Witchcraft and Magic in Europe*, 6, W. de Blécourt, R Hutton, J. La Fontaine, *The Twentieth Century*, London, 1999, 176–180; J. Devlin, *The Superstitious Mind: French Peasants and the Supernatural in the Nineteenth Century*, New Haven, CT, 1987, 100–119.

37 The *sudden infant death syndrome* (SIDS) describes the abrupt and inexplicable death of those born under the age of 1 year. The syndrome is still the leading cause of healthy children death today. See B. Levack, "The Decline and End of Witchcraft Prosecutions," in *The Oxford Handbook of Witchcraft*, 435.

38 O. Davies, "Witchcraft Accusations in Nineteenth- and Twentieth-Century Europe," in *The Routledge History of Witchcraft*, 290. "Until the twentieth century English villagers continued to scratch, swim and even murder suspected witches. There was a lynch as late as 1945," see M. Gaskill, *Witchfinders: A Seventeenth-Century English Tragedy*, London, 2005, 285.

19

THE DISENCHANTMENT OF THE WORLD

The themes of suffering and harm in our investigation have been analyzed as the intentional result of a will to do evil, the neurobiological roots of which found fertile ground for development in agricultural civilizations. We consider it essential to continue this quite often secretive history of the witchcraft system with an episode from the recent past.

The case points to malefic agency as the mental result of the personalization of the damage, to the burden of closeness and intimacy of little groups in village communities in the deep French countryside. The sudden impact of the way of life of the enlarged urban centers weakened the traditional aspects of the small community based on kinship ties, on duties and solidarity of neighborhood, on the constraints of shame culture. All this was confirmed by an ethnographer who in the 1970s investigated the persistence of malefic spells in the *bocage* areas, with residential settlements scattered across farms and hamlets. When asked about witchcraft beliefs, a farmer replied: "[It is not clear] under what pretext city dwellers should cast incantation with each other, since among them any real contact or knowledge is lacking."[1] The European countryside is thus under fire. And its inhabitants, labeled as a "sack of potatoes" in the merciless words of Karl Marx, drag their existence into the "idiocy of rural life."[2]

City dwellers, then. They are the leading actors of this chapter, giving substance to a conjecture. By developing known concepts, we argue that European urban civilization, accelerating the evolutionary potential of human neurophysiology, triggers conflicting ways and criteria of evaluation in respect to theories and behaviors.[3]

***

In Thomas Mann's *Doctor Faustus*, Serenus Zeitblom meditated: perhaps there is a "psychic disposition of the city,"[4] almost as if the matter of urban space, like the time spent in the city, is not so much a property of the physical world as a presupposition

DOI: 10.4324/9781003414377-21

of new human experiences. People live in a sensate world whose reality is described in terms of relations that are basic to the understanding of our perceptions. Therefore, let us seriously consider the idea, "that there is something psychic in everything."[5] We want to reflect on the hypothesis of the influence of large residential centers in modeling human synapses in relation to magical beliefs.

In the century of the Enlightenment, the scenery, the order of ideas is reversed. Magic convictions occur in a state of ambiguous silence which can conventionally be alluded to in Max Weber's words, the disenchantment of the world, an allusive, fortunate label, even if too widespread. To understand the cerebral foundations of the persistence of witchcraft it is worth checking whether in the very modern age, among the multiplicity of factors that contributed to a new vision of the world, some strong links that ended up accelerating the path of people towards this alleged disillusion of minds are identifiable. We will select the spatial and demographic factors, questioning what function urban centers played in stimulating human synaptic connections, multiplying the cultural practices that alter and influence body/brain chemistry and directing them towards additional/alternative interpretations of worldly things.

The problem is to be accessed from its origins. We want to focus on Adam Smith's remark: the journey of man towards better living conditions involved the intervention of factors of discontinuity with respect to the organization of the economy based on tilling the land that had characterized the ancient and medieval world. It is no coincidence that "since the fall of the Roman empire, European political systems have been in favor of the arts, manufacturing and trade, which are the activity of the city."[6] With these words, from the opening pages of the *Inquiry into the Nature and Causes of the Wealth of Nations* Smith anticipates a concept he will repeat several times, namely that trade in medieval and modern cities ended up reversing the spontaneous course of things in the production of goods. Consumption, comforts, and luxury of urban centers hindered man's natural inclinations indicating that subsistence comes before comfort and luxury. In the development of modern European states, things went differently because of the growing detachment of trade and commercial cities from the surrounding countryside.[7]

What Smith underlines is the disturbance of the natural order of things in the economy brought about by medieval urban reconstructions that characterized the economic expansion of the European continent. The witchcraft system, organic to agrarian civilization, had encountered no structured obstacles capable of limiting its operation in classical cities. When towns were re-founded in the second millennium of Christian era, supported by the yields of the expanding countryside, their mold is new and behavioral similarities with rural areas constantly slow down. Is this the embryogenesis of the new psychic disposition on which *Doctor Faustus*'s character is mulling? The question to be asked is simple then: are man's immediate inclinations (cerebral predispositions) undergoing an adaptation because, due to the Anthropocene, a different mental mood is generated in cities? In the following paragraph, we would like to speculate on a late medieval German proverb, city air makes you free, projecting its perceptions forward.

The Air of the City Makes You Free

In addition to some residual rural servitude, what could a city atmosphere be free from? From the perspective of an extended, multi-thousand-year period, the role played by demographic factors and the distribution of men on the land has been underlined, specifying that housing conglomerates represented a nursery favorable to the formation of potential witchcraft agency. The stabilization of semi-nomadic groups catalyzed the essential emotional ingredients of witchcraft agency. Proximity and neighborhood tested man's basic emotions. Empathy, shame and envy, the seedbed of interpersonal confrontations, are found in villages as much as in the sophisticated milieu of ancient cities. In fact, even larger urban centers were well ingrained in the magical vision of the world and could not significantly develop skeptical social figures corroding the dominant ideology. These remained latent intellectual phenomena. There is no consensus on the nature of an urbanization which, although strongly developed in the imperial age, retained a rural imprint.[8]

Still, whatever the case may be, the early Middle Ages demographic collapse swept away all trends, intervening in European history as a profound discontinuity bringing the Continent closer to a protohistoric social and economic context. The repopulation of the continent after the year one thousand produced new situations that fueled the ways of reasoning of city dwellers in divergent directions. On one side, in smaller towns and cities the relatively large urban environment might have proven to be a fertile ground for witchcraft accusations and prosecutions.[9] But on the other, the direction of development of the social context of the demographically most important urban centers was different. And here we refer once again to Max Weber and his "rational city" as an ideal typology.[10] In the first European urban flowering seeds leading to different attitudes are to be encountered, bringing out the contrasting potential of the residential centers where a humanistic culture favored by "courts, universities, religious groups could germinate. [...] The skepticism towards the belief in witchcraft had its roots in this same atmosphere."[11] The culture of a "civic rationalism" fueled an attitude of doubting peculiar to the centers of Humanism and the Renaissance. These potentials materialized beyond a certain demographic threshold. Unquestionably, some fields insinuated themselves into medieval and even modern urbanizations. But in the end, taking care of the land involved much more than working it; it tied to kinship organizations, to the neighborhood of trade and belief, to the tribe, the temple, the village, the guild and the church.[12] A whole human tissue breeding ground of magical convictions. When cities became a more complex sociological structure, they paved the way, step by step, for the future disenchantment of the world. Two national examples highlight the direction of change.

***

A differential geography of European economic, demographic, social and cultural changes shows divergent rates of urbanization. A decisive advance took place in the English countryside where possessive individualism was about to replace the community ethic of neighborhood support. For no nineteenth-century Old Continent nation as for England could one talk about of a disappearance of the peasants, now completely transformed into wage laborers. After so much "walking under-ground," the old mole of capitalism – to use Karl Marx's abused expression probably inspired by a passage in *Hamlet* – clearly came into the open, marking an alteration of the social grammar inherent in the relationship among men.[13] The transition from a way of life based on traditional agriculture to one oriented towards the pursuit of private profit marks a profound break with the environment in our *Homo sapiens*. It was a painful change for the subsistence of many who lived in the countryside affected by a change. From an economic point of view, the theoretical debate caused by the tragedy of common lands, necessary for the livelihood of the poorest, is far from exhausted.[14] But there were benefits, too. They accelerated a redistribution of people's empathic gra-dient in a direction that would separate the city from the countryside, the center from the periphery. The detachment marks a fading of the embedded-ness of witchcraft. Between 1550 and 1750, conditions were created for a more significant growth of the urban population and focus must be placed on the multiplication of centers with more than ten thousand residents. A city/coun-tryside relationship was activated in which it was the city that influenced the countryside. It marks the beginning of a critical trend that undermined the well-established system of witchcraft and ended up making it lose its reason for being in the face of the new social relations promoted by the city. On one hand, the moral economy of the countryside was pressed by a competitive political economy and the socio-economic mechanism of a self-sufficient pea-sant world, forged by natural control, physiological to the equilibrium of small communities, gradually gave way to a culture dependent on the opportunities that cities offered. On the other, those who went to live in the cities began to adapt to the new fundamentals of human relations generated by the most marked forms of urbanization. It was a slow mutation. No doubt, traditional forms of spells, those to which Shakespearean *Merry Wives* allude colorfully, had not waned in the countryside or the small towns and continued. However, even before the middle of the seventeenth century, with one exception, trials were no longer instructed by the same state justice.[15] At the beginning of the twentieth century, residents in cities outnumbered those in the countryside and the consolidation depended on the number of medium and medium-sized centers, considered the critical demographic threshold for an urbanization of behavior.[16]

The English example is substantially confirmed in the Dutch case that anticipates this trend. In the interconnected urban area, the Randstad, Amsterdam, Leiden, The Hague, and other centers had moved away from the closed and corporate medieval atmosphere. Cities became legally, physically, and economically more open; social centers that stimulated a variety of consumption that developed integrated systems producing an impact in social relations.[17]

The English and Dutch cases are certainly exceptions in Europe. It remains to be specified and interpreted in which way cities, by triggering different types of activities and habits, favored what is called a *behavioral urbanization*.[18] As a set of balanced powers, in urban centers the witchcraft system appeared as a crippled social formation, because the anti-witch mediator figure gets weakened in the new communication contexts where differently qualified competitors were operative. We know that in large or exceptionally large cities there is no trace of extensive repression. What made Hamburg, London, Vienna, Paris, Venice, or Madrid different? The answer is clear: these sociological monsters became centers of innovation and creativity to transform the attitudes of the inhabitants towards basic issues like of health and bad luck, spreading them in the centers of some high demographic consistency. Among the factors most responsible for the change the intrusion of the state into communities in view of an improvement in personal safety and forms of assistance, the bettering in food production and supply and the spread of new products should be listed. It has been argued that the discovery of spirits, the arrival of tobacco, sugar, coffee, and tea in Europe have led to great revolutions in customs.[19] In short, there were novelties that reshaped urbanized people, if still linked to conformism of any autarchic culture, leading to a series of inter-related circumstances that alter the entire context of communication.[20]

An example taken from the sphere of health throws light on the probable formation of a different collective attitude. During the eighteenth century in a flourishing economic center like Bristol – whose population was around 25,000 – the wealthy classes no longer turned to fortune-tellers of the witchcraft system to solve unknown sicknesses but rather to socially respectable professionals as a symbol of their belonging to the wealthy classes. It was an additional hard blow dealt to the pillars of the system because these experts were doctors from a discipline that had left behind the propensity to understand mysterious diseases as malefic evil, practiced with diabolical artifice.[21] In developed urban milieus an evaporation of the natural control of witchcraft was highly likely under way. What changed was the intellectual perception of soothsayers "no longer seen as servants of Satan but rather as cheaters."[22] Testimonies like such a transformation of reasoning abound and all move in the direction of a reappraisal of arguments on the sensitive issues of health and harm.

The Psychic Disposition of the City

The formation of an urbanized, "bourgeois" way of thinking has a long history that had already found an early and detailed arrangement in Leon Battista Alberti: "an amalgam of successful practices with theoretical-normative elements, but it is not an abstract intellectual concept. It was favored by certain reasons and values that facilitated thinking, individualism and achievements."[23] The Weberian typology of a rational city is enriched by emphasizing the psychic nature embodied by its material qualities. The urban space finds a concrete definition in its multiple and structured articulations: institutional, ethical, recreational. Thomas Mann's insight of a "psychic disposition of the city" finds a neurobiological explanation in the plasticity of the human brain, stimulated by new environmental situations.

At the sunset of the Paleolithic, *Homo sapiens*'s anatomically completed cerebral matter got remodeled in response to the economic, social, and cultural transformations introduced by the incoming agrarian civilizations. To measure the brain's slow adaptations that developed over millennia, distinguishing by geographical area and social classes remains objectively difficult. Nonetheless, in this line of examination based on long duration factors, the impact of the early modern growth of cities, due to their multiple novelties, marks a powerful discontinuity that further affects the plasticity of human grey matter. What will a neuro-historical examination look for behind the *behavioral urbanization* established by current studies (Chapter 28)?

A large field of adaptations is to be evaluated, including the rise of public street lighting, altering the rhythms of daily life.[24] Changes in the quality and quantity of human consumption of available calories resulting from basic nutrition and a wide range of products available are to be considered. New neural configurations were generated that altered the states of the body–brain system and evolved into distinct thinking of which evidence abounds. The interactions between body–brain and environment–body define people's subjectivity (their mind) as an ongoing process.[25] Reactions to the growing prominence of the media and a commercial culture produced by a thriving exchange economy are well known. They are effectively summed up in a generalization: "they contributed much more to the marginalization of witchcraft in the most advanced European regions than any direct political, legal or ecclesiastical action dictated by the throne or the altar."[26] Historical research documents that in bigger flourishing urban centers residual witchcraft ideas were now accompanied – ending up being overshadowed – by an interpretation of human relationships destined for a perennial future, that of consumerist capitalism. Inside the protean nature of a market-oriented cosmogony a disguised continuance of false beliefs is attested.

Impasse

As mentioned in the previous chapter, it is not our intention to leave the question of early modern witch hunts as a cognitive puzzle without an attempt to answer it. For this purpose, it is worth asking: since in many parts of Europe there were no formal witchcraft accusations and trials, what was happening among the populations of those areas? We do not know. In face of dearth of documentation historians rarely initiate a search. "Obviously, research can only go so far when sources are missing or were never generated from the start."[27]

As it is known, the study of witchcraft has called for various methodological approaches that crossed the boundaries of other disciplines including law, cultural history, and anthropology. A little more than fifty years after the publication of Hugh Trevor-Roper's lively essay, which in a way started a series of new interpretative waves of the early modern witch hunts, perhaps the time is ripe to argue that there is something in the minds of men that often generates this cultural institution: the understanding of a mental phenomenon such as the malefice is incomplete if its brain roots are neglected. A global approach to the study of evil witchcraft will consider not only the "system of differences" between the countries where the phenomenon is documented, but also the differences with the same European countries where witch hunts are not at all attested.[28]

Most recently further exhortations have come from scholars: a role is to be played by active spectators, because of historians' "familiarity with an enormous wealth of behavioral data and the interpretative challenges they raise [...]; new concepts, methods, approaches will need to be found."[29] These solicitations are valid even for areas that have left no written trace of witchcraft agency. In these large parts of Europe, due to a biological homogeneity of the population, brain functioning does not differ, and people experience the same feelings of jealousy, envy, retaliation, wickedness, seed bed of interpersonal animosity. What, then, were their reactions to mysterious, unexplained misfortunes of any kind that happened in life? How do we proceed without judicial sources?

In any scientific enterprise it is worth taking risks, venturing into the unknown and reformulating a question. What result could extensive exploration strategies, in areas not affected by crises, give? Local studies of this kind, aimed at indexing all sources, secular and ecclesiastical, could verify the existence, dimensions, fluctuations and quality of discourse on abstract concepts, on evil and the possible ways of controlling it, on the spread of controversies following defamation, on the extent empathic sentiments buried in testaments, on popular skepticism probably hidden in the behavior of those *esprits forts* never absent in any community.[30] Almost half a century ago this experiment was put into practice in England in the parish of Earls Colne (700 souls) from 1380 to 1750, aimed at measuring the recurrences of the term "evil" and related topic.[31] Such enterprises are now made feasible and less expensive by "a set of digital tools designed to analyze the huge amount of paper documents that can be relevant to any large survey."[32]

For the same neuroscience, the realization of the Human Genome Project has revealed enormous potential. The implications for Medicine in general are evident and include the evolution of famous pathogens (origins of leprosy, tuberculosis, the Black Death bacterium). Cognitive advances are to be expected for the evolutionary biology of the brain. What will happen when we have genome-wide data of populations that lived shortly after the transition to agriculture?[33] Studies of ancient DNA stimulate research into natural selection and the rhythm and nature of human adaptation in recent historical ages. Investigating changing human biology in relation to the gelatinous gray mass is on the agenda of neuroscience. The hunt for the gene is extended to hereditary genetic differences that underlie individual differences in psychological traits to find pathways that from genes, through the brain, lead to behavior.[34] Closer to one specific critical point of our book, the equation witch = woman, perhaps genetic probing might give a basis to (or definitely refute) the thesis of an "essential difference" of the female brain from the male one, to which we return in Chapter 24. In conclusion, it seems advisable to maintain that the exploitation of the identical quarry represented by man's primary and secondary emotions, reported by early modern witchcraft trials, is improved using neuroscientific knowledge. Everything pertaining to witchcraft and religion ends up being abstract if bio-psychological premises underlining their persisting strength and articulations are neglected. In the future, hopefully, a consilience of humanistic and scientific disciplines will promote such research directions.

And in this book, with reference to the said cognitive puzzle of early modern large witch hunts? Are we satisfied by the vague explanation given above: namely, they were a series of occasional brain short circuits in the nature-culture dynamic, fostered by "the many reasons" that upset an "iron century," after which a new balance, characterized by the definitive triumph of *thinking slow*, was restored? There is a bias in this reasoning. On purpose, the warning of the eminent Laureate is to be recovered: "it's time to say goodbye to simplicity."[35]

In fact, we fear that an anatomy of a mental representation of witchcraft and witch hunts, attentive to the neural mechanisms that underlie reasoning, should also beware of the hypothesis on the oscillations of human thought and behavior regarding evil and superstition: there is no reason to ignore that in our mental life there are incomprehensible things, at least with reference to causality, and the known laws of nature.[36]

Then, causality be damned, we repeat. It has been a huge evolutionary advantage for our species. The inclination of man to link facts together for predictive purposes, necessary to protect himself, to solve the puzzle of evil and damage, has however had as a side effect assigning meaning to situations where there seems to be the intervention of chance or chaos. Alas, a conclusion is inevitable: a rational comprehension of the sudden early modern huge pyres shows limitations, including our attempt to draw on neurobiological understanding of what drives behavior.

Perhaps, the analysis of a cerebral phenomenon such as witchcraft requires the use of distinct theories that are complementary to each other. Recent decades in cognitive studies have seen an increasing recognition of the importance of the body, and of the relationship between body and matter to our intelligence of the mind.[37] There is an extended feeling of co-presence, of overlaps and interactions in human mental processing. There are conflicting but complementary descriptions of reality which apply as much to physical world as to thought. Our nature is partly free, partly determined, partly subject to chance, and we are in obvious difficulty in understanding the oscillations of man's counterfactual beliefs.[38] We have declared our bias and are aware of the objections to our ability to understand our mental life in terms of known natural laws.

The anatomy of counterfactual cultural institutions points substantially to the theoretical complexities already mentioned. It is certainly important to explore the differences in the reasoning of individuals and of groups in sociological terms, yet in the final analysis they do nothing but refer to a neurobiological question that crosses time: the very existence of cognitive dissonances in single mind. In other words, we must try to understand why not only in different groups and historical periods but sometimes in the same individuals, beliefs that at first sight appear incompatible coexist, and why they adopt conflicting methods and criteria of evaluation regarding non-evident ideas.[39] It is a problem for cognitive neuroscience: that is a complementarity in human mental processing which, alluding to a separateness of the things of the world, invites us to think about it in an integrated perspective. This coexistence would imply the recognition of epistemological statutes relating to two parallel and independent fields of activity due to the difference in their approach to reality. Rather than science and magic religious ideas having different areas of investigation, coexistence and complementarity would realize in the mental life of individuals a synthesis "not understandable in terms of known natural laws."[40] So, despite all that we have written so far, this impasse may signal something relatively simple. There are different disciplines studying different aspects of the human quest for understanding. The limits of our comprehension are the fact that human brains evolved to solve savanna-induced problems, not to engage in the ultimate quest for the nature of reality. "We know that there are cognitive limits to the power of the human mind, and perhaps at least some of the disciplinary boundaries that have evolved over the centuries simply reflect our epistemic limits."[41]

Notes

1   J. Favret-Saada, *Deadly Words: Witchcraft in the Bocage*, Cambridge, 1980, 81.
2   K. Marx, *The Eighteenth Brumaire of Louis Bonaparte*, 1851; and *The Communist Manifesto*, 1848.
3   G. E. R. Lloyd, *Demystifying Mentalities*, Cambridge, 1990.
4   Thomas Man, *Doctor Faustus*, VI.
5   C. Rovelli, *Helgoland*, 163.
6   Adam Smith, *An Inquiry into the Nature and Causes of the Wealth of Nations*, London, 1776, I, 1.
7   ODS, "Neuropsychological Origins of Witchcraft Cognition. The Geographic and Economic Variable," in *The Oxford Handbook of Witchcraft*, 507–527.
8   J. W. Hanson, *An Urban Geography of the Roman World, 100 BC to AD 300*, Oxford, 2016, 18–21.
9   B. P. Levack, *The Witch-Hunt in Early Modern Europe*, Harlow, 2006³, 137–141.
10 B. Roeck, "Urban Witch Trials," in *Magic, Ritual, and Witchcraft (MR&W)*, 4, 2009, 82–89. See ODS, *Inquisizione, stregoneria, medicina. Siena e il suo stato (1580–1721)*, ch. 10, "Tipologia urbana (Urban Typology)," *Documenti di Storia*, M. Ascheri, ed., Siena, 2000, 157–163.
11 B. Roeck, "Urban Witch Trials," 87.
12 K. Polanyi, *The Great Transformation*.
13 Marx's passion for Shakespeare is well known: "Well said, old mole! Canst work i' th' earth so fast? A worthy pioneer! Once more remove, good friends!"; W. Shakespeare, *Hamlet*, I, sc. v.
14 J. Radkau, *Nature and Power. A Global History of the Environment*, Cambridge, 2008, 36–41. In sixteenth and seventeenth century England neighborly values collapsed: see A. Wood, *Faith, Hope and Charity*.
15 In England, with 1630 the trials declined, except for the massive hunt in East Anglia in 1645–7, due to a legislative lapse of the central power. A precursor in the decline of witchcraft prosecutions was the Parliament of Paris, from 1600 onward.
16 J. de Vries, *European Urbanization 1500–1800*, Cambridge, Mass, 1984, 11–12; and ODS, "On the Neuropsychological Origins of Witchcraft Cognition: The Geographic and Economic Variable," in *The Oxford Handbook of Witchcraft*, 514.
17 In Holland, the last witchcraft trial took place in 1659. There is a significant connection between the decline of the trials and the increase in defamation complaints by those who were called witches; W. de Blécourt, *Termen van toverij: De veranderende betekenis van toverij in Noordoost-Nederland tussen de 16de en 20ste eeuw*, Nijmegen, 1990.
18 J. de Vries, *European Urbanization*, 12, 30, 36, 45.
19 L. Smail, *On Deep History and The Brain*.
20 O. Davies, *Witchcraft, Magic and Culture 1736–1951*, Manchester, 1999.

21 J. Barry, "Piety and the Patient: Medicine and Religion in Eighteenth Century Bristol," in *Patients and Practitioners. Lay Perceptions of Medicine in Pre-Industrial Society*, R. Porter, ed., Cambridge, 1985, 146. On non-conformist physicians, P. Elmer, "Medicine, Witchcraft and the Politics of Healing in Late Seventeenth-Century England," in *Medicine and Religion in Enlightenment Europe*, O. P. Grell, A. Cunningham, eds., Aldershot, 2007, 223–241.

22 O. Davies, *Cunning Folk*, 37.

23 H. Rindermann, *Cognitive Capitalism: Human Capital and the Wellbeing of Nations*, Cambridge, 2018, 183. See Leon Battista Alberti, *I libri della famiglia* (1433/4 and 1440).

24 C. Koslofsky, *Evening's Empire: A History of the Night in Early Modern Europe*, Cambridge, 2011, 130. In 1660 no European city had stable street lighting, but already at the beginning of the new century Amsterdam, Paris, Turin, London, and many French provincial cities and in the Holy Roman Empire, from Hamburg to Vienna had it.

25 D. L. Smail, *On Deep History and The Brain*; L. Hunt, *The Self and Its History*, 1582.

26 R. Porter, *Witchcraft and Magic in Enlightenment, Romantic and Liberal Thought*, 243.

27 L. Ann Homza, "Witch Hunting in Spain. The Sixteenth and Seventeenth Centuries," in *The Routledge History of Witchcraft*, 134.

28 H. Trevor-Roper, *The European Witch-Craze of the 16th and 17th Centuries*, Harmondsworth, 1969; P. Burke, "The Comparative Approach to European Witchcraft," in B. Ankarloo, G. Henningsen, eds., *Early Modern European Witchcraft. Centres and Peripheries*, Oxford, 1990, 434–491.

29 T. Robisheaux, "The German Witch-Trials," in *The Oxford Handbook of Witchcraft*, 197; W. Scheidel, *Evolutionary Psychology and the Historian*, 1575. "An evolutionary approach gives us a whole set of new questions concerning the structural permanence of social tensions, which take on their full importance when we insert them into their environment": see G. Hanlon, "Evolutionary Psychology & Human Ethology for Historians (2006)," unpublished, in *Academia.edu*, 2023, 20.

30 The potentialities to seek out new material in other archives are shown by the achievements of a monograph that throws new light on witch hunts in Spain; see L. Ann Homza, *Village Infernos and Witches' Advocates: Witch-Hunting in Navarra, 1608–1614*, Philadelphia, 2022.

31 A. Macfarlane, M. Spufford, *Reconstructing Historical Communities*, Cambridge, 1977. It might be "telling that in some regions of early modern Germany, the term "evil people" was used as an equivalent of "witches"": see J. Dillinger, "Germany – 'The Mother of the Witches'," in *The Routledge History of Witchcraft*, 98.

32 D. Armitage, *Manifesto per la storia: Il ruolo del passato nel mondo d'oggi*, Roma, 2016, 181.

33 R. Plomin, *Blueprint: How DNA Makes Us Who We Are*, London, 2018.

34 D. Reich, *Who We Are*.

35 G. Edelman, *Wider than The Sky*.

36 R. Trivers, *The Folly*, ch. 14.

37 G. Declerck, O. Gapenne. "Actuality and Possibility: On the Complementarity of Two Registers in the Bodily Constitution of Experience," in *Phenomenology and Cognitive Sciences*, 2009, 8 (3), 285–305. ff10.1007/s11097-009-9128-4; U. Peters, "The complementarity of mind-shaping and mind-reading," in *Phenom Cogn Sci* 18, 2019, 533–549, doi: 10.1007/s11097-018-9584-9; T. Zawidzki, *Mindshaping: A New Framework for Understanding Human Social Cognition*, Cambridge, MA, 2013. See also Núñez, R., Allen, M., Gao, R. *et al.* "What happened to cognitive science?," in *Nat Hum Behav* 3, 2019, 782–791, doi: 10.1038/s41562-019-0626-2

38 C. Rovelli, *Helgoland*, 175–185.

39 G. E. R. Lloyd, *Demystifying Mentalities*, ch. 2.

40 C. Rovelli, *Helgoland*, 184.

41 M. Figliucci, "The Limits of Consilience and the Problem of Scientism," in *Darwin's Bridge*, 259.

20

THE OTHER MONOTHEISMS

Jewish and Islamic

As we have seen, large parts of early modern Europe did not experience any witch hunts and remained immune to the slow blast wave of the "nuclear explosion," symbolized in Exodus 22.18: "do not allow a sorceress to live"; a peremptory prohibition with fatal repercussions for the future of Christians. But what happened to the faithful of the other two vigorous monotheistic religions, the Jewish and the Islamic ones?

If we ask how *maleficium* cases were resolved within Hebrew communities scattered throughout the Old Continent, the answer is embarrassing: we have no precise idea, due to lack of documentation. In the rich witch hunt dossier of Christian Europe there seems to be almost no evidence of open legal actions against Jewish witches.[1]

And what happened to the faithful of the Islamic vigorous monotheism, formed some 600 years after the Christian one, which was also based on a scripture inspired by divine thought, on the Qur'ān? People of Muslim faith, unless throughout history their gray brain matter had developed differently, were subject to the same emotions and drives, and the same cauldron of counterfactual beliefs. What forms of malefic witchcraft control, then, were practiced among these believers? A comparison could throw some additional light on the reasons for the repression in Christian lands.

An Islam without Witch-Hunting

Unfortunately, specific monographs are lacking on the subject. In Islam we do not come across significant cases of witch hunt, and for lack of trial papers, even the system for the informal control of *maleficium* cannot be reconstructed. Available studies are in fact built on folk tales and ethnographic testimonies unusable for outlining a sociological profile of the phenomenon (sex, age, marital status, social status of witches and sorcerers) and the formation of the "making of the witch"

DOI: 10.4324/9781003414377-22

concept, or types of crimes in different geographical areas of the vast Ottoman dominion, or a probable prevalence of men among those who practiced spells and of women among those who committed malefices.[2] How can we, for example, get an idea of what trajectories in the Islamic world did the Mediterranean misogyny (Jewish, Greek, Roman and Christian) have, partially responsible for the equation witch = woman? How can we use Leo African's, a Berber convert, notes? In his *Description of Africa* (1550) he left a too short portrait of three types of magicians and diviners active in Fez (Morocco), practicing spells like those found in Christian lands. It would be risky to generalize about a group of women charmers who boasted a friendship with spirits (jinn) in Fez.

> The third species are women, who make common people believe that they keep friends with certain demons of different sorts, because some are called red demons, some are called white demons and others are called black demons. And when they want to guess [...] they use perfumes with certain fragrances and then, as they say, the devil they call enters their person, so that they immediately change their voice, pretending that the spirit is what speaks for their language [...][3]

There are other disadvantages. From the comparative point of view, namely that of identifying an exact definition of witchcraft in the Abrahamic texts, a comparison encounters two further obstacles. The first concerns the different level of studies to which the sacred texts of the three monotheisms have been subjected. There is no Qur'ānic equivalent of the nineteenth- and twentieth-century biblical and New Testament exegesis which have greatly illuminated the historical background of Judaism and Christianity. Islam has resisted such a critical analysis and the Qur'ān is presented as a revelation that cannot be doubted. "For Islamic intellectual and cultural history, the line between magic and religion does not follow the same course that defined the Enlightenment, with its critique of magic as primitive superstition."[4]

The second disadvantage: to this different approach to the founding sacred texts of monotheistic religions, the fact that the human sciences have timidly entered the Arab intellectual scene must be added.[5] The processes of historical–cultural analysis that have so widely developed in Christian countries and elsewhere, seem to have a weak course in the Islamic world, at least the public one, and even today in Islamic countries there are few translations of scientific literature concerning society, religion, psyche, sex, history.[6]

This sum of documentary and theoretical obstacles stands in the way of a comparison between the reality of witchcraft in Christian and Islamic mono-theism. Yet, despite many setbacks, a crucial knot that differentiates the two faiths can be identified. We propose an interpretation of the absence of exten-sive witchcraft repressions in Islamic lands based on the ambiguous role magic occupies in the Qur'ān in contrast to the explicit condemnation contained in the Bible.

The Ottoman Phase in Europe

Christians and Muslims had not come into contact for the first time in the heyday of witch hunting. Muslim civilization had settled on the margins of Christianity, in Bulgaria, Serbia and finally Hungary. New land borders were established from the Balkans to Bulgaria by multiplying a common historical space that produced acceptance, competition and, with reference to our theme – the formal State control of witchcraft – perhaps a substantial indifference or ignorance of what was happening in the opposite field.[7]

In the southern Slavic countries that fell under the Turkish regime (roughly the current Bosnia, Serbia, Montenegro, Macedonia, Albania, and Bulgaria), no State and Church persecutions similar to the ones that occasionally occurred in Western and Central Europe, can be found. Rulers cared little about how malefices were seen by the dominated populations. There are no traces of legal norms and trials. By contrast, the case of Transylvania (part of today's Romania), a vassal state of the Ottoman Empire, is significant. In the principality, whose rulers were of the Calvinist or Protestant faith, we note different cultural models and have sources relating to trials from the end of the sixteenth century.

With reference to southern Slavic countries, some historiographical discussions, unsubstantiated by any monograph, claim the existence of accusations of witchcraft and more generally of supernatural phenomena such as vampires in Ottoman lands. Those who communicated with the supernatural to predict the future or to heal were not considered witches or sorcerers and even if criticized by religious authorities, were not persecuted. "No doubt, there is no evidence of massive and systematic persecution of magic and witchcraft by the Ottoman authorities."[8]

The absence of a flow of accusations and consequent judicial proceedings in Ottoman lands is a silence that remains unexplained.[9] We will move accordingly based on the line of reasoning: a capital condemnation of witchcraft did not fall within the religious horizon of the Ottoman dynasties as it was considered alien to their faith; and laws could not even be produced to monitor malefices because there were no clear legislative precedents.

The Qur'ānic Difference

Islamic magic and demonology did not arise ex-novo but was grafted on to ideas of previous magical-religious contexts: pre-Islamic and Bedouin Arab, Coptic, and Jewish culture. The real protagonists were the jinns, aerial or fiery bodies, intelligent and imperceptible. They were spirits of both sexes, although not made of flesh and blood; it is believed that they ate, drank, and could be killed. They interfere with human beings and if they wanted, they could cause material damage and misfortune to people. It would be wrong to call them evil spirits; better to regard them as morally neutral demons.[10]

The existence of jinn was officially recognized, as the Prophet had them integrated into the Qur'ān, which makes continuous references to them. Iblis / Satan, the perverse version of the jinn, is the evil "whisperer" of temptations (Sura 114). In short stories, in religious literature, in works of a juridical nature, the nature of the jinn is often misunderstood out of an evident concern to respect the Qur'ān, which actually speaks of them in an opaque way. It has been observed that, "Islam by conferring an official and prominent place on belief in demons opens the door to the magician."[11] This opacity of the Arabic sacred text is added to the essential basic fact: invoking the jinn with an imperative and severe language, through extremely long rituals, they are forced to obey the magician, because they remain servants of Allah: "Those who invoke [...] are Allah's servants"(Sura 7.194). Magicians derive their strength from the control they can exert over these ambivalent demons. That witchcraft (*sihr*) exists is a dogma supported by the Tradition of the sayings of the prophet; a tradition that is based on another chapter (Sura 2.102): "The demons taught the peoples magic." The crux of licit and illicit magic, then, was the control of demons. Conversely, the sorcerers made offerings to the jinn; gifts that displeased Allah. On this point there is doubt: even if blamed, was evil magic to be punished with death?

The idea that God has his enemies is present in the Qur'ān as well as in the Old and New Testament. In the Qur'ān the adversaries of God are defined as non-believers and infernal fire awaits them (Suras 2.98; 41.19–28). Not unlike Judaism and Christianity, the Qur'ān insists on a cosmic clash between good and evil, light and darkness. In the three religions we find the enemy, the archetype of God's antagonist, Satan. Giving in to his temptations means becoming an apostate, and apostasy is punished with death. As we have seen, in Exodus, Leviticus and Deuteronomy, the Bible sanctioned sorcerers and witches with death and the entire spectrum of anti-witchcraft punishments. On these points there is no coincidence among the great monotheistic religions. The Qur'ān lacks an equally explicit exhortation to the killing of the malefic people and, above all, there is no condemnation of the beneficial use of magic. Recent interpretations on the origins of the Islamic holy book suggest the hypothesis of a selective assimilation of Pentateuch books that would not have allowed the Bible lethal prescriptions against the witch to enter the Qur'ān.[12]

Therapeutic Magic

A clue to understand the differences between monotheisms is provided precisely by these cases related to people's health. In other words, can we infer that the Qur'ānic acceptance of therapeutic magic, introducing a substantial element of tolerance, has anesthetized the persecution of evil witchcraft? Let us examine the point.

The power of magicians found wide application in healing the sick. The line between its beneficial and evil force is thin, nevertheless magic, and its use to heal was accepted by Tradition, *hadith*. There was no harm seen in magical spells aimed at healing a sick person. Medicine was often misunderstood as a form of counter-witchcraft, and the word *t'ibb* in classical Arabic means as much magic as medicine.[13] Not unlike the Christian West, it was believed that various work activities (that of executioner, blacksmith, barber) involved occult skills to operate as healers. To sum up, it seems possible to conclude that the Qur'ān, not prescribing punishments for those who practice magic for healing purposes, does not prohibit it. The difference with Christian lands could not be more striking.

Muslims were subject to the anxieties and fears caused by envy and the evil eye, just like the faithful of other religious beliefs. In all lands where Islam spread, magic, in forms like that of Christian lands (therapeutic, divinatory, protective, maleficent) performed the function of solving the general complications of daily life and alleviating or eliminating those caused by the malevolent intention of antisocial people or people endowed with an innate negativity (carrier of the evil eye, "aïn"). And here lies the obstacle: we cannot say much about how the presence of evil men or women was managed in practice. The opinion of Ibn Khaldūn, a fourteenth-century North African philosopher and historian, that the work of sorcerers should be sanctioned with death penalty, did not have any effect.[14] The point is not discussed in legal texts. For some founders of Islamic law schools, learning or teaching magic was considered a crime of apostasy (but a significant exception was made with respect to those who invoked demons to cure epileptics). For the same authors, a magician who caused an injury was punished with death and the decision had a Qur'ānic value, it was not an application of the lex talionis. Other jurists disagree.[15]

Be this as it may, what were the outcomes of these divergent positions? Again, a flaw in historical research prevents an answer. There are only some Iraqi testimonies according to which under the Caliphate of Umar (643) there were three executions for evil (the sex is uncertain).[16] But later, regarding the execution of a sorcerer, Caliph Uthman declared that according to Islamic law it had been a mistake.[17] In practice, although magic remains one of the most serious infractions to be shrouded by the suspicion of apostasy, there is no evidence to assert that "capital punishment is the rule, as in all ancient religions, especially in Judaism."[18] The absence of bloody witch hunts is not surprising, given the particular role that therapeutic magic had assumed within the Muslim religion, making any systemic repressive actions at least contradictory. An absence perhaps partly due to the natural control of the occult crime. However, we have no sources to prove it.

How to summarize? Although witchcraft "was generally considered a capital offense in juridical discourse, historically Muslim society did not participate in anything akin to the persecutions of witches [...] that shapes significant chapters in medieval and early modern European history."[19] Nothing similar is recorded in Muslim lands, where for an uncertain number of supposed witches, men, and women, casting spells did not cost their lives. And this seems to us no small balance; outcome due to the embedding of magic in the Qur'ān that made those bloodbaths unworkable.

Notes

1 A case of Sienese inquisition seems to be "an absolute rarity" (W. Behringer, personal communication). See ODS, "Finizia detta la Sciabacca, una strega ebrea di Pitigliano

(1666)," in *Le Inquisizioni cristiane e gli ebrei*, Atti dei Convegni dei Lincei, 191, Roma, 2003, 431–448.

2 R. Irwin, "Islamic Witchcraft and Magic," in *EW*, II, 569–563.

3 L. Africano, "La descrizione dell'Africa," in G. B. Ramusio, 'La descrizione dell'Africa di Giovan Lioni Africano," in Id., *Navigazioni e viaggi*, M. Milanesi, ed., Torino, 1978, I, 192. Our translation.

4 T. Zadeh, "Magic, Marvel, and Miracle in Early Islamic Thought," in *The Cambridge History of Magic and Witchcraft*, 238.

5 "Even though themes such as occult sciences, a fixation on the metaphysical, magic, demons, and the devil are mentioned in both state-centered documents and diaries or travelogue texts in Ottoman historiography, these concepts have not yet been closely examined as the research subjects of historians"; in F. Yaşa, "Güneşin Altında Yeni Bir Şey Yok: 16. Yüzyılda Osmanlı İmparatorluğunda Define Hikâyeleri (Nothing New Under the Sun: Stories of Treasure in the 16th Century Ottoman Empire). Osmanlı Mirası Araştırmaları Dergisi," abstract.

6 N. Wade, *The Faith Instinct*, 172–187, S. Pinker, *Enlightenment*, 440. See *L'orientalisme aujourd'hui*, in "Annales. E.S.C.," 35, 3–4, 1980, 415. A delay that persists after decades; see Adonis, *Violenza e Islam. Conversazioni con Houria Abdelouahed*, Milano, 2015, *passim*; E. Galli della Loggia, "Le troppe parole che l'Islam non dice," *Il Corriere della Sera*, 11 luglio 2016.

7 From the small number of Muslim visitors to Christian Europe, no comments were received on any acute phase of witch hunts. The few studies on the West written by authors of that faith, such as that of the Ottoman historian and scholar Kàtib Celebi (1655), lack information on events of this type.

8 M. Sariyannis, "Of Ottoman Ghosts, Vampires and Sorcerers: An Old Discussion Disinterred," in *Archivum Ottomanicum*, 2013, 191. On pre-Ottoman Islamic magic, see *Annales Islamologiques*, 11 (1972), 287–340; G. H. Bousquet, "Fiqh et sorcellerie: Petite contribution à l'étude de la sorcellerie en Islam," in *Annales de l'Institute des Etudes Orientales*, 8 (1949–50), 230–234.

9 A. Tunc Sen, "Practicing Astral Magic in Sixteenth-Century Ottoman Istanbul: A Treatise on Talisman Attributed to Ibn Kemal," in *MR&W*, 12, 1, 2017, 66–88.

10 They were like the capricious and unpredictable Sicilian *donni de fuera* (women from outside). For example, jinn and donni "have the inspiration of exchanging children and the replacement is deduced from sudden changes: the child withers [...] Both the jinn and the ladies sometimes decide to give them back, or because they change taste (both are fickle) or because the child's relatives have managed to propitiate them." E. Panetta, *L'Italia in Africa: Studi italiani di etnografia e di folklore della Libia*, Roma, 1963, I, 139.

11 E. Doutté, *Magie et religion dans l'Afrique du nord*, Paris, 1994 (1908), 54. See *Magic and Divination in Early Islam*, Emilie Savage-Smith, ed., Trowbridge, 2004, xvii–xx.

12 Y. D. Nevo, J. Koren, *Crossroads to Islam. The origins of the Arab Religion and the Arab State*, Amherst, New York, Prometheus Books, 2003, pp. 224–226, 340–344. Only future research will validate these perspectives on which scholars' consent is lacking. The revisionist theses basically refer to J. Wansbrough, *Koranic Studies*, New York, 1977.

13 E. Doutté, *Magie et religion*, 36–40.

14 Ibn Khaldūn, *The Muqqaddimah: An Introduction to History*, London, 1967, 392.

15 M. W. Dols, *The Theory of Magic*, 96–97.

16 M. G. Morony, *Irak After the Muslim Conquest*, Princeton, 1984; Id., *Between civil wars; the caliphate of Mu'awiyah*, Albany, 1987.

17 M. W. Dols, *The Theory of Magic*, 98.

18 E. Doutté, *Magie et religion*, 337.

19 T. Zadeh, "Magic, Marvel, and Miracles," 238. The rare evidence of a witchcraft system in Islamic lands was possibly due to the fact that pastoralists were a considerable portion of the Ottoman population.

PART III
In the Laboratory

There were people ill-intentioned towards their neighbors and willing to harm them by resorting to witchcraft. Let us investigate the documented reality of a deliberate evil agency and the anxious tortuosity of human intelligence by drawing more closely on perceptions coming from brain science laboratories.

DOI: 10.4324/9781003414377-23

21

CASE STUDY 1

The Personalization of Damage

> I don't know whose eyes make my tender lambs sick.
>
> *Virgil*

Witchcraft accusations of the sixteenth and seventeenth centuries prove the persistence of ancestral patterns of thought in which some sudden, unpredictable misfortunes are not traced back to events of the same type (to other deaths or damages of people, animals, things) but to different causes, not to objects but to subjects, not to things but to persons. Medium and large-scale witchcraft trials – due to the multiplier role played by suspects of complicity in the diabolical plot that expanded the number of criminals – tend to hide the psychological reasons that were established between the injured parties and offenders, because the *noise*, "the undesirable variability in judgement of the same problem" they generated makes the examination difficult.[1] Individual proceedings, on the contrary, shed some light on "the background of continuing suspicions, accusations, harassment, insults and local scandals that never reached the stage of a formal complaint or trial."[2] Single trial protagonists show the psychological logic driving their behavior: a personalization of the damage suffered, that we have argued is supported by automatic modalities of processing information. Here are some examples.

Why, around the year 39 BC, did Virgil complain in an eclogue that his lambs died, struck by someone's evil envy? Why, sixteen centuries later, in 1589, in England, did a Southampton tanner complain that his pigs had suddenly died after dancing and jumping very strangely, as if they had been bewitched and suspected that those deaths were the evil work of a neighbor? Why, in 1605, in Tuscany, did the noble parents of an infant, found dead in cradle, with a pang in his head and the right side of his chest bruised, conclud that the little one "had died from witchcraft [...] that Gata and Gioma are publicly suspected of similar crimes and atrocities in that place"? Why was the fifty-year-old Maddalena accused in the Modena area? In 1651 a witness reported:

DOI: 10.4324/9781003414377-24

I have never heard that she is a witch, only I have understood that she goes to beg in houses as that she is poor and that when they do not give her charity some misfortune happens to them. In Giovanni's house he asked for milk, and it being denied all his cows gave little milk for about ten days. In Giuseppe's house he asked for a chicken and being denied it three other chickens died immediately.[3]

Why were people not wondering how the damage had occurred but who had done it? Why was the guilt personalized? The search for an answer takes us back to that primordial thinking originated in the depth of prehistory, when for our ancestors coping with potentially dangerous situations could be a life-or-death problem. Human decisions, when they occur in conditions of uncertainty, are biased by psychological, biological, idiosyncratic and contextual factors. And the intentionality of an event (such as the spell) tends to exclude chance,[4] perhaps more so if the human predictive brain might be more prone to computation errors (attributing certainty to the spell) under more volatile environments.

Explaining Misfortunes

Between Thinking Fast and Thinking Slow

It is advisable to remember that in trials in which the personalization of misfortune occurred the context remains ambiguous. The mental oscillations of the offended parties hardly appear. It follows that such personalization drive is not precisely the result of an automatic attribution of responsibility. In fact, the problem of causation appears in a complex, blurred way. To clarify the point, recalling what has been previously explained when dealing with human reasoning mechanisms and the *fast thinking* and *slow thinking* phases, will help. In order to explain misfortune, the brain does not by default privilege a sequence of reasoning leading to systematic *ad personam* specification of what caused serious trouble, but rather finds itself tossed between conflicting solutions.

The organ of thought, formed in the prehistoric predatory world, specified through an elastic wiring that invariably leads to articulated hypotheses: it is an irreproducible software considered as a set of modules or cognitive systems and derived from the human biological endowment functioning in the environment where people live.[5] These systems, being activated, in turn set in motion brain devices responsible for searching agencies.

In the entire physical, animal, and human universe, essences are imagined from which one can expect positivity or negativity. The result of multiple interactions of the brain systems is a mind working to simulate various and complex scenarios relating to the intentions of mysterious presences (people, animals, spirits). Our hominins, for hundreds of thousands of years prone to suggestions from multiple agencies, at the critical moment of evolution with the appearance of the *Sapiens*, found themselves enriched by specific mental endowments required by community life:

We have special equipment to recognize our relatives in a group, we know how to deal with group members and outsiders, we have insights into trustworthy people, we have inferential systems that pay particular attention to those who deceive and to not cooperate and which generate particular emotions when the principles of social exchange are violated.[6]

The tendency to personalize the damage certainly found fertile ground for spreading with the transition from societies made up of cohabitation of small non-kin groups or tribes to chiefdoms where conflict resolution began to obey agreed norms in line with the most complex network of social relations. But such explanation of misfortune was strongly conditioned by the neural mechanisms activated by the *fast thinking* that had imprinted itself in the prehistoric predatory environment.[7] The life-saving intuitions of *fast thinking* produced the side effect of thinking in causal terms, in contrast with the slow reflection on the information available relating to the occurred misfortune.

These stages of mental development and cognitive processing can only be hypothesized, and we must allude to them in terms of probability. The impression persists that in witchcraft crisis, what trial sources present as a clear link between personalistic thought and causal thought is the dilated effect of a document's distortion that tends to ensnare historical analysis. The explanation of misfortunes often unfolds in a continuum that goes from one extreme of wholly human and personal causations, to others "rather abstract, from half human to mechanical and inhuman: [that is] the ancestors, witches, fairies or other little spirits, God or the Devil, the stars, 'science,' fate and chance."[8] It would be misleading to see plaintiffs as not affected by such a sequence of ideas, which can be reasonably inferred from the exceedingly long time that elapses between the harmful action and its denunciation.

In 1597, in a trial against Barbara di Antonio, a widow in her seventies, for forty years residing in the Sienese area, nine women were summoned, who gave similar depositions. They tell of several pregnancies and of the few children who survived suspicious diseases; they describe the long and conflicting doubts, lasting twenty years, and up to the infamous mental construction of a witchcraft accusation.[9]

Similar cognitive processes were at work in the Modenese in Sassatella, in 1634. Reports Maria, a witness at the trial against Pellegrina:

It will be 20 years since I heard that the Pellegrina's mother was a witch and it was also suspected that her daughter was a witch, but for four years I have heard clearly from everyone that the said Pellegrina was a witch as well as two years later I have commonly heard that Maria, her daughter, is a witch [...] too. I heard my mother say when she was alive that Pellegrina's mother was a witch but she did not tell me what or how; as for Pellegrina and her daughter, I don't know what originated this.[10]

Examples where plaintiffs wait years before turning to justice can be multiplied. The long chronological intervals possibly refer to mulling minds, to unstable certainties.

It is known that the reputation of being a witch should not be seen as an immediate mental construction, but rather as a long and incoherent one, full of second thoughts. The idea and the suspicion take shape through reasoning without a precise and linear trend that "does not require logical coherence, nor systematic application of the principle of non-contradiction, nor consequentiality of correlation between causes and effects."[11] The time factor, acting on the memory, induces second thoughts that oscillate following a multiplicity of hypotheses. The victims' brooding on facts follows a narrative scheme: the experiential self (the *fast thinking*) and the mnemonic self (the *slow thinking*) are the protagonists. Cognitive psychology emphasizes that *slow thinking* proceeds by remembering. Memories are the only think victims keep of their distant experience. Decisions that follow, influenced by the immediate emotional reaction to harm, end up producing a cognitive illusion activated by *slow thinking* when choosing either an accusation or letting go. Perhaps reaching the conviction that misfortune was the result of chance or bad luck.[12]

In some cases, people's long inner debate is connected to the attempt to fix *maleficium* through the traditional operational code according to which the spell could only be canceled by those who had operated it (*qui scit destruere scit sanare*), restoring an ambiguous neighborhood cohabitation in villages for variable time intervals that an unforeseeable negative event could interrupt, setting in motion an increasing tide of suspicions: a succession of major or minor witch crises. In the logic of this cerebral activity, the propensity to blame a specific person appears as the inevitable corollary of a movement between the contrasting neural mechanisms of the individual brains and their being inserted into intersubjective relationships. The reaction to fear, a primary emotion, materialized around a prevalent social context in that predatory prehistoric environment, the fear of other human beings which then turns out to be the most widespread defining peculiarity of witchcraft.

Notes

1 See D. Kahneman, O. Sibony, C. S. Sunstein, *Noise: A Flaw in Human Judgement*, London, 2021, 36.
2 See E. Midelfort, "Witch Craze? Beyond the Legend of Panic," in *MR&W*, 6, 2011, 21.
3 Virgil, *Eclogues*, III, 103, "Nescio quis teneros oculus mihi fascinat agnos"; K. Thomas, "The Relevance of Social Anthropology to the Historical Study of English Witchcraft," in *Witchcraft*, M. Douglas, ed.; ODS, *Autunno*, 131; Archivio di Stato di Modena (ASMo), 128, 23.
4 D. Kahneman, P. Slovic, A. Tversky, eds., *Judgment under Uncertainties: Heuristic and Biases*, Cambridge, 1982.
5 M. Gazzaniga, *Human*, ch. 4.
6 P. Boyer, *Religion Explained*, 226–227.
7 Dealing with the concept of causality, Hans Kelsen wrote that personalistic thought and causal thought cancel each other out. Primitive men when want to explain something, do not ask: "how did that happen?"; but "who did it?" The interpretative scheme of

facts leads the individual to explain misfortune based on social norms, and particularly based on the *lex talionis*; Id., *Society and Nature*, ch. 2.

8 A. Macfarlane, "The Root of All Evil," in *The Anthropology of Evil*, 58.

9 ODS, *Autunno*, 174–178.

10 ASMo, 97, 1, 119v-120.

11 E. Brambilla, *La giustizia intollerante: Inquisizione e tribunali confessionali in Europa (secoli IV–XVIII)*, Roma, 2006, 146.

12 See D. Kahneman, *Thinking, Fast and Slow.*

22

CASE STUDY 2

Ambiguities of Malefice – The Evil Eye

A.: I did neither good nor bad to your baby because I didn't even touch him.
F.: It's true that you didn't touch him, but you saw him with your own eyes.

Agia and Francesco (1673)

Albert Einstein versus Niels Bohr

How was a spell cast? There was a considerable variety in the perception of the ways in which a malefice could be practiced or passed on. By widespread belief, its mysterious force found a preferential course of action in gifts of food. Charms were activated by offering things to eat or drink which were suspected of being manipulated. There are plenty of testimonies of sudden illnesses or discomforts caused by ingesting edible stuff. The illusory cause of misfortune through a donation, due to psychosomatic reactions, resulted in serious ailments. A "mixture of a subliminal communication of hostility and psychological influences on the disease contributed to the victim's illness."[1]

The typology of a presumed agency for harming people involves touching, speaking, and seeing. Speaking and seeing cases are situations regarding a concept defined as the locality principle by physics: separate objects can influence each other through causal intermediaries (gestures, glances, words) that bridge the distance. "The idea of locality emerged early in the history of science. For Greek atomists it meant what distinguished naturalistic explanations from metaphysical ones."[2] It is known that Albert Einstein, in a debate on quantum mechanics which in 1930 put him in opposition to Niels Bohr, reserved some peppery reflections on the principle of locality: he dismissed the distant – non-local – influence of voodoo spells with the phrase: "action at a distance of a specter."[3] Quantum physics did not give up and started to shuffle the cards again. Recent studies have shown that among masses of a fixed system there is a "wave function" that collapses in a

DOI: 10.4324/9781003414377-25

strange way. The experiments reflect years of research on quantum entanglement, in which particles are connected in a mysterious way even when separated.[4] The equations aim to describe how a physical system influences another one and that physical reality is given by interaction.[5]

We lack, alas, adequate qualifications to understand and comment. Far be it from us to use quantum mechanics to interpret human beliefs. Perhaps, "claims about the nature of reality are not yet possible, even if they are well substantiated mathematically and philosophically."[6] We would still be stuck in what Bertrand Russell hypothesized almost a century ago: "The raw material of which the world is made is not of two types, matter and mind; it is only arranged in structures different from its inter-relations: some structures we call mental, others physical."[7]

But given the protracting doubts and conflicting hypotheses, why have we slipped into this cognitive labyrinth? After all, the answer comes simply: Einstein's iconic line is a perfect reminder to introduce the evil eye, above quoted as exergue, of which a woman, Agia, was accused more than three centuries ago. We must therefore necessarily dwell on the evil eye obsession, which remains the most mysterious and least studied of all apparent malefice cases.

Apparent Cases of *Maleficium*: The Evil Eye

I'm sure, the eyes do not have the strength to hurt. This is what the snobby Phoebe says at the end of a dialectical tirade, in *As You Like It*. [8] But are you sure, little shepherdess? We must therefore understand why a few human acts have been (and still are) endowed with dark force able to harm through the aggression of the eyes.

What does this peculiar spell consist of? It is understood as a hostile power that proceeds from someone's negative gaze: a psychic condition of impediment and inhibition, a being acted upon by a powerful and occult force that cancels the autonomy of the person, his capacity for decision and choice. A psychic power idea deemed capable of being activated unintentionally, that is, regardless of the will of the bearer. Although the association with witchcraft is uncertain, "it is part of the same ideological order."[9]

***

"That there are men capable of doing evil with their eyes is a universal belief, widespread in ancient and modern societies, and still today."[10] Precisely the evil eye proximity to envy has led anthropologists to speak of its universality, on the other hand peremptorily denied in various studies: "the evil eye is not a universal phenomenon."[11] A more systematic historical and anthropological research, in a survey carried out on 186 societies, identified 67 cultures, 36 percent of the total sample of the entire planet, highlighting its presence. By contrast, 190 cultures display no belief in the evil eye.[12] The dissent remains.

There are divergent assessments on the spread of the evil eye in its presumed homeland – the Middle East – and on its pernicious face. According to a commonly held opinion the idea would have been widespread in Mesopotamia: "The evil eye could wipe out one's family, their means of subsistence and their own life."[13] But others dispute it:

> In Mesopotamia there are surprisingly few spells or medical prescriptions against the evil eye, compared with the abundance of material against witchcraft in general. Most likely this is due to its less dangerous nature. As Sumerian spells show, the evil eye caused harmless daily accidents: the breaking of a tool or a vase, the tearing of a fabric, the spoiling of food and the like.[14]

As we move westward, other disparities of assessment are encountered in Judeo-Christian monotheisms. In the Scriptures, "the phenomenon of the evil eye is attested only in some passages";[15] in a few punctual warnings in which envious and selfish men and women are explicitly condemned: in Deuteronomy (28.54; 28.56), in Proverbs (23.6), and in Matthew (20.15).[16] Others, on the contrary, point out that the Holy Scriptures contain no fewer than 24 references to the evil eye, although "this aspect is obscured by most modern translations of the Bible."[17]

Let us stay in the Fertile Crescent for another millennium. Surely, the evil eye does not have a marginal position in the Qur'ān. Such an innate quality must have been a widespread view in pre-Islamic societies, where sudden deaths of infants associated with this spell are clearly attested to.[18] And in particular, among the various ways in which damage can be inflicted, it is believed that the influence of evil is transmitted more generally through the gaze. The universal nature of the evil eye (and not evil tongue or malevolence) is probably explainable in psychological rather than sociological terms.[19] It is not clear how these psychological formulations are distinguishable from other psychic forces that define malefic spells.

Landing on Greek shores we encounter reflections that intend to tackle the evil eye not from a moral but from a scientific point of view. An admirable documental primacy must be ascribed to poetry. Thanks to Apollonius Rodius's inspiration we are indebted to the oldest Greek text describing the effect of the evil eye. An anticipation that in verses explains the powers inherent in Medea's gaze:

> Here he invoked and propitiated himself with spells
> the deadly chere, the swift bitches of Hades,
> who roam all over the ether, chasing the living. with spells,
> thrice with prayers, and, creating for himself an evil heart,
> bewitched the eyes of the bronze man with enemy eyes.[20]

The scene, which refers to an ancient tradition, is painted on the famous Ruvo crater.[21] An extensive theoretical discussion was left by Plutarch in the *Moralia*. The topic is not ridiculed as superstition but addressed seriously during a mealtime conversation.[22] The dialogue specifies the virtues of eyes. They are believed to be an active rather than a receptive organ, from which flows of particles and atoms loaded with evil hatched in the heart are projected into the air through a physical mechanism that is activated by an extramission theory popular among the educated

Democritean elite.[23] A natural event that can be explained based on logical physical principles was indicated with the term *baskania* (evil eye). And the link with envy was so close that the two terms were used as synonyms. Those who carry it were considered to be mischievous. Speaking of witchcraft, Plutarch does not refer to the evil eye and Pliny the Elder does not mention it in his digression on magic.[24] An insistent distinction between the evil eye and witchcraft seems to span the entire classical era and to give substance to an identification by sex of charmers, bearers of the evil eye, proves impossible; whereas on the contrary the association witch = woman is a reality, to be discussed shortly. Lastly, it should be noted that the widespread apprehension of misfortune caused by the evil eye "left few traces of such accusations."[25]

***

The evil eye is part of the same order of phenomena as witchcraft although its role in social organization is not as well defined and evident (or rather, well studied) as that of witchcraft.[26] "Although evil eye and witchcraft beliefs often overlap, they are usually perceived as distinct."[27]

Considering its mechanics, it could fall into "a whole series of intermediate forms [of wanting to hurt], which fade towards the pole of an intentionality of doing evil expressed or realized, so to speak, at a distance."[28] The persistent conviction of its power would escape without deepening the impact that vision had as a means of communicating negative intentions. In demonological literature – it must be remembered – the evil eye was not the subject of a particular treatment, and this even though witchcraft has left "a profound mark [in] the history of the senses, and in particular of the sense of sight."[29] There is no shortage of references to witches who can be recognized by the eyes. The persuasion that exceptional personalities with the power of their imagination could radiate a destructive fluid with their gaze spans centuries and after St. Thomas was popularized at the beginning of the witch hunt by Heinrich Kramer's *Malleus maleficarum*.[30] It is certainly no coincidence that the fluid, the nefarious psychic energy of the witch causing illness and death was a strong concept, much debated in medical literature and in demonological treatises of the age of witchcraft trials.[31] The Jesuit demonologist Martin Del Rio (1551–1608) wrote about eyes that have the power to bewitch: they can have double pupils, or one can see a horse or a dog, marks of Satan, inside them.[32] In trial sources, the transmission of emotions, both the expression of whoever sends the signal of malevolence and of whoever receives it, is documented as a fact that occurs spontaneously and unconsciously in face-to-face interactions. Testimonies abound.

In 1594, at the Cotone, in the Maremma area, at night, Tommelone made eye contact with the old and feared Manfilia who was wandering around a cemetery. His blood "froze" (*gelò*), dismay petrified him, he fell into illness "and he died with all his kin."[33] Years later a similar bewitchment struck Ruggiero crossing his gaze with same Manfilia: "He remembers that when he was in a big city about 12 or 15 years ago, his eyes met Manfilia's over and over again: and he knew [...] that during mass Manfilia had goggled his eyes."[34] In Grosseto, in 1604, Ruffino and Antonia la Palandrana, a well-known witch, caught a glimpse of each other at night, "and Ruffino was so afraid that he fell ill and died in five or six days."[35] In the Modena area, in 1639, Genesio recounts that Melegara, famous as a witch active in the Carpi countryside, caught her gaze: "While she was led in prison, when passing in front of my house, being in the courtyard, she greeted me, and I got worse."[36]

In the early modern episodes referred to here, Democritus's theory of flows was unconsciously applied. It is useful to delve much deeper, into un-documentable prehistoric realities, to try to understand this cognitive persistence.

***

The beholder's eyes allow us to speculate on his intentions and emotions. But why is our brain extremely sensitive to the direction of the gaze? Our mind processes the visual information stored during life, it analyzes this information in the light of experience and generates an internal representation, a perception of the external world. A targeted action in response to the information received is initiated. This sensory information is converted into neural codes, that is, into potential action patterns generated by nerve cells although we have not yet understood the details of the neural mechanisms of a symbolic representation.[37] If this reasoning is correct, we have a clue to follow, in order to formulate a hypothesis on the brain foundations of the idea of the evil eye: the conjecture is given by the strong gaze ancestral situation, the staring attacking gaze.

In fact, our hunter–gatherers have been benched too quickly; in the dawn of humanity hominins were burdened with the first half of the match, the critical confrontational game between nature and culture. The staring eye is a special anxious sign of the threat of predators based on an ancient and general biological program. Nature invented the eye to search for food. The fear of the eye is present in many animals, as a functional reaction to being hunted by sharp-sighted predators.[38]

Studies of gazing eyes show the reasons why the ancients might have found the notion of an active organ of sight plausible. A belief persists of "a provocative source of social stimulation," represented by ocular aggression accompanied by a "bio-psychological nervous excitement in almost all species of the animal world."[39] Not unlike predators, humans communicate with their eyes, conveying fear, anger, or other emotions. It is plausible to speculate that *Homo sapiens* may have had an early knowledge of this force transmitted by the fixity of the gaze.[40] We will have to make conjectures about its origins in neurobiological terms, due to the action of neurons that are particularly sensitive to different facial expressions and the direction of the gaze.[41] For example, it is believed that the face fusiform area (FFA) of our brain requires a lesser degree of activity to consciously recognize staring faces rather than faces looking elsewhere.[42] We are disposed, at a neural level, to become more easily warned of the presence in the environment of a fixed gaze as a fundamental social signal. Deciphering the gaze seems to be one of the building blocks of the ability to mentalize, or to interpret the mood and intentions of others (as already seen, it represents the first layer of empathy in the matryoshka); and the neural basis of reading gazes seems to be altered at least in certain individuals with empathy deficits.[43]

Referring to the previous observations on faunal and human context in which Pleistocene hunters/gatherers lived, it does not seem unreasonable to infer that the myth of the evil eye has its roots in feline biological strategies when "they inserted the prey into their visual field."[44] Tommelone and Ruffino cases, whose blood froze at the glance of a witch, appears homologous to the paralyzing effect of the predator's eye on prey. It is difficult to say whether more advanced scientific instruments will permit us to argue that human superstition in the face of the evil eye appears rooted in a defensive biological mechanism. There is no present consensus on such speculations.[45]

Hallucinations: The "Old Witch" Syndrome

Extreme brain sensitivity to the queen of senses, the sight, takes the investigation to other collateral effects induced by the fear of *maleficium*, apparent or real: we refer to frequent hallucinations of people involved in witchcraft dramas. The anguish of being bewitched produced violent emotions and bodily reactions to be defined as psychosomatic, in a word then ignored, although medicine was already investigating the dialectic between mind and body.

In 1701 the whole Tirli, a Tuscan Maremma hilltop village, was tormented by the threats of a woman, Pellegra, considered a witch. Gioberto Viligiardi, physician, reports:

> Reverend father, one can find in Tirli an old woman called Pellegra having a son and three daughters [...] who are very ugly, and all this family is said to practice the art of witchcraft. On the morning of August 10 [...] at the first crowing of the cock, a son of mine named Giacinto, about two years old, went to bed healthy in the evening, and kept his mother after midnight on [her] side, and she felt like someone was pulling the baby out of bed with great impetus. The mother woke up, although she was still asleep, began to shout for me to help her because she felt the baby being pulled out of bed. And I with great effort pulled him up, and the said baby began to say, as children are used to say, "dad, pain," and after I pulled him up he looked very pale and unhealthy, while before he was in good health, and was rotten and in few hours passed away at that very cock-crow, and at once his right arm turned black, and his kidneys were discovered black when he became cold. And that very morning when he passed away it looked as if all the cats of the world were roaring around the house.[46]

At San Cascian de' Bagni, in 1595, Alessandra told the inquisitor:

> This May spent being in my house [...] and in bed with my husband [...] and with a small son who could have been three or four days old [...] being awake

and my husband sleeping and my door being locked at home [...] as the lamp was still lit, I saw two women appear in front of me and I met them, one of whom was Donna Augustina di Biagio and Donna Bonifatia both from San Casciano, and having seen them so suddenly I was amazed and my flesh and hair crawled and most of all I saw them disheveled and I began to say Jesus and to cross myself and I said [...] to one of them what ... do you come to harm me [...] and not having their answers I stood up in bed [...] and then the two women turned into two women from Celle [...] I replied the same words [...] and having returned to their first being, they replied that if I had not said anything I should not be afraid for my little son.[47]

Giovanni, in the Modenese area, experienced a similar terror. A woman suspected of being a witch had touched him and then sent him an offer:

Two eggs that I drank [...] and then I began to feel ill and after a few days thinking of nothing else I dreamed that said Virginia was on me and was squeezing me hard.[48]

The physical oppression was even more evident in the deposition of Giacoma, at Chiusi in 1598:

Since I was not sleeping in the bed and a grandson of mine called Giuliano was with me [...] about two years old, I heard a person climbing the stairs of my house who arrived at the bed, I was unable to speak or say anything, he threw himself on me and sucked me, and forcing myself to speak it was never possible except that with the heart I was saying Jesus and I felt certain explosions with the mouth from the left where there was the putto ...Stayed like this for a third of an hour and then I felt that the person got out of bed from the left side and then having found my speech again I imagined that she was a certain woman Agnesa seeming to know from her breath [...] And I said Agnesa, Agnesa I didn't believe this about you when people told me [that you were a witch], and then she replied: be quiet or you will regret it and afterwards I heard that she went down the stairs.[49]

These experiences as well as visual are visceral, auditory or tactile, and are accompanied by a sensation of suffocation or pressure on the chest, the perception of a malignant presence, and the general impression of being helpless and in desperate terror.[50]

***

Nothing better than Henry Füssli's perverse and visionary dimensions of human figures helps introduce a reflection on the sensitive appearances universally known as the "old witch" syndrome.[51] The interpretation benefits from a cautious use of retro diagnosis. In the "old hag" set of physical conditions "the person who appears initially taken by a hypnopompic paralysis, [...] generally reacts with fear [...] and imagines through hallucinations and afferent bodily reactions to be crushed by some agent. This is the sequence usually reported by people."[52] From a physiological point of view, the cardinal qualities of the nocturnal nightmare – symbolized in a painting by Füssli, where a monkey lies crouched on the abdomen of a sleeping girl – can actually be described as a "sleep paralysis closely related to REM atony, the paralysis that occurs as a natural aspect of REM sleep."[53]

A convergence between source material and what the neuroanatomy of feelings says about the fundamentals of a human conduct, may help. There is some coherence between sources and neurobiological interpretations of the syndrome. From the modern study of "experiential models" it seems logical to infer those aspects of contemporary pathologies and disorders are comparable with semblances that are glimpsed in depositions and interrogations of trial actors: accusers, accused, witnesses:

> If physiology can only account for sensation and cultural beliefs reflect the generalized content of experience rather than creating it, the experiential model seeks roots in common human experiences that recreate similar experiences from similar circumstances. More specifically, the emotion of fear or the idea of a witch attack does not in itself require a cultural link and can be considered as universal.[54]

Some specific reactions of those who in various ways were involved in witchcraft contexts share a persuasive comparison with the reading of contemporary syndromes of the same type that come from neuroscience laboratories. In other words, these historical sources document serial psychological phenomena and, by substance and tone, configure clinical cases and comparison with the studies of our days.

In the human dramas recorded by trials, the perception of a negative influence exerted by evil individuals is amplified into visual hallucinatory syndromes of which there is evidence over time. They are fears with complex ramifications, as in the description left by Lucretius Caro:

> [Hallucinations are] simulacra of bodies. These, like membranes torn from the surface of things, fly here and there through the air, and they terrify souls by appearing to us in wakefulness and sleep, when we often see prodigious figures and ghosts of the dead, which several times aroused us in fear while we languished asleep.[55]

Contemporary psychiatry, fighting against the same psychoses, moves in the direction of discerning the psychobiological roots of such sensitive appearances. By this we do not mean that victims and perpetrators of malefices were psychotic in the contemporary diagnostic sense, since psychosis refers to a sensory thought or experience that is inconsistent with beliefs shared by the subject's cultural context. Rather, we are interested in exploring how from a phenomenological point of view, the experiences reported in witchcraft contexts are placed within a possible psychotic spectrum or dimension, where there is no categorical distinction between normality and pathology but a continuum of experiences. In this sense, it is worth asking: should the victims' visual sensations (also related to hearing and touch) of being attacked be interpreted in the light of contemporary theories of psychotic phenomena? One prominent theory of hallucinations hypothesizes alterations of the dopaminergic system whose neurons intrude in an unorthodox way.[56] This dopaminergic dysfunction would lead to a lack of filtering of sensory stimuli attributing an erroneous relevance ("aberrant salience") to marginal sensory stimuli, up to the production of hallucinations, and falsifying the cognition of meanings and values, as an attempt to give meaning to the new reality of aberrant sensations.[57] Another potential mechanism leads back to a dysfunction in the predictive brain, based on the hypothesis that perceptions result from constructive processes balancing external sensory input and prior expectations. Hallucinations may occur from errors in this process when prior expectations are too strong. This is exemplified in an old experiment where individuals are told to expect hearing a song, while they're played a recording of white noise: a small percentage of the population will report hearing the song, signaling that the expectation outweighed the sensory signal in the brain's final computation. More sophisticated experiments suggest that a similar mechanism is more likely in individuals who hear voices in their daily life.[58]

Dreams, hallucinations of pregnant women or of women who have recently given birth, refer to a common substratum of knowledge, about witches with supernatural powers, which translate into repeated surreal experiences, with a greater frequency in situations of high tension. The evident element of socialization of these dreams possesses a communicative effectiveness and transmits stylized descriptions conforming to traditional schemes modeled on schemes of local civilization.[59] Experiences are reported that in the eyes of the dreamer and the listener take on the weight of an objective reality. The structure of dreams, visions, hallucinations, memories of noises, lights that go out, of strange gestures (such as the testimonies of having seen and dreamed of disheveled women who anoint themselves and invoke the sun or the stars or the devil) appears determined by counterfactual beliefs and confirms them in turn, starting a spiral that feeds itself. The trial reports refer to stories handed down and transformed into knowledge not only of a single individual but of a social group that receives, transmits, adapts them to its values through a process of cultural, memetic replication.[60] They are hallucinatory experiences whose spread is due to universal primary physiological mechanisms in the brain, linked to local excitation, a release phenomenon, a neurotransmitter disorder or any other factor.[61] Such a picture recalls the symptomatology of the "so-called doxasm – the deception of feeling constantly influenced" – interpreted as "an important symptom of schizophrenic collapse" similar to those witchcraft situations in which the very presence of an evil person generates an atmosphere of suspicion and anxiety.[62]

Malaise generated by malefic witchcraft was a reality. In villages where witches were active there were people who had an intermittent feeling that their minds were exposed to the eyes of those who, endowed with extraordinary powers, could look inside and take control of them. It would certainly be misleading to believe that small communities lived in constant restlessness that a fellow countryman would cast an envious gaze on them or that one lived in a condition of perpetual anxiety of being bewitched. And yet, these mental states, whose frequency we ignore, are placed in a social tissue in which concepts of nuclear family, home, privacy were substantially fluid, and could ultimately materialize in widespread panic states arising from the occurrence of sudden misfortune. Individuals eased psychological difficulties by connecting with neighbors and talking about witchcraft agency during community sociability. As it happened in 1588 to a young Sienese nobleman, Aspremio Borghesi, who, agitated by a nightmare, woke everyone in the house causing a commotion. During a vigil, the case of a local witch, Lisa, had been reported and when he went to bed in the evening with this fantasy she showed up in his sleep and he jumped up screaming and drew his sword to defend himself and creating a turmoil in the house.[63] In that lost rural world, solidarity coexisted with opposite emotions that fostered an atmosphere of gossip, suspicion, mutual control, and malice.

Notes

1 E. Bever, *The Realities of Witchcraft*, 11–37; Id., "Bullying, the Neurobiology of Emotional Aggression, and the Experience of Witchcraft," in *Emotions in the History of Witchcraft*, L. Kounine, M. Ostling, eds., London, 2017, 194.

2 Jim Holt, "Something Faster Than Light? What Is It?," in *NYR*, 2016.

3 R. Arianrhod, "Einstein, Bohr and the origins of entanglement," in *Cosmos*, 75, 2017.

4 H. M. Wiseman, and others, "Experimental proof of non-local wave function collapse for a single particle using homodyne measurements," in *Nature. Communications*, 6665, 2015, doi: 10.1038/ncomms7665. On the debate, see F. Laguisa, *La realtà al tempo dei quanti: Einstein, Bohr e la nuova immagine del mondo*, Torino, 2019, 79–148.

5 "The subjective nature of conscious feelings (phenomenal experience, or qualia in philosophical terms) has yet to be explained scientifically, theorists appealing to either higher order emergence, or lower-level panpsychism, the latter suggesting qualia are intrinsic features of matter, or deeper levels of reality. These deeper levels somehow give rise not only to qualia, but also to matter, as well as electrical charge, magnetic spin, and the various constants and parameters which govern the universe. In approaching these deeper levels another mystery arises, that of quantum mechanics and collapse of the wave function." See S. Hameroff, "The Quantum Origin of Life: How the Brain Evolved to Feel Good," in *On Human Nature*, 350.

6 A. Ananthaswamy, "What Does Quantum Theory Actually Tell Us about Reality," in *Scientific American*, 175, 2018.

7 B. Russell, *The Analysis of Mind*, London, Macmillan, 1921.

8 "there is no force in eyes / That can do hurt"; W. Shakespeare, *As You Like It*, act 3, sc. 5.

9 E. De Martino, *Sud e magia*, Milano, 1998, 15, 130; W. de Blécourt, *The Witch, her Victim, the Unwitcher and the Researcher*, 196.

10 W. Deonna, *Il simbolismo dell'occhio*, Torino, 2008, 57.

11 A. Dundes, *The Evil Eye: A Casebook*, Madison, 1992, 191, as opposed to E. Schoeck, "The Evil Eye: Forms and Dynamics of a Universal Superstition," ibid., 192–200.

12 "A more restricted dissemination" would seem established; J. H. Elliot, *Beware the Evil Eye: The Evil Eye in the Bible and the Ancient World*, I, *Introduction, Mesopotamia, and Egypt*, Eugene, 2015, 39.

13 J. H. Elliot, *Beware the Evil Eye*, I, 107.

14 M.-L. Thomsen, *Witchcraft and Magic in Ancient Mesopotamia*, 42–43.

15 F. H. Cryer, "Magic in Ancient Syria–Palestine and in the Old Testament," in *Biblical and Pagan Societies*, 140.

16 J. H. Elliot, *Beware the Evil Eye*, I, 95.

17 Id., *Beware the Evil Eye*. I, *Introduction*, 1.

18 *Magic and Divination in Early Islam*, xix.

19 B. Spooner, "Evil Eye in Middle East," in *Witchcraft*, M. Douglas, ed.; Ibn Khaldūn, *The Muqqaddimah*, 395–396.

20 Apollonius Rhodius, *Argonautica*, IV, vv. 1665–1670, in *Arcana Mundi*, I, *Magia, miracoli, demonologia*, a cura di Georg Luck, Milano, 1998, 93, 441. Our translation.

21 T. Rakoczy, *Böser Blick, Macht des Auges und Neid der Gotter eine Untersuchung zur Kraft des Blickes in der griechischen Literatur*, Tubingen, 1996, 160–164; J. H. Elliot, *Beware the Evil Eye*, II, *Greece and Rome*, 133.

22 Plutarch, *Quaestiones conviviales*, 5.7.2–3. J. H. Elliot, *Beware the Evil Eye*, II, *Greece and Rome*, 49.

23 Plutarch intervenes in the debate quoting Democritus who says that these images (eidola) are emanations emanated not entirely unconsciously or unintentionally by malevolent subjects and are full of evil and envy.

24 Even if the Bad (see Medea in the verses of Apollonius), could be endowed with such a powerful negative force; Pliny the Old, *Natural History*, L, 30; M. Dickie, *Magic and Magicians*, 130–131; J.H. Elliott, *Beware the Evil Eye*, I, 61–66.

25 J. H. Elliot, *Beware the Evil Eye*, II, 131.

26 B. Spooner, *Evil Eye*.

27 W. Ryan, "Evil Eye," in *EW*, II, 332.

28 F. Remotti, "Maleficio," in *I concetti del male*, 151.

29 S. Clark, "La storia della stregoneria e il senso della vista," in *"Non lasciar vivere la malefica."* *Le streghe nei trattati e nei processi (secoli XIV-XVII)*, D. Corsi, M. Duni, eds., Firenze, 2008, 97.

30 *Malleus maleficarum*, vol. II, I, Q. 2, 65.

31 C. Webster, *From Paracelsus to Newton*, Cambridge, 1983. There is no census to hazard regional/national characterizations. For example, no case of evil eye is attested in the Essex studied by A. Macfarlane, *Witchcraft in Tudor and Stuart England*.

32 Del Rio, *Diquisitionum Magicarum*, L. III, p. 282 (http://books.google.com, *Diquisitionum Magicarum…*, p. 308). L. Cherubini, *Strix*, 131–139.

33 ODS, *Autunno*, 133.

34 Ibid. In 1531 in a Swiss village a peasant was psychologically dominated by the occult force of a woman named Stürmlin: "Once in church Stürmlin gave him such a look that his hair stood on end."; see N. Cohn, *Europe's Inner Demons*.

35 ODS, *Autunno*, 133.

36 ASMo, 113, 7, 38v.

37 E. R. Kandel, *The Age of the Insight*.

38 W. Burkert, *Creation of the Sacred*.

39 R. Coss, "Reflections on the Evil Eye," in A. Dundes, *The Evil Eye*, 182; T. Siebers, *The Mirror of Medusa*, Berkeley, 1983, 29–35.

40 J. Meerloo, *Intuition and the Evil Eye*, 120–122.

41 P. G. Enticot, P. J. Johnston, S. E. Herring, K. E. Hoy, P. B. Fitzgerald, "Mirror Neuron Activation is Associated with Facial Emotion Processing," in *Neuropsychologia*, 46, 2008, 2851–2854; T. Nielsen, "Felt Presence: Paranoid Delusion or Hallucinatory Social Imagery?," in *Consciousness and Cognition*, 16, 2007, 975–983, and debate, 984–991; R. J. Itier, M. Batty, "Neural bases of eye and gaze processing: the core of social cognition," in *Neurosci Biobehav Rev*, 33, 2009, 843–63. doi: 10.1016/j.neubiorev.2009.02.004.

42 A. R. Madipakkam, M. Rothkirch, M. Guggenmos, A. Heinz, P. Sterzer, "Gaze Direction Modulates the Relation between Neural Responses to Faces and Visual Awareness," in *Jour Neurosci*, 35, 2015, 13287–99. doi: 10.1523/ JNeurosci.0815-15.2015.

43 R. J. Holt, L. R. Chura, M. C. Lai, J. Suckling, E. Hagen von dem, A. J. Calder, E. T. Bullmore, S. Baron-Cohen, Spencer M.D., "Reading the Mind in the Eyes': An fMRI

Study of Adolescents with Autism and their Siblings," in *Psychol Med*, 44, 2014, 3215–27. doi: 10.1017/S0033291714000233.

44 J. Meerloo, *Intuition and the Evil Eye*, 122.

45 R. Sheldrake, "The Sense of Being Stared At." 2: "Its Implications for Theories of Vision," in *Journal of Consciousness Studies*, 12, 2005.The author's theses are strongly discussed.

46 ODS, *Autunno*, 27.

47 Ibid, 316.

48 ASMo, 131.3.

49 ODS, *Autunno*, 317.

50 O. Sacks, "Narcolepsy and Night Hags," in Id., *Hallucination*, London, 2012.

51 "Damn Nature! She Always Puts Me Out." See C. Fraylings, "The Nightmare: Somewhere between the Sublime and the Ridiculous," in *Gothic Nightmares. Füssli, Blake and the Romantic Imagination*, M. Myrone, ed., London, 2006, 11.

52 E. Bever, *The Realities of Witchcraft*, 34.

53 See A. Cheyne, T. A. Girard, "Spatial Characteristics of Hallucination Associated with Sleep Paralysis," in *Cognitive Neuropsychiatry*, 9, 2004, 281–300.

54 E. Bever, *The Realities of Witchcraft*, 34.

55 Lucrezio, *De rerum natura*, IV, vv. 30–36.

56 The theory, initially proposed by Shitij Kapur (Institute of Psychiatry, Psychology and Neuroscience, London) has been the subject of thousands of experimental studies and numerous reviews, which nevertheless confirm a central (albeit not exclusive, and not without exception) role of aberrations of the dopaminergic system as a way where numerous possible causal factors converge; a summary and brief recent discussion in T. T. Winton-Brown, P. Fusar-Poli, M. A. Ungless, O. D. Howes, "Dopaminergic Basis of Salience Dysregulation in Psychosis," in *Trends Neurosci*, 37, 2014, 85–94. doi: 10.1016/j.tins.2013.11.003.

57 K. Jaspers, *Genio e follia. Strindberg e Van Gogh*, Milano, 2001, 64. The slow evolution of such a psychosis through a series of stages is an interpretation that was anticipated by Karl Jaspers. With literary talent in his *Pathography of Strindberg* (1922) a phenomenological inventory of symptoms was offered which allows us to detect significant analogies with our argument: "I hear someone in the shadows [...] spying, [...] touches, [...] feels the heart, and sucks ... The feeling that someone [...] is standing behind the chair. "" The sentences quoted belong to the playwright's delusions. These emotions match with the sensitive experiences of people involved in local paranoia.

58 A.R. Powers, C. Mathys, P.R. Corlett, "Pavlovian Conditioning-Induced Hallucinations Result from Overweighting of Perceptual Priors," in *Science*, 11,357(6351), 2017, 596–600, doi: 10.1126/science.aan3458.

59 E. Dodds, *The Greek and the Irrational*.

60 J.-C. Schmitt, *Le corps, les rites, les rêves, le temps. Essais d'anthropologie médiévale*, Paris, 2002.

61 O. Sacks, *Hallucinations*. Strindberg's hallucinatory syndromes provide a new point for comparison. Let us reflect on the words of the play writer, what he imagined he saw: "the people at the window peering with grim eyes [...] and then withdrawing; [when] he had a constant fear of being watched. He saw searching eyes everywhere; traps everywhere [...] No, they will not exterminate me, it is I who will exterminate my neighbors." See K. Jaspers, *Genio e follia*, 51.

62 Today, even though we are aware of the complexity of the brain, we do not hesitate to describe a mental problem, such as Strindberg's, with the precision with which a prostate tumor is analyzed. The playwright's delirium can be read using the DSM-V *Delusion* entry: "Delusions are fixed beliefs that are not amenable to change in light of conflicting evidence. [...] Delusions are deemed bizarre if they are clearly implausible and not understandable to same-culture peers and do not derive from ordinary life experiences. [...] The distinction between a delusion and a strongly held idea is sometimes difficult to make and depends in part on the degree of conviction with which the belief is held

despite clear or reasonable contradictory evidence regarding its veracity." American Psychiatric Association: *Diagnostic and Statistical Manual of Mental Disorders*, Fifth Edition. Arlington, 2013. With reference to DSM-IV, 2000: 821, see T. Bayne: "A Long Standing Debate Is whether the DSM Definition Is Right to believe that Deceptions Are, or Must Be, Beliefs"; Id., "In Defense of the Doxastic Conception of Delusions," in *Mind and Language*, 20, 2005, 163. The controversy rages on the DSM-V; see Bessel van der Kolk, *Il corpo accusa il colpo: Mente, corpo e cervello nell'elaborazione delle memorie traumatiche*, M. S. Patti e A. Vassalli, eds., Milano, 2015.

63 ODS, *Autunno*, 31–32.

23

CASE STUDY 3

The Reality of Malefice

ORIZIA.: Why don't you waste?
FAINA.: I can if I want [...] We cast spells on whoever we want.

(ODS, Autunno della stregoneria)

All in all, the little shepherdess of *As You Like It* was not wrong. Phoebe was not completely mistaken arguing that "the eyes do not have the strength to hurt." As a matter of fact, nightmares or lethal glances of a suspected witch did not bring about any trial and could at most be used as circumstantial evidence.

Profoundly different was the impact on jurisprudence made by oral intimidation attesting the intention of acting badly. It would make no sense to conclude a primacy of the magical power of the word over that of the gaze, as responses of individuals depended on subjective variables. On the other hand, it is certain that verbal threats were considered a voluntary performative act and people were aware of the risks of uttering or mumbling expressions such as: you will regret it, you will pay for it. Similar verbal confrontations could result in an appeal to local authorities. The case of Domenica Mattioli is paradigmatic and shows that the option of witchcraft over victimhood to use the power attributed to her was a matter of survival. Haunted by a thirty-year reputation of being a witch that forced her to wander from one place to another in the Modenese countryside, in 1676 her exasperation reached its peak and the woman retorted imprudently to the inquisitor:

> she said that she wanted to resent those of Gaggio and that they would have paid for it and among others threatened [three names follow] and said that three more of Panzano who had offended her had died and that this would also happen to the aforementioned ones from Gaggio, threatening them strongly.[1]

DOI: 10.4324/9781003414377-26

Curses or threats of revenge could trigger physical symptoms of a disease whose psychological origin may be likened to contemporary manifestations of the so-called somatic symptom and related disorders category; similarly, for the gifts of food received from neighbors on whom there were suspicions of malefic will. In both cases, the victims obviously did not receive any explanation from physicians of the time who, not accustomed to the differential diagnosis, interpreted such symptoms as being induced by supernatural causes. It should be acknowledged that to date, the underlying mechanisms and neurobiology of psychopathology characterized by physical ailments where the relationship between a medical cause (if at all present) and the functional impact is disproportionate remain poorly understood.[2] Contemporary evidence suggests that interpersonal context (such as feeling rejected) modulates brain activity in pain perception areas,[3] and hyper-arousal in emotion processing circuitry could affect brain areas controlling movement (for example in functional neurological disorders)[4] shedding a light on how the dense emotional milieu and interpersonal conflicts of malefice might explain its "actual power." Whether or not a curse-induced disease should be considered on the spectrum of somatic symptom disorders, the "predictive brain" framework could help again explain the phenomenon, as a result of an inference failure in brain computations whereby an actual perception (of a symptom) emerges from an unduly certain top-down belief.[5]

In addition to the intentional malefic incantations communicated verbally, a substantial number of spells refer to the discovery of objects denoting the will to harm, and in various episodes this intention was even admitted. Witchcraft agency, the choice to perpetrate evil, appears tangible in cases where objects are discovered, and they sometimes denote specific regional characterizations. In Emilia, for instance, numerous defendants admitted of being experts in practicing the so-called "levar la pediga" (to take the footprint) technique:

> Boasting of being able to kill a man and a beast by taking his footprint [pediga], and attacking the earth taken from the footprint and putting it in a basket and attaching it to the fireplace and while the earth taken from the foot was drying, with four words that the man or the beast from which she had taken the print would go to extermination that is to death.[6]

However, a similar Mesopotamian testimony could make one speak of universal value: "From the house of man, an enchantress will take the dust of his footprint to [practice] witchcraft."[7]

A trans-regional value had findings with traces of organic substances, or holy objects endowed with a suggestive enchanting power if manipulated with art, such as hosts or blessed candles, or artifacts such as the trouser strings for magical ligatures aimed at inducing impotence, or other objects pierced with pins, the meaning of which refers to today's use of voodoo dolls. And it is appropriate not to overlook the fact that the same jurisprudence of the time did not ignore the problems posed by the reality of the *corpus delicti*: in the decades at the turn of the 17th century the judges of the Roman inquisition consulted the instructions about specific finds having a value for cases of *maleficia*, available first in manuscript and then in print.[8]

In 1608, in the Modenese area, in the house where Domenica, a prostitute known as Ningola lived, the Inquisition found in a hole in the wall a piece of meat pierced with five nails and five needles covered by two images of Jesus and the Virgin Mary.[9]

A search carried out in 1595 in Istia d'Ombrone by the Sienese agency in the house of the "Santefioresi," two women to be met again, revealed the ingredients of a kit for malefic witchcraft:

Human hair, a piece of rope, some coals, and more pieces of human nails, [...] three pieces of skull known to be of a human skull [...] a piece of a human shin [...], a piece of wrapped diaper and sewn together, dyed with a certain mixture, which seems to be [menstrual] blood, with a stiletto inside.[10]

If intimidation and discovery of magical paraphernalia represented a significant circumstantial factor of existing criminal intentions, in several cases there are explicit admissions of perpetrated malefices. In 1624, Jacopo, in the Modena area, confessed the fault and described the technique:

The garlic bulbs were stolen from my garden. The footsteps went to Battista's house [...] Margherita, my sister-in-law, took off his pediga and we attached it to the fireplace. Battista fell ill [...] In the end I resolved to throw away [the pediga] and he recovered.[11]

In 1602 Maddalena Bignardi, called la Bozzacchia, admits the malefice:

About three years after having been beaten [...] to take revenge I took off his pediga [...] and in three days the said Hieronimo threw himself into bed sick [...] and his wife came [to beg me] if I knew how to do something [...] and I didn't look at the offense he had done to me, and moved by compassion I took the earth away from the chimney [...] [And always] for revenge other times I did the same.[12]

The Santefioresi, mother and daughter, in whose home the corpus delicti was found, are among the proven admissions of guilt.

[On the spells to Isabella declares a witness]: "Going to the river for water one day I found the Santefiorese still taking water from there. As I was not far away, I heard Camilla say "mother, if we hadn't done what we had to Isabella I wouldn't want us to do it because now I love her" [...] The mother replied: "What is done cannot be undone." And as I arrived, they were immediately silent.[13]

At Viadana, on the Po River, in 1616, Isabella Noliani e Giovanni Caleffi were tried by the Domenican inquisitor "for a deadly attack against Giovanni's wife so that he could marry Isabella." Crying, Caleffi recognizes that he has performed the spell:

> because this woman kept my brain roasted, I was out of myself and mad and mad, [we then put] a piece of earth where the said [wife] had put her foot into a handkerchief and we fried it with some ferns in a bowl and then we attached it to the chimney chain.[14]

Love magic includes a conspicuous part of proven episodes of criminal intentions brought to completion. This refers to circumstances in which investigators find manipulated objects attesting the determination to coerce the will of the desired person. And there are plenty of cases in which certain proofs of spells are followed by spontaneous admissions of guilt. In 1658 Modena, Maria admits the spell "so that her lover could no longer perform carnally with his wife."[15]

> Maddalena in 1629, [confesses that] she had some baptized beans and she fed them to her husband so that he would not go with other women [...] She dipped the bread in her husband's seed and gave it to him to eat with words.[16]

At Montisi, in the Sienese area, in 1624, Laura la Starna says:

> I do not mean that I did not do something [spell] so that Maestro Giovanni would not leave me. [And he said:] that if you want the wedding between two spouses not to follow, that is, between a man and a woman who love each other, you take a string, and you make three knots on it, and then the same string has to be touched by the bridegroom [...], and that while the priest joins them [...] that or that person who wants to have said effect on the said string and spouses has to say "you lie by the throat," and this word must be said at the same moment as the phrase is uttered in the Church by the priest, and thus the groom and the bride will never love each other. [And Laura herself said to Giovanni that he could not have carnal intercourse with her:] why don't you look if you find anything? [...] And he, looking minutely around the house, looking between the barrels, found a white patch full of menstrual fluid which he brought me [...] and told me: look what I found in the barrels, I found a patch full of menstruation blood [...] I took it, thinking it was charmed I burned it, and immediately after burning it he knew me carnally.[17]

The knowledge of how to build a love spell was obviously provided by prostitutes against which the Inquisition performed occasional raids.[18] In 1654, Isabella, a prostitute expert in such incantations, explained to the inquisitor that: "my exercise is to do evil for a fee."[19] Malice for a personal interest is clear in some cases, though. At Monticiano, a Sienese village, in the second decade of the seventeenth century, a dialogue between prostitutes in conflict over a lover is revealing:

Question: "Why don't you harm?" Answer: "I can if I want [...] I may cast the spells on whoever I want."[20] A question is to be anticipated: do these words reveal a guilty mind (*mens rea*)? We will come back to this in Chapter 26.

A list of admitted malefices could be prolonged: it is known that casting spells was not unusual. We are not looking for a quantification of crimes knowingly perpetrated out of the total number of recorded *maleficium* cases. Witch-trials abound with false cases of malefices, spontaneously confessed for fear of the torture by the inquisitors, too: some memories were implanted in the defendants by leading questions or intimidations by the judges.[21]

The difficult question arises again: were all the above perpetrators conscious of the assumed *maleficia*? Research has asked this question in various ways and our answer is yes.[22]

However, the reasons for wickedness remain under our investigation, to challenge the absurd attempt to understand evil that Augustine of Hippo equated with "wanting to see the darkness." The pivotal aim of the book has been stated: an anatomy of the intentional evil interpreting it as a gradual depletion of empathy towards one's neighbor, the psychological outcome of an obligatory choice.[23] The topic is not dealt with in the following chapter. First, we must face the most obstinate of historical serialities: the gender specificity of the accused, the tried and executed. As already anticipated, in percentages sometimes higher than about 80 percent, they were women. Why?

Notes

1   ASMo, 165. 3.
2   M. Browning, P. Fletcher, M. Sharpe, "Can Neuroimaging Help Us to Understand and Classify Somatoform Disorders? A Systematic and Critical Review," in *Psychosomatic Medicine*, 73, 2011, 173–84. doi:10.1097/PSY.0b013e31820824f6
3   A. Landa, B. A. Fallon, Z. Wang, Y. Duan, F. Liu, T. D. Wager, K. Ochsner, B. S. Peterson, "When it Hurts Even More: The Neural Dynamics of Pain and Interpersonal Emotions," in *J Psychosom Res*. 128, 2020. doi: 10.1016/j.jpsychores.2019.109881.
4   S. Pick, L. H. Goldstein, D. L. Perez, T. R. Nicholson, "Emotional Processing in Functional Neurological Disorder: A Review, Biopsychosocial Model and Research Agenda.," in *J Neurol Neurosurg Psychiatry*, 90 (6), 2019, 704–711, doi: 10.1136/jnnp-2018-319201.
5   M. J. Edwards, R. A. Adams, H. Brown, I. Parees, J. J. Frston, "A Bayesian Account of Hysteria," in *Brain*, 135(11), 34–95–512, doi: 10.1093/brain/aws129.
6   ASMo, 122. 2.
7   M. L. Thomsen, *Witchcraft and Magic in Ancient Mesopotamia*, 31.
8   See *Instructio pro formandis processibus in causis strigum* [1593?–1594], handwritten text; and E. Masini, *Sacro arsenale, ovvero pratica dell'uffizio della Santa Inquisizione (1625²)*, Roma, 1730, 297–303. ODS, "Instructio pro formandis processibus in causis strigum," in *Dizionario storico dell'Inquisizione*, A. Prosperi, V. Lavenia, J. Tedeschi, eds., II, Pisa, 2010, 845–847; F. Motta, "Verità del maleficio. Alle origini dell'abolizione della tortura giudiziaria," in *Il caso Beccaria. A 250 anni dalla pubblicazione del "Dei delitti e delle pene,"* V. Ferrone, G. Recuperati, eds., Bologna, 2016, 275–276.
9   ASMo, 32/4.
10 ODS, *Autunno*, 100, 347.
11 ASMo, 74. 14
12 Ibid.
13 ODS, *Autunno*, 101, 346.

14 ASMo, 46.3
15 ASMo, 138.5.
16 ASMo, 129. 5.
17 ODS, *Autunno*, 250–252. On the magic power of symbols in cognitive and neurophysiological perspective, E. Bever, *The Realities of Witchcraft*, 159–161.
18 ASMo, 8/21. Nine prostitutes investigated for "superstitiones ad amorem."
19 ASMo, 131/5.
20 ODS, *Autunno*, 258–259.
21 G. Modestin, "Can Contemporary Science of Memory Shed Light on Late Medieval Witch-Trials?," *Academia Letters*, Article 2084, doi: 20935/AL2084.
22 But see E. Pócs, *Between the Living and the Dead*, 12.
23 S. Baron-Cohen, *Zero Degrees of Empathy*, ix, and *passim*.

24

CASE STUDY 4

The Stereotype Witch = Woman

For our lengthy past has much to say
about men's lives as well as ours

Euripides, Medea

"Houston, We've Had a Problem"

The well-known call transmitted in April 1970 by astronaut Jack Swigert from *Apollo 13* spacecraft is now taken as a metaphor for difficulties that arise in any undertaking, intellectual or material. We wish we had only one problem in writing this book! Yet none of them proved to be as intractable as trying to understand the reasons that may have led to the formation of the witch = woman stereotype, responsible for sex-selective witchcraft persecution. Where did it all come from?

"I tell ya, it's a whole different sex!" This is what in *Some Like it Hot* the unforgettable Daphne, Jack Lemmon disguised as a woman, realized while staggering on uncomfortable high heels.[1] What use can be made of the hilarious truism in our work? We intend to develop the meaning of such an evident platitude by putting forward the conjecture that the commonplace, a meme, of the equation witch = woman may have neurobiological bases and that an "essential difference" of the female brain can be associated with the formation and repetition of mental states favorable to the emergence of witchcraft situations. Before proceeding with the hypothesis, let us delve into a more detailed check of our knowledge than what anticipated in Chapter 3. How do things stand in history and in neuroscience?

DOI: 10.4324/9781003414377-27

Prehistoric Antecedents, Historical Evidence

So, why was witchcraft especially associated with women? Why in the millennia of recorded history has the image of woman been constructed as having a disposition to witchcraft? Some fundamental aspects of the equation witch = woman may be brought out by elaborating on two reflections of differently famous women: Simone de Beauvoir and Medea. In *The Second Sex*, the title lines cited in the exergue, "a woman is not born but is made" set the problem.[2] Medea's thought is expressed with the voice of the Chorus, just before Jason enters the scene, in Euripides' tragedy. Let us taste it:

> Phoebus, God of song and singing,
> never put into our minds the gift
> of making sacred music with the lyre,
> or else I would have sung a song
> in response to what the male race sings.
> For our lengthy past has much to say
> about men's lives as well as ours.[3]

The race of males, the long past: how much rancor! There is much more: Medea's resentment contains an explosive heuristic power, because precisely in the millennia of prehistoric times, as we have argued, the material and psychological premises for the destiny of women were being built, preconditions for the fatal cliché witch = woman.

Preliminarily, however, we must clean the ground of false notions. Scholars know well that man-made witchcraft has always existed. Modern research shows that the prevalence of witches as women on average in early modern Europe could fluctuate between 70 and 80 percent of the total. In German lands, the percentages fluctuate between 20 and 30 percent of people tried and sentenced overall; in France, the *Parlements* of Paris and Dijon saw a slight majority of male witches; in Finland and Estonia there is a balance; in Iceland and Russia the majority were men. Witches as men were therefore a concrete reality, certainly not unknown in previous millennia. Still, the fact does not seem to have in the least affected the formation and consolidation of the cliché witch = woman. All that remains is to try to trace the formative stages of this pre-established and generalized opinion.[4]

***

"One of the most enduring historical errors is the idea that Christianity was responsible for the fear of witches. In reality, witches were feared in the Greco-Roman world."[5] In classical antiquity, perhaps the stereotype of the witch = woman was not predominant, but the spread of the archetype among the popular and educated classes is undisputed.[6] Given the almost total absence in the ancient world of systematic persecutions activated by State tribunals, no statistics by sex are available. One fact remains: either in creations where the prevailing topic are love affairs, or in those involving evil witchcraft with infanticide or other bloody splatters, "almost all the detailed and distinctive portraits of witches in the main classical literature are of women."[7] The nefarious performances of the Telchines, the mythical blacksmiths who made the trident of Poseidon, and of the Dactyls, also metal workers, did not stimulate the imagination of poets: "both groups declined in the state of curiosity, material for local historians."[8] If these literary inventions come from a meme (and perpetuate it) what originated as a cultural concept so powerful as to condition the imagination of poets such as Homer, Euripides, Theocritus, Horace, Ovid, etc.?

> Since it is unlikely to have been invented out of thin air [...] the obvious but not the only answer is that the historic literary figure of the enchantress has its roots in a type of woman with whom men and women were totally familiar.[9]

How a woman is made, then? It seems to us that the plot of her daily existence is involved, in all its ramifications, from the primal ones of being the source of desire and the generator of life, to the private sphere to tend to the home administration, to the public one of the expert healer, the procuress, the prostitute. Women observed every day appeared to the classical poets as the outlet of a *gynecopoiesis*, the result of their biological, mental, material and professional evolution in the course of that lengthy past, as described by the poet.

But afterwards Zeus who gathers the clouds said to him in anger:

> "Son of Iapetus, surpassing all in cunning, you are glad that you have outwitted me and stolen fire – a great plague to you yourself and to men that shall be. But I will give men as the price for fire an evil thing in which they may all be glad of heart while they embrace their own destruction."
>
> So said the father of men and gods and laughed aloud. And he bade famous Hephaestus make haste and mix earth with water and to put in it the voice and strength of humankind, and fashion a sweet, lovely maiden-shape, like to the immortal goddesses in face; and Athene to teach her needlework and the weaving of the varied web; and golden Aphrodite to shed grace upon her head and cruel longing and cares that weary the limbs. And he charged Hermes the guide, the Slayer of Argus, to put in her a shameless mind and a deceitful nature.
>
> So he ordered. And they obeyed the lord Zeus the son of Cronos. Forthwith the famous Lame God molded clay in the likeness of a modest maid, as the son of Cronos purposed. And the goddess bright-eyed Athene girded and clothed her, and the divine Graces and queenly Persuasion put necklaces of gold upon her, and the rich-haired Hours crowned her head with spring flowers. And Pallas Athene bedecked her form with all manners of finery. Also, the Guide, the Slayer of Argus, contrived within her lies and crafty words and a deceitful nature at the will of loud thundering Zeus, and the Herald of the gods put speech in her. And he called this woman Pandora (All Endowed), because all they who dwelt on Olympus gave each a gift, a plague to men who eat bread.[10]

Hesiod's verses related to body and mind formation describe a cultural model of what pertains to historical female species: Pandora's deceptive words and aptitude for artifice are attributes that qualify witches of Greek and Roman classical poetry.[11] But the making of woman is a process that certainly began well before the Pandora myth gave it a fine narrative form. The Greek historian Xenophon provides the temporal dimensions of the phenomenon, describing the private and practical side of the making of the feminine, in his *Oeconomicus*, a treatise on the rules for house administration.

> The god, from the beginning [...] has also adapted natures: those of the woman to the activities and cares inside the house (and those of the man to the jobs and external activities): [...] preparing the fallow [...], sowing, planting, tending the cattle [pertaining to] the male body and soul.[12]

The line *from the beginning*, and Medea's *lengthy past*, have an enormously extended retroactive value, expanding the time span of research on the genesis of man's proprietary concept of women. Did the ingredients of the historic association of witchcraft with women pre-exist Proto history, too? Could we spot them in the gender differential in hunter–gatherers' everyday life, that in historical times became the seed bed of biased psychological relationship between men and women? The question has no answer, but we can hypothesize the trend of a development.

Endowed with a lower physical complexion, women in hunter–gatherer society possibly carried out fewer heavy and risky tasks which, for the needs required by offspring, could gravitate around places of shelter. Within the prevalent context of kinship and village gender cooperation, in prehistoric times macho power still maintained a considerable reach. It is pointless to ask whether hominin females could have teamed up against the alpha males to restrain them when selfishly too assertive (admittedly an eventuality practiced among primates by bonobos): "it is unknown whether women have been able to support each other."[13] If the tendency is correct, thousands of years consolidating a spatial and occupational separation of women had psychological and behavioral consequences in both sexes.

The likely specialization of women in foragers will make them expert connoisseurs of plant and mineral nature. In agricultural civilizations, their reputation as healers is certainly no coincidence. Circe, a manipulator of filters and Medea "very expert by nature" in destroying enemies with poison have already been met. Other less famous women were equally learned, and their knowledge refers to a variety of daily family practices inherited from the Pleistocene: mostly healing, the critical point in the relation to the cognitive ambiguity of witchcraft.

And there is more. Deep in time, the very generator of life can also be imagined as possible dispenser of death to infants, a cannibal witch, like in Ovid's *Fasti*: a fantastic, mythopoetic projection of real infanticides. How many Pleistocene mothers, not unlike those of a twentieth-century !Kung tribe had "not only a demanding newborn to care for but also the constant intrusion of an angry and emaciated two-year-old"?[14] Difficult moments to manage and, as it happens in historic times, lethal for female births.[15] Something must be added about infanticides, which abound in the statistics of the crimes in early modern witchcraft trials. An impenetrable darkness envelops the murder of newborns in prehistoric times. We will never know if women came to the decision autonomously or if male impositions already weighed on them. Later, in historical times, these could become the husband's instructions, like those of a devoted Roman soldier of the first century AD in a letter to his wife: "I ask and pray to take good care of our infant […] If he is a boy, keep him, if he is a girl, get rid of her."[16]

There is a further peculiarity which could be traced back to the witch = woman association when female biological aspects are called into question. Menstruation, pregnancy, menopause brought women closer to the mutability of the natural world, differentiating them from the male world devoid of such changes and challenges. Fears of woman's body nourished by men are known. "Taboos upon menstruating women, and their potential defilement of men's hunting equipment, are widely reported in the literature on hunter gatherers and may leave the impression of an almost universal suppression of women via magico-religious sanctions."[17] It is likely that male fear of female demonic characteristics existed since the dawn of time. The high culture of Western civilization has been imbued with this theme since the time of the Greek tragedies.[18] There was indeed such an association but how to substantiate it with in-depth studies? And how many thousands of years does it go back?

Ultimately, returning to the question we asked ourselves, women's biological dimension, spatialization and prohibitions appear as good components to give rise to the formation of the prejudice that sees the existence of dangerous, malefic potentialities in women.

***

As we have seen, in the evolution of *Homo sapiens* it is difficult to find clear traces of the beginning of male/female spatial delimitation of work functions. But roles will become more specific when in historical times the days were dedicated to work in the fields, the prevailing prerogative of men for most of the year. The very existence of a humanity that feeds on cereals implies a strong agency of those social and economic forces that have activated and deactivated neural and hormonal circuits that motivate the formation of the couple and parental investment in the long term. "The advent of agriculture changed the ecological conditions in such a way that monogamy became the option of a reproductive strategy."[19]

This interpretation comes to the aid of studies that address the problem of the long-term impact of the traditional use of the plow on gender relationships, as in Mesopotamia between 6000 and 4000 BC.[20] Women had certainly taken care of fields and gardens where cereals grew: much depended on their hoeing the soil and taking care of the harvest. Men had been first hunters and later herdsmen. Later they took possession of the plow, which only they were allowed to use.[21] The transition from cultivating the soil with the hoe to that with the plow has long been considered a key factor in the relationship between the sexes: in arable and mixed farming regions women and men seem to have worked apart, women's labor was restricted to small plot of land or to the household compound, but the subject needs fuller study.[22] Specific investigation has shown that "individuals, ethnicities and countries whose ancestors used the plow have beliefs that today show greater inequality and have less female participation in non-domestic activities such as market employment, entrepreneurship and politics."[23]

The transition to societies dedicated to agriculture with the different cultivation techniques and the domestication of animals sanctioned a specialization of functions within the management of the household, starting, as in the verses of the poet, a feminine compensatory universe made of aesthetic values of the body (the "beautiful hair"), dressed up with expensive objects that enhance it ("golden necklaces"); and regulated by women's style of power, because "often criminal stepmothers collected and mixed [poison] with herbs and not harmless words."[24]

***

If it remains complicated to reconstruct how much and how a possible proprietary conception of women, from the depths of the Pleistocene reaches the Axial age, the outcome is clear, it appears marked by a separation of spaces as outlined by Xenophon: on the one hand the female domestic one, on the other the male public one which will exclude and marginalize women's access to politics (the public sphere) for millennia. Distinctions, undoubtedly, are necessary and useful, yet they should not sidetrack us by blurring the general significance of the historical trend. We read poets of classicism inspired by women's daily life, which appears open to limited options: the wife for sex on demand and the mother who feeds children; the pimp, the prostitute, the seer, and wise women capable of healing and harming, generating terrifying narratives of distant things that happened. Judeo-Christian theology added much of its own to this process of *gynecopoiesis*, starting with Eve's weakness in the face of temptations. The highest admonishment came from the apostle Paul: "I do not permit a woman to teach or to exercise authority over a man; rather, she is to remain quiet."[25] A destiny towards an inferiority on which Aristotle had already made himself clear seeing women as biologically imperfect human beings.[26]

The witch = woman stereotype consequently would appear to come from a sequence of connected circumstances. Women's daily separate sphere led to the formation of predominantly female social situations, to microcosms of femininity produced by the coming together of the young, adult or old, pregnant, post-natal or menopausal, widows or spinsters; potential seedbed of bitterness and envy that, not by chance, abound in witchcraft trials.[27] If this analysis is correct, it would seem logical to deduce that the psychological dynamics that arose in female environments led to the witch = woman topos.

Female microcosm does not mean that gender variables alone determined the psychological atmosphere favorable to witchcraft suspicions. There is no counterproof that the same would not have happened among groups of men if they had remained segregated, employed in activities but mainly in nurturing and in conditions of extreme proximity where social confrontation was constant. Unable to test this hypothesis, we just speculate that due to a greater amount of time devoted to social interactions, women would seem to be more capable than men at interpreting other people's intentions, non-verbal signals, and potentially better at understanding deception and practicing it. Were women most skilled in subterfuges? There is no evidence of such a systematic female ability.[28] But wouldn't it be a derivative of being more empathic? Certainly, they were believed to be more empathic. This widespread conviction eventually penetrated the eighteenth- and nineteenth-century European narratives and is symbolized in nineteenth-century Italy by the words of Kite (*il Nibbio*), in Alessandro Manzoni's novel *The Betrothed*: "Compassion is a story a little like fear: if one lets it take possession, he is no longer a man."[29]

***

At the current state of research, the above prehistoric traces of the witch = woman stereotype remain conjectures. Ironically, it will be precisely the advent of agrarian civilization that constricting women in the sphere of the management of the household will mark the beginning of their gender consciousness and of the fatal cliché. The historical origins of the misleading homologation record little new and substantial, although significant facets have been introduced by the vast number of studies on the history of women appearing in the two decades that close the twentieth century and in the following one. This is research that has produced much knowledge for the whole of ancient history. But we should not "get lost in the delights of the accumulation" of new intelligence, forgetting the core of male domination.[30] The relationship between men and women was built on a natural datum on which the construction of politics took precedence. The new knowledge, if it introduces significant distinctions, does not scratch the hard substance of patriarchy, which resulted in a heavy public incapacity of women, who "largely excluded from public religious life were driven back to specific rites, indeed to all religious deviations [...] The appeal that superstition of all kinds exercised on women was a commonplace in Roman literature."[31]

And there was politics within the family. Noting that in the classical age of the witch hunt most people accused and convicted were women, we consider it useful to reflect on a connection according to which royal absolutism could favor a specification as to the sex of malefic people. It is not a discovery that the decades of the great pyres overlap chronologically with the strengthening of patriarchal values (hierarchy and authority in general) of the first centuries of modernity. The persecution coincided with a "reinforcement of masculine privilege, an attempt to confine women more strictly than before within the bounds of [men's] 'propriety,' meaning, first and foremost, the control of their sexual impulses."[32] The *Res publica*, writes Jean Bodin in *Les six livres de la République* (1576), is built around a strengthening of man's power within marriage. An assumption consistent with the meaning he gave to his *Démonomanie des Sorciers*: witches must be burned to strengthen the State, because they play a ruinous role for the cosmological order centered on the political power that is transmitted from God to the sovereign.[33] Closing the treatise, Bodin overcame the *Malleus maleficarum* by alluding to the bestial sexual greed of women. The *Démonomanie* "became a manual for the legal profession, probably cited even more often than the *Malleus Maleficarum* in the judicial practice of witchcraft trials."[34]

Patriarchy must not be absolved from its sins. An indirect connection between its principles and the witch hunt was not absent, particularly in the psychology of men in office, who had leadership functions, whether they are bishops/inquisitors or witch hunters.[35] Unfortunately, by amplifying its extension, the reality is misunderstood. It is forgotten that in the face of misfortune, the accusations of malefices arise on the initiative of women and men. Historical research has not had an easy time refusing the idea that witch hunt was a persecution of women to further strengthen men's power. We must accept the fact that the patriarchal organization of society was not a cause but a "necessary precondition for hunts that mainly produced female victims."[36] The role of such a social system was particularly important in relation to the functioning of the Law whose expensive activation was in the hands of men. Furthermore, we must remember patriarchy's general addiction to the use of male physical force, understood as a natural fact, exemplified by that passage of a founding text of power, which pertains to politics and family, when the Florentine Secretary in chapter XXV of his *The Prince* states that "luck is a woman, and to keep her under it is necessary beat her and hit her."[37]

Let us conclude by going back to the origin of magical and religious ideas as a result of brain creativity. We wonder if David Hume's reflections are not congruent when, asking himself which sex was more disposed to superstition he sought logical support in the authority of Strabo, giving himself an identical answer:

> Examples of every kind of superstition are women. It is them who incite man to prayer, to supplications, to the observance of days dedicated to the gods. It is difficult to find someone who lives far from women, and yet insists on such practices.[38]

It is also known that Darwin, although Hume was one of his main sources, underestimated the role of women in the genesis and evolution of religious sentiment.[39] Studies and debates in this field are new; empirical evidence seems to "favor Strabo and Hume rather than Darwin: women having on average a higher level of religiosity and a higher percentage of religious affiliations and volunteers, which successfully ensure their reproductive and cooperative interests."[40]

If the arguments raised are valid, the other more pressing questions still follow: how strong was the anchoring of the female brain (as our predecessors would have called it) to the long past recalled by Medea? How much did it weigh on the development of social emotions such as empathy, shame and envy, the seedbed of witchcraft situations? Are its genetic foundations identifiable? Jean Bodin himself provided the answers describing the anatomical differences between man and woman:

> for we see the visceral parts greater in women than in men, who do not have such violent cupidities. And on the contrary the heads of men are much bigger

[...] than women: What the Poets have figured when they said that Pallas Goddess of wisdom, was born from the brain of Jupiter.[41]

Little more than three centuries pass and around 1900, in a clinical–neurological milieu, a Swiss doctor, Paul Julius Moebius, argues on the indisputable fact of the smaller female skull:

> it is completely demonstrated that in women portions of brain are less developed than in men, portions which are of the utmost importance for psychic life, such as the convolutions of the frontal and temporal lobe [...] Instinct in women dominates in a much wider field than in men [...][42]

Fortunately for us, neurosciences today know how to investigate better. The witch = woman association is a phenomenon that has universal features and to understand it we propose to verify whether questioning it as artificial and historically determined should exclude "naturalizing" it.[43]

Neurobiological Evidence

"What the hell are we going to do in this mess?"[44] We give voice to Molière at the beginning of a dubious enterprise from which it is difficult to emerge satisfied. Because the presumption that something genetic, during hundreds of thousands of years, would have shaped the female of the species awaits substantial experimental tests. The word, then, passes to biology and the investigation concerns the changes of the organization of the mental modules of the brain that could lead to distinctions by sex. The starting point could be the following: there are sex-based differences in the human brain. What we still do not know is how these relate to behavior.[45]

In the third millennium AD, the assumption of woman's brain diversity does not raise the turmoil it would have produced in the years of roaring proto feminism. The topic is addressed with specialized studies whose provisional conclusions pouring into science trade books amplify stereotypes that are no less tenacious and can be summarized in a cliché: "the female brain is mainly wired for empathy. The male brain is mostly wired to understand and build systems."[46] The debate remains heated (with not a few accusations of "neuro-sexism") and it is important to underline that even in empirical research ideological assumptions influence method and conclusions.[47]

The sustainability of the interpretative proposal that the cliché witch = woman has a neurobiological foundation is based on the premise that "the male and female ancestors occupied rather different niches and had quite different roles. If this is true, it is likely that the selective pressure was very different for both and may have led to the evolution of different types of cognitive specialization."[48] If sex-based differences are due to biological causes and these are encoded in the genes, the hypothesis must be formulated in terms of evolutionary theory because the process would have conferred advantages from the point of view of survival and reproduction. It may have been adaptive or advantageous for the species to develop a set of on-average female-type brain characteristics which found the decisive imprint in the pregnancy-lactation cycle and in subsequent parental role that made women the main provider of childcare. All of this makes sense and helps to explain the reason for an "empathizing" female peculiarity: low levels of fetal testosterone would lead to a female brain of type-E (programmed for empathy) while average levels produce a balanced brain and high levels a male type-S brain (programmed for systematizing). "Furthermore, these physical differences result in differences in cognitive and emotional skills and style that are statistically significant." In short, there would be an "essential difference" in the female brain type, a neurobiological reality with all the consequences that a high empathic gradient entails: greater inclination to socialize; greater disposition to verbal communication and gossip, etc.[49] But is it so?

A fine-tuning of the matter is necessary, given the constant updating typical of neuroscience. Some obvious things, for starters. The brain consists of groups of independent cells, interacting with each other and influenced by internal and external factors:

> This is abundantly true for hormonal modulation, with an evocation of numerous and varied signals that from hormones modulate brain development and function. As a result, it is almost literally impossible for the brain to assume a uniform masculinity or femininity. The brain, on the other hand, is a mixture of relative degrees of masculinization in some areas and feminization in others which can also vary over time for example under the influence of stress.[50]

Secondly, there is an organizational effect of hormones in the brain, or which we have growing detail at different micro-levels involving a specific receptor, protein cascade, or type of brain cell, but the general integrated picture of how this plays out into the brain function and how it is expressed at different life stages is far from clear.[51] Admitting the validity of this premise, from the point of view of evolution it seems that two conflicting opportunities ensue: on the one hand, this organ adapts and qualifies with some degree of masculinization or feminization depending on environmental factors; on the other hand, through a complex channeling of factors, a concept developed by evolutionary biology, the brain retains a prevalent masculinization or feminization. Third, more specifically, males and females have neural circuits that are not "male or female" but use them differently in response to certain signals related to the sphere of instinctive social behavior. There are indisputably overlaps of male / female properties as well as sexual differences in brain functioning. On the other hand, it is not clear how great these variations can be and with what repercussions in daily life … "A mosaic of mainly small differences […] creates a mosaic of personality traits."[52] And each biological endowment undergoes a channeling effect reinforced by social, parental, and cultural factors.[53] Fourthly, there is a substantial body of research focusing on testosterone that "has debunked some supposed sexual differences concerning the brain, hormones, and behavior."[54]

A no minor downsizing concerns a molecule, oxytocin, produced by the hypothalamus which acts on the emotional and reward systems of the brain. Initially known as the peptide that enforces the components of motherhood including birth, breastfeeding and the care of the baby, the focus then shifted to its broader role in pair bonding and reproductive behavior. From the initial focus on the role in pair bonding, oxytocin has been involved in a variety of functions beyond reproductive behavior. It appears that during evolution this hormone has extended its potential to create a favorable ground for many forms of pleasant human interrelationships favored by a greater empathic gradient, with questions on its potential role in the alleged female empathic advantage:

> But this comes with a big caveat – these hormones only increase pro-sociality towards an US. When we are in relationship with them, they make us more ethnocentric and xenophobic. Oxytocin is not a universal love hormone. It is a hormone with parochial value.[55]

Its evolutionary role in regulating the survival function of social behavior appears to be both broader and more context-dependent than the original pro-empathic hypothesis, and so comes greater nuance in any sex-based effect.

Advances in research would seem to produce a significant scientific change, shifting the angle of the questions to be asked. No longer or not only: "How does this sexual difference in the brain and hormones make males and females think or act or behave differently?"; but also "how can males and females so often behave alike despite biological differences?"[56]

In fact, one of the recent assumptions is that structural differences between male and female brains have the function not of distinguishing behavior, but of ensuring that in the face of an average brain volume smaller in women (the only robustly replicated sex-based difference), it can perform functions equivalent to the male one.[57] So much attention is required:

> If we want to talk about the cerebral difference between the sexes we must proceed with caution, carefully sift the evidence and taking care not to overestimate the conclusions that can be drawn from it, [which would be] a leap in the dark made by the imagination in the absence of exhaustive data.[58]

In short, does the hypothesis of an "essential difference" hold? Let us look at another angle. The conjecture would posit a different genetic programming of male and female brains. Currently, no study has the strength to support attributions of this high caliber, but the lines of investigation disclosed by the studies on the human genome might clarify some of the elements on which stereotypes relating to the female sex are based.[59]

But then, are empathy genes really identifiable?[60] What evidence is there that the social brain is sexed and in particular that the female brain is genetically more predisposed to understanding social signals, which would be the basis of a greater inclination to social emotions of empathy, envy and shame?[61] There are a number of experimental studies that suggest that women have a greater ability to understand social intentions, for example to interpret movements and body language and to recognize emotional facial expressions, and that this may be underpinned by differences in brain functioning and neural structure. The truth is that up to a decade ago, neuroscience neglected sex differences and none of these experiments have been replicated sufficiently and in large enough samples to give a definitive answer. In fact, it is argued that neurosciences need to learn from gender studies in social sciences an embed specific methodological adjustments to inform a future generation of more reliable research into sex/gender-based neurobiology.[62]

And even if these biological bases of disparity were confirmed, would we be really hardwired by them? This is a questionable statement because the brain is modified by the thinking and social context of everyone. The activity of genes is a completely different story because they are activated or deactivated depending on what happens in the environment. The heuristic utility of the "wiring" is weakened, because it expresses fixity and appears inadequate to the domain of neural circuits that change and learn in response to life.[63] To make the picture even more complicated there are recent studies that revolutionize biology and argue that individual specificities can be transmitted from one generation to another through a previously unknown method, genetic inheritance, that is, a mode of transmission of the expression of genetic heritage in which the environment plays a role. Epigenetics could support another troublesome issue, the relationship between nature and culture, as it acts as a channel through which environmental factors produce biological changes that last a lifetime. In this way it provides a molecular basis for affirming that education has a strong impact on biological functions and behavior, and in some cases even stronger than genes:

> The concept of epigenetics offers further explanations of the individual differences that arise from life experiences; and one of the most striking examples is that of identical twins who have the same genotype but different physiological or behavioral responses or disease propensity.[64]

Epigenetics could give substance to the assumption that our identity (self) and our body emerge in a conspicuous way from the dynamics between congenital and cultural, but in varying proportions.

Let us carry these scientific distinctions/clarifications into one of our witchcraft contexts: innate and learned characteristics would make women more likely to adopt accusatory defensive strategies in moments of crisis.

> The point is not that the brain is asexual, or that we shouldn't study the effects of sex on the brain [...] As several neuroscientists have argued, since genetic and hormonal differences between the sexes can affect brain development and function, at every level (and through the brain, rather than in some reproductive circuits), investigating and understanding these processes can be

particularly critical to understanding why one sex may be more vulnerable than another to certain brain or mind pathologies.[65]

Now, going back to the pivotal enigma of the chapter: are there objective facts that support the equation witch = woman? As much as there is too much we do not know to confirm or exclude that the stereotype witch = woman is associated with biological factors, present accounts rather suggest that the strength of context and experience in shaping the expression of small biological differences is a most likely explanatory factor of any "essential difference."

The historical investigation, if correct, argues that the *gynecopoiesis* probably resulted in the tendency to develop that dark side of empathy that corrodes interpersonal relationships. From the point of view of a conflict between innate disposition and the educational process, Simone de Beauvoir's aphorism "one is not born a woman but becomes a woman," possesses a compelling and legitimate hermeneutic force. But the significance of scientific research cannot settle on what has historically happened. The dangerous distinction of "us" versus "them," interfaced with women's separate space outlined above, predisposed the female brain to be more receptive, subject to developing social emotions such as envy and shame constantly present in witchcraft cases. Maybe. From an evolutionary perspective the question remains: what would happen of the witch = woman stereotype if there was a zeroing the societal constraints that made it possible? In the last chapter we will look for an answer.

Notes

1 In Billy Wilder's movie *Some Like It Hot* (1959).
2 S. De Beauvoir, *The Second Sex*, New York, 1973.
3 Euripides, *Medea*, vv. 499–505, Jan Johnston's translation.
4 L. Apps, A. Gow, eds., *Male Witches in Early Modern Europe*, Manchester, 2003; A. Rowlands, ed., *Witchcraft and Masculinities in Early Modern Europe*, Basingstoke, 2009.
5 D. Purkis, "Witchcraft in Early Modern Literature," in *The Oxford Handbook of Witchcraft*, 123. For different opinion see J. L. Brain, "An Anthropological Perspective on the Witch-Craze," in A. C. Lehnman, J. E. Myers, *Magic, Witchcraft, and Religion: An Anthropological Study of the Supernatural*, New York, McGraw-Hill, 2005, 208–214: "In Europe before the association of witchcraft with heresy, witchcraft was considered bad but of minor importance," 211.
6 F. Graf, *Victimology*.
7 G. Luck, *Witches and Sorcerers in Classical Literature*, 62.
8 R. Gordon, *Imagining Greek and Roman Magic*, 180–181.
9 M. Dickie, *Magic and Magicians*, 11.
10 Hesiod, *Works and Days*, vv. 53–83. Translated by H. G. Evelyn-White. Of the original *kyneon noon* see a different translation, full of meanings for the construction of the woman image: C. Franco, *Shameless: The Canine and the Feminine in Ancient Greece*, Oakland, 2014.
11 L. Cherubini, *Strix*.
12 Xenophon, *Administration of the House (Oeconomicon)*, VII, 22, our translation.
13 R. Wrangham, *The Goodness Paradox*, 139.
14 S. B. Hrdy, *Mother Nature*, 101.
15 G. Hanlon, *Death Control in the West 1500–1800: Sex Ratios at Baptism in Italy, France and England*, London, 2022.

16 S. B. Hrdy, *Mother Nature*, 321.

17 R. Jarvenpa, H. J. Brumbach, "Hunter-Gatherer Gender and Identity."

18 E Shorter, *A History of Women Body*, London, 1982.

19 K. Harper, *The Sentimental Family: A Biohistorical Perspective*, 1559–1560.

20 F. Braudel, *Mediterranean in the Ancient World*, London, 1998.

21 E. Boserup, *Woman's Role in Economic Development*, London, 1970.

22 B. Smut, "The Evolutionary Origins," 16.

23 A. F. Alesina, P. Giuliano, N. Nunn, "On the Origins of Gender Roles: Women and the Plough," in *The Quarterly Journal of Economics*, 469–530. Working Paper 17098, www.nber.org/papers/w17098.

24 "Quod saepe malae legere novercae miscuerunt herbas et non innoxia verba," Virgil, *Georgics*, III, 283.

25 St. Paul, *1 to Timothy*, 2. 11–13.

26 Aristotle, *Politics*, 1–13.

27 See *Womanhood*, in L. Roper, *Witch Craze,* 125–178.

28 R. Trivers, *The Folly*.

29 A. Manzoni, *I promessi sposi*, ch. XXI.

30 P. Schmitt Pantel, "La 'storia delle donne' nella storia antica oggi," in *L'antichità*, P. Schmitt Pantel, ed., 544, 547.

31 J. Scheid, "Indispensabili straniere," in *L'antichità*, 450, 447.

32 R. Muchembled, *EW*, I, "Forword," xxviii.

33 Bodin mentioned more male than women witches, though.

34 R. Hagen, "Bodin, Jean (1529/1530–1596," in *EW*, I, 129.

35 M. Hexter, "Patriarchal Reconstruction and Witch Hunting," in *Witchcraft in early modern Europe*, J. Barry, M. Hexter, G. Roberts, eds., 288–308; W. Behringer, *Witches and Witch-Hunts*, 163.

36 A. Rowlands, "Witchcraft and Gender in Early Modern Europe," in *The Oxford Handbook of Witchcraft*, 453.

37 N. Machiavelli, *Il Principe*, ch. XXV. Our translation.

38 D. Hume, *Natural History*, 55. Strabo, *Geography*, VII, 3.4.

39 C. Darwin, *The Descent of Man*.

40 M. Blume, "Evolutionary Studies of Religiosity and Religions, started by Charles Darwin," Lecture at the 13th Congress of the European Society for Evolutionary Biology (ESEB), Tübingen, 22. August 2011.

41 "car on voit les parties visceralles plus grandes aux femmes qu'aux hommes, qui n'ont par les cupiditez si violentes. Et au contraire les testes del hommes sont plus grosses de beaucoup [...] que les femmes: Ce que les Poetes ont figure quant ils ont dict que Pallas Deesse de sagesse, estoit née du cerveau de Juppiter.": J. Bodin, *De la Démonomanie des sorciers...*, Paris, M. D. LXXXVII, 246.

42 P. J. Moebius, *L'inferiorità mentale della donna: Una fonte del razzismo antifemminile (The Mental Inferiority of Woman*, 1904), Torino, 1977, 7, 8.

43 K. Stratton, *Naming the Witch: Magic, Ideology, and Stereotype in the Ancient World (Gender, Theory, and Religion)*, New York, 2007, 178; Ibid., *Daughters of Hecate*, 3.

44 "Que diable all[ons-nous] faire dans cette galère?," (J-B. Poquelin) Molière, *Les Fourberies de Scapin*, a. II, sc. VII.

45 E. R. Kandel, *The Disordered Mind*.

46 S. Baron-Cohen, *The Essential Difference*, 1.

47 Larry Cahill, "Equal ≠ The Same: Sex Differences in the Human Brain," in *Cerebrum*, 2014, 5.

48 S. Baron-Cohen, *The Essential Difference*, 117.

49 Ibid., *passim*.

50 M. McCarty, "Sex Differences in the Brain," in *The Scientist*, October 1, 2015.

51 For example, the development of masculinization of the brain leads to significant structural differences of the organ in the two sexes. "Some regions of the brain are larger in males, others smaller. Collections of cells that make up nuclei or sub-nuclei of the brain

differ in size due to differences in the number and / or density of cells, as well as in the number of neurons expressing a particular neurotransmitter. In addition, the pattern of length and branching of dendrites and the frequency of synapses vary between males and females – in specific ways and in specific regions – as does the number of axons forming projections between nuclei and across the cerebral hemispheres." Ibid.

52 C. Fine, *Testosterone Rex*, 105–107.
53 P. Griffiths, "The Distinction Between Innate and Acquired Characteristics," in *The Stanford Encyclopedia of Philosophy*, Stanford, 2009, E. N. Zalta, ed., http://plato.stanford.edu/archives/fall2009/entries/innate-acquired.
54 R. M. Sapolsky, *Behave*, 266. See also 99–136; 174–222.
55 Ibid., p. 135.
56 C. Fine, *Testosterone Rex*, 179.
57 A. Gabrowska, "Sex on the Brain: Are Gender-Dependent Structural and Functional Differences Associated with Behavior?" in *Journal of Neuroscience Research*, 95, 2017, 200–212.
58 S. Baron-Cohen, *The Essential Difference*, 160, 161.
59 See V. Warrier et al., "Genome-Wide Meta-analysis of Cognitive Empathy: Heritability, and Correlates with Sex, Neuropsychiatric Conditions and Cognition," *Molecular Psychiatry* 23, 6, 2018, 1402–1409, doi: 10.1038/mp.2017.122; They identify a genetic locus that is associated with scores on the Eyes Test in females. They found significant genetic correlations between scores on the Eyes Test and three phenotypes: anorexia nervosa, cognitive aptitude and educational achievement (anorexia nervosa, cognitive aptitude and educational attainment), and a disposition to experience. Phenotypic sexual differences regarding the Eyes Test may be partly due to a different genetic architecture in males and females that interacts with postnatal social experience.
60 The identification of "empathy genes" is anything but an established fact of knowledge, although 4 empathy genes have been identified. Surely "a beginning is a beginning," and therefore we do not believe it impossible that in the near future the scanning of the entire Genome (consisting of about 30 thousand genes) will lead to their identification: S. Baron-Cohen, *Zero Degrees of Empathy*, 54; M. McGrath, B. Oakley, "Codependency and Pathological Altruism," in *Pathological Altruism*, ed. By B. Oakley, 59. And yet we now know that no behavioral trait is determined by one, or a group of genes, but by a mosaic of gene variations of which each contributes a small part.
61 M. A. Pavlova, "Sex and Gender Affect the Social Brain: Beyond Simplicity," in *Journal of Neuroscience Research*, 95, 2017, 235–250.
62 G. Rippon, R. Jordan-Young, A. Kaiser, C. Fine, "Recommendations for Sex/Gender Neuroimaging Research."
63 C. Fine, *Maschi=Femmine*, 218–229.
64 I. M. Mansuy, S. Mohanna, "Epigenetics and the Human Brain: Where Nurture Meets Nature," in *Cerebrum*, 8, 2011. Published online 2011 May 25., PMCID: PMC3574773.
65 C. Fine, *Testosterone Rex*, 92.

25

CASE STUDY 5

An Envious and Factional Community

Father [inquisitor] we envy each other.

An elderly villager

The proposition

The proposition of an essential difference of the female brain, its pronounced emotional attributes facilitating the experience of envy, remains a case open for scientific research. But the pernicious social sentiment, the most intense of the "affects" aroused by witchcraft, was not a prerogative of women. Two dramatic trials in which economic greed and malicious envy are intricate prove it. Also, they give us a documentary basis to go over the case of intentional evil in humans whose enigma has absorbed us.

Envy

The action takes place in Tuscany, in the decades after Pope Sixtus V's campaign against magical superstitions. In 1588, at Monticiano, a village of some five hundred souls (360 adults) in the Sienese countryside, the sudden death of many infants generated panic among mothers, triggering a flood of witchcraft accusations eventually leading to a trial. Under the pressure of the local *parroco* (parish priest), the Inquisition instructed the case against a woman, Leonarda.

Fire smoldered under the ashes. Within twenty years, the village was the limelight of another major confrontation, in 1609, against another woman, Antonia. Not a few of the inhabitants, actors or spectators of the first psychodrama, played a role in the second, too.

Leonarda was jailed, underwent three interrogations, and for the duration of a *paternoster* she was also tortured. She was eventually acquitted, because part of the inhabitants, the parish priest included, testified in her favor, witnessing she was a pious church goer and generous donor to a local Company.

DOI: 10.4324/9781003414377-28

During the trial, the "making of the witch" process does not unfold in all its significance. An accident occurred some twenty years before, when an infant died while she was nursemaid, but suspicions did not multiply. We wonder whether without the panic unleashed by cases of infant mortality the crisis would take place. In fact, other feelings brooded in the minds of inhabitants. Let us investigate Leonarda's personality.

She was not really a free rider, but a human character reticent to gregarious conduct. Isolation, unfortunately for her, proved risky, emphasizing the tortuous doubts concerning witchcraft belief. Wealthy, having already been a wet-nurse for many years, Leonarda appeared partly integrated among co-villagers. It is to be emphasized that she did not have a reputation for healing infants wasted by witches: no heal/waste dichotomy, fatal for many healers of the time, was mentioned by accusers. Leonarda was viewed with malevolence because she was well off, and aloof, reluctant to participate in village sociability and gossip.

The dreaded Roman court's initiative breaks the village. Witnesses of both sexes declare about her: "She is hated and unwelcome because she does not delight in being liked too much, and so she doesn't even ask, and they hate her for this effect, because she has something."[1] Dramatic showdowns between the opposing factions, for or against her innocence, follow. An elderly man allows himself an admission that leaves us breathless making the reader relive the community drama: "Father [inquisitor], I'm sorry for the bad feeling of this place, because we envy each other."[2]

A creeping corrosiveness of malevolent voices exudes from the proceedings. It is true that chatters play the role of glue, a tool for maintaining social balance by blaming those who act in disharmony with the tacit local understandings. But in Leonarda's affair, would backbiting, acting in tandem with envy for her wealth, acquire a disruptive force to the point of turning into hostile acts such as blaming her for causing the death of infants? The question remains open. The comment of the old neighbor subtly alludes to parallel mental mechanisms hidden in trial documents of this kind. On one hand, malignancy for Leonarda's anomalous demeanor that shuns conformity is revealed; on the other, the very envious resentment of neighbors demolishing individual empathy and leading to defame, remains in the shadow.

And there was much more underneath: some of the contrary testimonies turned out to be false. Here we have a hot point. The study of witchcraft allegations is complicated by extant traces of downright fraud. In the records of this same case, references emerge to men who were unreliable, because in other situations, had been convicted of perjury.[3] How are treacherous charges to be interpreted? Must instances of frauds "be recognized as essentially parasitic to the witch belief"?[4] Or should we accept that they were "more firmly engrained in early modern culture"?[5] Do they constitute an essential lymph, inherent in human nature? How to explain malice, out of envy or selfishness or greed? Perhaps it is not only due to a lack of sources that the interpretation of critical situations appears so difficult for historical research. Ultimately, the roots of evil lie in a pathological dimension of a single mind. We have already met Augustine of Hippo's definition of evil, in a philosophical-religious frame: as he noted with frankness, he once wanted to do a bad action without having any other reason to be evil than wickedness. The 1609 trial takes us even further into the Saint's crude remark.

Greed

Indeed, it was the worst of time for the village. The end of the century disclosed an even more dramatic decade. In the trial of 1588 Antonia had testified in favor of Leonarda: she is charitable and gives to the church, "but they hate her because she has something."[6] After little more than twenty years, in 1609 at the age of seventy, she experienced the sting of other people's envy on her own skin: she was accused of malefic witchcraft and imprisoned. Let us examine Antonia more closely, making a comparison with Leonarda.

Antonia was wealthy and would make loans to co-villagers. She was a devout churchgoer and used her economic resources to give alms to the church, too. The common traits of the two women end there, because their personalities could not have been more different. Antonia had an opinionated and moralizing character, perhaps a common feature of many village elders. She prophesied about every aspect of daily life, and about sensitive issues of existence, such as anomalous aspects and course of an inhabitant's illness, or the sex of a pregnant neighbor's unborn child. This peculiarity backfired on her, eventually fueling the suspicion that her guessing was due to some witchcraft. In 1606, a secret preliminary investigation was devised by Antonia's main enemy, one Lepido Vannuccini. He was a wealthy villager, owed Antonia money and had been calling the shots for years, eventually being stopped by the *parroco*. Finally, in 1609, the next parish priest caved in to pressures and reported to the Inquisition that Lepido had been bewitched by Antonia. The woman, first jailed, was then placed under house arrest.[7] The fight between the two *coqs de village* involved the inhabitants; dozens of them were questioned. Most of the accusers, of both sexes, had received loans from Antonia. No surprise they sided with Lepido. One debtor, a 22-year-old boy, admitted he had made a false deposition, too. The trial dragged on. It was eventually resolved, and Antonia acquitted, with the intervention of two Sienese nobles, landowners in the area, who took sides.

***

Noting that deep economic conflicts and clashes between factions are a characteristic of witch trials is certainly not new: the European scenario abounds in cracks in the social fabric of a community. The little Tuscan village is no exception.[8] The complexity of witchcraft conviction permeates both trials, but it is worth stressing that neither of the two women was suspected of being able to heal; no figures of cunning men, the pivotal corollary in most trials to find the witch and coerce her to withdraw the malefice, appear; no clear cut "making of the witch" process can be glimpsed. The cases were triggered by different causes, but both exploded and found fuel on the creeping economic contrasts since long riveting the inhabitants.

Now, in fairness, we must underline that Monticiano judicial proceedings, as well as many other big trials, present situations that do not fit with the focus we have given to millenary village witchcraft, ruled by the natural control of malefice. Moreover, the evasiveness of the informal control says nothing about the thousands of anonymous women suspected of being witches who would use the power ascribed to them to carry on a critical coexistence, not immune from occasional fall-out, possibly due to some deliberate bad move. Perhaps, as wished by considering the research *impasses*, in-depth studies based on all the sources of a village, will be able to dispel some darkness on the intrigue of drives and emotions affecting human relationships in a community.

Be it as it may, the conundrum of understanding a guilty mind stands. Certainly, the intricacies of envy and greed have found documentary evidence in Monticiano, showing much intentional malice hidden in witchcraft agency. This seems to confirm neurosciences direction of investigation to understand the mystery of evil as a biological drive with intricate connection to the social environment, as an action taken to resolve psychological impulses produced by envy or to gratify deeper inborn inclinations for antisocial agency that remain unknown.[9] The faculty of the dangerous feeling would appear in the human brain as the case of an indissoluble contradiction: a problem of individual psychology with possible genetic bases, inseparable from concrete social implications, capable of rewarding or reinforcing or punishing the psychological variations of each individual. The following chapter addresses these issues more closely.

Notes

1 ODS, *Autunno*, 187, 190–191.
2 Ibid.
3 Ibid., 187–188.
4 See K. Thomas, *Religion and the Decline of Magic*, 646. The point is debated in J. Barry, "Introduction: Keith Thomas and the Problem of Witchcraft," in J. Barry, M. Hester, G. Roberts, eds., *Witchcraft in Early Modern Europe*, 13–14.
5 E. Bever, *The Realities of Witchcraft*, 229.
6 ODS, *Autunno*, 190–191.
7 Ibid., 223–240.
8 These factional struggles have some affinity with medieval political sorcery.
9 J. W. Buckholtz, R. Marois, "The Roots of Modern Justice: Cognitive and Neural Foundations of Social Norms and their Enforcement," 665; W. Irons, "The Intertwined Roles of Genes and Culture in Human Evolution."

26

CASE STUDY 6

Anatomy of Witchcraft

Angelica, Angelica, if this girl dies, I want you burned.

Pompilius

Basics on Reductionism

Man's predisposition to be cooperative determined the price paid by evolution, because once he became *Sapiens*, he himself defined "other individuals and groups as outsiders, potential adversaries or enemies."[1] During prehistory, the expanding dimensions of human aggregates made the appearance of a greater number of individualists, profiteers reluctant to accept agreed rules, inevitable. The altruistic punishment of free riders to force good collective behavior contains an evolved instinct in which an anticipation of the harsh control of antisocial people such as sorcerers and witches could be traced. This very consideration does not exclude a problem, which consists in the difficulty of explaining how such a behavior could have evolved through natural selection. Perhaps altruistic selection strengthened through a kind of group selection (groups that include punishing people fared better than others).[2] The collateral effects summarized by Hesiod's verses on fatigue and suffering, disclosed by developed agrarian civilizations, cannot be forgotten. On one hand, various tribes, allying themselves to confront the material aspects of existence, reaped the psychological advantages of being together: sympathy, gratitude, mutual trust. On the other, they experienced the complex obstacles produced by fear, anger, dislike, envy, sense of shame and guilt; that is to say by the social emotions we encounter in the development of interpersonal relationships disclosed by witchcraft trials.

This objective relevance of the emotional load buried in court papers raises a problem of method. In the face of the intricate reality of evil, which unites the perpetrators and their victims in tortuous psychological connection of a reciprocal

DOI: 10.4324/9781003414377-29

and disguised hostility, shouldn't a neurobiology of emotions get rid of Émile Durkheim's well-known conceptual *diktat*? The great intellectual authority of the French sociologist imposed a muting on this mental sphere, arguing that whenever a social phenomenon is directly explained by a psychic phenomenon, the explanation turns out to be false, because the cause of a social fact must be sought among previous social facts.[3] For the entire twentieth century there aren't many historians or social analysts who have not made extensive use of this theoretical statement, generating large areas of conceptual uncertainty from which it is difficult to escape. For a long time history, among human sciences, has disdained any kind of psychological argument: historians often speak of psychological reductionism, but never of a sociological or cultural one.[4] The blank slate theory underpinning Durkheimian positions, rejecting everything that is innate in man, is no longer tenable, though; it collides with the new knowledge of brain functioning opened by research on the role played by emotions.[5] Renaissance and Baroque Europe witch-hunts reveal veins of human sentiments in which malefic witchcraft is enveloped.

Looking for a taxonomy of malefice, this case study highlights psychological, material and cultural factors: such as reasons for economic contrasts, community power strategies, desire for revenge, conflicting "ideologies," mere evil. A human capacity emerges, driven by neurobiological roots organized in the multiplicity of principles that form man's morality: roots hidden in a tangle of unravelling neural reactions and neuroanatomical connections.[6] There is more. The reality of witchcraft, namely a possible inborn existence in individuals of a *mens rea* (guilty mind), is contrasted with the hypothesis of their intentional evil as the outcome of a decrease/disappearance of empathy with regard to people.[7]

The Causes of Evil: An Empathic Deficit?

Probing into witchcraft, we looked to Montaigne for inspiration, although his reflections seem to barely touch it. The well-known passage on witches in his *Essays* records an ill-concealed evasiveness. It is easy to see that he is arguing against pyres, but it is difficult to establish what he is in favor of. He gives the impression of wanting the reader to draw conclusions that are never explicit in the text. He says that it is better to incline to doubt than to be confident in things that are hard to prove and dangerous to believe.[8] He does not deny the existence of the witch and even accepts common stereotypes, when he sees "an old woman, truly a witch for ugliness and deformity." And when, showing ancient medical wisdom, he suggests that "in good conscience, I would have ordered them [the witches] hellebore rather than hemlock," he does not explicitly make them crazy, but his wording continues to remain ambiguous.[9] One remains perplexed. And the same reality of evil in human nature is vague. Montaigne addresses it always tangentially, walks away doubtfully and as often happens, leaves the readers alone. His great mind is of a little help for our purpose. As anticipated, we aim to deal with man's faculty to intentionally commit a crime and to delve into the hypothesis of a redefinition of evil as a zero degree of empathy.

***

From an evolutionary perspective scholars agree that *Homo sapiens*'s reciprocal altruism became a human universal that helped the psychology of hunters and gatherers to survive and genetically reproduce. It was a suitable cultural terrain for developing new emotions. Complex cooperative actions were the result of a complicated set of chemical and neural responses defined as empathy: a biological endowment that learning and culture would enrich giving it the new meanings already encountered. The role of empathy in the development of civilization should not be overestimated.[10] But all in all, in the age of witch hunts, people were potentially owners of Hume's "particle of the dove" and in interpersonal relationships their actions may fall within an empathic spectrum from a minimum to average and maximum value.

If we accept the assertion that "people believed to be bad or cruel are simply at one end of the empathic spectrum," it will remain to establish the genetic, hormonal, neural and environmental factors determining where on that spectrum the individual agency falls.[11] This is a key step in laboratory investigations. From this corner point any evil action, whatever the physical or verbal means by which it is perpetrated, can be measured with neuroscience tools: they show that at the very moment of an evil action the empathic circuit goes down.[12] Alas! The very crossroad where experimental and historical sciences seem to separate without remedy is here.

For scientists, in the laboratory, the question of *if* and *how* the empathic circuit collapses to a hypothetical zero degree, which makes deviance possible, can be scientifically faced. For historians such an investigative procedure is obviously denied. However, it can be replaced by arguing that a malevolent action is the product of a human psychological construction, that is, of a biography strewn with adverse events. When someone's serial malefic agency threatens or harms a neighbor, what should we lay the blame on: a defective childhood, adolescence and education, a hostile social context? Historical sources rarely allow us to delve into the biography of these women, the witches, belonging to a complex human typology. Individual and family precedents, physiological and pathological, of the previously encountered witches such as Grana, Meleagra, Manfilia, the Santefioresi, Battista are unknown to us no less than their semblant. How do we proceed then? Ultimately, St. Augustine, due to his experience of things and men, hit the mark arguing that there is no efficient cause of evil "but a deficiency." Neuroscience could say a lack of empathy.

This may have been the case of Angelica, whose serial misbehavior can be reconstructed in a most substantial trial instructed by Franciscan Inquisition. Our considerations on radical evil, understood as a possible genetic predisposition of some free riders, will be supplemented with information and plausible conjectures relating to the biography of our protagonist, long suspected and finally accused and tried for having harmed many infants by working as a healer. We will hazard scrutinizing her mental profile, deducible from *how* she addressed others; that is, with menacing verbal messages whose repetition we interpret as result of a deliberate inclination to confrontation. Also, her appearance will not be neglected, due to the psychological consequences that a physiognomy can generate in human relationships. In short, the thesis regarding the formation of an empathic deficit will be looked at carefully.

Angelica's Life

At the time of her interrogation by the Sienese Holy Office in 1584, Angelica remembered her age quite well: "I'm 74 or 75 years old." She was born at Radicondoli, a high hill village that around the year 1640 had 91 families, with 729 souls. Located between the Elsa valley, the Cecina valley and the Merse valley, Radicondoli was part of the diocese of Volterra; for lay justice, it depended on Casole, one of the eight criminal districts of the New Sienese State.

Sixteenth century Europe's final decades, from Lorraine to Bavaria to Scotland to the Netherlands to Switzerland, are considered the roaring years of a witch hysteria. Counter-Reformation Italy was no exception. After the 1586 papal bull, *Coeli et Terrae*, the Inquisition hunted down with insistent zeal anyone suspected of exercising any form of magic. Change was in the air. Within a few years, various smaller parishes near Radicondoli (Montalcinello, Gerfalco and Belforte) were hit by paranoid reactions, in a growing spiral of panic fueled by the action of ecclesiastical authorities urging parish priests to incite the faithful to report cases of infants suffering from unexplained ailments or sudden death, and all sorts of *maleficia*. Fiery sermons went viral from the pulpit. A letter from Andromaco d'Elci, an exorcist, introduces the case:

> Very reverend Father Inquisitor, finding myself here in Radicondoli, I was forced with the permission of the bishop to exorcise many people oppressed for spells by spirits [...] He committed me to [investigate some witches.] and in particular an old woman called Angelicona [big Angelica]. And all this village is upside down against her, and so it is said of one of her daughters [...] And there are trials of great things, with the death of many creatures; and medicated creatures, wasted by witches, led to death [by them], and with their mouth they confess it [to cure] It is important to put Angelica and Antea her daughter in prison, both of which are kept for witches [...] This will be a matter of great importance and all these villages as well as this land, which is full of charmed and spoiled children, will be treated. And they all shout that this big Angelica is the cause [...] Everyone is afraid of their witchcraft and spells and on one hand they are right because they have experienced the bite of the wolf for many years. And they threaten those who will testify [...] and me also threatening stabs, and the old woman goes on to say that [for all my conjurations in church] I am more of a sorcerer than her [...].[13]

Local factions are involved in the trial. Economic contrasts between parental groups remain in the background. There is no open fight. Competing powers, magical and religious, disguised as local health policy, are confronted. Angelica and her daughter Antea are jailed. From numerous testimonies of fellow villagers, we can reconstruct some of Angelica's biographical data and the complex of emotions that are expressions of her individuality. We will use them to probe her "self" and consider which mental mechanisms offer insights for a reflection on evil.

Twelve Years Before

An episode that occurred some years before, around 1572, illustrates the psychological atmosphere of the village, regarding magic and witchcraft. A vividly theatrical scene is recalled by the scribe's transcript of the interrogations: Maco del Bolgia, a powerful cunning-man, addressed Angelica as a witch in public. A witness reports:

> Already ten or eleven years ago, finding myself one day in the wash place at Radicondoli where there was still a woman Maria, Angelica, and others whom I don't remember, and there being an astrologer in Radicondoli, [Maco del Bolgia] the sorcerer of Casole, who spoke to madonna Francesca wife of Pompeo Berlinghieri, who wanted to see her hand to predict her future in spite of her reticence. He then turned to us women [sitting] in a circle and said, in this circle there is a witch, and then Angelica added and said, if it is so why do you not mention her, and then the said astrologer said hush that it would be you, showing it to the others present there, by putting a hand on her shoulder; and seeing this Angelica began to mumble and the said sorcerer or astrologer said be quiet that my soul would be enough [I have the power] to make you stay all this day in this street that you never move [...] We all stepped aside, and Angelica without ever changing as motionless as she was, stayed in that place for a good while, and then we left, being all awed that after the words occurred as above she stood still at the words of the said astrologer.[14]

The cunning man, Maco del Bolgia, came from a dynasty of *indovini* (magicians/ soothsayers) and enjoyed an extensive and almost regional fame for being able to heal malefic misfortunes. He was proud of possessing "secrets" that would be read in a memoir book. Maco passed his art to descendants traceable up to the mid-seventeenth century.[15] The arrival of such an astrologer at Radicondoli is remembered after more than a decade and details of gathering impressed the village collective memory.

Let us analyze the testimony as a film, reviewing this written clip in slow motion. Unwinding the paper footage, several critical moments emerge in separate time sequences. In the circle, the natural control of witchcraft ingredients faces each other in a sculptural pose, Maco and Angelica, anti-witchcraft and witchcraft. During a brief tacit confrontation of powers, Maco breaks the delay saying, "in this circle there is a witch." Angelica challenges him: "why don't you name her." Maco affirms his superior power: "Hush, it would be you," and touches her shoulder. Angelica, displaced, "mumbles" something, provoking Maco's final blow, sanctioning his power: "my soul would be enough [to immobilize you]."

What were the facial expressions of bystanders in the circle when the magician turned to them? What happens in such situations? Maco observes and reads thoughts in the faces. He intuitively sees Angelica's and bystanders' emotions and their state of mind, based on the vitality expressed by postures even in the short spans of an episode. Villages or small-town neighborhoods resemble the limelight of a theater. Intimate impulses, despite attempts at dissimulation, are exhibited, acted out in front of everyone. In Europe's ancient regime, from the top to the bottom of the social ladder, we find the need to communicate emphasized through gestures and movements of the limbs. It is an overbearing use of body language, of face and eyes: what Erwin Goffman called an idiom of individual appearance and signals.[16] In every small community microcosm, the way to exist in the eyes of others is unescapable: glances, words, mimes appear as cultural automatisms aimed at defining one's individuality and social status. Eyes are protagonists in social life, they catalyze feelings. There is no detail of individual daily gestures that does not occur under the gaze of all inhabitants and is not subject to a decoding of the *vitality forms*, by virtue of an instinctual endowment that comes from the depth of time.

Cognitive neuroscience seeks an updated empirical support and integrates previous explanations with that of an acute ability for mind reading. In our footage, Maco's gaze penetrates, like a fever, the veins of Angelica, who only mumbles something; he immobilizes her with a sort of psychogenic paralysis and conveys his karma to the awed bystanders. The clash between Maco and Angelica has really become an icon carved in the village memory for years.

Healer and Witch

A biographical sketch of Angelica and her family needs to be attempted now. There is little good information. In general, we notice an evanescence of male figures. Angelica's husband is never mentioned; of a son there is trace of a sentence for intemperance of character, a family connotation. Most significantly, Betta, her mother, had been a healer, too. She passed her knowledge to Angelica who in turn introduced her daughter Antea into the practice. Betta had assets; she handed down the reputation of a witch to Angelica: "a fame going forty years back," according to the sworn testimony of a local noble.[17] Not really a surprise: in every corner of Europe, witches were usually thought to "group themselves into families: a mother, a daughter, a granddaughter. Their power is inherited."[18] Old village women confirmed such reputation, recalling Betta's bragging: "She boasted [that] by spitting on someone [she could] bewitch him and make him do her wish."[19] Such intangible endowments could hardly be refused.

Angelica possessed land and cash, and, according to accusations, practiced usury. She certainly consolidated her wealth practicing as a healer for a fee. But a testimony hints at a glimmer of compassionate spirit, though. A witness reports: "Angelica used to tell me, 'I don't want anything from you because you are poor.'"[20]

What kind of illnesses did Angelica cure? According to common opinion, she was a sort of *ante litteram* pediatrician; those centuries could be defined as year zero of neonatology. In 1708 a soothsayer and healer remarked that to infants who are ill "the surgeon, for being so small, doesn't usually go there, because he can't do anything."[21] Angelica perfected herself in treatment of infants who, when their illness dragged on inexplicably, were considered to have been wasted by witches. Despite the 1586 papal bull prohibitions, parishioners "send infants to the sorcerers," because "putti [infants] cannot be allowed to die."[22] Mothers would go to wise women and healers. The legitimacy of this popular practice was socially accepted. Some evanescent figures active as doctors are attested in Radicondoli area.[23] But with a sick infant mothers would go to Angelica. There are no differing opinions on this point among villagers. Let us follow some of them closely:

- "All of them availed themselves of the work of this woman, because it was customary here to resort to her, because in the infirmity of putti it is said that she has a good hand."
- "In this village, they avail themselves of the work of this woman in treating sick and damaged children. It is publicly held that she medicates them daily."
- "In this village it is universal, as we know that putti are rotten, they must be brought to Angelica, who heals them."
- "By common opinion in this place as we know that when the putti are wasted, they must be brought to Angelica who heals them."[24]

A succession of repetitive statements that pair with others fatally denigrating Angelica's practice of restoring health that she herself has wasted:

- "At present time we have knowledge of the said woman Angelica who is called to tidy up languishing infants, because it is the opinion [...] that she is the one who spoils them."
- "She wastes the putti, and they give them to her with that mind that only she can treat them."[25]

Testimonies moved towards the widespread dichotomous belief healing/destroying that keeps a theater of lies alive. People lived in a sphere of dissimulation and deception. Mothers could not address Angelica claiming to have a putto/a wasted by a witch knowing she could not accept infants: because if she agreed to treat him/her and heals him/her, automatically it would imply she was the one who caused the disease. The conviction of wasting/healing dichotomy is exemplified by Alexandra's case:

Nine years ago I had a putta (she-baby) which according to my opinion had been damaged, she had more holes in one arm that looked like bites [...] I went to Angelica not [telling her] that the putta was damaged but that she had some other infirmity; but I took everything as an excuse, since I knew the putta was wasted, and so the next morning Angelica was called and held the putta on the neck and stretched her arms and legs and then released her [...]

and since she came into her hands she went on improving and she lived about two more years, and then she died of another disease.[26]

Such mental ruminations were common among mothers of sick babies. It is to be noted that in this enduring theater there is no trace of the key figure in the witchcraft system, the cunning-man. Perhaps, the long monopoly of healing exercised by Betta and Angelica made its function redundant, attesting to a state of mental confusion caused by fear. With shams and cautions mothers turned directly to them for the spells to be withdrawn.[27]

***

Some non-marginal details can improve Angelica's personality profile. She was a woman of above average built, as indicated by her name augmentative name, and "very ugly" in the opinion of the Elci friar: "this Angelicona who is enough to see her to realize she is a witch, no need of other witnesses."[28] The friar's aesthetic consideration is not of trivial value. If, in fact, "Beauty is a great element of esteem in human relationships; it is the first means of reconciling with one another, and there is no man so barbaric and grim who does not feel somehow touched by its sweetness."[29] Likewise ugliness, its opposite, is a reality that strikes observers and affects the self-image of those who unfortunately carry it as a dowry. A pervasive cultural fear of elderly and ugly women may have been a centuries old legacy that influenced even great minds. Not long after Montaigne's reflection, Johan Kepler – the astronomer and mathematician investigating the laws regulating the movement of planets – occasionally became a lawyer to defend his seventy-year-old mother whose repugnant physical appearance frightened people to the point of inducing them to accuse her of witchcraft (1616–1622).[30]

For villagers, aesthetic appreciations were anything but irrelevant when considering marriage alliances, too. It is certainly no coincidence that Betta was considered a witch for having managed to marry another daughter, Caterina, casting spells on a certain Tiberio, a tailor. A scandalous local misalliance, "for disparity of goods, age, parentage, and fame, and the whole *terra* (village) turned around so that he wouldn't take her." Villagers would brand the girl with telling words: "and the said daughter Caterina had a monkey's face and was aged, and short."[31]

At her advanced age Angelica's way of reasoning seems to be clear and coherent. The traits of harsh character attributed to her – anger, penchant for threatening and insulting – may have been the result of some pathology veiled to us. Lucky are contemporary historians and social analysts! Similar serial situations can take into consideration biological factors and verify if in cases of chronic family deviance wrongdoers are found to possess low activity genetic variants of the MAO-A enzyme making "antisocial genes."[32]

Be that as it may, Angelica would use her natural endowments as a deliberate strategy, as a weapon to intimidate co-villagers, impose one's will and strengthen her status. The very style of her serial aggressive behavior seems to owe much to a mental predisposition that influences her *vitality forms* and the *how* she interacts with villagers. Testimonies of her prevaricating, threatening arrogance are a leitmotif of the trial.

Having been denied the assignment of an infant as wet nurse to which she aspired, she frightened Arminia, the chosen one, screaming. A witness reports her words:

> You tried to prevent, and you prevented me from having this baby to wet nurse, I do not want you to have any happiness with it [...] And she repeated it in anger ten times, in the presence of witnesses, and within ten days [my baby] began to vomit with repugnance every time I gave him milk, appearing weaker every day.

Another mother testifies that she had been addressed with hateful words that connote a family animosity, too.

> [Angelica threatened me saying:] I want you to regret it when you least expect it. A few days [later], doubting that I was bewitched, I went to father Andromaco, so that he would know it, [...] Returning home Antea daughter of said Angelica said these or similar words: you went to see the friar, if I had to drink blood, I would like to drink nothing but yours.

And these are by no means cases of predominantly female conflicts. We have seen the stabs that the exorcist was threatened with. Evidence of Angelica's aggression comes also from fellow male villagers. Emanuele, a weaver, declares:

> One day she came to my house to threaten me because of a cloth given by her to weave in Belforte because we had refused to work it here and said that I was the one who had said not to work her cloth [...] and in this she began to threaten me.

At Radicondoli, when exorcisms of Alexandra in the church had become a daily affair and the priest managed to make the possessed pronounce the name of the person who tormented and frightened her, another witness tells us how Angelica reacted:

> Angelica once came to our loom and without anyone telling her anything she said: Who will be that cuckold or that slut that said that I am a witch and that I have threatened [her]? I replied that I wanted to say it because I had heard her say it, and she told me that she wanted to strangle me if she knew I was ever talking about it again.

Of this very exploit we have a more telling report from another witness. Once Angelica faced the gossips and went to the loom where many women were gathered and proudly bragged of her threats. The result is one momentous show-down during which she reminds everyone: "I scared her [Alexandra], my vendettas will take place, and twenty more devils will enter her body."[33]

The show down reveals what is at stakes in interpersonal relationships between villagers, the wielding of sway, the degree of dependence that an individual is prey to or can manipulate.[34]

So, Angelica actually cast the spell she boasts about. Certainly, the woman was herself aware of being considered a witch. Eventually the choice of an evil agency was the result of her natural disposition.

Empathy Deficit or a *Mens Rea*?

The information available on Angelica's past makes it difficult to argue that her serial, criminal threatening behavior is a result of an empathic gradient that has reached its lowest point. True, her agency could fall within the temperamental excesses of a woman subjected for the entire course of her existence to the psychological pressure of an infamous reputation that corrodes her potential empathy. After all, once Angelica proves she still has a thin residual "dove particle" when she does not accept money from a poor neighbor. Unluckily, trial papers hide the possible biological mechanism of a slippery slope toward a zero degree of empathy. A steady empathy reduction may have started at some point, long before the falling out with the Maco del Bolgia that made Angelica's witch nature public, and it shrank to nothing eventually making her a serial wrongdoer. We do not want to rule this trend out.

In fact, the empathic deficit hypothesis goes hand in hand with the assumption that evil is a biological drive with intricate connection to the social environment. The core of emotions on which the psychological atmosphere of Radicondoli pivots comes from the fear of malefice that Angelica has the power to inflict and remove. It is tempting to recover the notion of *proactive aggression* referred to by reflecting on a primary emotion such as anger: the serial nature of Angelica's attacks leads us to assume a premeditation for the extortions of advantages.[35] For sure, the long duration of her practice as a pediatrician cannot be explained without the acquiescence of villagers, perpetuated precisely by virtue of her reputation of having a good hand in the care of infants. Good hand versus malefic hand: the two-faced Janus dichotomy, *qui scit sanare scit destruere*, stands. And is not this ambiguous conviction just a window of opportunities, one of the many possible ones, in which the selfish interests of all free riders (possible witches) thrive?

Is the guilty mind hypothesis strengthened by the crime she herself claims: "I scared her"? The boast was by no way a snap decision; it alludes to an awareness and to the will to act certifying a property that comes from intentionality.[36] The woman was what her brain made her to be, and her manipulative demeanor was consistent with familism, factional alignments, struggles for management of local power. At the individual level, we may think of Angelica's vendettas as a peculiar mental impulse simply devoid of Hume's "particle of the dove" assumption: a deficiency of empathy hard core of evil. Why is that? The origins are in the neural mechanisms of human mind to grasp.

Notes

1 A. T. Beck, *Prisoners of Hate*, 35.
2 P. Bloom, *Just Babies*.

3 É. Durkheim, *The Rules of Sociological Method*, 1895.
4 L. Hunt, *Inventing Human Rights*, New York, 2007.
5 S. Pinker, *Blank Slate*.
6 S. Pinker, dealing with the neurobiology of violence connects "the psychological phenomenon to the neuroanatomy"; Id., *The Better Angels of Our Nature*, 500–508; A. Raine, *The Anatomy of Crime*, ch. 5.
7 S. Baron-Cohen, *Zero Degrees of Empathy*.
8 P. Burke, *Montaigne*, New York, 1982. Montaigne's mother was a Spanish Jewess.
9 Montaigne, *Essays*, III, cap. XI. Hellebore is an herbaceous plant of the *Ranunculaceae* and a decoction of its roots was considered a remedy for madness. Montaigne obviously has Horace in mind, *Satire*, II, 3, v. 82. Not dissimilarly Johan Weyer, in "De praestigiis daemonum," in *Witches, Devils, and Doctors in the Renaissance*, G. Mora ed., Temp, Arizona, 1988, XXVII, "A juridical summary concerning Lamiae," 561–576.
10 C. Heyes, "Empathy Is Not in Our Genes," in *Neuroscience and Biobehavioral Review*, 95, 2018, 499–507.
11 S. Baron-Cohen, *Zero Degrees of Empathy*, 10.
12 Ibid., 100–119, and *passim*.
13 ODS, *Inquisizione, stregoneria, medicina*, 181–187. Factions siding alongside noble Sienese landowners such as the d'Elci and the Berlinghieri, on one side, and the Landucci, and the Vieri and the local parish priest, on the other side, with the two women.
14 Ibid., 203.
15 On The del Bolgia, see ODS, *Autunno*, 204–209.
16 E. Goffman, *Interactional Ritual: Essays on Face-to-Face Behaviour*, New York, 1967.
17 ODS, *Inquisizione*, 185.
18 J. Demos, *The Enemy within*, 17.
19 ODS, *Inquisizione*, 205.
20 Ibid.
21 Id., *Autunno*, 381.
22 Ibid., p. 161.
23 ODS, *Inquisizione*, 194–195.
24 Ibid.
25 Ibid.
26 Ibid., 202.
27 Assuredly, the extent to which bewitchments were attributed to unwitching specialists is a point of debate among historians. Among villagers all forms of magic were fundamentally ambiguous: R. Muchembled, *Sorcières. Justice et société aux 16ᵉ et 17ᵉ siècles*, Paris,!987, 149–155. The relationship between protective (or remedial) magic and malevolent witchcraft was so close "that historian have come to see them more and more as the two inseparable halves of the world of popular culture": S. Clark, *Witchcraft and Magic in Early Modern Culture*, 112.
28 ODS, *Inquisizione, stregoneria, medicina*, 181–187.
29 Michel de Montaigne, *Essais*, II, XVII. Our translation.
30 U. Rublak, *The Astronomer and the Witch: Johannes Kepler's Fight for His Mother*, Oxford, 2017.
31 In cases where there is a conspicuous difference in social status between the spouses, the accusation is made that the marriage is due to love magic spells; see ASMo, 196/7.
32 See above, Chapter 10, note 29.
33 For all previous quotations, ODS, *Inquisizione*, 200–205.
34 C. Larner, *Natural and Unnatural Method of Witchcraft Control*, 138.
35 "The neurobiology of proactive aggression has not been extensively studied in humans [...] The better we know its biological basis, the better the opportunities to reduce aggression." R. Wrangham, *The Goodness Paradox*, 38.
36 G. M. Edelman, *Second Nature*.

27

CASE STUDY 7

Treasure Hunting or the Simulator Brain

There is the treasure there.

Mephistopheles

Enveloped in Chats: Memes

Malefic spells have monopolized our book. However, witchcraft can take many forms. It used to have a utilitarian face and in its multiple versions, aspects qualifying it as a technological resource, something intrinsic to human nature and the laws of evolution, have been found. It is a reasoning modality that connects Spinozian appetites, critical core of the human psyche, leading to beliefs. This hunger for knowledge, resulting in the high and low practices of magic, found constant nourishment in the widespread awe of a sublunar world populated by demons and spirits. "The wonderful remained a central category of investigating" and intellectuals debated and disagreed on those essences and the extent of their powers but did not question their existence.[1]

One goal of the wide repertoire of magical activities was to find out about what had happened, was happening or would be in the world: in every age divination was a central element of occult activities. Magic, representing an objectification of desire, focused on the attempt to shed light on what is unknown, or far away in space and time. In each community, specialists were used for a variety of purposes, such as searching for lost or stolen objects, missing persons, predicting the sex of an unborn child, progress of business or asking questions about the election of a doge or a cardinal. Maybe no ruler, from a petty despot like the Sienese Pandolfo Petrucci (1452–1512), to a Habsburg king like Rudolf II (1552–1612), governed without the help of an astrologer. Learned magic was held in high esteem, but that knowledge, moving away from larger cities, lost its depth while retaining only a functionalistic aspect. Among villagers,

DOI: 10.4324/9781003414377-30

the ambitious cognitive purposes of Renaissance and Baroque Europe magicians spread into a multitude of customs aimed at achieving personal goals, and the world of demons or the souls of the dead were accessed through bastardized rites over the centuries. Precisely this public use would prove to be the greatest corrosive agent of magical rituals. Consumers took refuge in abbreviated formulas for which there was no need for a soothsayer, but to find a lost object they resorted to domestic divination by observing reflective surfaces (mirrors, crystals) or to hydromantic clairvoyance, like looking into a bucket full of water. A do-it-yourself practice mixed cabals already inspiring Ovid's hexameters: "Et obscurum verborum ambage novorum / ter noviens carmen magico demurmurat ore [and muttered a mysterious incantation, dark with strange words, thrice nine times, in magical utterance]."[2] High and low knowledge transmitted by the flow of technical manuals which came out of the presses of the sixteenth century, induced by the boom that followed the invention of printing. But the diffusion mostly took place orally through the mechanical repetition of formulas.[3]

We have often insisted on a specific cognitive spiral: personal experiences, people's emotions, end up being translated into stories. Ancestral plots of hunting prowess or of loves and lusts or of the bloody wickedness of witches and demons or of any other kind of prodigies were told and listened to during the sociability of the vigils in the frescoed caves of the Pleistocene. Such narratives, delivered orally, aroused empathy, and dominated communication.[4] They constitute the oldest layer of human memories and the origin of all tales. From them, a plurality of situations, gestures and actions emerged, which are repeated in whole or in part, unpacked and adapted, resulting in survivals, fragments, cultural amalgams that are shaped in the various human and ecological contexts. These are pieces of information, also called memes, which have a very satisfying effect on the mind, related to occurrences that strike the imagination and "consequently are easily memorized, [a] further bonus for their distribution in the cognitive market."[5]

The entire history of humanity is full of "false news, in the multiplicity of their forms - simple tales, impostures, legends." Errors that propagate and amplify the condition that they find in the society in which they spread "a favorable breeding ground." In these tales, myths, legends, etc., "men unconsciously express their prejudices, their hatred, their fears, all their strong emotions."[6] Many environmental conventions related to various kinds of beliefs were reinforced in the ancestral attitude of humans to relate, tell stories, and transmit behaviors. Sequences attributable to some fundamental attribute of the mind, inherent in its astonishing capacity to become infected. We will not attempt a study of memes avoiding a territory strewn by traps, because the beginning and the accumulation of culture remains difficult to explain and different views abound among scholars. There is no agreement on which "infections" have been most adaptive for the human psyche, but on the other hand a propensity for contagion is indisputable.[7] Also, we cannot entirely exclude neural logic underlying the repetition of many similar phenomena. As for their possible biological substrate, we prefer to put a stop to it.[8]

But a curious form of contagious idea (we would not know how to better define it) deserves to be told and scrutinized in detail: treasure hunts. The countless number of court cases to which they gave rise make an analysis possible.

Goethe's Treasure Digger

Thousands of lively trials deal with a different typology of hunts, related to a niche witchcraft, the search for buried treasures, extravagant enterprises whose charm may have spanned millennia without leaving many documentary traces before the early modern age.

Spreading adventures caught Johann Wolfgang von Goethe's artistic imagination and his ballad "The Treasure Digger" (1797–1800) introduces the story:

All my weary days I pass'd
Sick at heart and poor in purse.
Poverty's the greatest curse,
Riches are the highest good!
And to end my woes at last,
Treasure-seeking forth I sped.
"Thou shalt have my soul instead!"
Thus I wrote, and with my blood.
Ring round ring I forthwith drew,
Wondrous flames collected there,
Herbs and bones in order fair,
Till the charm had work'd aright.
Then, to learned precepts true,
Dug to find some treasure old,
In the place my art foretold
Black and stormy was the night.
Coming o'er the distant plain,
With the glimmer of a star,
Soon I saw a light afar,
As the hour of midnight knell'd.
Preparation was in vain.
Sudden all was lighted up
With the lustre of a cup
That a beauteous boy upheld.
Sweetly seem'd his eyes to laugh
Neath his flow'ry chaplet's load;
With the drink that brightly glow'd,
He the circle enter'd in.
And he kindly bade me quaff:
Then methought "This child can ne'er,
With his gift so bright and fair,

To the arch-fiend be akin."
"Pure life's courage drink!" cried he:
"This advice to prize then learn, –
Never to this place return
Trusting in thy spells absurd;
Dig no longer fruitlessly.
Guests by night, and toil by day!
Weeks laborious, feast-days gay!
Be thy future magic-word!"[9]

When Goethe composed his moralistic poem, those peculiar hunts were near the end of a probable eighteenth-century heyday recorded in thousands of trials.[10] The weird excavations had been soon accompanied by a notable accentuation of their legal significance. Was it lawful to unearth treasures? And who did they belong to? These the basic questions raised by secular and ecclesiastical jurisprudence.[11]

So, this seductive chimera, was considered a crime, to be analyzed asking questions posed by every judicial fact. What is a buried treasure? Where do you dig for it? Who are the treasure hunters? Do those excavations go through periods of greater and lesser intensity? And, above all, why did the diggers insist for so long on seeking hidden riches that never came to light?

Facts

What was a buried treasure? Before defining such an apparent reality, we note that the myth of underground hidden fortunes has universal dimensions, as is amply "testified by the recording of the theme of the *Treasure Trove* in the folkloric repertoire of Aarne-Thompson [...] which covers almost every continent, listing ninety-nine possible variants of the motif in question present [...] in fairy tales and popular sagas."[12] In a very strict sense by treasure we must mean material goods with monetizable value: gold, silver, jewels. Protecting one's wealth by hiding it underground does not appear strange in an age without the banking facilities that today allow for the deposit of such assets. The word "treasure" also had a metaphorical meaning that we find in the Bible and in Christian theology. In the New Testament, treasure means the kingdom of God:

> The kingdom of heaven is like treasure hidden in a field. When a man found it, he hid it again, and then in his joy went and sold all he had and bought that field. Again, the kingdom of heaven is like a merchant looking for fine pearls. When he found one of great value, he went away and sold everything he had and bought it.[13]

Leaving the Gospels aside, even if for many men reaching upwards, to the kingdom of heaven, represented the most coveted wealth, the end of life,[14] for as many, the greatest desire was to own land and money. According to an economic opinion of the time, the goods available to men were in finite quantities and could not be increased. This meant that the economy was a zero-sum game; a concept contrasted by possessive individualism until its definitive decline with Adam Smith.[15] In traditional societies, the sudden enrichment of a single person could come from the impoverishment of another, who perhaps had buried his possessions. From the perspective of economic calculation, it does not appear illogical that to find new wealth one ended up looking underground. And "seeking," a crucial drive intrinsic to the magical cosmos, includes everything. Therefore, a labyrinth of direct or tortuous connections tied the search for buried treasures to alchemy, astrology, and necromancy.[16]

But where to dig? If theoretically a hidden treasure could lie anywhere, there were ideal places for concealment, such as near ruined castles and monasteries. Fortunes were expected to be found even in rural areas, especially if moving armies had camped there:

> Primitive mounds or piles of earth were particularly favored [...] Their excavation in the hope of quick enrichment was so common that "hill-digger" had become a recognized insulting term for a man seeking personal gain.[17]

And some hillocks really had to be pierced like a Swiss cheese, because the essence of the buried treasures was their intrinsic mobility. This was the case in the Verona area where, under the orders of the Venetian patrician Giulio Morosini, three expeditions of hunters alternated in the excavations between 1579 and 1580.[18] Open spaces prevailed but cellars of ancient buildings were dug, too.[19]

Hidden riches were guarded by spirits who moved them. Here comes again the common opinion that the world was populated by unreal entities and the most important guardians of treasures were ghosts. Shakespeare's Horatio stressed: "if thou hast uphoarded in thy life / Extorted treasure in the womb of earth, / For which, they say, you spirits oft walk in death, / speak of it: stay, and speak!"[20] The matter was very risky, then. Not so much for the attitude of secular and ecclesiastical justice that was, after all, long bland towards the crime; nor because there was widespread hostility of people towards diggers, although there is no lack of evidence of ringing tocsin when groups of strangers suddenly appeared on the spot armed with hoes and spades. In 1655, a witness reported to the Modena inquisitor:

> In the countryside, at Groppo, a villa under the jurisdiction of Sestola, [...] Five people were discovered where they were put to flight by the sound of bells [...] Then they returned after a few months [...] We went to observe them and we just had a few scuffles with them but they withdrew under some mountain rocks, and it was at night [...] They dug a little earth under a stone [...] making a wide circle almost two arms long.[21]

The principal risks came from sinister ritual procedures and fear of ghosts' revenge against the desecration.

Protagonists

Who were the diggers, these brave men, tenaciously attracted to such an ambiguous, perilous, delusional adventure?[22] These risks (even economic ones) were not a matter for women, men are mostly encountered.[23] Let us outline a sociological profile of the individuals involved.

The leader of an excavation should not have been without a smattering of magical erudition necessary to conceive the undertaking. It was necessary to bring together a mixed team, with specific skills inherent in the procedures that preceded and accompanied the organization and material execution of such a singular venture. The project almost always involved a small group of six / seven persons with different roles and among them the real treasure hunter stood out.

In Europe, these leaders share three or four common traits. The organizer or impresario could be (a) some wealthy person of notable extraction, owner of the castle, land, or other place to dig in; (b) a kind of fortune-teller, often poor, itinerant, and potential fraudster; (c) a socially high-ranking supporter; (d) and in urban areas support could come from ranks of intellectuals. "In seventeenth-century Bavaria, the upper classes and even the members of the city council organized treasure hunts."[24] Therefore, excavating hills was not intended as a small challenge and certainly not suitable for everyone. But pathetic and isolated cases of the do-it-yourself type appear, too. Like that penniless Sienese noblewoman who in 1676 wandered alone around one of her farms, using a lighted candle, dead bones, and a wand.[25]

The real leader needed managerial skills to finance the treasure search, find the instrument for divination, and bring together the protagonists of the pursuit: priests to exorcise spirits and access the riches released through notions of ceremonial magic (drawings of circles, recitation of spells and psalms, use of arcane symbols); fortune tellers; and pure subjects, not contaminated by sin, such as adult virgin women or pre-pubescent youngsters, with a central role in invoking the ghost, communicating with him by reading in a jug or in a mirror or on their uncontaminated hand, while in the meantime someone was holding a lighted candle and a would be metal detector: A pivotal role was played by a divining rod, a forked wooden stick (*furcilla*), already used in prehistoric times for identifying water sources. The wand had to be discovered in wooded areas and the procedure to build it was elaborate:

> Go where there are branches of olive tree or hazel laurel [...] and get on your knees and bare head and look fixedly at the sticks and tell us the gospel of St. John [...] and have a new knife and cut a stick saying *egredietur virga* from its roots [...] the chopsticks need to be at least half an arm long and must have a fork on the extremity, that is to say it is done with a knife [...] they are held in this way [...] the morning before sunrise [...][26]

An ardent prayer of heavenly protection opened and closed the magical invocation:

I implore you, wand, and mirror, in the name of the holy trinity that you open and show me the truth about this treasure which lies here in the area of a common street of the village and show and teach me where exactly it is hidden without any deceit on the part of evil spirits, amen.[27]

Next comes the crucial question. Why were there so many hunters in the early modern age? We can speak of a treasure hunt craze if we give weight to statistics from the Continent. The data also highlights a discrepancy: the declining late seventeenth and eighteenth-century State or Church justice interest in witch hunts, and the growing persecution of treasure hunters, particularly in German lands.

The proliferation of singular excavations reveals a signal of economic potential within a static agrarian society. The excessive eighteenth-century increase spreads to a fashion, like a meme, which ended up turning into a sort of speculative bubble. No surprise, then, that treasure hunting degenerated into a scam. The frauds were confirmed and were a corruptive fact not to be overestimated, though. Faced with the general good faith of those seeking to enrich themselves, during the eighteenth century the profiteers ended up multiplying among the leaders, attracted by the money of the company's financiers. In the end, their fraudulent intent would end up undermining the excavations.

Two Adventures

In these serial sources we come across surprising reports and narratives of crimes in which the minds and bodies of diggers act under pressure of that neurotransmitter that became part of brain flesh a few million years earlier: dopamine, source of man's *animal spirit*, that prompts action, curious craving, repetition of what we like. We will try to glimpse the dopaminergic pressure that fueled the desire pushing to seek and repeat risky deeds. Let us summarize the hunts told by Ranuccio (1652), a 34-year-old bricklayer[28] and Tommaso Paccioni (1657), a 38-year-old gunsmith subject of the Gonzaga in Mantua.

> [Ranuccio]... In July I was called by Captain Giovan Battista Melloni [second-in-command, aged 24]in Mantua. He wanted us to extract some money that was hidden in a vault of the Rocca della Pieve [...] In September we went there in the company of some strangers in number of five people among whom there was a woman dressed as a man and a 13 year old putto [lad].
>
> Once at the Rocca one [...] Francesco Benedetti [25 years old] who was always the main one and was the Chief [...] opened the boy's hand and anointed it with oil and stained it with a black dye saying certain words and then placed the third and fourth finger of that hand a lighted candle of human fat and then spoke into his ear. I then understood that he called a spirit called Uriel by name and that putto said he saw him in the form of a man on horseback [...]

The putto said that he saw the Spirit on his left hand [...] and Uriel said let me see the Fortress of the Pieve di Cento. The putto primed [by the leader] asked if there is any jewel or other precious stone [...] He asked the Spirit how many thousand scudi [there were]. Show me a hand. If there are a hundred thousand, show me one finger, if there are two hundred thousand show me two fingers, if there are three hundred thousand show me three fingers, if there are four hundred thousand show me four fingers. The putto said that [the spirit] showed four fingers [...] And when the Spirit was angry and did not want to obey [the leader and the putto] said those words [...] Uriel, Potestas, Seraphin, Potestas, Anglati, Anglata, Cala, Cala. [And the putto said] Uriel astringo [bind] you for my Virginity that is in front of you and for all the Angels, Archangels and for all those Angels who dominate you, that you declare the truth to me [...] He was still told how many feet the treasure was at the bottom, and that it showed as many fingers as the treasure was below, and the putto said that the Spirit showed seven fingers [...] He asked him again if there was any guard, and the Spirit did not show any [...]

The same is done many other times in different [times and] places. [... Another time] the enchantment was done again in the same way, and the [leader] made a large circle and asked the Spirit if the Treasure was in there and the putto said that the Spirit answered yes. [...] In the beginning we gave three or four strokes [of pickaxe and shovel] and we found nothing. It is true that we did little, and because the day was near, the Spirit left us [...] It is true that when they began to strike and dig two of us who had remained below said that they had heard a noise from below [...] They had heard a noise like a roar [...][29]

Tommaso Paccioni in January was in Turin on duty:

[One day,] having gone to an apothecary I was asked what country I was from. Having replied that I was Mantuan, I was told that the Germans on the occasion of the wars had taken away great treasures from those places. And I replied that it was true, but that there were still many more treasures buried there [I continued] telling them that I knew where they were buried, and I named them to be in the place of Carbonara on the river Po near Mantua. This speech, heard by a Dominican father [...] about my age, present in that shop, said that if there was money buried in those places named by me, he would find them through a Secret that he knew. And so, it ended.[30]

In the following days we grew in number and in the shop of another apothecary the Secret was translated into practice and was found an eight-year-old prepubescent putto who was instructed by the priest. Also, it was essential to get a rooster with all black feathers which, having hung a bulletin with the words Jesus Nazarenus Rex Iudeorum around his neck.[31]

[...] A month later I organized the team again in Mantua. [There are other expenses to be financed in order to fill the ranks and finally proceed to the executive stages of the enterprise.] We left the mainland to get to Carbonara by boat on the Po and faced the river at sunset [...] The excavation could not begin before midnight.

[The pleasure derived from the choice to act, anticipated in the long times of conception and preparations, undergoes a transformation, accelerates, and is replaced by new times and rhythms. The palpitations are diluted within two/three days during which the magical procedures were started, interrupted, and resumed several times but then refocused, reaching a climax, in a few hours, in the critical moments of the magical procedure. On the spot, wands are swinging. The putto, during the dialogue with the spirit, was constantly primed.]

We started digging, hands on the spade. [Repeated recitation of psalms and the pronouncements of conjurations alternate with ever new blows of the pickaxe, while the black rooster wanders at random. Then the spell ends. The release of dopamine decreases, the euphoria dies down.] Finally all of us were disappointed in our hopes, the work was finished and there was no other test, and everyone returned to his own business.[32]

What Meaning: Economic Risk or Cognitive Drive?

If the meanings of these human stories were predominantly economic, the moralistic tone of Goethe's ballad ("Pure life's courage drink! ... Guests by night, and toil by day!") would have centered its substance, proposing to bring men back to the non-apparent realities of daily activities and friendly sociability enjoying honest life with dignity. Examined instead from a psychological point of view, the verses leave one unsatisfied. Is that all, supreme poet, a moral sermon only? Better spare us the irony, because he pulled out the cognitive claws elsewhere giving the floor to his Mephistopheles:

You all feel the secret action
of the always powerful nature
and from the lowest regions a living clue creeps in.
When you feel your limbs bite,
when it upsets you, in a place, restlessness,
on then, decided, with spade and peak!
Over there is the dead; there is the treasure there.[33]

Thanks, damn figure, your tirade penetrates the heart of the nature/culture dichotomy, displacing the reasons for a choice: the rational calculation that invites us to get out of misery by working, yields to demonic words, captured by the stimulus of risk and uncertainty, by their incessant charm.

We will try to scrutinize which neural realities may be hidden behind a human event that spread through cultural replication, organizing collective beliefs and actions. In the *alea* of treasure hunting a conspicuous inconsistency stands out: the almost total failure of all the enterprises appears in stark contrast to the obstinacy of diggers not to give up picks, spades, and magic mirrors. Such persistence drags the meaning of diggers' conduct onto the terrain of a mental pathology. "Once again it appears that [an] economic problem becomes a psychological problem,"[34] and the illogicality of treasure hunters drags the analysis into the field of the force of collective illusions.

***

In descriptions left by the diggers the succession of events is confused. The very temporality of emotions plays an important role in the study of this financial operation in which pleasure and trepidation are closely intersected. Sometimes months before the date of the excavation it is rather obvious to imagine a mixture of passions stirring in the heads of the leaders; they imagine and anticipate emotions of what will happen in the actual moment of the exploration on site; emotions already directly savored or learned from the experiences of others.

We can hypothesize that mental imagery, which we discussed when dealing with the "simulator brain" and its "creativity," returns to play a role here again. Leaders, continually worrying about an upcoming event, anticipate future performance with their mind's eye; they hear in their heads the noises of the excavation, the menacing warnings of the ill-disposed spirit, they imagine the moment when they will find the hidden treasure.[35]

Experimental psychology research suggests a key role of mental simulation in desire and behavior that can push towards the desired object while ignoring its risks. For example, the more vivid a mental image of food is, the more salivation is activated, and the frequency of involuntary mental images of alcoholic beverages is associated with a greater risk of relapse in abstinent alcoholics.[36] At the neural level, imagining desired substances activates the areas of the brain that respond to pleasure and reward.[37] This power of mental simulation is exploited by innovative therapeutic proposals, which seek to harness its potential to promote adaptive behaviors.[38] The power of suggestion and self-suggestion is clear, a particular mood determined by different facts that put protagonists in a psychological condition, in an enchantment amplified by the rituals.

We are left speculating that the treasure hunt leaders may have been particularly susceptible to the reward anticipation of finding a treasure "as if it was already real." It is unknown how they would have performed in contemporary, real-world laboratory experiment, such as the Iowa Gambling Task, where participants must select cards from a variety of decks that present varying levels of economic gain or loss and risk. The test measures parameters such as the willingness to risk in the face of a greater immediate gain and the ability to learn (quickly) which decks of cards are most advantageous economically in the long term.[39] Neural responses during the IGT reveal a plurality of activations. At the heart of the performance is the activity of the ventromedial prefrontal cortex, a hub that integrates emotional information (inherent to pleasure / pain, anxiety, fear, etc., coming from the amygdala, the hippocampus, the basal ganglia) with cognitive control functions ("that deck has the highest scoring cards but also the greatest risk of losing everything").[40] While the neural details remain debated by neuroscience, it can be concluded that the test measures the balance between pleasure and the motivation system, regulated by dopamine and endorphins, and the cognitive control system, representing a model of how individuals take "affective" decisions when there are loss, gain and uncertainty at stake.[41] Unsurprisingly, both performance and neural activity during IGT change with age, maturing in the transition from adolescence to adulthood, suggesting a neurobiological basis for the greater risk propensity of adolescents. These same circuits also seem to vary according to the individual temperamental traits of individuals, such as sensitivity to gain and pleasure (reward seeking). The personalities who respond more intensely to gain end up losing more money (in the test) when they must make choices under conditions of greater risk.[42]

Alongside psychology studies, neuroeconomic investigation has used this task to understand the brain's appetite for economic risk. While the discussion remains open on which aspects of "risk" are measured by the task, it emerges with substantial clarity that the perception of risk in an economic-speculative decision activates a neural circuitry other than that which represents the hoped-for gain. And indeed, the risk involves areas of the brain responsible for higher cognitive functions, such as some parts of the prefrontal cortex and the anterior cingulate cortex that preside over the processing of conflict situations.

... Or Addiction?

Treasure hunting is much more than a purely intellectual affair in which the seduction of the occult and economic calculation is mixed, then. "Recent developments in neuroscience have shown that when we take a risk, including a financial risk, we do more than just think about it. We prepare for it physically."[43] Our bodies wait for action, influencing our way of thinking. The dynamics of body and brain provide these adventurers with stamina, an ability to withstand prolonged physical and mental exertion. The narratives of the trials provide a repeated series of concrete situations configuring the construction of a witch-like context and its alluring spell. We have the repetition of rituals made up of acts and words that induced in the participants an alteration of their state of consciousness, a sort of trance, in which their thoughts and perceptions were translated, for a certain period, into a readiness to get results. Maybe.

In fact, things could not have turned out this way. It is perplexing to allude to a conscious manipulation of the nervous system. Not unlike what can be observed when dealing with therapeutic magic, in the human search for buried treasures the phenomenal world with all its invisible and mysterious essences and the individual's psychological and neurobiological characteristics are confronted and interact. In the case of healing magic, many positive outcomes can be seen coming from the mutual influence of the interested parties, with certified psychological relief. In the case of buried treasures, after the almost hallucinogenic phase of excavation we do not know what to imagine. The disarming words of the Duke of Mantua's armorer apply: dejected each digger left for his own business. So why did many of them start again? Was it an addiction?

Let's return for a moment to the balance between risk assessment and anticipation of earnings measured by the IGT. We will never know whether hunting leaders would fit into the high reward seeking profile of contemporary personality questionnaires whose risk control circuits appear dysfunctional. Or if they were eternal teenagers whose response circuits to pleasure were hyperactive. And if it were "addiction," what would it be due to? To find an answer, we can return to the analogy with the contemporary financial speculative bubble. In the project of an excavation, as in the world of reckless stock market operations, we hypothesize that the dominant psychological factor is not the calculation of monetizable advantages of the undertaking. On the contrary, the excitement given by the cognitive mystery of the action prevailed over the pleasure of waiting for the gain. But then, Gordon Gekko, the ruthless financier in the movie *Wall Street 2*, was right, and his words lead to the heart of a psychological problem: "It's not about the money. It is about the game."[44] It's not so much money that matters as much as the thrill of the game, of the risk.

We could consider the compulsiveness detectable in the actions of some serial treasure hunter as a state of addiction, a disease that has neurophysiological bases quite like those defined by the studies conducted on pathological gamblers, where behavior shifts from goal-directed to becoming insensitive to negative consequences.[45] We doubt that this chimera of buried treasures is configured as any pathology. However, the neuroscientific studies of clinical populations offer at least suggestive insights.[46]

The neurobiological interpretation presents elements of a contradiction that reflect the complexity of attempts to understand human decision-making mechanisms and their apparent deformations: cognitive risk assessment, simulation of future gain, distortion of risk as pleasure, habit-driven behavior. We are left with speculations as to what the brain of the treasure diggers did when faced with choices. The memory that actualizes the emotions experienced by subjects in the past constitutes a reserve of affective experiences that they recall when choosing.[47] By combining the observation of actual choices with a mapping of neural activity, current research illustrates well how the emotion evoked by a word or a vision encapsulating the anticipated excitement and distorting previous losses, filters into the final choice.[48]

Notes

1 S. Clark, *Thinking with Demons*, 253.
2 Ovid, *Metamorphosis*, XIV, vv. 57–58. Our translation.
3 W. Eamon, *Science and the Secrets of Nature*, Princeton, NJ, 1994.
4 W. Burkert, *Creation of the Sacred*.
5 G. Bronner, *La democrazia dei creduloni*, Ariccia, 2016, 17.
6 M. Bloch, "Réflexions d'un historien sur les fausses nouvelles de la guerre," in Id., *Mélanges historiques*, I, Paris, 1963, 43, 44.
7 On the concept of infections see R. Dawkins, *The Devil's Chaplain*; E. Bever, "Current Trends in the Application of Cognitive Science to Magic," *MR&W*, 7, 2012, 7–8.

8 "We don't know how to define memes in a way that is operationally useful to the practicing scientist, we don't know why some memes are successful and others not, and we have no clue regarding the physical substrate, if any, of which memes are made. Memes, as it turns out, are an intriguing metaphor, but they do not come close to providing us with even a sketch of a theory of cultural evolution"; see J. Burman, "The misunderstanding of memes: Biography of an unscientific project, 1976 to 1999," in *Perspectives on Science,*20, 2012, 75–104.

9 J. W. von Goethe, *Schatzgraeber*, translated into English verse by Alfred Baskerville, 1853.

10 The exact number is unknown, J. Dillinger, *Magical Treasure Hunting in Europe and North America: A History*, Basingstoke, 2012, 5.

11 Ibid, 9–27.

12 M. Leonardi, "Inquisizione, tesori, angeli e demoni in Sicilia tra etnografia e testimonianza storica," in *Bruniana & Campanelliana: Ricerche filosofiche e materiali storico-testuali*, XIX, 2013, 91.

13 Matthew 13.44–46. New International Version.

14 K. Thomas, *The Ends of Life*, 110–146, 226–268.

15 G. M. Foster, "Treasure Tales and the Image of the Static Economy in a Mexican Peasant Community," in *Journal of America Folklore*, LXXVII, 1964, 39–44; Id., "Peasant Society and the Image of Limited Good," in *American Anthropologist*, LXVII, 1965, 293–315; Id. "Reply to Frans J. Schryer: A reinterpretation of treasure tales and the Image of Limited Good," *Current Anthropology*, 17, 1976, 708–9, 710–713. J. Dillinger, *Magical Treasure Hunting*, 190–194.

16 The Arab-Islamic tradition was particularly rich, as evidenced by the reflections of the philosopher al-Kindī active in Baghdad in the mid-ninth century; see C. Burnett, K. Yamamoto, M. Yano, "Al-Kindī on Finding Buried Treasure," in *Arabic Sciences and Philosophy*, 7 (1997), 57–90. In sixteenth-century Naples such synergies were rife: see J.-M. Sallmann, *Chercheurs de trésors et jeteuses de sort: La quête du surnaturel à Naples au XVIe siècle*, Paris, 1986.

17 K. Thomas, *Religion and Decline of Magic*, 279–280.

18 R. Martin, *Witchcraft and the Inquisition in Venice 1550–1650*, Oxford, 1989, 88–89.

19 In Siena, in the 1630s and 1640s, we have news of excavations. ODS, *Autunno*, 77–78

20 Shakespeare, *Hamlet*, I, i, vv. 136–139.

21 ASMo, *Inquisizione*, 133, 9; 136, 10. At Confortino, near Bologna, around 1513–14 there was a treasure hunt that had "a resonance in Modena like few other magical enterprises of the time"; see M. Duni, *Tra religione e magia. Storia del prete modenese Guglielmo Campana (1460?–1541)*, Firenze, 1999, 244.

22 J. Dillinger, *Magical Treasure Hunting*, 96.

23 Statistic of treasure hunting trials records only 4 certain cases of female presence; see ODS, *Autunno*, 77. The prevalence of men is instead total in the Modenese trials. A persistence of women in this keeping away from economic risk is reported: "Women, at most, account for 5% of those who work in the financial world"; J. Coates, *The Hour between Dog and Wolf. Risk-Taking, Gus Feelings and the Biology of Boom and Bust*, London, 2015, 252–257.

24 J. Dillinger, *Magical Treasure Hunting*, 149.

25 ODS, *Autunno*, 77. See V. Tedesco, "Treasure Hunt – Roman Inquisition and Magical Practices *Ad Inveniendos Thesauros* in Southern Tuscany," in *Witchcraft Demonology and Magic*, M. Montesano, ed., in *Religions*, 2019, 10, 98–108.

26 ASMo, *Inquisizione*, 136.

27 J. Dillinger, *Magical Treasure Hunting*, 96.

28 ASMo, *Inquisizione*, 136, 3.

29 Ibid., 129, 2, 1–10v.

30 Ibid., 136, 3.

31 Ibid.

32 Ibid.

33 J. W. von Goethe, *Faust II*, I, vv. 4985–4992.

34 M. Bloch, "Pour une histoire comparée des sociétés européennes," in Id, *Mélanges historiques*, I, 26, n. 1.

35 S. M. Kosslyn, G. Ganis, W. L. Thompson, "Neural Foundations of Imagery," in *Nature Reviews Neuroscience*, 2, 2001, 635–642.

36 J. L. Ji, D. J. Kavanagh, E. A. Holmes, C. MacLeod, M. Di Simplicio, "Mental Imagery in Psychiatry: Conceptual & Clinical Implications," *CNS Spectr.* 24, 1, 2019, 114–126. doi: 10.1017/ S1092852918001487.

37 C. D. Kilts, R. E. Gross, T. D. Ely, K. P. Drexler, "The Neural Correlates of Cue-Induced Craving in Cocaine-Dependent Women," in *Am J Psychiatry*, 161, 2004, 233–41.

38 J. May, D. J. Kavanagh, J. Andrade., "The Elaborated Intrusion Theory of Desire: A 10-Year Retrospective and Implications for Addiction Treatments," in *Addict Behav*, 44, 2015, 29–34. doi: 10.1016/j.addbeh.2014.09.016.

39 The *Iowa Gambling Task* was invented by Antoine Bechara, António Damásio, Daniel Tranel e Steven Anderson. See Bechara A, Damasio AR, Damasio H, Anderson SW, "Insensitivity to Future Consequences Following Damage to Human Prefrontal Cortex," in *Cognition*, 50, 1994, 7–15.

40 Ibid.

41 C. Schmidt, *Neuroeconomia. Come le neuroscienze influenzano l'analisi economica*, Torino, 2013, 178.

42 B. Almy, M. Kuskowski, S. M. Malone, E. Myers, M. Luciana, "A Longitudinal Analysis of Adolescent Decision-Making with the Iowa Gambling Task," in *Dev Psychol*, 54, 2018, 689–702. doi: 10.1037/dev0000460.

43 Ibid.

44 Michael Douglas in *Wall Street: Money Never Sleeps*, directed by Oliver Stone.

45 R. Z. Goldstein, N. D. Volkow, "Drug Addiction and its Underlying Neurobiological Basis: Neuroimaging Evidence for the Involvement of the Frontal Cortex," in *Am J Psychiatry*, 159, 2002, 1642–1652; A. E. Goudriaan, J. Oosterlaan, E. de Beurs, W. Van den Brink, "Pathological Gambling: A Comprehensive Review of Biobehavioral Findings," in *Neurosci Biobehav Rev*, 28, 2004, 28, 123–41.

46 We would find that the structures and neural systems involved with different functions in the pathological search for treasures are likely to be like those of gamblers. Both performance and neural function during IGT are altered in individuals suffering from a wide range of impulsive / compulsive behaviors, including gambling and obesity. In gamblers, the disorder is even more serious, the more hyperactive is the response of the dopamine circuits of pleasure and gain, when they lose but were about to win (in tests that simulate roulette); that is, it is the "risk of winning" (albeit accompanied by a monetary loss) that seems to give pleasure. In addictions induced by substances of abuse that act directly on the dopaminergic circuits of the brain, brain alterations are triggered for which the response to pleasure or gain (for example monetary) is desensitized, and the behavior is no longer driven by motivation but chained (through alterations of the cerebral circuits) by the habit of looking for the substance of abuse indifferent to any risk. See H. W. Chase, L. Clark, "Gambling Severity Predicts Midbrain Response to Near-Miss Outcomes," in *J Neurosci*, 30, 2010, 6180–7; D. J. Nutt, Lingford-Hughes A, Erritzoe D, P. R. Stokes, "The dopamine theory of addiction: 40 years of highs and lows," in *Nat Rev Neurosci*, 16, 2015, 305–12. doi: 10.1038/nrn3939; K. D. Ersche, C. M. Gillan, P. S. Jones, G. B. Williams, L. H. Ward, M. Luijten, S. de Wit, B. J. Sahakian, E. T. Bullmore, T. W. Robbins., "Carrots and Sticks Fail to Change Behavior in Cocaine Addiction," in *Science*, 17, 2016, 1468–71.

47 C. Schmidt, *Neuroeconomia*. All this is perhaps combined at the level of that prefrontal ventromedial cortex that synthesizes the excitement promoted by the amygdala and the anticipation of pleasure in the basal ganglia with the self-control provided by the anterior cingulate and other frontal areas of the brain.

48 D. Kahneman, *Thinking, Fast and Slow*.

PART IV
Millennials

The attractive powers of urban and industrial civilization marked the spatial marginalization of witchcraft within global cosmology. But in the third millennium AD, the same forces have been undergoing too many accelerations and developments. In relation to counterfactual beliefs, it is difficult to end our analysis by tracing it back to the other opening assumption of the book: *after looking so far back how far forward can you see*? Unless we want to turn into an unlikely Nostradamus, the uncertainty of ancient cartographers is preferable: when drawing an unknown territory, they would write *hic abundant leones* ("lions abound there").

DOI: 10.4324/9781003414377-31

28

A LOOK FROM ABOVE

About 36,000 km high on the vertical of the equator and on the Greenwich meridian, a geostationary satellite scans and photographs the planet with its radiometers. In a nocturnal image of the Old Continent bright spots highlight the dense constellation of inhabited centers and introduce some final considerations.

Ten thousand years after the settlement of the first agricultural societies and the beginning of the Holocene, Millennials crossed the threshold of the Anthropocene. This phase of life defining the centrality of human species is marked by an over-building of the countryside. Before the nineteenth century, urban public spaces were insufficiently illuminated.[1] If similar snapshots were achievable for significant moments in our narration, from antiquity to medieval and modern times, maybe only a few pale eighteenth-century lights isolated in total darkness would deliver the tangible example of a close link between the shrinking embeddedness of witchcraft in a cosmogonic scenery and the different times of the distribution of population on the Continent. The image retrospectively confirms the prospected evolution: "the dividing line between city and countryside stands out as the most striking geographical feature of the origins of witchcraft cognition."[2]

Returning to the rational city, the effects of modern age behavioral urbanization show a better distinction between the public and private spheres, with an impact on the moral autonomy of individuals regarding the persuasions tyrannically imposed by a culture of shame. On one hand, in the countryside, "what is public and what is private remained as undifferentiated as ever"; on the other, in the cities, the educated classes developed different ways of reasoning in domestic privacy, proposing themselves as a model for illiterate classes.[3] It was an intertwining of human relationships produced by the contraction of space and time in city habitat: the rich amalgam of the nineteenth and twentieth centuries, a bourgeois ideology kept the culture of rural spells at a distance, except for sporadic survivals. But the third millennium AD is proposing much more: a creeping metamorphosis from a "rational" city to a "smart"

DOI: 10.4324/9781003414377-32

one, due to unexpected dimensions and speed of information and communication technologies, with all their economic and cultural repercussions.

An Unpredictable Cosmogonic Revolution

The image taken by the satellite suggests that due to technological innovations people, adding up to 75% of the global population, who work and live in cities interact with each other, creating an atmosphere of logical participation and inclusiveness that increases involvement. It is not just as an exponential growth of the economy like the ones that occurred in nineteenth- and twentieth-century Europe, mainly based on the use of energy. The transition from a rational city to a smart one alludes to a future defined by the power of information and communication technologies in "hyperhistoric" societies whose advancements depend on intangible assets based on knowledge.

It has now been established that the qualitative gap of the 2000s occurs in the ability to process the information acquired; a decisive expansion, which has made the leaps forward of the previous two centuries obsolete.[4] Surveys, forecasts, analyses, measurements are multiplying at an exasperating rate. The speed with which a genetic knowledge is acquired implies that we may be able of inventing modifications of our gene complexion.[5] Here the will to forestall the worst future, to control it with calculation, is to be noted. The cognitive frontiers opened by the industrial scenarios of tomorrow (4.0, 5.0, 6.0) eliminating distances and times of connections between men, invite us to reconsider the nature of experience and how the brain constructs the mind.

Now, if it is correct to have identified in the notion of space, time, knowledge, in the relations between humans and nature, between individuals and men and women, some salient features of the universals typifying the cosmology of an era, it seems undeniable that something profoundly new is taking place in the life of individuals. The pressure of such a multiplicity of situations shapes human psychology to adapt its cognitive abilities to meet new challenges and goals. The urge to seek has always been an impulse that has distinguished *Homo sapiens*; its intrinsically informational nature has powerfully expanded in this third millennium after Christ. The acceleration promises a mutation that may unpredictably impact the primary and secondary emotions, which prepare the breeding ground for abstract concepts in the functioning of our gelatinous brain flesh. All of this concerns a future that analysts measure with immoderate faith in the blessed/cursed algorithms, whose gender-related variables may affect the current millennium cosmogony.

But if in seeking we identify the even more expanded figure of the future new *Sapiens*, we can no less foresee a re-edition of that prehistoric spiral of reasoning that prepared the emotional terrain of abstract thought through the gears of the "ape problem." To seek, but for what? Cinema and good and bad dystopian literature anticipate future sets based on mathematical projections of the current advances in science: bioprinters, nanotechnologies, genetics, artificial intelligence, etc., etc. Algorithms, again, will define an existence that overcomes past imperfections:[6] the unbridled faith of the techno-fixers that technology will ease human existence.[7] A whole series of achievements that, according to some, in an indefinite distant time, will remove *Homo*'s biological hardware by eliminating the defective parts of his genome, leading to a transhumanism that comes as the latest search for a desire for immortality.[8] It no longer makes sense to think in terms of evolution, relating to the time span that was necessary for the advent of *Homo sapiens*. Given the geometric progression of recent innovations, some hundred generations would be deemed necessary for the appearance of a similar new species.[9]

Let us stop here. The acceleration of change exceeds our ability to predict timing and effects of a different perception of experience on the plasticity of the organ of thought.[10] We are not equipped to turn into unlikely Nostradamus and are reluctant to draw a future map filled with conjectures based on artificial intelligence. Instead, in the short span of a century, we believe *Sapiens* will remain entangled in something of the past, in neural sedimentations that lead us back to issues that have hitherto committed us: to fear, anger and the corollary of emotions magma of counterfactual explanations.

Farewell to Nearly All That?

Did a legacy of the age of witch hunt reach the third millennium AD? Some ambiguous similarities are worth reflecting on.

Ambiguous Similarity 1:*This Is a Witch Hunt*

Indeed, we live in a paranoid world, which believes in conspiracies.[11] Millennials still seem to be trapped in the psychological dimension of fast thinking versus slow thinking that characterized reactions to evil witchcraft in past centuries. Let us consider the expression this is a witch hunt! The claim recurs in the language of politics, of mass-media and of ordinary people. A former president of the USA tweeted the expression hundreds of times during his presidency; words that have become a catch phrase for any human imbroglio. The contemporary universal use of the assertion is a metaphor for the prosecution of situations, and "harass, convict or otherwise penalize a group of people who have become the object of wide-spread fear."[12] Witch hunt has become a disposable meme that illustrates the force of human imagination to create a stereotype and its unwillingness to query the stereotype once it is accepted.

The case of migrants is significant. The evanescence of neighborhood crime has left a void filled with new fears and anger, when another type of neighbor bursts into the daily landscape, generating an anxiety for personal safety or job and goods: a continent-wide malaise, amplified by the web, that multiplies the inborn brain propensity for viral contagion. The case of LGTBQ+ people is momentous, too. The polyfunctionality of the meme is at work here to indicate an angry disgust towards certain categories of persons judged to be dangerous based on prejudice alone. Palimpsests of man's psychic structure resurface. The neural response to perceived threat leads to an eruption of defensive stress, to a badly restrained rage, to an abstract personalization of harm. Motions of the soul are not oriented either by urban rationality or by statistical accounting on the actual dimensions of the danger. As the projection of fear and anger fueled the emotional bases of witchcraft agency, so any kind of a difficult contemporary situation in public life is likely to be characterized as a witch hunt. And, no surprise, *fast thinking* continues to exert its pre-eminence by producing disordered reactions. But our understanding of how prejudice is formed also shows that its expression is very malleable to social context and is starting to equip us with more refined means to combat it.[13]

Ambiguous Similarity 2: The Neighborhood Crime

Did, then, the twentieth-century French farmer mentioned above, suggesting that familiarity between people was the prerequisite for evil spells, grasp the situation? Does the Millennials' anonymous proximity in great urban centers of the Continent prevent them from bewitching each other? The answer cannot be totally affirmative with reference to the meaning given to malefice as neighborhood crime. Some phenomena of contemporary society raise the problem of their affinity with the intentional spell of the age of the witch hunt. Starting from the sixties, a series of studies by ethnographers, folklorists, criminologists, and anthropologists revealed that witchcraft accusations were still being made in Europe, although the phenomenon is marginal (or less studied) in urban areas.[14]

We have seen that after the decriminalization of malefice during the nineteenth century with extensions to subsequent years people continued to take the law in their own hand with regard to dealing with witches, and this led to what has been called "witch trials in reverse."[15] Nevertheless, in general, in Europe public witchcraft accusations became uncommon events by the mid-twentieth century. Despite this, the scenario remains ambiguous: finding traces of active bewitchment is impossible, but since the fear of malefice continues to stir people's minds, some presence of malevolent agency cannot be excluded.

If we focus on evil agency, understood as a degradation of empathy or as an inborn personal endowment, a similar destructive drive can be found in the pathology of haters on the web, no less devoid of the deliberate malevolence peculiar to neighborhood crime. Let us assimilate two distant actions. Consider the *levar la pediga* malefice (taking the footprint of a hated local enemy) perpetrated against a neighbor a few centuries ago. What feelings could the contemplation of that small bundle containing earth devised by Jacopo and Margherita and kept hanging over the fireplace arouse? Imagine their cerebral response recorded by an fMRI. Now, think about the angry Millennials writing texts filled with hatred on a personal computer or cell phone. Even their inner psychological satisfaction would be recorded by an fMRI, as "whatever the nature of the act (be it physical un-empathic acts [...] or non-physical un-empathic acts – deception, mockery, verbal abuse, etc.), at the very moment of the act, the empathy circuit goes down."[16]

Both neural reactions are induced by malignant agency, driven by fear or anger or envy or a competitive urge to make the other succumb in revenge or to preserve one's own advantage or, ultimately, by a mere evil nature.

The astonishing animosity characterizing public life in our third millennium marks the obsolescence of the centuries old divide between the countryside and the city in respect to the malignancy inherent in the neighborhood crime: hatred on the web knows no geographical demarcation. All in all, Hugo Grotius was right: wickedness is the daughter of familiarity in the update meaning it finds in the cosmology of the third millennium AD. We are genetically wired to think in group terms, us versus them. Expanding the closeness among people, the social media have contributed to the multiplication of inborn blind evil in which a single tweet can destroy a person. The social media effect would appear even more pernicious as it combines unboundaried closeness in time and space to anonymity and distance, such that there's no visual cue of the victim's embodied response to restrain an aggressor.

Ambiguous Similarity 3: The Witch = Woman Factor

Within the development perspective promoted by smart cities, will the cliché witch = woman, for millennia a salient feature of the embedding of witchcraft in cosmogonic systems, still keep finding a breeding ground favorable to a lasting reproduction?

After the heyday in *ancien régime* Europe, patriarchal societal preconditions of a *gynecopoiesis*, which have for centuries favored the persistence of the stereotype, are thinning out with a moderate but constant progression. About a hundred years ago a Thomas Edison's prophecy marked a good turning point in women's life prospects as depicted in Xenophon's *Oeconomicus*:

> The housewife of the future will be neither a slave to servants nor herself a drudge. She will give lesser attention to the home because the home will need less; she will be rather a domestic engineer than a domestic laborer, with the greatest of all handmaidens, electricity, at her service.[17]

Therefore it is worth asking: what does the twenty-first-century smart city offer from a gender perspective? How deeply can the new opportunities be harnessed to purposefully address challenges of most concern to women and turn upside down the historical process that "made" them?[18] Should Millennials then consider patriarchy to be completely agonizing, and with it the infamous cliché, good only to feed the "cultural" tourism scattered in many small cities around the globe, a legacy of the age of witch hunts: which are the best small towns for witches to visit?

There are niche areas where the sick equation and its pernicious adhesions seem to persist. "A sample of English 'witch trials in reverse' dating from the eighteenth century to the twentieth century indicates that 91% of the accused witches were women," and similar European percentages are given for roughly the same period.[19] Despite the emancipations extorted from the supremacy of a male governance, women are still the target of derogatory epithets and prejudice, related to a latent drive for the male to reduce them to their sexuality, in fact limiting and de-legitimizing their participation in public life.[20] But how indicative are such situations? Much research will be necessary to verify whether the social, cultural, and economic reasons of the new millennium are at play to make the cliché obsolete.

From a neurobiological angle, the scientific debate on the levels at which sexual dimorphism is expressed at the cerebral and cognitive sphere remains heated. The female brain performs functions equivalent to the male one.[21] But we do not know to what extent and in what exact directions will the basics of different characteristics possibly governing the cognitive functions of female brain be affected by future interactions between genetics and high-speed environmental change. Do opportunities offered to women by smart cities affect a creeping trend? According to a 2020 survey, three out of five Millennials were willing to delay their pregnancy until they reached a certain job title or level within their career.[22]

Ambiguous Similarity 4: Suffering and Damage

An ambiguous proximity between religion and science characterized the nineteenth and twentieth centuries. The ambivalence about religion, the co-existence of the scientific and the supernatural, remains a feature of contemporary societies, though today the mix is certainly different, and societies are more divided between believers and non-believers, with the latter having acquired a more institutionalized status since the Enlightenment.[23] The third millennium AD seems to promise a further acceleration towards a pre-eminence of rationalistic-scientific-skeptical thought. Will it be separated from a further masking of religion and the propensity for counterfactual reasoning? The health-factor seems to prove it.

Homo sapiens have always had a complex relationship with the causes of pain produced by disease, to which magical-religious ideas, monozygotic twins, owe much of their persistent vitality. On one hand, the reality of suffering, no longer understood to be of mysterious origin, is mainly addressed by turning to medical science; on the other, in the face of treatments enduring fallacies, comfort is likely to continue to be sought and found in the providential framework of faith in miraculous divine interventions, faith perhaps not separated from the use of pseudo-scientific therapies of no less magical matrix. In the 1960s, the Italian parliament and the labor minister were involved in a collective psychodrama concerning the fight against cancer. With public money, the activity of a would-be doctor was financed. The pressure of the press forced the therapist to reveal his recipe against cancer on a live broadcasting, eventually halting the secret treatment.[24] After a few decades, another treatment against advanced neoplasm stages, now equipped with self-styled scientific cloaks, captured the hopes of many patients and was the subject of a nation-wide scientific debate and political discussion.[25] To be fair, these therapies were sometimes rewarded by the blessed placebo effect, which has probably been the dominant benefit during the two thousand years of Western medical science.[26] The fluctuations of this reasoning – that escapes measurements re-proposing an etiology in terms of the increase or decline of one or the other mental attitude – remind us of Plautus's Cappadoce tirade: if medical science doesn't heal me I try something else. Perhaps the balance will be shifted once medical science takes a deep dive into understanding and intentionally integrating the "something else": making use of those cognitive and neural mechanisms that we have touched upon throughout the book to shift brain computations and generate expectations, from which perceptions, motivation and change in physiology could emerge.[27]

And what about harm, those mysterious spells that made Virgil's tender lambs die, curdle cheese, pigs or other beasts go crazy, etc.? Have education, communication, technological knowledge, neutralized the tendency to blame witchcraft in the face of unexplained damage and malfunction? In long-term evaluation, the sudden and misunderstood minor or bigger misfortunes still haunting everyday life have gradually seen their impact on the modes of reasoning canceled out. The spread of a technical-scientific culture has prepared the ground and transported thought from elaborating a theory of misfortune to the impersonal causality of the Law of Entropy, "widely acknowledged in everyday life."[28] And so, theories of explanation of misfortune have travelled a very long journey from St. Augustine's "doctrine of the punishment of the human race for the sin of Adam" to Murphy's law,[29] in sayings such as: if something can go wrong, it will, a current currency and minimum cognitive cost in every twisted occurrence.

Ambiguous Similarity 5: Seeking

If we concentrate our reflection on the cauldron from which evil agency draws nourishment, that is, on primary and social emotions, it is easy to notice ambiguous affinities in people's contemporary ways of behaving, reminding us of the peculiar scenarios of past centuries. Maybe the hostility polluting the web also disguises some people's resentment against harm and suffering mysteriously inflicted by unspecified contemporary malefic *free riders*. Trying to identify a common denominator within the corrosive emotional forces pervading the air, we register situations in which they, the haters, consider themselves as the victims of badly discerned strong powers. "Many people find it easy to direct their anger against an allegedly cosmopolitan and rootless cultural elite."[30] The misfortunes one has to endure and combat are not intended as a consequence of problems and difficulties "which are inevitable in an indifferent universe but as malevolent designs of insidious elites, minorities, or foreigners."[31] The idea of secret conspiracies increases the paranoia of those who, influenced by fake news, are convinced that it is all a deception in the interest of no one knows who. It is a concrete yet intangible fear, vaguely named and personified in abstract entities: in globalization, in multinationals, in the algorithms of finance, in the hidden plots of powerful cliques. How distant are we from the sixteenth-century machinations of the phantasmatic sects of witches, theorized by Jean Bodin's *Démonomanie des sorciers*, and labelled as enemies of the Christian state and of common wealth? The main novelty of today's secret plans devised to accomplish selfish and treacherous ends consists in the planetary diffusion enabled by the research tools of the network. In such delusional theories, the common element is certainly recognizable in the fierce details, devoid of critical scrutiny, with which the theses of conspiracy pacts are documented.

Yet, the conspiracies demonized by haters on the web could conceal a rationale: certain forms of rancor, an indignation at the breaking of an ethical principle that has universal dimensions and is deeply buried inside humans' mind. In our discourse, Rousseau's disgust with inequality between men has a decorative importance, though it is worth noting it fueled a debate on the social grammar of centuries to come, providing the "basic psychological vision of those who perceive themselves as abandoned or rejected."[32]

How many people think their life has been betrayed and there is no morality in profit? How many carry something of the acrimony that found root in Rousseau's eighteenth-century anger at the wounds that the commercialization of society inflicted on the human soul? Why not recognize a deontological substratum, some affinity with the distant formation of a communal morality originating in a Pleistocene era? Why not suggest that imprints of primordial reciprocal altruism persist in human mental conformation, of those principles of sharing that led to the elimination of cheaters and parasites enriching themselves without respecting the rules? Why cannot today's ire towards the selfishness of individual and corporate tax evasion and avoidance be compared to the prehistoric hostility towards the parasitism of free riders?

These are by no means abstractions. The misdeeds at which a moral economy is indignant would be nothing more than the intentional result of a global market economy which, after having stripped ordinary people of some of their ancestral values, is now preparing to devour them completely with the witchcraft of algorithms and their stellar speed.

Yet, behind speculations about malicious plots and designs of insidious elites, we glimpse a brain process: conspiracy beliefs tap into fundamental aspects of human psychology, formed in the predatory environment of prehistory that generated the "ape problem." Indeed, causality, despite all its evolutionary advantages, is once again in the dock; searching for causal explanations of events is a side effect of the brain's incessant drive to seek. In an evolutionary logic, the universe built by men turns out to be the outcome of their nature.

Mimicking Humphrey Bogart, one may exclaim: it is capitalism, baby, with all its Protean mutations, and there is nothing you can do about it. And go find out what future is reserved for humans.[33] In the truly short run, *Homo* species seems mired in its primordial conformation: selfish for 50 percent and familyist for 25 percent. What about the remaining 25 percent? Alas Hume! Your better angels of human nature have no choice but to keep making a living with what is left to reach the goals of reciprocal altruism.

Notes

1 C. Koslofsky, *Evening's Empire*, 128–156.
2 W. de Blécourt, *The Witch, her Victim*, 202.
3 K. Thomas, "Behind Closed Doors," in *NYR*, November 9, 1989; Id., *In Pursuit of Civility: Manners and Civilisation in Early Modern England*, New Haven, CT, 2018, 80–81, 186–187.
4 L. Floridi, *La quarta rivoluzione: Come l'infosfera sta trasformando il mondo*, Milano, 2018, 4, 6, 9, 109; M. Tegmark, *Life 3.0: Being Human in the Age of Artificial Intelligence*, ePUB, 2017.
5 See some of the recent ground-breaking gene therapies for spinal muscular atrophy or cystic fibrosis, and beyond. G. Conroy, "How Gene Therapy is Emerging from its 'dark age,'" in *Nature* 612, 2020, S24–S26. doi: 10.1038/d41586-022-04210-5.
6 Algorithms: the range of predicted outcomes has expanded to cover medical variables; economic measures; questions of interest to government agencies; the likelihood of other forms of violent behavior; and miscellaneous outcomes. Each of these domains entails a significant degree of uncertainty and unpredictability and they are called low-validity environments, and in those environments, simple algorithms matched or outplayed humans and their "complex" decision making criteria, essentially every time; see D. Kahneman, *Thinking, Fast and Slow*.
7 S. F. Johnston, *Techno-Fixers: Origin and Implication of Technological Faith*, Montrial, 2020.
8 M. Tegmark, *Life 3.0*.
9 G. Pacchioni, *L'ultimo Sapiens: Viaggio al termine della nostra specie*, Bologna, 2019.
10 M. Walker, "Transhumanism," in *Future on the Edge. The Coming of Age of Quantum Biology*, J. McFadden, Al-Khalili, eds., New York, 2017.
11 Joshua Cohen, in "The Gods of Chaos and Stupidity: Joshua Cohen interviewed by Daniel Drake," *NYR*, November 5, 2022.
12 B. Levack, *The Witch-Hunt*, 292.
13 I. K. Rösler, D. M. Amodio, "Neural Basis of Prejudice and Prejudice Reduction," in *Biol Psychiatry Cogn Neurosci Neuroimaging*, 7(12), 2022, 1200–1208. doi: 10.1016/j.bpsc.2022.10.008.
14 O. Davies, "Witchcraft Accusations in Nineteenth- and Twentieth-Century Europe," 296.
15 Ibid., 290.
16 S. Baron-Cohen, *Zero Degrees of Empathy*, 110.
17 Quoted in S. Pinker, *Enlightenment*, 252. See *In a New Light: Histories of Women and Energy*, A. Harrison Moore and R. W. Sandwell, eds., Montreal, 2021; essays that focus on the significance of gender in the history of energy, and of energy transitions in the history of women and gender.
18 P. Bruckner, *Un colpevole quasi Perfetto: La costruzione del capro espiatorio bianco*, Milano, 2021; N. Gill, "Bringing Women's Voices into the 'Smart City Just City' dialogue," in *OpenGlobalRights,* June 13, 2019.
19 O. Davies, "Witchcraft Accusation," 294.
20 From the observation of a scarcity of female scientists at the elite universities, it has been possible to assert that it could be "a function of intrinsic aptitude [sic!]'." See M. Pickett, "I Want What My Male Colleague Has, and That Will Cost a Few Million Dollars," *The New York Times Magazine*, April 18, 2019.
21 A. Gabrowska, *Sex on the Brain*.
22 A. L. Scagliusi, "Women and Work: The Decision to Have a Child Whilst Pursuing a Career: Can We 'Have it All' at Once?," in *Vanity Fair*, September 2, 2021.
23 J. Goody, *The Theft of History*, 16.
24 M. Pavone, "Sulla terapia dei tumori: in particolare sul Metodo Vieri," *Urologia*, Dec 1, 1967, doi.org/10.1177/039156036703400612.
25 The first words of the therapy were "wine vinegar"; see G. Traversa et al., "The Unconventional Di Bella Cancer Treatment," *Cancer*, 86, 10. 1903–1911 doi.org/10.1002/(SICI)1097–0142(19991115)86:10<1903:AID-CNCR5>3.0.CO;2-X.
26 R. Trivers, *The Folly*, ch. 12.

27 M. Peciña, J.K. Zubieta, "Molecular Mechanisms of Placebo Responses in Humans," in *Mol Psychiatry,* 20(4), 2015, 416–23. doi: 10.1038/mp.2014.164.

28 S. Pinker, *Enlightenment,* 16.

29 P. Brown, *Sorcery, Demons,* 28.

30 P. Mishra, *Age of Anger. A History of the Present,* London, 2018, 334.

31 S. Pinker, *Enlightenment,* 333.

32 P. Mishra, *Age of Anger,* 112.

33 There are only three possible futures: (a) the continuous development of the consumerist capitalist way of life towards greater complexity, (b) collapse of the planet, or (c) a new way of living: S. L. Lewis, M. A. Maslin, *The Human Planet.*

CONCLUSIONS

More than half a century ago, reflecting on the genesis of witchcraft as a collective psychological event an English anthropologist raised the issue of brain's imaginative activities in the form of neuro-electrical events, but concluded that the current state of knowledge regarding this organ, the most complicated system known in nature, is still relatively superficial and partial.[1] This is no longer the case. Advances in research promoted by neurobiological and cognitive sciences over the decades at the turn of the twentieth century make an outline of a better scenario possible.

In the depths of the emergence of *Homo sapiens*, the idea of witchcraft turned out to be a mental representation produced by the human brain. A somewhat per-emptory statement has opened our book: the brain builds the mind; from the plastic properties of the cerebral cortex, the mind emerges as a biological phenomenon.

Still, the blend of psychology, computer science, linguistics and philosophy that goes by the name of cognitive science has grown enormously, and our assertion is to be advanced carefully, given the extraordinarily complex concept of the nature of thought, reasoning, meaning and their relationship with perception.[2] The translation of neurobiological phenomena into psychic life undoubtedly remains a land strewn with mines. The reduction of mental facts to physical facts has been challenged, resisting the attempt to understand consciousness as a biological phe-nomenon. It is perfectly possible that the truth is not only elusive but completely out of our reach by virtue of our intrinsic cognitive limitations at the present stage of the intellectual development of humanity.[3] On the other hand, the data that, connecting brain events to mental experiences signal that the reality of the mind consists in the flesh of the brain, begins to add up significantly. To get closer to understanding how the brain works a great deal of theoretical effort will be needed to bridge the gap between brain and mind, given the billions of neurons in the human brain that are activated at the moment of conscious perception. Only a mathematical theory can explain how *mental* becomes *neural*. A model of the brain

DOI: 10.4324/9781003414377-33

will require many levels of explanation. Neuroscience needs a series of bridging laws, analogous to the Maxwell-Boltzmann gas theory, which link one domain to another. This is not an easy task: the condensed matter of the brain is perhaps the most complex object existing on Earth.[4]

Perhaps the entire human decision-making process of the future is destined to be revolutionized. "The age of large-scale 'mass cooperation networks' based on written language, money, culture and ideology – products of carbon-based human neural networks – is giving way to a new era of silicon-based computer networks based on algorithms."[5] Although the aversion to the idea that algorithms will make decisions capable of influencing men is deep seated, the studies of cognitive psychology over several decades, debating the dynamics between "intuitions versus formulas", invite us to conclude that whenever we can replace a human judgment with a formula, we should at least consider doing it.[6] If the destiny of human coexistence proceeds in this direction, responsibility seems to fall on the operational complexities caused by the enduring disharmony between *slow thinking* and *fast thinking*. In the future following the Third / Fourth / Fifth Industrial Revolution, scenarios will be produced in which we imperfectly know to what extent the governing of humanity falls back on emotionless robots, if the evolutionary advantage of fast and biased heuristics will fall.

The direction of research, subject to so many cautions, seems to move towards ascertaining that psychological phenomenon must be investigated physiologically because much depends on their physiology. In the dark hours for European and world history Marc Bloch questioned the future of his discipline: historical facts are essentially psychic facts. Therefore, as a rule, they find their antecedents in other psychic facts. Faced with the present condition of investigation on mental life and its dark depths this is further proof of the eternal difficulties that sciences encounter in order to remain exactly contemporary one to the other.[7] These are additional horizons to explore. More generally, applying the perceptions deriving from the various branches of psychology ends up accounting for the two sides of witchcraft, as deception and reality.[8]

And yet, after spending a few hundred pages to illustrate which brain mechanisms could underlie the various aspects of witchcraft, we still struggle with a doubt: on one hand we are convinced that neurobiology really is adding heuristic value to psychology and to our original question, even if the point remains open among mind and brain scientists themselves.[9] On the other we fear that our knowledge is too limited. Differences in people's ways of reasoning stubbornly do nothing but refer to a cognitive and neurobiological question that inhabits nineteenth-twentieth century modernity and is found much more enhanced in the twenty-first: the persistence of cognitive dissonances in single minds. In other words, we must try to understand why not only in different groups but sometimes in the same individuals, beliefs coexist that at first sight appear incompatible, and why they adopt contrasting methods and criteria of evaluation as to magical and religious ideas. This is the knot of cognitive neuroscience already touched upon: the sensation of copresence, of a complementarity in human mental elaboration which, alluding to a separateness of the things of the world, invites us to think of it in an integrated perspective, considering overlaps and interactions. No synthesis is available yet, perhaps "there is no reason to suspect that there must be something in the mental life of individuals, not understandable in terms of the known natural laws".[10]

From Stanley Kubrick to William Golding to Caliban

Taking our leave of the book, we offer the reader a conclusion that still, in the short run of time, sees the human mind hovering over the past and the future. In the contemporary world, post-apocalyptic science-fiction filmography, television serials, and mere fiction paint scenarios of humanity's regressions when, in the aftermath of some apocalyptic disasters, the institutions of society crumble and the material conditions of existence return to primitive levels. We come across stories set in virtual or futurized worlds after the collapse of civilization; texts or scenes that describe landscapes of a degraded, semi-desert nature, crossed by bands of raiders dressed in animal skins. A descent into the abyss of Prehistory (and maybe we fear that the latest data on impending climate change makes such images less dystopian than expected). But here, for a final consideration, we draw on a fictional work that with its highest caliber has the power to stimulate not only literary observations. We refer to William Golding's *Lord of the Flies*.

The novel's plot is simple. A group of boys from good English families, preteens or younger, are affected by a mental reversal and we witness their relapse into primordial scenarios. Survivors of a plane crash find themselves abandoned on a deserted tropical island. As protagonists we do not have hominins but educated contemporary humans, suddenly enveloped by a wild nature in which, not unlike the Pleistocene, a vivid light and deep darkness prevail, and the great contrast affects sight and thought, altering their perceptive faculties. The boys are divided into small rival gangs reproducing the forms of command, hierarchy and violence seen at the opening of the book that are imagined, looming among the prehumans in Stanley Kubrick's *2001: A Space Odyssey*. Darkness and fear generate the psychological atmosphere of a predatory context and in the thoughts of children and adolescents the ape syndrome doubt is stirred up: somewhere a beast is hiding, a threatening monster. Summoned to the sound of a large shell by one of the leaders, the little ones gather in assembly and debate on how to face the mysterious danger. They ask each other: what is it about? Is it a ghost? Yes, of course, the "beast" is only a ghost, some say. Unreal explanations alternate with skepticism. Ralph, one of the leaders, proposes:

> We'll have a vote on them; on ghosts I mean [...] I'll say here and now that I don't believe in ghosts. Or I don't think I do. But I don't like the thought of them. Not now that is, in the dark. But we were going to decide what's what. [...] Who thinks there may be ghosts?[11]

How do we want to comment on this drama in which actors seem to be precisely "evolved and abandoned" and the *fast thinking* seems to prevail? Ignoring the Nobel laureate for literature, the scientific answer fulfills its role. Bound by the burden of evidence, in the words of an eminent primatologist, science pronounces and asserts that there is no shred of proof that this is what children left on their own would do.[12]

Maybe! Note, however, there is room for disagreement among scientists:

> Take a hundred people anywhere, put them on a desert island where they will have a purpose to work together, and they will make really good use of them. Maybe they will break up into two groups of fifty trying to exterminate each other, but if the common problem is a hostile environment or a hostile group, working together as a group is a natural outcome of our species.[13]

The metaphor of the ghost in that tropical atoll evokes another island, inhabited not by a ghost but by a man-monster in flesh and blood, full of freckles: Caliban. The words of his master underline the inevitable presence of evil and the enduring nature/nurture contrast. Prospero warns: Caliban is "A devil, a born devil, on whose nature / Nurture can never stick; on whom my pains, / Humanely taken, all, all lost, quite lost."[14]

And so, the book returns to the critical fulcrum it started from, which remains an unsolved knowledge problem.

Notes

1 R. Needham, *Primordial Characters*, Charlottesville, NC, 1978.
2 G. M. Edelman, *Bright Air, Brilliant Fire: On the Matter of the Mind*, New York, 1992.
3 T. Nagel, *Mind and Cosmos: Why the Materialist Neo-Darwinian Conception of Nature is Almost Certainly False*, Oxford, 2012.
4 Despite all these difficulties, over the past fifteen years Jean-Pierre Changeux, Lionel Naccache and S. Dehaene have begun to bridge the gap. S. Dehaene, *Consciousness and the Brain: Deciphering How the Brain Codes Our Thoughts*, New York, 2014.
5 N. Ferguson, *The Square and the Tower*, 13–14.
6 D. Kahneman, *Thinking, Fast and Slow*.
7 M. Bloch, *The Historian's Craft: Reflections on the Nature and Uses of History and the Techniques and Methods of Those Who Write It*, London, 1964, ch. 5.
8 P. Elmer, *Science and Witchcraft*, in *The Oxford Book of Witchcraft*, 559.
9 See https://thepsychologist.bps.org.uk/volume-28/april-2015/what-has-neuroscience-ever-done-us; see also A. Diamond, D. Amso, 2008, "Contributions of Neuroscience to Our Understanding of Cognitive Development," in *Curr Dir Psychol Sci*, 17, 2008, 136–141, doi: 10.1111/j.1467–8721.2008.00563.x.
10 C. Rovelli, *Helgoland*, 184.
11 W. Golding, *Lord of the Flies*, ch. 5.
12 H. de Waal, *Bonobo: The Forgotten Ape*, Oakland, 1997.
13 D. Sloan Wilson, *Darwin's Cathedral*, 26–27.
14 Shakespeare, *The Tempest*, act IV, scene 1, 188–189.

INDEX